ENTERED MAR 2 2 1995

ESSAYS IN AMERICAN MUSIC
VOL. 1

AMERICAN MUSICAL LIFE IN CONTEXT AND PRACTICE TO 1865

GARLAND REFERENCE LIBRARY
OF THE HUMANITIES
VOL. 1583

ESSAYS IN AMERICAN MUSIC
JAMES R. HEINTZE AND MICHAEL SAFFLE
Series Editors

AMERICAN MUSICAL LIFE
IN CONTEXT AND PRACTICE
TO 1865
edited by James R. Heintze

AMERICAN MUSICAL LIFE IN CONTEXT AND PRACTICE TO 1865

edited by
James R. Heintze

GARLAND PUBLISHING, INC.
New York & London / 1994

Copyright © 1994 James R. Heintze
All rights reserved

Library of Congress Cataloging-in-Publication Data

American musical life in context and practice to 1865 / edited by James R. Heintze.
    p. cm. — (Essays in American music ; vol. 1) (Garland reference library of the humanities ; vol. 1583)
  Includes index.
  ISBN 0–8153–0816–7
  1. Music—United States—19th century—History and criticism. 2. Music and society. I. Heintze, James R. II. Series. III. Series: Garland reference library of the humanities ; vol. 1583.
ML200.4.A4 1994
780'.973'09034—dc20   93–44465
                                      CIP
                                      MN

```
780.97309034 A512h


American musical life in
   context and practice to
```

Printed on acid-free, 250-year-life paper
Manufactured in the United States of America

CONTENTS

Series Foreword	vii
Introduction	ix
Music and Dance in Philadelphia's City Tavern, 1773-1790 Sterling E. Murray	3
Peter Erben and America's First Lutheran Tunebook in English Edward C. Wolf	49
Gaetano Carusi: From Sicily to the Halls of Congress James R. Heintze	75
Edward Little White, Professor of Music Barbara Owen	133
The Anthem in Southern Four-Shape Shape-Note Tunebooks, 1816-1860 David W. Music	149
The 1838-40 American Concert Tours of Jane Shirreff and John Wilson, British Vocal Stars Katherine K. Preston	173
Catholic Church Music in the Midwest Before the Civil War: The Firm of W. C. Peters & Sons Richard D. Wetzel	203

The Origins of Music Journalism in Chicago:
    Criticism as a Reflection of Musical Life
        James A. Deaville   231

An American Muse Learns to Walk:
    The First American-Music Group
        Richard Jackson   265

The Beginnings of Bach in America
    J. Bunker Clark   337

Index   353

Contributors   367

SERIES FOREWORD

Essays in American Music celebrates the rich and varied heritage of this country's music by bringing together articles written by distinguished scholars, researchers, and teachers about significant and unique musical events, persons, and places. Although the historiography of American music has advanced considerably since the first calls went out in the early 1800s for the collecting of historical data, and today, readers may now choose from a vast body of literature on American music, including several excellent histories and surveys, numerous critical studies and facsimile editions, monographs on individual musicians, topical studies, reference works, including bibliographies, indexes, encyclopedias and dictionaries as well as articles in journals devoted specifically to American music, the content of the subjects addressed in the articles contained in this series offers evidence for the fact that there is still much to discover about this country's musical past. The purpose of this series is to provide a sampling of areas of research currently under pursuit and, nearing the onset of the twenty-first century, to provide a stimulus for future research into American music.

The volumes in the series progress chronologically, beginning with the period prior to 1865. Volume two focuses on 1865-1918 and subsequent volumes examine the remainder of the twentieth century. All of the contributors to the series are recognized authorities in their respective areas of investigation and represent prominent organizations devoted to the study of American music, including, for example, the College Music Society, Sonneck Society for American Music, Hymn Society in the United States and Canada, and others. Within the space allotted to them, all contributors have provided essays on topics of their choice and were encouraged to apply their own critical points of view.

James R. Heintze
Michael Saffle

INTRODUCTION

American Musical Life in Context and Practice to 1865 covers a wide cross-section of topics, individuals, groups, and musical practices representing various regions and cities. The subjects discussed reflect the religious, ethnic, and social plurality of the American musical experience as well as the impact on cultural society provided by the arrival of new musical immigrants and the internal movements of musicians and musical practices. The essays are arranged principally on the basis of the historical chronology of the cultural practices and subjects discussed. Each article helps to shed additional light on cultural expressions through music in eighteenth- and nineteenth-century America.

Sterling E. Murray presents a vivid example of secular musical life in Philadelphia in the late 1700s, and the significance of the City Tavern as a place where gentlemen met and concerts and balls were given.

Two of the essays discuss different denominational contributions to musical life in America: Edward C. Wolf traces the development of American Lutheran hymnody through the work of Peter Erben, a New York organist and organ-builder, and his publication of the first Lutheran tunebook published in English in 1817; Richard D. Wetzel describes the significance of the publisher W. C. Peters in making accessible published Catholic church music in the Midwest. Another aspect of the impact of publishing on the development of music in America is given by David W. Music who examines in detail the occurrence of the anthem in four-shape shape-note tunebooks published in the South and offers a compilation of anthem repertory and sources for the works cited.

James R. Heintze introduces Gaetano Carusi, an Italian immigrant musician who was active principally in the mid-Atlantic area from Philadelphia to Norfolk and who, through persistence and initiative, successfully established his musical identity in America and left his mark on the cultural development of several cities.

The essay contributed by Barbara Owen on Edward Little White, the Massachusetts organist, teacher, composer, arranger, and publisher, provides valuable insight into this versatile musician.

Katherine K. Preston addresses the significance of the European influence on American music by the travelling virtuosi Jane Shirreff and John Wilson and chronicles their success as performers in the United States. An enlightened contextual comparison of the enthusiastic acceptance by American audiences of European musicians like Shirreff and Wilson versus the struggling attempts by American musicians—such as Charles Jerome Hopkins, Charles Hommann, and others—to have their works heard emerges with a reading of Richard Jackson's extensive essay on the first organization devoted to the performance of American concert works—the short-lived but historically significant, New York American-Music Association.

James A. Deaville examines the nature of the music press in Chicago during the mid-nineteenth century and describes the manner in which the press reflected the development of music in that city.

J. Bunker Clark completes this volume with an informative essay on how Johann Sebastian Bach was introduced to Americans through both publications and performances in the nineteenth-century.

I would like to extend my sincere appreciation to Michael Saffle of Virginia Polytechnic Institute and State University for his suggestions and to all of the contributors whose research has enriched our understanding of the American musical heritage.

James R. Heintze

American Musical Life in Context and Practice to 1865

MUSIC AND DANCE IN PHILADELPHIA'S CITY TAVERN, 1773-1790[1]

Sterling E. Murray

Late in August 1774, delegates to the First Continental Congress started to gather in Philadelphia. For many the journey was a long and exhausting one. Writing in his diary, John Adams, a delegate from Massachusetts for whom fate had reserved a particularly important role in the forthcoming meetings, recalled his entrance into the city in the following words:

> We . . . rode into town, and dirty, dusty, and fatigued as we were, we could not resist the importunity to go to the Tavern, the most genteel one in America. . . . Here we had a fresh welcome to the city of Philadelphia.[2]

Eighteenth-century taverns were common meeting places for gentlemen, and it is not surprising that Adams and his companions headed there first. The particular establishment referred to here is City Tavern, located on the west side of Second street north of Walnut, which at that time was under the management of one Daniel Smith, an Irishman of imposing stature, known as "Little Smith."[3] Only six months before, Smith had first announced that his establishment was open for business:

> DANIEL SMITH, begs leave to inform the PUBLIC, that the Gentlemen Proprietors of the CITY TAVERN have been pleased to approve of him as a proper person to keep said tavern in consequence of which he has completely furnished it, and, at a *very great expense* [*sic*], has laid in every article of the first quality perfectly in the style of a London Tavern.[4]

Although in August 1774, City Tavern was less than a year old, it had already begun to etch its place in history. Earlier in the summer, when Paul Revere brought news to the city of the closing of Boston's port, a mass meeting was called in the second-floor room of the tavern to discuss a plan of response. In the days before the convening of the Continental Congress, delegates gathered unofficially at Smith's tavern to meet one another and begin to share their ideas. Only a short walking distance from Carpenter's Hall, the tavern remained a favorite gathering place for the delegates, and it is likely that some resolutions were hammered out and agreed upon here before they reached the floor of the debates. Several delegates took their meals here and gathered in the common rooms during the evening to continue their discussions in smaller groups. During its long history, the tavern on Second street played host to many of the founding fathers of our country. Among those who knew its rooms well were George Washington, John Adams, Thomas Jefferson, Benjamin Franklin, the Marquis de Lafayette, Peyton Randolph, and Richard Henry Lee.

EIGHTEENTH-CENTURY PHILADELPHIA AND ITS INNS AND TAVERNS

City Tavern was only one of the many impressive public buildings of eighteenth-century Philadelphia. Travelers seeing the city for the first time in the early 1770s might well have been stunned by its size and splendor. By the mid-eighteenth century, Philadelphia's population had swollen to over 30,000, making it the second largest city in the English-speaking world. Among the estimated 3,600 dwellings within its limits, there were many that would compare well with contemporary London town houses. Neatly situated on the straight streets laid out in interlocking grids that stretched from the Delaware River west to the State House and beyond, these imposing structures stood as symbols of a confident and assured culture.[5]

A cosmopolitan city, Philadelphia offered its citizens amenities that some visitors coming from small towns and rural environments must have found surprising. The pebblestones that paved the city's streets not only cut down on the choking dust in dry weather and splattering mud in the rainy season but also helped to reduce the deafening street noise that plagued most eighteenth-century cities. Brick-paved sidewalks were lighted at night, and the city had both a police force and several fire companies. Among its many public buildings Philadelphia could boast a lending library, a theater, a hospital, and a prison.[6]

Like other cities of its size, Philadelphia also included many inns and taverns.[7] An eighteenth-century inn or tavern was a public house licensed to sell food and drink, care for horses, and often provide lodgings.

Traditional names—such as Bay Horse, Bull's Head, White Bear, Turk's Head, and Golden Swan—provided subjects for the colorful and artistic signs that hung over their doorways as an aid to those who could not read as well as a prominent place to display the license number required by law.[8] Travel in the eighteenth century was both difficult and dangerous. The lights of the tavern must have seemed a welcome beacon to a traveler seeking food, shelter, and protection for the night. For the local residents taverns were the central focus of social life—an informal place to gather, smoke a pipe, read a newspaper, eat and drink, and enjoy the company of friends and colleagues.

Larger taverns often set aside special rooms where small groups of men with similar interests could meet regularly to dine, drink, play cards, and engage in conversation. Most eighteenth-century gentlemen belonged to at least one of these clubs and some held membership in several. Especially popular were "glutton" or eating clubs, while others focused upon literature, sports, and the arts. No matter what the special interest, conversation eventually turned to politics.

The range within this general definition was considerable. Some taverns offered excellent kitchens, fine wines, and comfortable accommodations, while others were of a meaner sort that catered to a less discriminating population. All types could be found in Philadelphia.[9] Although spotted throughout the city, the most prominent taverns seemed to have been grouped in the area west of Second street, between Walnut and Arch.[10] The licensing histories of Philadelphia's taverns indicate that while most remained in business for only a short time, some—often under a number of different innkeepers—flourished for many years. Several shared the same name (the Indian Queen being a good example), while others changed names more than once. The tavern opposite the State House (now Independence Hall) was known to the members of the Federal Convention as the Half Moon, but older residents would have better recognized it as the Coach and Horse, the State House Inn, or Clark's Inn. During the British occupation of the city, the Indian King on Market street between Second and Third, which had been operated by John and Sarah Biddle, was taken over by Peter Lennox and renamed the British Tavern.

Characteristic of the city's better taverns was the Bunch of Grapes (previously known as the Bull's Head), located on Third street between Market and Arch. The description of this establishment printed in the *Pennsylvania Packet* provides an idea of what the best of the city's trade could offer:

> ... A LARGE convenient TAVERN, situated on the east side of Third-street near Arch-street, commonly known by the name of the Bunch of Grapes, with two parlours, seven chambers, a large dancing room, two garrets, two kitchens, with a house at the end

of the lot and stables for thirty horses.[11]

Not all Philadelphia taverns provided lodging for their guests, but among those that did the Indian Queen (southeast corner of Market and Fourth streets) and The Sign of the Conestoga Wagon (south side of Market street above Fourth) enjoyed reputations excellent enough to attract the business of delegates to both Continental Congresses. Francis Lee's Indian Queen was a particular favorite of both George Mason and James Madison, but it also played host to John Rutledge and Charles Pinckney of South Carolina, Alexander Hamilton of New York, and others. From the following description taken out of the *Pennsylvania Gazette*, one can imagine why accommodations at Lee's tavern were in demand:

> . . . five large rooms on the first floor, to entertain companies, two large kitchens, cellars under the whole, 16 lodging rooms on the second and third stories, besides four large garret rooms for servants; four rooms in the house can be made into two, which will entertain from 80 to 100 gentlemen; the stables will hold 83 horses, all plank floors, and laid into four feet stalls . . . the loft will hold from 80 to 100 tons of hay; coach-horses and sheds for carriages; graineries [*sic*], which will hold from 100 to 1500 bushels of grain, large dung hole; a straw house; and a large flat for drying clothes. . . .[12]

In a tavern like the Indian Queen a guest could anticipate first-class treatment. In July 1787, when the Reverend Manasseh Cutler (1742-1823) arrived in Philadelphia to appear before Congress to request the sale of millions of acres of land north of the Ohio river, he took lodgings there. In his diary Cutler left a vivid picture of the reception one might expect at one of the better Philadelphia taverns:

> Friday, July 13. As soon as I had inquired of the bar-keeper, when I arrived last evening, if I could be furnished with lodgings, a livery servant was ordered immediately to attend me, who received my baggage from the hostler, and conducted me to the apartment assigned by the bar-keeper, which was a rather small but very handsome chamber (No. 9), furnished with a rich field bed, bureau, table with drawers, a large looking-glass, neat chairs, and other furniture. Its front was east, and, being in the third story, afforded me a fine prospect toward the river and the Jersey shore. The servant that attended me was a young, sprightly, well-built black fellow, neatly dressed—blue coat, sleeves and cape red, and buff waistcoat and breeches, the bosom

of his shirt ruffled, and hair powdered. After he brought up my baggage and properly deposited it in the chamber, he brought two of the latest London magazines and laid them on the table. I ordered him to call a barber, furnish me with a bowl of water for washing, and to have tea on the table by the time I was dressed.[13]

THE CITY TAVERN

Although the City Tavern shares features with the other Philadelphia taverns just described, in several ways it was exceptional. No matter how elegant the services provided within, most eighteenth-century taverns were designed with a practical plan in mind as places of business with minimal concern for appearance. From its inception, City Tavern challenged this assumption. Described as the "largest and most elegant" of taverns in pre-revolutionary America, Philadelphia's City Tavern was an imposing structure of five stories, whose design was reminiscent of that used for the spacious and fashionable coffee houses of London.[14] The building's appearance was unhampered by any need to accommodate to practical requirements typical of other inns. The original design called for only a few lodging rooms on the upper floors, and no accommodation was made for a stable or an open courtyard for carriages.[15] Unencumbered by conventional restrictions, the building could be designed with an appeal to elegance rather than utility. There were no outbuildings. The bottom floor, recessed halfway below the ground level, housed the tavern's kitchen and storage areas. The main entrance was on the second floor, reached by a set of vaulted stairs raising from the street level. A front door placed in the middle of the facade was flanked by two windows on either side. The five windows across on the upper levels balanced the format of the second level. In the rear a balustraded porch ran the full width of the building, with stairs connecting it to a garden.

Also unlike most Philadelphia taverns, City Tavern was built by subscription.[16] The list of subscribers included the names of fifty-two of Philadelphia's most prominent citizens, each of whom purchased one or two shares at £25 each, to which Governor John Penn contributed an additional £1000. The subscriber's investments would be paid off through a yearly rental fee charged the innkeeper. Only after the mortgage was paid would the shareholders receive their dividends. Among the subscribers were prominent lawyers, merchants, public officials, and physicians. This select roster of the city's elite reads like a roll call of Philadelphia's great families—Penn, Mifflin, Cadwalader, Shippen, Hill, Wharton, Chew, Allen, and Tilghman, among others. From this group, seven trustees were selected to oversee the affairs of the venture and act as agents for the larger body. Included among this smaller fraternity were a signer of the Declaration of Independence, the first Treasurer of the United States, and a Colonial Chief Justice of the Pennsylvania Supreme Court.[17] It is clear that with such a backing City Tavern was destined to enjoy the patronage of Philadelphia's leading gentlemen.

Normally, the running of an eighteenth-century tavern was a family affair—husband, wife, children, and close relatives fulfilling multiple functions in catering to the needs of their customers. Once again, however, City Tavern's history poses an exception. The subscribers were good businessmen, who expected a return on their investment, but none of these "gentlemen of the city" intended to become involved with the day-to-day operations of the tavern. Although they maintained a keen interest and probably kept a close watch over the affairs of the tavern, innkeepers or managers were chosen to see to its daily operation. In all, City Tavern had six managers, three of whom served during the period considered here. The first, Daniel Smith, was associated with City Tavern from its opening through the war years and the British occupation of Philadelphia. His tenure ended in December 1777. Smith was followed by Gifford Dalley, who announced the reopening of the tavern in August 1778. Dalley continued at his post until 1785, when he was replaced by Edward Moyston who served as manager until March 1796. In the early 1780s, George Evans was employed as the innkeeper, but he does not seem to have ever been a manager.[18] The last two innkeepers were Samuel Richardet (1796-99), and James Kitchen (1799-1808).

Although certainly interested in this project as a sound business venture, the proprietors who conceived and put up the money for the City Tavern were also men with a vision for their community. All were well educated and cultivated gentlemen of their day. Several had traveled and studied in Europe where they were exposed to the latest fashions in art, music, and dance. Armed with a greater familiarity with and appreciation for the arts, they returned home to Philadelphia with a desire to use the fruits of their experience to enhance their own city. In part, these men of learning and cultivation conceived City Tavern to serve as an elegant center for the social and cultural life of their city—an appropriate setting in which the artistic accomplishments of their community could be featured and encouraged.[19] Its very name proclaimed the building as a symbol of the city, like the other City Taverns in New York, Boston, Annapolis, and Georgetown. More than merely providing an appropriate meeting place for the gentlemen of the city, City Tavern could also house banquets and other special entertainments or serve as a comfortable setting for concerts and balls.

The interior of City Tavern was designed with these needs in mind.

On the entrance floor a central hallway gave access to four public rooms. The two on the left, called coffee rooms, were also used for dining. The room on the back right side housed the bar, and the "subscription room" in the front right side functioned as a waiting area where newspapers were made available. On the floor above, reached by a center staircase, there was a great room that extended the full width of the front of the building. Usually referred to as the "Long" or "Assembly" Room, it was narrow and long and could easily accommodate itself to concerts and balls. Heated on cold winter evenings by fireplaces at each end and elegantly illuminated, the long room could also, if desired, be partitioned into two smaller individual chambers:

> . . . it contains several large club rooms, two of which being thrown into one make a spacious room of near fifty feet in length, for public entertainment.[20]

This practical space-saving arrangement is very much in keeping with the times. Francis Lee's Indian Queen boasted two such adaptable chambers.[21]

In the back of the second-floor level there were two smaller rooms flanking the central staircase. Normally they were used for club meetings of groups like the Sons of St. Patrick, the Jockey Club, St. Andrew's Society, the Freemasons, St. George's Society, and the Society of Cincinnati. On evenings when a ball was taking place in the long room, the smaller back chambers were set aside for cards. The upper stories housed bed chambers for lodgers and servants.

Before City Tavern, Philadelphia had no appropriate gathering place ideally suited to the needs of concerts and balls. Dances had been held in Hamilton's warehouse and stores on Water street and, along with concerts, in the structure on Lodge alley known as the Masonic Assembly Rooms.[22] Ballad operas were performed first at William Plumstead's warehouse at Pine and Water streets and then later at the Southwark Theater on Cedar street. The London Coffee House probably hosted some modest musical performances, and Henry Epple's Sign of the Rainbow Tavern on Race street is known to have been the home of the amateur concerts, but in general even the largest taverns did not have a room spacious enough to accommodate public concerts and balls. None of these locales could boast the elegant surroundings provided by City Tavern.

It did not take long for the expectations of the subscribers to become realized. After its opening in February 1773, City Tavern soon became a center for Philadelphia's social and cultural life. Until about 1790 it was the scene of special entertainments, state banquets, brilliant balls, and many public concerts.

MUSIC AT CITY TAVERN

A great deal of music making in eighteenth-century taverns was informal and, as a result, left undocumented. In this regard City Tavern was probably not unlike other establishments of its time and type. Popular songs of the day received an enthusiastic audience among tavern patrons. Sung in a robust manner, unaccompanied or to the sound of a dance fiddle or other single instrument, these songs capture for us an element of the elusive popular culture of their day.[23] Within this context simple tunes could be borrowed and easily reset to new words to change an innocent popular song into an instrument of political criticism or satire. Such *contrafacta* frequently found their way into newspapers,[24] and undoubtedly many of the political lyrics preserved in eighteenth-century Philadelphia newspapers were well-known in their contraband musical settings in the taverns of the city. Given City Tavern's close association with the politics of its day, it seems reasonable to assume that such politically-motivated music also resounded within its walls.

Some European taverns of the day featured regular performances by small instrumental ensembles. Especially favored were wind ensembles (called *Harmonie*) that performed selections from popular stage productions.[25] Such practices were also known in Philadelphia[26] but have not been linked specifically with City Tavern. Although no records have been found to establish that City Tavern employed any musicians to perform there on a regular basis, professional performers were sometimes brought in for special events.

As the site of numerous political rallies and meetings, City Tavern played a special role in the shaping of American democracy. When figures of national importance like George Washington and John Adams visited Philadelphia, they attracted local attention and on more than one occasion were provided with special escorts through the city. Thus, for example, when John Adams arrived at the outskirts of Philadelphia on his way to the meeting of the Second Continental Congress in May 1775, he was greeted by a party of prominent Philadelphia gentlemen and, to the accompaniment of music provided by the band of the local militia, paraded into the city, down Second street, and directly to City Tavern.

Like other Philadelphia taverns, City Tavern was also the scene of special dinners sponsored by clubs and lodges to distinguish a particular occasion or honor a visiting dignitary. For some of these entertainments music was provided. On 24 June 1777 Smith's Masonic Lodge, No. 3, held a dinner at City Tavern to celebrate St. John's day. After the meal, there were thirteen "proper toasts" followed by "an anthem, accompanied with a Grand band of music."[27]

On 4 July 1778, as part of the celebration of American independence, a special dinner was given at City Tavern for members of Congress and other dignitaries. Arrangements for this important event were entrusted to Gifford Dalley. Perhaps this was an "audition" as only days later Dalley would be officially named the tavern's new manager. Dr. Samuel Holten, a delegate from Massachusetts, reported that during the meal eighty guests were entertained by "an Agreeable band of Musick."[28] Also in attendance that day was Chief Justice Thomas McKean, who described the event in the following terms:

> ... the Anniversary of Independence was celebrated at the new Tavern, where there was an elegant entertainment, and a fine band of musick, the firing of a vast number of cannon proved that there was no want of powder. . . . [29]

Rhode Island's William Ellery, who also attended this celebration banquet, considered the entertainment "elegant and well conducted." He left this somewhat fuller description of the musical ensemble in his diary:

> As soon as the Dinner began, the Musick consisting of Clarinets, Haut–boys, French horns, Violins and Bass Viols, opened and continued making proper pauses until it was finished. Then the Toasts followed each by a discharge of Fieldpieces, were drunk, and so the afternoon ended.[30]

The musicians who entertained for the Fourth-of-July banquet at the City Tavern are not identified in any of the newspaper references, but they were probably members of the regimental band under the command of Colonel Thomas Proctor.[31] On 5 December of the same year, the *Pennsylvania Packet*, in describing a procession from the state house to City Tavern four days before, established that "a band of musick belonging to Col. Proctor's regiment" provided the entertainment.[32] Proctor's band seems to have been in demand. Several weeks later they played at a Masonic celebration at Christ Church. In the parade between the college and the church the band played Masonic melodies. The service continued with an anthem consisting of "A GRAND SYMPHONY," a chorus, three arias, and a trio, all "accompanied by *The Organ* and other instrumental music."[33]

Born in Ireland, Proctor settled in Philadelphia sometime before December 1766 when he was married to Mary Fox in Zion Lutheran Church.[34] He was employed as a house carpenter by Samuel Powel. Proctor enjoyed a close affiliation with City Tavern. A portion of the lot that City Tavern sat upon had at one time belonged to him. Evidence also points to the fact that Proctor was probably the builder of City Tavern.[35]

On 6 August 1778 Gifford Dalley, now the official manager of City Tavern, arranged an elegant entertainment there following the reception by Congress of Conrad Alexander Gérard, Minister Plenipotentiary from the court of King Louis XVI.[36] The event, described by Holten as "grand & elegant," was also quite expensive; Dalley presented the Congress with a bill totalling $1424. Among the itemized entries was payment to "Furedge, Spanganbay, Miller, Schulz and Schultz for their Services as Musicians."[37] Furedge may be a creative spelling of Forrage. Stephen Forrage is known to have performed on Philadelphia concerts in the 1760s with Francis Hopkinson, John Penn, James Bremner, John Beals, and others. He played the Armonica or Musical Glasses, an invention that was improved by Benjamin Franklin.[38] The musician identified as "Spanganbay" is probably Conrad Spangenberg, about whom more will be said later, and "Schultz" is likely to be the violinist for whom a benefit concert was held at Henry Epple's Tavern (The Rainbow) on Race Street in April 1789. Both Schultz and Spangenberg were associated with Proctor's ensemble but probably as civilian musicians as their names do not appear on the band's 1779 roster.[39]

PROFESSIONAL MUSICIANS AND PUBLIC CONCERTS AT CITY TAVERN

The most substantial musical events of eighteenth-century Philadelphia were public concerts featuring the talents of professional musicians.[40] Before the Revolution, Philadelphia had attracted a modest number of professional musicians. Figures like Giovanni Gualdo (d. 1771) and John Bremner (d. 1780) were influential in establishing a tradition of musical cultivation in the city. But much of the music making in Philadelphia before the war was characterized by enthusiastic amateur participation, spearheaded by "gentlemen amateurs" like Francis Hopkinson and John Penn. After the war, the number of professional musicians arriving in the city increased substantially. Ships docking at Philadelphia brought with them musical émigrés trained in Germany and France as well as the mother country—all seeking to establish their careers and find their fortune in America. These musicians were to populate the theater and concert orchestras, advertise their talents as teachers and instrument makers, and leave their distinctive mark on the musical culture of the city. Most were well-trained performers, and some were gifted composers. In the mid-1780s, the concert life of Philadelphia was dominated by four such figures: William Brown (fl. 1783-1788), Alexander Juhan (1765-1845), Henri Capron (fl. 1768-1794), and Alexander Reinagle (1756-1809). Each was associated at one time or another with City Tavern.

Brown was a flutist, who came to America in 1782 or 1783. He settled first in New York, where he gave a benefit concert on 8 August 1783. According to a New York newspaper Brown had previously "exhibited on the German flute, in most parts of Europe."[41] Brown remained in New York only a short time; by October he had relocated in Philadelphia, where on 16 October he announced a benefit concert at City Tavern. Perhaps Brown was enticed to Philadelphia by the harpsichordist John Bentley, in whose house he took rooms.[42] It is likely that Brown is identical with Wilhelm Braun, who played flute in the Kassel *Hofkapelle* of Landgrave Friedrich II from 1770 to 1780.[43] Although the Philadelphia Brown never used the German form of his name, he maintained close professional contact with several of Philadelphia's German musicians, such as the violinist Philip Phile.[44] Brown was recognized as a skilled performer. According to one observer, his "power over the German flute has astonished Americans, and would give additional grace to any royal band in Europe."[45]

The violinist Alexander Juhan also arrived in Philadelphia in 1783. He probably came here from Charleston with his father, James Juhan, a keyboardist.[46] On 6 August of that year Alexander Juhan gave a benefit concert at the Assembly Rooms on Lodge Alley.

Two years later the French cellist Henri Capron made his first appearance in the city's musical circles. On 23 March 1785, Capron advertised a benefit concert in the Assembly Rooms, which had to be postponed until the following month. In newspaper announcements Capron claimed an ignorance of the English language, and it is therefore plausible that his appearance in Philadelphia marked his arrival in this country. The suggestion that Henri Capron was a student of Pierre Gaviniès (1728-1800),[47] a violinist whom Fétis places on the 1768 *Concert spirituel* in Paris[48] is incorrect. The French violinist was named Nicolas Capron.

The fourth member of this group, Alexander Reinagle, was the last to arrive in Philadelphia and the one to make the greatest impression on the city's music. Reinagle was one of the most talented of the emigrant professional musicians who contributed to the early development of concert music in this country.[49] He received his early musical training in Edinburgh where his father was employed as a master in the Edinburgh Musical Society.[50] Reinagle studied with Rayner Taylor (1742-1825), whom he later convinced to join him in Philadelphia. He was employed as a professional musician in both Glasgow and London before sailing for New York at the age of thirty. In June 1786 Reinagle, billing himself as a "Member of the [Royal] Society of Musicians in London," first advertised his services as a teacher "in singing, on the Harpsichord, Piano Forte and Violin."[51] The following month he arranged a concert at the Assembly

Room on Broadway. Appearing along with Reinagle on this concert was the Philadelphia violinist Philip Phile. Perhaps it was Phile who convinced Reinagle to abandon New York and try his luck in Philadelphia. Phile probably introduced Reinagle to the principal musicians of his new city—Brown, Juhan, and Capron. His Philadelphia debut in a benefit concert for Henri Capron at City Tavern was an immediate success, and just three weeks later Reinagle had his own benefit in the same hall. In both concerts he was joined by Brown, Juhan, and Capron.

As a group, these four musicians are characteristic of the professionals who shaped the musical life of our young republic. All had received traditional musical training in Europe and—at least in the instances of Brown and Reinagle—had already established themselves in the musical life of their homeland before they left. Versatile and flexible, they played several different instruments, all of which they were prepared to teach, and each was a capable composer.[52] In order to achieve even a modest success, these musicians had to be energetic, enterprising, and more than competent business men. All four pursued active performance schedules while at the same time negotiating heavy teaching commitments. In addition to subscription and benefit concerts in Philadelphia, their performance commitments required extensive travel, often bouncing them around between Charleston, New York, Boston, and Baltimore.

Their musical success brought these musicians into contact with individuals of wealth and influence. By dedicating his *Three Rondos for the piano forte or harpsichord* (March 1787) to Francis Hopkinson, William Brown was linking his name with the highest level of Philadelphia society. The subscription list for Brown's keyboard rondos included the names of such other important Philadelphians as John Penn, Stephen du Ponceau, and Alexander Hamilton. While in Philadelphia for the Constitutional Convention in 1787, General George Washington attended Reinagle's concert at City Tavern and was impressed enough with his talent to later engage him as music teacher to his granddaughter Nelly Custis. This duty was then inherited by Henri Capron.[53] Reinagle's services were also sought after by Robert Morris and Peyton Randolph.[54]

Several of this group must have been difficult personalities—a trait perhaps fanned by inflated egos. Brown, for example, was involved in arguments on different occasions with both Bentley and Capron, and in 1787 Juhan and the singing-school master Andrew Adgate (1762-1793) engaged in a public airing in the local press of their differences concerning a proposed concert of music to benefit the poor.[55]

Eighteenth-century public concerts fall into three general types: amateur, benefit, and series. Amateur concerts are the least well documented of the group. It is known that during the 1780s Epple's tavern was the site of a series of amateur concerts, but as newspaper references are for the most part reduced to simple announcements and do not generally include the specific programs, it is difficult to evaluate the personnel or repertory of these performances. It is clear, however, that upon occasion professional musicians performed on these programs.[56]

Although some "benefit concerts" were designed to raise money for those in need,[57] in most instances it was the musician who organized and advertised the concert who would "benefit" from it. The sponsoring musician rented a hall, hired the orchestra, selected the program and advertised the event. The audience, heavily stocked with friends and pupils, purchased individual tickets. After all expenses were paid, profits from the ticket sales ended up in the pockets of the sponsoring musician. Benefit concerts could be a highly profitable venture, depending on the artist's popularity. Capron wrote of Brown that "every concert for the benefit of that Gentleman, opens a scene of considerable profit."[58]

Subscription concerts are closest to the model in general use today. A series of concerts spaced about two a month for a total of ten to twelve performances was offered on a subscription basis. The series was advertised in the newspapers, and before the evening of the performance individual tickets were made available at a variety of locales.[59]

There is no documentation of amateur concerts taking place at City Tavern, but the other two types were common occurrences there. The height of the involvement of City Tavern in public concerts occurred between 1783 and 1790. As early as October 1783 Brown proposed two benefit concerts to be performed under his direction at City Tavern on 16 and 18 October at which he indicated that he would "perform some well-known and approved Scotch airs, with variations."[60] These appear to be the earliest professional concerts performed in City Tavern. At this time the Assembly Room located just to the west of City Tavern was the preferred concert setting. Juhan performed there on 6 August 1783, and in December 1783 a series of new amateur concerts was announced to take place there.

Between 1786 and 1788 City Tavern was also the site of a subscription series referred to as the "City Concerts." This series had actually had its beginning several years before when in October 1783 Brown and Capron joined forces with Bentley to establish a series of biweekly public concerts which continued through April 1784.[61] Their venture must have met with some success, as a second series was announced to begin in October 1784. The project was, however, not without its critics. A South-American visitor to the city, Francisco de Miranda, found the performances of the first season rather unexceptional. In January 1784 he wrote that "among the performers the flautist Brown, of middling merit, distinguishes himself." Both seasons were held in the Assembly Room, about which de Miranda could only say "not badly decorated."[62] Each concert was followed by cards and dancing. The last performance of the second season took place on 26 April 1785.

The 1785-86 season was scuttled as a result of a disagreement among the managers. As there were so few musicians of professional calibre, all were interdependent for their livelihoods, and personality squabbles could not last long. Brown, Capron, and Juhan continued to perform on each other's benefit concerts during the winter season, several of which took place in City Tavern.

By the fall of 1786, Bentley had separated himself from the others. Capron, who had been in Charleston, returned to Philadelphia in the late summer and on 21 September 1786 he teamed up with Brown and Juhan for a benefit performance at City Tavern. Also appearing on this program was a new face for Philadelphia music lovers: Alexander Reinagle. Three weeks later, Reinagle announced his own benefit concert at City Tavern. Again Brown and Capron were included on the program. By this time the four musicians had decided that they would attempt to resurrect the defunct City Concerts.[63] At the same time the decision was made to move their enterprise from the Masonic Assembly Rooms to City Tavern. The previous spring Gifford Dalley had terminated his contract with the proprietors, and the building was put up for sale. Samuel Powel purchased it on 12 April 1785 and appointed Edward Moyston manager. Moyston appears to have been sympathetic to the arts, and under his management City Tavern was the scene of many concerts and balls.

The 1786-87 season at City Tavern opened on 19 October and continued for the next five months. In all, there were twelve concerts, the final one occurring on 23 March 1787. Reinagle, Juhan, Brown, and Capron were featured in some way on each program. Sandwiched amongst the subscription programs, the musicians found time to schedule their own benefit concerts both at City Tavern and the Assembly Rooms. Concert activity at City Tavern continued in the second-floor long room through April, May, and June.

September and October found Reinagle in New York, where he was involved in trying to establish a similar concert series, also to be known as the "City Concerts." As a result, the 1787-88 season in Philadelphia started late (22 November 1787) and the total series was cut back to ten performances, the last of which took place 13 March 1788. Benefit concerts for a singer named "Rehine" (28 November 1787, postponed from 25 November) and Brown (10 April 1788) were scheduled in Moyston's tavern, but the surge of activity was beginning to subside.

No information is available for the 1788-89 season. In December 1788 Reinagle played a benefit concert at City Tavern, in which he shared the program with "Mrs. Henry," the wife of John Henry one of the mangers and actors in the American Company. The number of performances at City

Tavern continued to decline over the next season and into the summer of 1789.

Both Reinagle and Capron were in New York in September of 1789 to direct the subscription series there. No record of the 1789-90 season has been found. By 1791 Reinagle had formed a partnership with a John Christoph Moller (1755-1803). Reinagle and Moller moved the performances out of City Tavern to Oeller's Hotel on Chestnut street a block west of the State House. Moller and his talented daughter Lucy dominated the keyboard performances on these programs. Moller was the organist at Zion Lutheran Church. He later opened a music store in association with Capron. During this time, City Tavern was booked for two performances in September by a group of French musicians.[64]

The 1792-93 season was the last for the series. Eight performances took place at Oeller's Hotel. By this time Brown apparently had returned to Europe, and Juhan was replaced by the Belgian violinist, Jean Gehot (1756-c1820). Reinagle, Capron, and Moller managed the series.

CONCERT PROGRAMS

The concerts at City Tavern were characteristic of their day.[65] Normally, they began at 7:00 p.m. and continued for about two and one-half to three hours, after which the room was cleared for dancing. The typical modern-day concert-goer would probably consider this a long evening. It should be remembered, however, that in the eighteenth century members of the audience were not expected to remain seated throughout the performance. At City Tavern, if one tired of the performance, it was acceptable to move to one of the smaller back rooms to watch or engage in a game of cards or to visit one of the downstairs rooms for conversation and refreshment.

A raised platform, called the "orchestra," was erected in the north end of the long room for the performers.[66] This platform apparently was large enough to accommodate an ensemble of about fifteen musicians as well as a piano. It was not a permanent fixture in the room; when not being used the orchestra was dismantled and stored (probably in the basement). A new orchestra was constructed as part of the improvements Reinagle negotiated with the management of City Tavern in preparation for the City Concert series in 1786.[67]

Programs for subscription concerts were usually printed in local newspapers. Occasionally, full programs for benefit concerts also appeared in the newspapers, although more often than not the advertisements of these events committed themselves to little more than "favorite pieces." Unlike the rather homogeneous modern-day concert program, these programs display a wide variety of pieces and solo performers. A typical program included nine selections. Although most of the music was instrumental, each concert normally included at least one song, almost always placed immediately after the opening selection. This is a pattern also followed in London concerts of the day. The core of the program consisted of symphonies, overtures, and concertos. Nestled within this standard format, however, one could also find duets, trios, quartets, and even solo sonatas.

Programs were divided into parts termed "acts." The standard procedure was to separate the evening's entertainment into two acts, but under the influence of Reinagle the City Concerts adopted a three-act division with two intermissions. Reinagle had become familiar with this format in Edinburgh.[68]

Concerts always opened with a symphony or overture. The use of the term overture is somewhat misleading. Although many so-identified works were in fact single-movement compositions originally intended to be performed before a stage production of some sort (such as William Shield's *Rosina*, which apparently had special appeal for Philadelphia audiences), some were actually three- or four-movement symphonies. It is possible that in the case of the multi-movement works only the first movement was performed, but there is no documentation to indicate that this was the common practice.[69] The opening selection served to alert the audience that the program was about to begin. In this sense it fulfilled a function similar to that of a theater overture. Programs normally closed with either another overture, symphony (often referred to as finale), or a concerto. Sometimes this final number was not preannounced and functioned somewhat in the manner of a modern-day encore performed "by particular desire." When a concluding symphony was identified as a "finale," only its last movement was played.

Eighteenth-century audiences came to concerts primarily to experience the virtuoso display of the soloist. Not surprisingly, the core repertory of both the subscription and benefit concerts were display vehicles—concertos or works simply identified as "solos." Naturally, the solo instruments encountered at City Tavern concerts were predetermined by the limited pool of capable performers. In addition to pianoforte, flute, violin, and cello concertos performed by Reinagle, Brown, Juhan, and Capron, the latter also performed solo works for guitar and Phile played violin concertos.

THE REPERTORY

There is considerable variety in the manner in which individual compositions are listed on these programs. In some instances, the composer is clearly identified, but frequently in the case of solo literature the name of the soloist appears where one might expect to find that of the composer. As a result, it is not always clear whether the work is composed and performed by the artist listed or that individual is simply functioning as soloist. Thus, for example, a concerto for violin linked with Juhan's name may be a composition written and performed by him or simply his rendering of a work by some unnamed composer. The apparent lack of concern for accuracy in crediting the composer is more often the case with concertos than other selections. This situation certainly results in part from the "star" status accorded soloists, but it is also possible that solo literature was not fully decided upon when advertisements were placed in the local newspapers.

Unfortunately, this lax attitude toward the precise identification of individual selections makes it difficult to reach any definitive conclusions about the nature of the repertory preferred by Philadelphia's audiences of the 1780s. However, even with incomplete information certain general preferences emerge. Like their European cousins, eighteenth-century Philadelphians had a taste for recent music. The symphonies programmed on the City Tavern concerts tend to favor works by Franz Haydn (1732-1809), Jan Vanhal (1739-1813), Carl Stamitz (1745-1801), and Johann Christian Bach (1735-1782). Also included are overtures and symphonies by Karl Friedrich Abel (1723-1787), Antonio Rosetti (1750-1792), Thomas Erskine, Earl of Kelly (1732-1781), Antonín Kammel (1730-1787), Carlo Giuseppe Toeschi (1731-1788), François–Joseph Gossec (1734-1829), and Ludwig Wenzel Lachnith (1746-1820). The concerto repertory is more varied and dependent to a greater extent on the personal taste of the soloists. Brown programmed the music of the Mannheim flute virtuoso Johann Wendling (1723-1797), Carl Stamitz, Ernst Eichner (1740-1777), Josef Fiala (1748-1816), Joseph Schmittbauer (1718-1809), and even Frederick the Great (1712-1786). The taste of Juhan, on the other hand, ran more toward the Italians. Although he also performed works by composers like Johann Baptist Cramer (1771-1858) and Vanhal, he preferred solo works by violinist-composers Federigo Fiorillo (1755-1823), Luigi Borghi (1745-c1806), and Giovanni Giornovichi (1735/45-1804). Capron—the Frenchman in the group—favored the music of the cellist Joseph Tillier (before 1750-after 1790), although on several occasions he performed a concerto by the elder Schetky. The *simphonie concertante* repertory, which was the current rage in Paris, is represented by a concerto for flute and violin (originally, two solo violins) with orchestra by Jean-Baptiste Davaux (1742-1822). Chamber music includes duets for violin and cello by Jean-Baptiste Breval (1753-1823), a string quartet by Kammel, a piano trio by Johann Samuel Schroeter (1750-1788), and isolated chamber music by Schmittbauer and Davaux. Piano sonatas by Haydn, Schroeter, and Reinagle were also included on some of the City Tavern concerts as well as Reinagle's benefit concerts. Vocal music heard on these programs includes songs by Andre Ernest Grétry (1741-1813) and Giuseppe Sarti (1729-1802).

Compositions are almost never identified in any specific manner on the programs. The general exceptions to this are overtures. Among the favorites in this category were the overtures to William Shield's (1748-1829) *Rosina* and *The Poor Soldier* (said to have been a particular favorite with Washington), Thomas Arne's (1710-1778) *Artaxerxes* (1762), Thomas Linley's (1733-1795) *The Duenna* (1775), and Pierre-Alexandre Monsigny's (1729-1817) *Rose et Colas* (1764), *Le déserteur* (1769) and *La bella Arsène* (1773). A special favorite was the *Overture to Henry the Fourth* (1774) by Giovanni Martini [Johann Paul Schwartzendorf, 1741-1816], known as "Martini il Tedesco." This work was popular enough with local audiences to be published by Capron and Moller in a keyboard reduction.[70] Among the few symphonies that can be specifically identified are Stamitz's "La Chasse" Symphony, composed in 1772, and a symphony by Abel from a set of six published as op. 14 in London in 1778. References to Stamitz's "Symphony 2d" (program of 28 February 1788) and "Symphony 15th" (20 December 1787) probably refer to works from op. 2 (Paris, 1768) and op. 15 (Paris, 1776), respectively. Such references suggest that the orchestra played from printed parts. Music published in London, Paris, Vienna, and other European centers was available from book shops, such as Henry Rice's on Market street between Second and Third and special shops like the one operated by Michael Hillegas.[71] Some of the items on these programs, like the flute concerto by "Fiolla" [Fiala], performed by Brown on 14 December 1786, were not available in print, and the musicians must have been reading from manuscript parts. Unfortunately, the library of the City Concerts has not been preserved in any single collection.

Most of these composers were favorites of their day, and their music was regularly programmed on public concerts in the capitals of Europe as well as this country. The particular choices reflect not only popular taste, but the personal preferences of the series managers and performers as well. Thus, Reinagle and Schetky may have been responsible for the continued popularity of the Mannheim composers on these programs, and the strong Bohemian representation is probably traceable to Brown.[72] In a similar vein it is probable that the inclusion of overtures and symphonies by the Scotch nobleman Thomas Erskine, Lord Kelly, can be credited to Reinagle, whose father was an associate of Erskine in Edinburgh.[73] With few exceptions, the composers of the repertory described here were still alive or only recently deceased when their works were performed on the Philadelphia series. This fact places in sharper relief the appearance of a concerto grosso by Arcangelo Corelli (1653-1713) within this literature. Typically, the concerts given by the Edinburgh Musical Society regularly programmed "ancient" music. Reinagle's selection of Corelli's concerto grosso may have been intended to duplicate this tradition.[74]

Somewhat surprising to modern audiences may be the fact that

Mozart's name appears only once (a piano sonata performed on 14 December 1788) among this repertory. This is characteristic, however. Judging from surviving documents, Mozart's music was not extremely popular in this country during his lifetime. This is, however, not true of the music of Haydn. One of the most interesting changes instituted in the programs of the City Concerts after Reinagle joined the management team was the persistent programming of Haydn's music. Reinagle first introduced Philadelphia concert audiences to the music of Haydn with two overtures (symphonies) performed on his first benefit concert at City Tavern.[75] Reinagle's "Grand Concert" in New York's Assembly Room just months before had included three overtures by Haydn, and it is likely that he reused two of these works for the City Tavern concert. After this, Haydn's music appeared on ten of the twenty-two programs in the subscription series as well as several benefit concerts performed at City Tavern. For the most part Reinagle selected Haydn's symphonies or overtures as opening or closing numbers, but he also performed a sonata by Haydn. (Since so little information is provided in the programs printed in newspapers, it is impossible to determine if multiple references to a "symphony" or "sonata" by a particular composer refer to different compositions or simply multiple performances of the same work.) Reinagle continued to include Haydn's music on the City Concerts after he moved the series out of City Tavern.

The City Concerts would be a natural opportunity for Brown, Capron, Reinagle, and Juhan to promote their own compositions. While it cannot be assumed that all anonymous concertos were composed by these performers, it was certainly not unusual for virtuoso performers of this period to write their own solo music, and the possibility that some concertos listed on these programs were written by the performer must be seriously considered. Although Brown, Juhan, and Capron all left behind compositions, none of the pieces that have survived can be linked directly with works advertised on the City Tavern concerts. The situation is different, however, with regard to Reinagle. On several of the city concerts as well as benefit concerts Reinagle performed solo piano sonatas, including what must have been some of his own compositions. It is tempting to suggest that one or more of the four sonatas preserved in manuscript in the Library of Congress were included in this group.[76] An especially striking feature of these concerts is the preference for the piano as the solo keyboard instrument. In Reinagle's first season with the City Concerts a composition for piano appeared on every program.

At the City Tavern concert on 16 November 1786 Reinagle and Juhan performed a sonata for piano and violin. They may have performed that evening from a print published in London (or Glasgow) three years before under the title *Six sonatas for the piano-forte or harpsichord with an accompaniment for a violin*. It is also likely that some of the songs sung by Reinagle on several of the City Tavern concerts in 1786 and 1787 were among those published in two volumes by John Aitken in *A Collection of favorite Songs, arranged for the voice and pianoforte* (Philadelphia, [c]1789).

ORCHESTRA PERSONNEL

The orchestra used for the performances at City Tavern in the 1780s probably included about thirteen to fifteen musicians: 2 to 4 violins, viola, 2 cellos, bass, flute, 2 oboes, bassoon, 2 horns, and keyboard. This ensemble would have been a blend of professional and amateur instrumentalists, with the precise personnel varying from one performance to the next.[77] In trying to recreate the complement of the City Tavern orchestra, it is necessary to engage in a good deal of speculation, as no program or receipt has been preserved that identifies performers by name. Reinagle probably presided at the keyboard or joined Juhan and Phile in the violin section; Capron and Reinagle's nephew J. George Schetky (1776-1831) played cello,[78] and Brown played flute.

A receipt for costs incurred for a celebration held in City Tavern on 15 September 1787 helps to shed further light on possible orchestra personnel. On this date the First Troop of Calvary of the City of Philadelphia hosted an entertainment in honor of General Washington, "members of the Convention & other respectable characters." This was a private party; officially, the tavern had not yet reopened after Dalley's departure. In addition to cataloging abundant quantities of wine, liquor, cider, and beer consumed that evening, the receipt also documents that meals were provided for sixteen musicians. The order, in the hand of Thomas Proctor (here acting in his capacity as a retired officer in the Calvary), instructs that payment be made to George Christhilf, director of the ensemble.[79] In addition to Christhilf, eight musicians are identified specifically on the receipt: Mr. Schultz, Mr. Treniner, John Keyser, William Hartung, Philip Rotti, David Kutzstock, John Bruner, and Conrad Spangenberg. It is probable that some—if not all—of these musicians were members of the orchestra that performed in City Tavern for subscription and benefit concerts. The pronounced German lineage of these names seems to support Miranda's claim that the performers on the City Concerts were "almost the same" group who performed on the German Concerts held in Lodge Rooms.[80] The theatrical dancer, John Durang, who during this period was a member of the American Company, later in his memoirs recalled that the orchestral musicians of the theater, under Phile's direction, also were primarily German.[81] Perhaps the instrumentalists who were hired to provide music for concerts and special events at City Tavern during the

1780s were enlisted from the Southwark Theater orchestra.

Christhilf, Schultz, and Treniner, who were paid more than the others, were probably professionals. The musician identified as "Treniner" is Fruntz (Fritz) Tremner, who along with Philip Pfeil [Phile] ran the following advertisement in the *Pennsylvania Journal* on 21 June 1783:

> THE Subscribers beg leave to inform the Young Gentlemen of this City, that they intend to instruct on the German Flute, Hoboy, Clarinet, Violin, Harpsichord, Spinet, Violoncello, and Guitar, any Gentlemen that pleases to enter, may be assured of the best attendance. Enquire in Race-Street, between Fifth and Sixth-Streets, at the Widow Forrage.[82]

Tremner is probably the cellist remembered by Durang as "Trimmer."[83] The proprietress of the house where inquiries could be made was the widow of the musician Stephen Forrage who had performed at City Tavern several years before as part of Proctor's group. Schultz is likely to be the violinist who in 1789 offered a benefit concert at Epple's Tavern on Race Street. It will be remembered that he and Spangenberg were members of Proctor's ensemble that entertained the French Minister at City Tavern in August 1778. Perhaps this is the "Nicholas Schultz" whose name appears among the subscribers to Brown's *Three Rondos for the piano forte or harpsichord*.[84]

Rotti is a misspelling for Roth, who described himself in an advertisement in the *Pennsylvania Journal* as

> Music Master . . . Teaches all kinds of Instrumental Music in the shortest manner, viz. Harpsichord, Piano Forte, Guitar, Flute, Hautboy, Clarinet, Bassoon, French Horn, Harp and Thorough-Bass.[85]

Roth's name first appears in the Philadelphia newspapers in 1771 when an overture of his composition was performed on a benefit concert for the flutist John McLean at the Assembly Rooms.[86] At that time Roth was identified as Master of the Band belonging to his Majesty's Royal Regiment of North British Fusileers (21st Foot).[87] During the war, he served as the music master of Henry Lee's "Partisan Corps" of the Continental Army.[88]

The Philadelphia City Directory of 1785 includes Philip Roth as one of three musicians so identified. The other two were Philip Malloney of Sugar alley and George Prunner of Race street.[89] Perhaps they were also members of the orchestra that provided music at City Tavern. Unfortunately, the instruments they played are not identified.

In 1792 Phile, Schultz, Tremner, Roth, Christhilf, and Spangenberg were all listed as instrumentalists on "A CONCERT OF VOCAL & INSTRUMENTAL MUSIC" at Vauxhall pleasure garden.[90] From this group only the names of Roth and Spangenberg appeared in the City Directory of 1791. Roth is listed as a musician living at 25 Crown Street, while Conrad Spangenberg is identified as a laborer residing at 359 N. Front Street.[91]

In the years between the opening of its doors in 1773 and the early years of the Federal Republic, City Tavern was the scene of a wide variety of musical entertainment, ranging from traditional tavern music-making to formal public concerts. The steady succession of subscription and benefit concerts that took place in the tavern's second-floor long room provided Philadelphians with musical experiences not unlike those enjoyed by fashionable London society. City Tavern concerts featured a thoroughly up-to-date repertory of vocal and orchestral literature performed by a capable ensemble of amateur and professional musicians. Moreover, these concerts were open to the public and recognized no social barriers.

SOCIAL DANCE IN EIGHTEENTH-CENTURY PHILADELPHIA

Next to concerts, balls were the most festive occasions at City Tavern to include music. Dancing was a special passion of the eighteenth century. It was advocated as healthy and considered an appropriate pastime for all ages. Philadelphians were no exception; in the words of one foreign visitor: "dance is their favorite entertainment."[92] Dancing in this period was not a casual affair, however. Balls were governed by an elaborate system of protocol. Where, when, what, and with whom you danced were factors of utmost importance. But deportment was not all; technique was equally important. A poorly-executed *pas de menuet* may exert detrimental consequences on one's social status. In order not to run the risk of public embarrassment, it was essential to secure proper instruction from an approved dancing master. To judge from the number of dancing masters who advertised their services in eighteenth-century Philadelphia newspapers, local society was fully committed to achieving perfection in this popular pastime.

Normally dancing masters also provided other types of instruction— most often in languages, but also fencing, art, and music. Some had studios, while others, like "Mr. Pike (Ten years a teacher in Charlestown, South-Carolina)" advertised that "Ladies and gentlemen may be waited on at their own houses, if agreeable, to be taught cotillions and other fashionable dances."[93] For gentlemen who were unavailable during the day, special evening classes were provided. Typical of newspaper advertisements offering the services of dancing masters is the following notice posted by William Francis (1762-1827):

> FRANCIS, DANCING MASTER, Will open a school at the Long Room, in White Horse Alley, on Thursday the 2d of December, for the accomplishment of young Gentlemen and Ladies in that genteel part of polite education. Those gentlemen and ladies who shall be pleased to intrust [sic] him with the education of their children, may be assured that he will take particular care of their behavior, as well as instruct them in every branch of dancing. . . . A night class will be opened for such young gentlemen as cannot attend in the day. N.B. Any Ladies or Gentlemen who are desirous of being taught the German and French languages grammatically, will be waited on at their places of abode, by sending to him at the sign of the Bear in Market-street.[94]

Having worked diligently through their instruction, dancers had ample opportunity to demonstrate their newly-acquired skills at private gatherings in the homes of Philadelphia's social elite:

> Mrs. Robert Morris and Mrs. James Allen are also wont to give nocturnal functions, limited to dancing and card playing, which they call "private parties" and are extremely pleasant. The company is select, the people know each other, and consequently there is more assurance and satisfaction.[95]

Dancing was also a favorite pastime in the home of Elizabeth and Samuel Powel on Third street,[96] and during the long winter months of 1784 balls were also given at the residence of the Spanish Envoy, Don Francisco Rendon.[97]

BALLS AT CITY TAVERN

One wishing to venture afield from this select company might try his or her luck in front of a larger audience at one of the city's many public balls. In addition to those that normally followed concerts, special balls were also arranged by individuals in a manner similar to that of the benefit concerts. While it was apparently possible for ordinary citizens to rent City Tavern's long room for dances,[98] it was most frequently the local dancing masters who sponsored balls there. A "Mr. Cenas" sponsored dances there many times in the years between 1785 and 1790. In 1788, Stephen Sicard, a musician and dancing instructor, hosted a series of "practicing balls" at City Tavern. Sicard operated a dancing school "at the Long Room in Elbow-lane, back of the Whitehorse [Tavern] in Chestnut-street." He claimed to be a pupil of "the celebrated Mr. Vestries, and assistant master of Mr. Gardelle, the first dancer of the Opera at Paris, Dancing Master of Her Majesty, the Queen of France and Royal Family."[99]

On these occasions the dancing master would demonstrate the newest dance steps or impress the company with his skill in executing the intricate steps of solo dances. In 1784 readers of the *Pennsylvania Packet* were assured that at a City Tavern ball Mr. Cenas "will have the honor to dance the solos and menuet." In 1789 a special ball under Sicard's direction in City Tavern featured his students dancing his own *Federal Ballet*. Sicard created both the music and the choreography for his dances. In 1788 "Mr. Atken [*sic*] opposite the City Tavern" published Sicard's *New Constitution March and Federal Minuet* in an arrangement "adapted to the pianoforte, violin and German flute, etc."[100] Aitken's advertisement claimed that "Mr. Sicard has also composed several new dances," but the only works known to have survived are *The President of the United States March* (Philadelphia: J. McCulloch, [1789]) and the melody to a "Cotillion Minuet."[101]

The elaborate etiquette associated with a formal ball provided a suitable opportunity to evoke and reinforce important social distinctions. As early as 1748 aristocratic Philadelphia banded together to establish an elite dancing society, known as the Philadelphia Dancing Assembly.[102] Membership was by subscription and open only to the highest levels of local society, with tradesmen and merchants denied access regardless of their material success.[103] Although no names of Philadelphia Friends appear on the original subscription lists, in later years Quakers did attend the assemblies, although apparently not to dance.[104]

In its early days, the Dancing Assembly (sometimes simply referred to as the "assembly") met in places like Andrew Hamilton's house and stores on Water Street, the long room of the State House (today known as "Independence Hall"), and taverns like Epple's Sign of the Rainbow. In the 1770s, assembly balls were announced in the local newspapers at the Assembly Rooms on Lodge alley, and it is very likely that even from its inception the Assembly held some balls in City Tavern.[105]

One of the busiest periods of dancing at City Tavern was during the British occupation, when British officers joined with Tory families still remaining in the city to continue a skeleton of the Assembly at City Tavern. When Lord Howe's forces, still flushed from their recent victory at the Battle of Brandywine, marched into Philadelphia on 26 September 1777, they were enthusiastically welcomed by the loyalists. Thus began a period of occupation that would last six months. British officers and soldiers quickly set out to provide appropriate diversion to help them confront the long winter evenings of their occupation duty. Dining and gambling clubs were established at several of the better taverns in the city. The Southwark Theater was reopened and used by "Howe's Strolling Players" made up primarily of General Howe's officers, among whose company the infamous Major John André (1751-1780) was prominent. British soldiers found that there was no dearth of Tory belles to accompany them to the theater and concerts or to serve as their dancing partners in a regular round of balls.

During the British seizure of the city, Smith kept his establishment open for business. This was, in fact, a prosperous period for City Tavern, which became the preferred gathering place for high-ranking British officers. With a group of officers appointed managers, the tavern's rooms were opened for gambling, concerts, balls, and general merry making.[106] In a short time City Tavern had become the center for the social whirl of the Tory-dominated city.

Improvements were made to the dancing area of the long room,[107] and City Tavern balls soon became a regular part of social life in the occupied city. The first of these took place on 29 January 1778[108] with the series continuing every Thursday evening until the end of April for a total of thirteen balls. Ladies were admitted free, but for all others an admission fee was charged.

The British balls at the City Tavern in the winter of 1778-79 stand out in stark relief against the hellish ordeal of the American army encamped north of the city at Valley Forge. Many were caught up in the swirl of gaiety that highlighted City Tavern that harsh winter. Johann Heinrichs, a captain in the Hessian forces, claimed that the merriment and entertainment "make us forget there is any war, save that it is a capital joke."[109] The young Tory socialite, Rebecca Franks, found the regular round of entertainments in the city much to her liking. She confided in her friend, Anne Harrison Paca:

> You can have no idea of the life of continued amusement I live in. I can scarce have a moment to myself. [I] am dressed for a ball this evening at Smith's where we have one every Thursday. . . . I know you are as fond of a gay life as myself—you'd have an opportunity of rakeing as much as you choose either at Plays Balls Concerts or Assemblys. I've been but 3 evenings alone since we mov'd to town.[110]

The Tory ladies who participated in these activities incurred the disdain of other Americans. Henry Livingston, Governor of New York, expressed the view of many when he wrote: "The Philadelphia flirts are equally famous for their want of modesty and want of patriotism in their overcomplacence to red coats."[111]

By the spring of 1778, it was clear that the occupation of Philadelphia was nearing an end. The mood turned dark, and City Tavern was now also the scene of several court martials. The last in the winter's series of balls on 30 April 1778 marked the temporary closing of the tavern. In May, Howe resigned as Commander of the British Troops, and to commemorate his service an elaborate farewell spectacle, known as the "Meschianza," was mounted by his officers.[112] This gaudy spectacle marked the end of the elaborate social spree of the occupied city. The British troops were placed under the command of General Henry Clinton, and, almost immediately, instructions were issued to evacuate the city and retreat to New York. By mid-May, the British had withdrawn, taking with them shiploads of Tory loyalists, including City Tavern's erstwhile manager, Daniel Smith.

The Continental Army that entered the city in May 1778 found it in a sorry state. During their last days there, the British troops had stolen what they could carry and destroyed much of the rest that was of value. The general abandonment that accompanied an occupied territory added to the stench, waste, and depravation that Clinton's troops left behind. City Tavern stood empty and abandoned, awaiting the next stage of its history.

The building was not to be dark for long. On 4 August the *Pennsylvania Evening Post* carried the following announcement:

> CITY TAVERN. On Monday next this well situated and commodious house, in Second-street, will be opened for the reception and entertainment of company, in large or small parties.[113]

ASSEMBLY BALLS AT CITY TAVERN

By the following autumn the city had started to return to its normal routine. As part of the rejuvenation effort, a group of subscribers met at City Tavern to reorganize the Philadelphia Dancing Assembly, which had been officially dormant during the war years. City Tavern was selected as the appropriate locale, and during the 1780s the tavern became the site of regular festivities under the direction of the Dancing Assembly:

> A few private balls were given in the course of the season, but most of the dancing was performed at what was called the dancing assembly, held by subscription at stated times in a room appropriate to that and other similar purposes at the Merchant's Coffee House in Second Street.[114]

The issue of loyalty was a sensitive one in the years following the British occupation. It was made clear that those who had consorted with the enemy were not welcome within the city's social set. Efforts of the French Ministers to mount a ball in honor of the king's birthday on 24 August 1778 were thwarted because the Americans "wish to establish an absolute line of separation between the Whigs and Tories, especially between the ladies."[115] In 1780, a ranking officer in Lafayette's command, François-Jean, Marquis de Chastellux (1734-1788), pointed out that at a City Tavern assembly a Miss Footman (one of the few women of "passable" appearance in the room that evening) was considered "a bit contraband, that is to say, suspected of not being a very good Whig, for the Tory ladies have been publicly banned from this assembly." Some Philadelphia ladies went to great lengths to proclaim their patriotism. At the same ball the Marquis encountered a "Miss [Mary] V[ining]" who "applies red, white, blue, and all possible colors, affects an extraordinary mode of dressing her hair and person, and, a staunch Whig in every point, she sets no bounds to her liberty."[116]

The lack of sufficient local beauties made it difficult to fully adhere to this philosophy, however. The *Pennsylvania Packet* of 29 August 1778 lamented that a city ball was "graced with Meschianza ladies equally noted for their Tory principles and their late fondness for British debauchees and macaronies," and Henry Livingston was appalled to note in January 1779 that "Tory-Girls" were well in evidence at the City Tavern subscription balls.[117] Gradually, distinctions were forgotten, and City Tavern was filled with the glitter and excitement of the assembly balls.

Biweekly the cream of aristocratic Philadelphia gathered in the second-floor long room of the tavern on Second street to dance and be seen. These balls were intended for a highly selective audience. Admission was restricted to subscribers and their wives and daughters who were received as guests.[118] Other ladies and "strangers arriving in the city" could be admitted only by letter of invitation.[119] Benefit balls sponsored by dancing masters were less restrictive. Tickets, usually at the cost of one dollar, could be purchased before the event at specified local taverns and coffee houses. Ladies could send their servants to these same establishments to request tickets for which there was no charge.

Dancers began to arrive at about seven o'clock, and they were shown to the second floor hall where the dancing took place. One of the first things they would have seen upon entering the large room at the top of the stairs was a prominently displayed portrait of John Inglis, one of the founding members of the Dancing Assembly, painted by Charles Willson Peale.[120] The orchestra was seated on the raised platform used for concert presentations at the north end of the hall. There are still uncertainties concerning the orchestra used for these occasions. It would seem likely that the musicians who played for the dancing were the same who performed at concerts, but this has yet to be fully established. It is possible that a smaller ensemble was used for the dances.

Assembly balls were governed by a strict set of rules, which were prominently displayed near the entrance to the room. For each season, subscribers selected four "managers" or "masters of ceremonies" who were responsible for the strict enforcement of the assembly's rules, which covered such matters as the distribution of tickets, regulation of the dances, and selection of the music.

Early in the evening the managers presented each dancer with a folded paper that contained a number that decided which partner one would have for the rest of the evening.[121] The ball officially began with a minuet. The privilege of dancing this first dance was decided upon by the managers in the case of the Dancing Assembly, but for balls sponsored by dancing masters, the opening dance was reserved for the teacher himself or his pupils. In advertising a ball at City Tavern on 19 December 1785, the dancing master "Mr. Cenas" specified that "two ladies will open the ball with the menuet and a menutt de la cour; after two countridances, two young ladies will perform the same minuets and each will dance a solo; one will dance another of a different kind, all of Mr. CENAS'S composition."[122]

At least one European observer considered Americans awkward dancers — "particularly in the minuet," and after the obligatory opening dance, the regular course for the rest of the evening was a series of country dances, contredances, cotillions, and quadrilles. Country dances are line dances in which the men and women form lines facing one another. The couple at the top of the line is the head or first couple. They move down the set performing the prescribed figures, while the other couples move up, eventually bringing the head couple to the bottom of the set and the last couple to the top. At the assembly balls, the arrangement of couples in the sets of the country dances was determined by the managers. Such decisions were extremely important, as they represented position and influence within the community. The position of first couple was reserved for individuals of rank and property. Writers of the period point out that Mrs. Robert Morris, reputed to be the wealthiest woman in the city, was often accorded this honor.

In advertising his ball on Thursday, 19 December 1785, Cenas identified several French "countridances" which he would demonstrate.[123] Sicard advertised that he was prepared to teach court dances (including various types of menuets and allemandes) as well as hornpipes and American country dances.[124] The contredanse was a French variation on the English country dance. It replaced the line formation of its English cousin with a square comprised of eight dancers. This version was also known in England as a cotillion. An early nineteenth-century *Treatise on Dancing* described the cotillion in the following words:

> The Figures of Cotillions, consist of two parts, the one is termed the change, the other the figure. There are ten changes, which are the same in all regular cotillions, but every cotillion has a different figure, which is performed between every change, and once after the last change.[125]

The most modern dance to be included on the Assembly programs was the quadrille. This dance was a close relative of the cotillion, being "a series of figures, usually five, performed without changes as in a cotillion but maintaining the square formation of eight performers."[126] The quadrille became increasingly fashionable after the turn of the century.

Dances were given names linking them to the music used. These names helped the dancers identify the combination and pattern of figures appropriate for that dance. In his commentary on his American travels the Marquis de Chastellux, who attended a Philadelphia Dancing Assembly in December 1780, pointed out that "dances, like the 'toasts' we drink at table, have a marked connection with politics; one is called 'the success of the campaign,' another 'Burgoyne's defeat,' and a third, 'Clinton's retreat.'"[127]

Apparently, not everyone in attendance danced. For those who preferred, at City Tavern there were tables set up in the back rooms for playing cards. About an hour before midnight a pause was taken for light refreshments of "tea, coffee, and chocolate . . . with biscuits and toasts." The dance then resumed and continued until about two or three o'clock in the morning. Miranda described the general atmosphere as rather relaxed.[128]

Although the entire membership of the Dancing Assembly did not attend each ball, there could be well over a hundred people for any particular ball, and, not surprisingly, there were soon complaints that the long room was too narrow for the fashionably-wide dresses and intricate step patterns of the newer dances. The suggestion of building an independent Assembly Room raised its head off and on. In January 1787, a meeting of the assembly subscribers was set in City Tavern to devise a plan for the financing of a new building. Newspapers as far away as Massachusetts carried notices of the meeting as well as an explanation of its need: "*The* LADIES and GENTLEMEN of this City having of late repeatedly testified their disapprobation of the present ASSEMBLY-ROOM, AT THE City Tavern as being in every way inadequate to the purpose."[129]

By the last years of the 1780s the popularity of the City Tavern assemblies was clearly on the wane. On 29 November 1790 the innkeeper, Edward Moyston, was obliged to announce in the *Pennsylvania Packet* that "The Dancing Assembly having lately procured a Hall for themselves, are removed from the CITY TAVERN."[130] The hall to which Moyston refers were the larger quarters at the newly completed Oeller's Hotel.[131]

Like special entertainments and concerts, balls had also found a welcome home at City Tavern. As a result, in the period from 1773 until about 1790 City Tavern functioned as a focal point for the polite society of the city. Philadelphia's wealthy and prominent gathered here not only to dance and enjoy music but also to reaffirm their heritage as ladies and gentlemen of a civilized and cultured society.

THE END OF AN ERA

In 1790 Philadelphia became the capital of the new Republic. In this early Federal period the city would continue to play a vital role in the cultural development of our country. City Tavern, however, was beginning to show its age. The complaints of the dancing assembly about the size of the facility could be echoed by those interested in the long room as a site for concerts. When Reinagle moved the City Concerts in 1791 to a larger and more opulent facility in Oeller's Hotel, he was signaling the end of an era for the building. The Assembly had left the previous year, and, with the exception of the concerts given by the visiting French musicians and a few isolated benefit performances, there was little concert activity in the building thereafter.[132]

Although once the showpiece of Philadelphia's cultural and social life, City Tavern had been eclipsed by other more modern halls. With its elegance faded and out of fashion and its size too limited to accommodate the public life of a capital city, the once-celebrated City Tavern had become little more than a symbol of a time that had passed. Although the building was to continue to function as a tavern and merchant's exchange until well into the nineteenth century, it was never again to experience the glory and renown it had known during the days of its brilliance in the 1770s and 1780s.

---

[1]In 1975 City Tavern was restored to its original appearance as part of Independence National Historical Park. Today the tavern is run by a commercial firm and serves meals in a recreated eighteenth-century atmosphere. Two studies compiled as part of the restoration process have been helpful in providing background detail for the present study: John D. R. Platt, *The City Tavern: Historic Resource Study* (Denver, Col.: Denver Service Center Historic Preservation Team, National Park Service, United States Department of the Interior, [April] 1973), and Penelope H. Batcheler, *City Tavern: Historic Structure Report* (Denver, Col.: Denver Service

Center, Historical Preservation Team, National Park Service, United States Department of the Interior, [October] 1973). I wish to express my sincere appreciation to the staff of the Research Library of Independence National Historical Park for permission to make use of materials from the research library and card index in writing the present study.

[2] Edmund C. Burnett, ed., *Letters of Members of the Continental Congress*, 8 vols. (Washington, D.C.: Carnegie Institution, 1921-36; reprint, Gloucester, Mass.: Peter Smith, 1963) 1:1.

[3] Smith's tavern enjoyed a prime location. Although within easy walking distance of shops and the marketplace as well as the commerce of the busy port's wharves, City Tavern also bordered on the residential area where many wealthy and socially-prominent Philadelphians lived. Second street was the primary north-south route through the city (known as "Old King's Road"), and, as such, travelers would have had little difficulty locating Smith's establishment.

[4] *Dunlap's Pennsylvania Packet, or the General Advertiser* [hereafter referred to as the *Pennsylvania Packet*], 14 February 1774. Construction on City Tavern began in August 1772 and by the following March *The Pennsylvania Journal and the Weekly Advertiser* [hereafter known as the *Pennsylvania Journal*], 31 March 1773, first announced "TO BE LETT, A LARGE commodious new HOUSE . . . intended to be kept as a genteel tavern." Smith, who had been a tavern-keeper in Dublin, was selected by the subscribers as early as July 1773 when his name was listed among those recommended for a license. Platt, *The City Tavern*, 7 n. 10.

[5] Some of these houses are still standing today and several have been restored as part of Independence National Historical Park and the Society Hill area of Philadelphia. By the 1770s the city had assumed the shape and appearance that have been preserved in the historical area today.

[6] For more information on Philadelphia in the eighteenth century, see Carl and Jessica Bridenbaugh, *Rebels and Gentlemen: Philadelphia in the Age of Franklin*, 2nd ed. (New York: Oxford University Press, 1965; reprint, Westport, Conn.: Greenwood Press, 1978); also helpful for a general background is Russell F. Weigley, ed., *Philadelphia: A 300-Year History* (New York: W. W. Norton, 1982).

[7] The terms inn and tavern were often used interchangeably, although the former seems to have been preferred in the northern Colonies. Robert Earle Graham, "The Taverns of Colonial Philadelphia," in Luther P. Eisenhart, ed., *Historic Philadelphia From the Founding Fathers until the Early Nineteenth Century: Papers dealing with its People and Buildings with an Illustrative Map*, in Transactions of the American Philosophical Society, vol. 43 (Philadelphia, 1953), 318-25. In the South, inns and taverns that

did not normally provide lodging were called "ordinaries." Jane Carson, *Colonial Virginians at Play* (Williamsburg, Va.: Colonial Williamsburg, 1965; reprint, 1989).

[8]If wine, liquor, or cider were served, the establishment had to be licensed by the Governor upon recommendation of the justices of the respective counties. In 1773 alone the July session of the Philadelphia court recommended 170 applicants for tavern licenses. Batcheler, *City Tavern*, 13. In addition, there were probably many more "tippling houses" functioning outside the law.

[9]The best sources of information on eighteenth-century Philadelphia taverns are Graham, "The Taverns of Colonial Philadelphia" and M. E. and Benjamin R. Boggs, "Inns and Taverns of Old Philadelphia" (unpublished typescript, Boggs Collection, AM 3032, Historical Society of Pennsylvania). The convivial atmosphere of Philadelphia tavern life of this period is preserved in various scenes from Andrew Barton's ballad opera, *The Disappointment*, first produced in the Southwark Theater in 1769. Barton drew his characters and locations from the world around him; the Tun Tavern on Water street just south of Chestnut probably served as Barton's model for the tavern scenes in his play. Patricia H. Virga, *The American Opera to 1790* (Ann Arbor, Mich.: UMI Research Press, 1982), 34. The Tun Tavern, which was operated by Peg and Thomas Mullen, was sometimes referred to as "Peg Mullen's Beefsteak House."

[10]In addition to those mentioned later in this study, among the more important Philadelphia taverns in operation during the period being considered here were the Black Horse on Black Horse Alley (which for a short time in the early 1770s was under the management of Francis Lee, who later ran the highly successful Indian Queen), the George Inn on the southwestern corner of Arch and Second streets, the Cross Keys on the northeastern corner of Third and Chestnut streets, the Harp and Crown on Elbow lane at Third street, the White Horse also on Elbow Lane, the Kouli Khan (or Turk's Head) on Chestnut between Second and Front streets, the King of Prussia on Market at Third street, and the Three Crowns next to City Tavern on Second street. A more extensive list is found as Appendix F to Robert E. Graham's unpublished study "Philadelphia Inns and Taverns, 1774–1780" (Independence National Historical Park, Research Library).

[11]*Pennsylvania Packet*, 15 December 1781. About a month later a second advertisement, this time in the *Pennsylvania Gazette*, 23 January 1782, added "a large room" and estimated the stables could accommodate forty horses.

[12]*Pennsylvania Gazette*, 3 January 1776.

[13]William Parker Cutler and Julia Parker Cutler, *Life, Journals and*

Correspondence of Rev. Manasseh Cutler, LL.D., 2 vols. (Cincinnati: R. Clarke, 1984) 1:253-54.

[14] Two important pictorial representations of the building have been preserved. In his depiction of the "Bank of Pennsylvania, South Second Street" the Philadelphia artist, William R. Birch, included a section of City Tavern. Birch's engraving was published in December 1800 as part of his set *The City of Philadelphia, in the State of Pennsylvania North America; as it appeared in the Year 1800, consisting of Twenty-Eight Plates*. Sometime around 1798 the English architect Benjamin Henry Latrobe did a watercolor drawing of the same bank taken from the same point of view. Both illustrations are included—along with modern-day architectural drawings—in Batcheler (see illustrations 3 and 6).

[15] There was a livery stable already to the west along the alley which was used by patrons of the tavern. Some outbuildings, including a stable, were added at a later date. In 1787 the small building on the south side of the tavern, which since about 1770 had functioned as a tavern called the Three Crowns, was purchased and used as an annex to provide additional lodging rooms for "the reception of such ladies and gentlemen as would chose to be more retired than they can be in the tavern." *Pennsylvania Packet*, 10 October 1787.

[16] The decision to use this manner of subsidy was probably suggested by the earlier success of a similar plan used to finance the construction of the London Coffee House at the corner of Front and Market streets. Coffee houses were primarily places for merchants and sea captains to gather and conduct business. The best of Philadelphia's coffee houses was the London Coffee House owned and operated by William Bradford, who was also the publisher of the *Pennsylvania Journal*. On the first floor there was a bar and a public room, where lemonade, coffee, wine, and spirits were sold, and smaller rooms were available upstairs for private or club meetings. Platt, 2 n. 2.

[17] The seven trustees were John Cadwalader, George Clymer, Samuel Meredith, Henry Hill, Edward Shippen, Jr., Joseph Shippen, Jr., and John Wilcocks. For more information on the proprietors and trustees of City Tavern, see Platt, 8-20.

[18] The role of Evans is not clear. Batcheler (Appendix G, 111) includes him as an employee of the tavern (1780-84) but does not list him among the managers. Platt, 156, writes that "From the evidence at hand, it appears that Dalley's successor received the keys to City Tavern sometime in November 1779." During the period of time when Batcheler placed Dalley as the manager of the tavern (1778 to 1785), Platt points out that Dalley held other positions in the city.

[19] An announcement that appeared in the *Pennsylvania Journal*, 11 August 1773, pointed out that City Tavern "has been built, at a great expense, by a number of gentlemen . . . without any view of profit, but merely for the convenience and credit of the city." Even private citizens had high hopes for the new tavern: "From the *Coffee House* and the *New Tavern* I expect abundant matter for speculation. The political, commercial, literary and religious interests of the province will there, no doubt be learnedly discussed by many a Knot of grave and sensible freeholders." *Pennsylvania Packet*, 24 October 1773.

[20] *Pennsylvania Journal*, 31 March 1773.

[21] ". . . four rooms in the house can be made into two, which will entertain from 80 to 100 gentlemen." *Pennsylvania Gazette*, 3 January 1776.

[22] The Masonic Lodge was described as a plain structure that stood on a lot between Lodge alley and Logan alley, which runs next to City Tavern, connecting Second and Dock streets.

[23] According to Bridenbaugh, "the circulating bottle at city pubs served as baton and tuning fork to lead many into song, and for gentry as well as common folk the tavern often became a musical center." *Rebels and Gentlemen*, 148.

[24] See Gillian B. Anderson, *Freedom's Voice in Poetry and Song* (Wilmington, Del.: Scholarly Resources, 1977).

[25] The best source of information on *Harmonie* ensembles is Roger Hellyer, "'Harmoniemusik': Music for Small Wind Bands in the Late Eighteenth and Early Nineteenth Centuries" (Ph.D. diss., Oxford University, 1973).

[26] In the summer of 1786, the manager of the Pennsylvania Coffee House announced a series of concerts of "Harmonial Music" to be given by an ensemble consisting of flute, two clarinets, two horns, and two bassoons. *Pennsylvania Evening Herald, and General Advertiser*, 17 May 1786. Performances were scheduled every Thursday evening from June to September.

[27] *Pennsylvania Evening Post*, 17 June 1777. Similar events were associated with taverns in other cities. Bridenbaugh reports that on 30 April 1773 while Josiah Quincy feasted at Bryne's Tavern in Boston he was entertained with music played by "three French horns, bassoon, three fiddles, etc., before and after dinner." *Rebels and Gentlemen*, 149.

[28] Samuel Holten, "Diary," as cited in Burnett, *Letters of Members of the Continental Congress* 3:320.

[29] Letter from Thomas McKean to William Augustus Atlee, 7 July 1778, as cited in Burnett, 3:321-22.

[30] "Diary of the Hon. William Ellery, of Rhode Island, June 28-July 23,

1778," *Pennsylvania Magazine of History and Biography* 11/4 (1887): 477.

[31]During the war Proctor served as Captain of the First Company of Pennsylvania Artillery, a militia unit, which included a band of at least six instrumentalists in addition to fifers and drummers. On 19 July 1777 Proctor's unit was incorporated into the Continental Army as the 4th Regiment of Artillery, and the following year he was promoted to Colonel, a title which he held until his discharge in 1781 or 1783. Proctor and his band were among the troops who survived the long and bitter winter at Valley Forge with Washington. For more information, see Raoul F. Camus, *Military Music of the American Revolution* (Chapel Hill: University of North Carolina Press, 1976), 137-41, and *History of the First Troop Philadelphia City Calvary* (Philadelphia: William F. Fell, 1948).

[32]*Pennsylvania Packet*, 5 December 1778.

[33]*Pennsylvania Packet*, 2 January 1779: "PHILADELPHIA: MONDAY last, agreeable to the Constitution of the Most Ancient and Worshipful SOCIETY of FREE and ACCEPTED MASONS, was celebrated as the Anniversary of ST. JOHN the Evangelist."

[34]Biographical information on Proctor is found in Benjamin M. Nead, "A Sketch of General Thomas Procter [*sic*]," *Pennsylvania Magazine of History and Biography* 4 (1880): 454-70.

[35]Platt, 26-27; Batcheler, 11-12.

[36]Gérard returned the favor with a banquet in celebration of the king's birthday, which was also held in the long room of City Tavern. Accounts of this festivity, however, make no mention of musical entertainment.

[37]Journal, Treasury Office and Auditor of Accounts, 16 April 1776 to 30 September 1781, p. 221, in Record Group 39, National Archives, as cited in Platt, 141 n. 253.

[38]Robert A. Gerson, *Music in Philadelphia* (Philadelphia: Theodore Presser, 1940; reprint, Westport, Conn.: Greenwood Press, 1970), 20; Oscar G. T. Sonneck, *Francis Hopkinson, the First American Poet-Composer (1737-1791) and James Lyon, Patriot, Preacher, and Loyalist (1735-1794)* (Washington, D.C.: H. L. McQueen, 1905; reprint, New York: Da Capo Press, 1967), 43; and *The New Grove Dictionary of Music and Musicians* (London: Macmillan, 1980), s.v. "Musical glasses," by Alec Hyatt King.

[39]According to Camus, Proctor's band in 1779 included twelve musicians: Charles Hoffman (clarinet), William Shippen, Peter Kalckhoffer (flute), Jacob Snell, Thomas Mingle, George Weaver, Samuel Hockuhoy, Michael Thurston, William Moore, Conrad Gropingeiser, Thomas Guy, and William Norton. Camus, 139.

[40]The best source of information on concert life in early America remains

Oscar George Sonneck, *Early Concert-Life in America (1731-1800)* (Leipzig: Breitkopf & Härtel, 1907; reprint, New York: Da Capo Press, 1978); also helpful are Harold Donaldson Eberlein and Cortlandt Van Dyke Hubbard, "Music in the Early Federal Era," *Pennsylvania Magazine of History and Biography* 69/2 (April 1945): 103-27 and Robert R. Drummond, *Early German Music in Philadelphia* (New York: D. Appleton, 1910; reprint, New York: Da Capo, 1970).

[41]*New York Gazette*, 2 August 1783.

[42]In a card addressed to Brown in the winter of 1785, Bentley wrote, "Did you not live free of every expense in my house for the whole of last Winter, and some months after the concerts were closed?" Sonneck, *Early Concert-Life in America*, 126. Very little is known about Bentley. He probably came to Philadelphia from England in the early 1780s. In 1785 he was hired as the keyboardist with the orchestra of Lewis Hallam's Old American Company at the Southwark Theater. In addition to his duties in the orchestra, Bentley also composed some new music for the company's productions, including songs for Hallam to perform as "Mungo" in *The Padlock* and dances for John Durang's black-face role as "Friday" in the pantomime *Robinson Crusoe*. Russell Sanjek, *American Popular Music and Its Business: The First Four Hundred Years*, 3 vols. (New York: Oxford University Press, 1988) 1:346.

[43]Carl Engel, "Introducing Mr. Braun," *Musical Quarterly* 30/1 (January 1944): 63-83. Perhaps the period of travel referred to in the *New York Gazette* would account for the years between 1780, when Wilhelm Braun left the Kassel *Hofkapelle*, and 1782-83, when Brown first appeared in this country. Quite possibly, Wilhelm Braun was related to the oboist Anton Braun (1729-1798) who, along with his sons Johann (1753-1811), Johann Friedrich (1758-1824), and Moritz (1765-1828), was employed in the Kassel court orchestra.

[44]Philip Phile, whose name is spelled in a variety of ways (Phyla, Phylo, Phyles, Fyles, Feyles), came to this country with the Hessian mercenaries. In the late 1770s, he conducted the orchestra for the musical stage productions put on in New York by British soldiers who identified themselves as "Clinton's Thespians." After the war, Phile remained in America. He moved to Philadelphia sometime around 1784. From this point on, Phile appears to have divided his performing career between Philadelphia and New York, finally settling in Philadelphia in 1789. Durang identifies him as the orchestra leader for the Southwark Theater orchestra. Phile died during the Yellow Fever epidemic in 1793. Drummond, 81-83.

[45]*Pennsylvania Packet*, 30 May 1786.

[46] *Pennsylvania Journal*, 28 June 1783. James Juhan advertised himself as a maker of "the great North-American Fortepiano, the mechanical part of them being entirely of his invention." He also claimed to be able to repair "all kinds of instruments in the neatest manner" and teach harpsichord, violin, and German flute. Alexander Juhan may also have been a keyboardist. In 1792 he proposed to publish a set of "Six Sonatas for pianoforte or harpsichord" (*Charleston City Gazette*, 13 June 1792), only three of which are known to have appeared. No copies of this print have survived.

[47] Sonneck, *Early Concert-Life in America*, 80 n. 1.

[48] Francois J. Fétis, *Biographie universelle des musiciens et bibliographie générale*, 8 vols. (Bruxelles: Leroux, 1835-44) 3:430.

[49] An excellent source of information on Reinagle is Anne McClenny Krauss, "Alexander Reinagle, His Family Background and Early Professional Career," *American Music* 4/4 (Winter 1986): 425-56; see also *The New Grove Dictionary of Music and Musicians*, s.v. "Reinagle, Alexander," by Frank Kidson and Robert Hopkins.

[50] Reinagle came from a musical family. His father, Joseph Reinagle (d. c1775) was a trumpeter; a younger brother, Joseph (1762-1825), played horn, trumpet, violin, viola, and cello; his second brother, Hugh (c1764-1785) was a cellist, as was his brother–in–law, Johann Georg Christoff Schetky (1737-1824), and his nephew, J. George Schetky (1776-1831). Another nephew, Alexander Robert Reinagle (1799-1877), was an organist.

[51] *New York Packet*, 12 June 1786.

[52] Although principally a cellist, Capron is featured on several concert programs in the 1780s as a guitarist and singer. Reinagle, while primarily a pianist, also appeared as a vocalist and he may also have played the cello, an instrument favored within his family. Listed on the program of his first New York concert is a "Duetto Violin and Violoncello" of "Messrs Phile and Reinagle." *Philadelphia Independent Journal; or, The General Advertiser*, 12 July 1786. The compositions of Brown, Juhan, Capron, and Reinagle are listed in Oscar George Sonneck, *A Bibliography of Early Secular American Music (18th Century)* rev. and enlarged by William Treat Upton (Washington, D.C.: Library of Congress Music Division, 1945; reprint, New York: Da Capo, 1964). A more detailed index of Reinagle's works appears in Robert Hopkins, "A Chronology of Known Works by Alexander Reinagle" in *Alexander Reinagle: The Philadelphia Sonatas* (Madison, Wisc.: A-R Editions, 1978), xvi-xxiii.

[53] "Washington's Household Account Book, 1793-1797," *Pennsylvania Magazine of History and Biography* 31/1 (1907): 70, as cited in James R. Heintze, "Music of the Washington Family: A Little Known Collection,"

Musical Quarterly 56/2 (April 1970): 289. Also helpful is Judith S. Britt, *Nothing More Agreeable* (Mount Vernon: The Mount Vernon Ladies' Association, 1984).

[54]Krauss, 443.

[55]Sonneck, *Early Concert-Life in America*, 124-26, 110-13.

[56]An advertisement in the *Pennsylvania Packet*, 26 January 1789, claims an "AMATEURS CONCERT For the Benefit of Philip Phile" to be held at Epple's tavern.

[57]In 1790 Reinagle participated in a concert at Epple's Tavern for the benefit of the "Society for the Relief of Poor Distressed Masters of Ships, their Widows and Children." *Pennsylvania Packet*, 29 December 1790.

[58]*Pennsylvania Journal*, 21 February 1785.

[59]In eighteenth-century Philadelphia this seemed to be a special function of Bradford's London Coffee House, where one could purchase tickets to plays, concerts, lectures, balls, and other public events.

[60]*Pennsylvania Packet*, 14 October 1783.

[61]A more extensive discussion of the City Concerts can be found in Sonneck, *Early Concert-Life in America*, 78-98; Drummond, 62-65; and Eberlein and Hubbard, "Music in the Early Federal Era," 106-10. The present study is concerned with the series primarily through the two seasons that took place in City Tavern.

[62]John S. Ezell, ed., *The New Democracy in America: Travels of Francisco de Miranda in the United States, 1783-84*, trans. Juson P. Wood (Norman: University of Oklahoma Press, 1963), 54. Miranda was apparently not alone in finding fault with the quality of the performances. In advertising the second season in the *Pennsylvania Packet* on 9 September 1784 Bentley promised that this season would "furnish a more elegant and perfect Entertainment than it was possible (from the peculiar circumstances of the time) to procure during the last winter." On 11 January 1787 Noah Webster attended the City Concert at City Tavern at which Juhan played a concerto by Luigi Borghi and Brown a flute quartet by Joseph Schmittbauer; Webster wrote in his diary, "Mr. Juhan on the violin—Mr. Brown on the flute are inimitable—But I am not amused." Noah Webster Papers, New York Public Library.

[63]Only a few days after Reinagle's benefit concert in City Tavern, the *Pennsylvania Packet*, 16 October 1786, published the following formal proposal: "that there shall be twelve concerts; to commence the 19th October, and to be continued once in two weeks. . . . That every subscriber shall be entitled to tickets for two ladies, besides his own admittance. . . . That each subscriber pay two guineas. . . . Strangers to be admitted on

paying one dollar each."

[64] The "company of French Musicians" arrived in Philadelphia in the summer and advertised "A GRAND CONCERT, VOCAL AND INSTRUMENTAL" assisted by Reinagle and members of the Amateur Concerts at City Tavern. *Pennsylvania Packet*, 27 July 1790. The group included a violinist named Emmanuel and a singer named DeListe, as well as Duport and his son "not yet ten years of age." A second performance—also in City Tavern—was scheduled for August. This program had to be postponed until the following month. *Pennsylvania Packet*, 28 August 1790. Members of the group also gave some performances at Gray's Garden. The appearance of these performers points to the decided turn toward a French taste in the arts in Philadelphia beginning in the 1790s.

[65] The full programs discovered thus far have been reproduced in Sonneck, *Early Concert-Life in America* and Drummond.

[66] In recalling the celebration on 4 July 1778, Ellery wrote "At the end of the room opposite the upper [northern] table, was erected an Orchestra." "Diary of the Hon. William Ellery of Rhode Island," 477.

[67] "A new orchestra is erected and the greatest care will be taken to make the room agreeable." *Pennsylvania Journal*, 18 October 1786.

[68] Krauss, 438.

[69] See discussion in Mary Sue Morrow, *Concert Life in Haydn's Vienna: Aspects of a Developing Musical and Social Institution* (Stuyvesant, N. Y.: Pendragon Press, 1989), 141-47.

[70] Martini il Tedesco's *Overture to Henry the Fourth* appeared as the fourth issue in *Moller & Capron's Monthly Numbers* (Philadelphia, 1793), 23-28.

[71] The following notice, which appeared in the *Pennsylvania Gazette* on 11 May 1774, provides some notion of the range of Hillegas's stock: "Imported and to be Sold by Michael Hillegas At his House, in Second-street between Arch and Race-streets; A neat Assortment of printed MUSICK Composed by the most eminent Masters, adapted for almost every Instrument now in Use; among which is a great Variety of Overtures, Concerto's, Quartetti's, Trio's, Duets, Solo's, Lessons, Voluntaries, Songs, Tutors, or Books of Instructions for Beginners, &c."

[72] Schetky's father was at one time in the service of the Mannheim court and certainly passed his familiarity with the work of composers like Stamitz, Eichner, and Toeschi on to his brother–in–law and son. During this period the small courts of Germany employed a number of musicians born and trained in Bohemia. Brown (or Braun) would have come in contact with this literature while employed in the Kassel *Hofkapelle* or during his travels after he left the Landgrave's service. The Bohemian composers represented on

these programs include Vanhal, Fiala, Rosetti (originally Roessler), Kammel, and Lachnith.

[73]Krauss points out that Erskine, who was director of the Edinburgh Musical Society, "used his influence to obtain for Joseph the post of trumpeter to the king [George III]." Krauss, 427. Erskine's music was known in Philadelphia before Reinagle's arrival, however. James Bremner adapted an overture by the Earl of Kelly for harpsichord. It is preserved today in the Hopkinson Collection of the University of Pennsylvania Library. Byron Adams Wolverton, "Keyboard Music and Musicians in the Colonies and United States of America before 1830" (Ph.D. diss., Indiana University, 1966), 103. Although Gerson claims that Bremner's arrangement was published by Willig in the 1800s (Gerson, 12), it is not included in Sonneck, *A Bibliography of Early Secular American Music*.

[74]Krauss, 426.

[75]*Pennsylvania Journal*, 7 October 1786. According to Irving Lowens, the first performance of Haydn's music on a public concert in this country was in 1782 when two of his symphonies were included on a concert in New York (*Royal Gazette*, 27 April 1782). Lowens, *Haydn in America* (Detroit: Information Coordinators, 1979), 49.

[76]Hopkins, *Alexander Reinagle: The Philadelphia Sonatas*; see also J. Bunker Clark *The Dawning of American Keyboard Music* (New York: Greenwood Press, 1988).

[77]Pupils of professional musicians were also included. On the City Tavern benefit concert for Juhan on 6 April 1784 a flute concerto was played "by a gentleman scholar of Mr. Brown."

[78]J. George Schetky was the son of Reinagle's sister, Anna Maria Theresa (Mary) and Johann Georg Christoff Schetky (1737-1824). He was born in Edinburgh on 11 June 1776 and received his early musical training from his father. The younger Schetky would have come to know his uncle well when he boarded with the family in Edinburgh in 1784. It is most probable that when the younger Schetky decided to emigrate to this country, he came directly to Philadelphia where he could be under his uncle's protection. Schetky first appears in Philadelphia in December 1787. In the 1790s, he formed a business partnership with Benjamin Carr. *The New Grove Dictionary of Music and Musicians*, s.v. "Schetky, J[ohn] George," by Anne Shapiro.

[79]"Col. Thomas Proctor to George Christhilf Dr. To Musical Permorance [sic] at the City Tavern the 15th instant," in First Troop Philadelphia City Calvary Archives, 1774.

[80]Ezell, *The New Democracy in America*, 54.

[81] John Durang, *The Memoir of John Durang, American Actor, 1785-1816*, ed. Alan S. Downer (Pittsburgh: University of Pittsburgh Press, 1966), 20-21: "The orchestra was composed of the following musicians: Mr. Philo [Phile] leader; Mr. Bentley, harpsichord; Mr. Woolf, principal clarinet; Trimmer, Hecker and son, violoncello, violins, etc. Some six or seven other names, now not remembered, constituting the musical force. *The latter were all Germans*."
[82] *Pennsylvania Journal*, 21 June 1783.
[83] Durang, *The Memoir of John Durang*, 20-21.
[84] Several of Brown's musical cronies are included on the list of subscribers: Alexander Reinagle, Fritz Tremner, Alexander Juhan, and Henri Capron.
[85] *Pennsylvania Journal*, 7 January 1789.
[86] *Pennsylvania Gazette*, 28 November 1771.
[87] Drummond, 76.
[88] Camus, 53, 147-48.
[89] Francis White, ed., *The Philadelphia Directory* (Philadelphia: Young, Stewart, & McCulloch, 1785). There were no directories before 1785, and the series was not continued until 1791.
[90] *Dunlap's American Daily Advertiser*, 5 June 1792. By the last decade of the eighteenth century Philadelphia had two pleasure gardens located on the periphery of the city: Gray's Gardens and Vauxhall Harrowgate. In summer months late-afternoon concerts often took place at both locations. Those wishing to visit Vauxhall Gardens could take the stage coach that departed each day from in front of Epple's tavern.
[91] Clement Biddle, *The Philadelphia Directory* (Philadelphia: James & Johnson, 1791).
[92] Ezell, 56.
[93] *Pennsylvania Packet*, 5 September 1774. Thomas Pike also taught fencing. Thanks to Kathleen Fernandes for this and the following reference.
[94] *Pennsylvania Packet*, 22 November 1773. Francis and Reinagle were colleagues. Sometime around 1801 George Willig published a collection of music by Reinagle based on dances of Francis's choreography as *Mr. Francis's Ballroom Assistant* (Philadelphia: G. Willig, [c1801]).
[95] Ezell, 55-56.
[96] The Powel house at 244 S. Third Street has been restored and is open to the public. The ballroom on the second floor in the front appears much as it might have for a dancing party in the 1780s. Samuel Powel served as mayor of Philadelphia both before and after the Revolution. He owned the land on which City Tavern was built. In 1785 he purchased the building as

well, and at his death both passed to his wife. Mrs. Powel was the daughter of Thomas Willing, who along with his business partner, Robert Morris, helped to finance the American Revolution.

[97] Ezell, 55.

[98] Within the Stockton Family Correspondence, now preserved at Princeton University, there is a letter—probably written in 1788—which claims that "Mr. Meade is . . . [the] subject of conversation, on account of a ball, which is to be given next Monday to a very large number of persons, at the City-tavern." Non-tavern settings for balls were also available. On 22 March 1786 the *Freeman's Journal or North American Intelligencer* advertised for rent an "ornamental Hall . . . communicating to Market Street and Church Alley" ideal for dancing and musical entertainments.

[99] *Pennsylvania Evening Herald, and General Advertiser*, 11 October 1786, "MR. SICARD, wishing to contribute everything in his power to accommodate his Pupils, has procured Mr. Duplesse's New Ball Room for the winter, where he means to teach seventy new Cotillions, and four new American Country Dances, on every second Saturday . . . he proposes likewise to give a Ball in the same Room every second Thursday."

[100] Sonneck, *A Bibliography of Early Secular American Music*, 290. John Aitken was a Scotch engraver, who settled in Philadelphia in the 1780s where he established a gold and silversmith business. Aitken engraved for publication Brown's keyboard works and much of Reinagle's music.

[101] Sonneck, *A Bibliography of Early Secular American Music*, 341.

[102] See Thomas Willing Balch, *The Philadelphia Assemblies* (Philadelphia: Allen, Lane, and Scott, 1916) and Joseph P. Sims, ed., *The Philadelphia Assemblies, 1748-1948: An Account of the Assemblies Printed for the Two Hundredth Anniversary, January 2nd 1948 by order of The Managers* (Philadelphia, 1947).

An earlier attempt at forming a Dancing Assembly in 1740 failed in part as a result of the efforts of George Wakefield (reported in Kellee Green, "The Politics of Dancing: Functions of Social Dance in Philadelphia Society, 1750-1800," read at the Sixteenth Annual Meeting of the Sonneck Society, Toronto, Canada).

[103] This restriction eventually led to the formation of a rival organization called the New City Dancing Assembly. Sims, 19.

[104] Miranda in describing an assembly dance in January 1784 wrote "The assembly, although small and in a very compact hall, was decent and pleasing, and for the first time I saw Quaker men and women taking part in this type of diversion, even though they themselves did not dance." Ezell, 60.

[105] Batcheler points out that Thomas Proctor, when advertising the building for sale, claimed that "The dancing assembly having been held there since the finishing of the building. . . ." *The Freeman's Journal: or the North-American Intelligencer*, 16 March 1785. Batcheler, 49 n. 17.

[106] John W. Jackson, *With the British Army in Philadelphia, 1777-1778* (San Rafael, Calif.: Presidio Press, 1979), 211.

[107] *Pennsylvania Ledger*, 25 April 1778. Rebecca Franks, an outspoken young woman of a loyalist family, reported to a friend that "you would not Know the room 'tis so much improv'd" (Letter from Rebecca Franks to Mrs. William Paca, 26 February 1778). "A Letter of Miss Rebecca Franks, 1778," *Pennsylvania Magazine of History and Biography* 16/2 (1892): 216-18.

[108] *Pennsylvania Ledger*, 24 January 1778.

[109] "Extracts from the Letter-Book of Captain Johann Heinrichs of the Hessian Jäger Corps, 1778-1780," trans. Julius F. Sachse in *Pennsylvania Magazine of History and Biography* 22/2 (1898): 139.

[110] "A Letter of Miss Rebecca Franks, 1778," 216-18. After the war, Miss Franks married Col. Sir Henry Johnson and moved to England. Jackson, *With the British Army in Philadelphia*, 214.

[111] Mary Guy Humphreys, *Catherine Schuyler* (New York: Scribner's Sons, 1897; reprint, 1968), 214, as cited in Green, "The Politics of Dancing," 12.

[112] The festivities began in the late afternoon of 18 May 1778 with a regatta that rowed down the Delaware River to the accompaniment of three bands of music to Howe's headquarters at the Wharton mansion near Old Swedes Church. There officers costumed as medieval knights engaged in a staged tournament replete with trumpet fanfares, followed by a ball, fireworks, dinner, and more dancing. The infamous Major André was instrumental in the orchestration of this extravaganza. Gerson, 24-25.

[113] *Pennsylvania Evening Post*, 4 August 1778. Even before City Tavern was officially opened for business, it was the site of a special celebration ball on 22 July 1778.

[114] James C. Whitehead, ed., "The Autobiography of Peter Stephen Du Ponceau," *Pennsylvania Magazine of Biography and History* 63/3 (July 1939): 334-35. Under the management of Gifford Dalley the tavern's front rooms on the entrance level were set aside as a merchant's exchange, and from this time on the building was sometimes referred to as the Merchant's Coffee House.

[115] Reported in Charles Sherrill, *French Memories of Eighteenth-Century America* (New York: Scribner's, 1915; reprint, New York: B. Blom, 1971), 36.

[116] *Travels in North America in the Years 1780, 1781 and 1782 by the Marquis de Chastellux.*, 2 vols. Trans. Howard C. Rice (Chapel Hill: University of North Carolina Press, 1963) 1:177 [entry dated 14 December 1780]. Included among the William Johnson Papers in the New Jersey Historical Society is a poem, entitled "The Belles of Philadelphia: Lines Written in Philadelphia Assembly Room," which mentions by name some of the ladies who regularly attended the assembly balls. It has been suggested that the poet was Benjamin Franklin's son, William.

[117] Henry B. Livingston to Susan Livingston, 28 January 1779, Livingston II Papers, Folder 1778-1781, Massachusetts Historical Society, as cited in Platt, 142.

[118] Only men could be subscribers. Eighteenth-century taverns were essentially a man's world. The only contact for women was as lodgers or at dances.

[119] Ezell, 54.

[120] Batcheler, 48, reports that on the back of the canvas there is a handwritten note which reads, "Painted by Charles Wilson [*sic*] Peale in 1770. To be hung in the Room of the City Dancing Assembly of which he was one of the Original Managers—and continued for many years."

[121] The Marquis de Chastellux observed that "Dancing is said to be the emblem of both gaiety and of love; here it seems to be the emblem of legislation and of marriage; of legislation, inasmuch as places are marked out, the *contredanses* prescribed, and every proceeding provided for, calculated, and submitted to regulation; of marriage, since each lady is supplied with a "partner," with whom she must dance the whole evening, without being allowed to take another." *Travels in North America . . . by the Marquis de Chastellux* 1:164 [entry dated 8 December 1780].

[122] *Pennsylvania Packet*, 19 December 1785.

[123] Ibid.

[124] *Pennsylvania Evening Herald, and General Advertiser*, 11 October 1786.

[125] Saltator, *A Treatise on Dancing* (Boston: The Commercial Gazette, 1802), as cited in Elizabeth Aldrich, *From the Ballroom to Hell: Grace and Folly in Nineteenth-Century Dance* (Evanston, Ill.: Northwestern University Press, 1991), 15-16.

[126] Alrich, *From the Ballroom to Hell*, 16.

[127] *Travels in North America . . . by the Marquis de Chastellux* 1:177.

[128] "Everyone comes or goes, plays or dances, talks or keeps quiet as he pleases. " Ezell, 54.

[129] *Massachusetts Spy*, 23 December 1786 (also advertised in the

Pennsylvania Packet). An architectural drawing of a building proposed as a replacement for City Tavern which would fulfill the combined functions of tavern, coffee house, dancing assembly, and merchants exchange has been preserved in the Library of Congress. Its design includes a long room attached to the back of the building in a manner similar to that of the Raleigh Tavern in Williamsburg, Virginia. Difficulty in raising the necessary funds put a moratorium on the project.

[130] *Pennsylvania Packet*, 29 November 1790.

[131] Oeller's Hotel was begun as a school building of the Episcopal Academy but completed as a Hotel. It replaced City Tavern as the most elegant of Philadelphia's gathering places until it was destroyed by a fire on 18 December 1799, that began next-door at Rickett's Circus. The long room in Oeller's Hotel was described as a "most elegant room, sixty feet square, with a handsome music gallery at one end." The long room in City Tavern was considerably smaller, measuring something close to fifty by approximately thirty feet.

The term "hotel" was probably introduced to Philadelphia by French emigrants. In 1789 Moyston was referring to City Tavern as a "TAVERN and HOTEL" (card found in Historical Society of Pennsylvania and included as illustration in Graham, "The Taverns of Colonial Philadelphia," 323).

[132] Concerts took place in City Tavern as late as 1801, but they were sporadic. Richard Lamar Bissett mentions a benefit concert there on 14 April 1801 in his "Journal of a Voyage to North America" (unpublished typescript, Independence National Historical Park, Research Library, 82).

PETER ERBEN AND AMERICA'S FIRST LUTHERAN TUNEBOOK IN ENGLISH

Edward C. Wolf

Publication of the *Lutheran Book of Worship*[1] in 1978 marked a true milestone in the history of American Lutheran hymnody. For the first time all the various national and cultural traditions within European Lutheranism were brought together and merged with the distinctly American hymnody which belongs to English-speaking Lutherans in North America. The *Lutheran Book of Worship* thus culminates over a century and a half of attempts to develop English-language hymnody that was both distinctively Lutheran and truly American. For many years the development of American Lutheran hymnody foundered upon the rocks of translation as well as upon the different national backgrounds which immigrants brought with them to this country. However, as early as 1816 Jacob Eckhard of Charleston, South Carolina took the first step toward providing hymn tunes for English-speaking congregations when he added a final page to his *Choral-Buch*[2] that listed 66 hymn texts in particular meter from the 1814 English hymnal of the Evangelical Lutheran Ministerium of New York that could be sung to tunes in his collection. Eckhard's collection was intended primarily for the Episcopal Church, but he himself was Lutheran, and obviously he was painfully aware of the problems facing organists when they played hymns for Lutheran congregations that worshiped in English. Perhaps inspired by Eckhard's example, Peter Erben of New York City published *A Collection of Church Tunes Composed and Arranged to the Different Metres in the English Lutheran Hymn Book, Now in Use Throughout the United States of America*. Erben's tunebook carries no date, but other evidence which we shall examine indicates that it probably appeared ca. 1817 and thus has the distinction of being the first tunebook published specifically for America's English-speaking Lutherans.

EARLY LUTHERAN HYMNALS IN ENGLISH

German Lutheran immigrants continued to come to America in large numbers until just before World War I. Quite naturally these immigrants brought along their language and customs of worship, and the constant flow of new immigrants into established congregations served to slow the shift from German to English worship. Similar conditions existed in the upper midwestern states, except that here the immigrants often were Scandinavian rather than German. Of course, so long as a congregation worshiped in the language of their homeland they simply used hymnals with their accompanying chorale books that they had known in Europe. It was only when churches began to shift to English worship that a need arose for new tunebooks that would fit either English translations or English hymns.

Lutheran churches in New York City and the surrounding area were among the first Lutheran congregations in America to make regular use of English worship. This was undoubtedly due in part to the fact that originally they were under Dutch patronage, using the Dutch language, and when immigration from Holland ceased the congregations naturally evolved toward using the dominant language of their area, namely English. Moreover, unlike German, Dutch was not a major European language; consequently, it had much less resistance to English than did German. Although it was not an official publication, the New York Lutherans were influential in publishing the first full-size Lutheran hymnal to be printed in English on this side of the Atlantic. This was a 1756 New York reprint of John Christian Jacobi's *Psalmodia Germanica: or, the German Psalmody*.[3] No music was included in the New York reprint despite the fact that the title page states that it includes melodies with their figured basses. However, the first line of the original German hymn and the name of its tune (if the original did not have its own tune, or if another tune was recommended) are printed before each hymn text. The editor, Jacobi, was associated with the German court chapel of St. James in London during the early eighteenth century, and the first edition of the *Psalmodia Germanica* was published in London in 1722. When the patriarch of American Lutheranism, Henry Melchior Muhlenberg, was in New York during 1751-52 in an unsuccessful attempt to heal a congregational schism created by language controversies over the use of Dutch, German, or English, he entered the following rather revealing passage in his diary for 28 July 1751:

> Having only one copy of the English hymn book [i.e., the *Psalmodia Germanica*] containing our hymns, I had to read each stanza separately and sing it for them. I soon observed that the English people did not know our tunes, so I selected familiar English melodies which fitted some of our Lutheran hymns; then the whole

congregation sang very pleasingly and inspiringly, for the English Church people here in New York know how to sing very beautifully and acceptably because they have a fine organ in their church and have been taught how to sing.[4]

Obviously the German tunes often did not fit English texts easily, so the solution was to use English tunes in an appropriate meter. Muhlenberg's reference to the English Church pertained to Trinity Parish, which in 1751 possessed an organ of twenty-six stops that had been built by Johann G. Klemm in 1739-40.[5]

In 1784 John Christopher Kunze, Muhlenberg's son-in-law, became the Lutheran pastor in New York and succeeded in reuniting the two Lutheran congregations that had resulted from the earlier schism. Kunze was anxious to use English worship, and in 1795 he edited *A Hymn and Prayer-Book for the Use of Such Lutheran Churches as Use the English Language*.[6] As he stated in the preface, many of the 240 hymn texts were taken from the *Psalmodia Germanica*, others were from an English Moravian collection printed in London in 1789, while some were translations or original hymn texts by either Kunze himself or two of his associates, John Frederick Ernst or George Strebeck. Although Kunze's hymnal includes no musical notation, a number precedes each text to indicate an appropriate chorale tune, of which sixty are listed in the back of the hymnal. Thus, an organist was expected to obtain music for these English hymns from the standard German chorale books. A more detailed examination indicates that many hymns did not fit the German tunes easily, and in some cases the translations were not very felicitous.

Consequently, only two years later Rev. George Strebeck published a new hymnal titled *A Collection of Evangelical Hymns Made from Different Authors and Collections for the English Lutheran Church in New York*.[7] Although originally a Lutheran from Baltimore, Strebeck had once been an itinerant Methodist preacher, but by 1794 he wished to return to the Lutheran fold. Since Kunze had been seeking an assistant who was proficient in English, he interviewed Strebeck and accepted him as an associate, and in 1796 the Lutheran Ministerium of New York ordained him as a pastor.[8] However, all was not well. In the preface to his hymnal Strebeck wrote:

> The unsuitableness of the metres of our English Lutheran Hymn Book, published in 1795 by Messrs. Hurtin and Commardinger, under the inspection of the Rev. Dr. Kunze, made it peculiarly necessary to provide another collection for the use of our English Lutheran Church. In the present collection I have endeavored to retain as many of the Hymns published in the former, as could be

done. All those have this mark * prefixed to them; — for the rest I am indebted to various Authors, and collections of reputation.

Strebeck's preface also states, "I hope none will be so bigotted to *mere name*, as to censure us for making selections from Authors who are not of our own profession in religion." These authors include prominent English writers like Watts, Doddridge, Cowper, and Newton, and their presence in a Lutheran hymnal demonstrates the strong English influences which were to overpower traditional German Lutheran chorales during the first decades of the nineteenth century.

The contents of his hymnal would seem to indicate that at heart Strebeck was more a Methodist or Episcopalian than a Lutheran, and this is further borne out by the fact that a short time after its publication he led a portion of the Lutheran congregation in New York into the Episcopal fold, and he himself became an Episcopalian. Strebeck's defection to the Episcopal Church was not as drastic a step as it might at first seem. Many American Lutherans around 1800 tended to think of the Episcopal Church as being simply an English version of the Lutheran Church. This thinking was so prevalent that when the New York Ministerium met at Rhinebeck in September 1797, the Lutheran pastors adopted a resolution which stated that because of the great similarities existing between the Episcopal and the Lutheran churches, the Ministerium would not recognize a new Lutheran congregation which used the English language in places where the ministration of an Episcopal church was readily available.[9]

The same year as the Rhinebeck resolution Kunze further expounded the current Lutheran views toward the Episcopal Church in the preface to a book of sermons honoring Lawrence Van Buskirk, a student of Kunze's who was preparing for ordination, but whose untimely death prevented him from fulfilling this aim.[10] After noting that "there is not a great difference in point of doctrine in all the protestant churches," Kunze proceeds to add:

> The reformed church of England was afterwards under Edward VI, and Queen Elizabeth so modeled and modified, that it bore the nearest relation to the church established in Sweden, Denmark, Saxony, Prussia, Hanover, Wurtemberg, &c. The Lutherans have bishops, superintendents, seniors and inspectors. The thirty nine articles fully agree with the Augustan confession and every Lutheran can subscribe them. The two German chaplains at St. James's use a German translation of the English liturgy. The king of Great-Britain, as a Lutheran is the head of the church of Hanover, and one of his princes on this account is entitled to the bishopric of Osnabrug. At the accession of George the I. the agreement of both churches was, by a conference of English and German divines investigated into and

pronounced to be as perfect as possible, which removed the doubts of this king, who is said to have declared, that he would not renounce his religion for a crown.[11]

This preface is signed: "John C. Kunze, D.D. Professor of the Oriental Languages in Columbia College, and Senior of the Lutheran Clergy in the State of New York." The close relationship which many Lutherans perceived to exist with the Episcopal Church explains why it was that Peter Erben published America's first English-language tunebook for Lutherans while he was employed as an organist-choirmaster for Trinity Episcopal Parish in New York.

Kunze worked with another associate, Rev. Ralph Williston, after Strebeck's defection. Apparently the Lutherans did not wish to continue using Strebeck's hymnal, so they asked Williston to make a new compilation, which he entitled *A Choice Selection of Evangelical Hymns*.[12] Williston's hymnal was partly an outgrowth of a resolution passed by the New York Ministerium at a meeting in Rhinebeck in October 1803, when the Ministerium resolved that a committee should consider collecting and printing an English hymnal for the use of the New York congregations.[13] This hymnal, therefore, was intended to be the official English hymnal for the New York Ministerium. Kunze, as Senior of the Lutheran clergy in the state, wrote an introductory paragraph endorsing the hymnal and stating that he had examined the hymns and found them to be compatible with Lutheran doctrine. Williston himself added a few prefatory remarks justifying the publication of the third different hymnal for New York Lutherans in only eleven years. He wrote, "A new edition, or a new compilation, became indispensably necessary, there not being a single copy to be had of the former collection; and the obvious deficiency of the former collection, determined us to make a new compilation."

Despite Kunze's reassuring remarks, the whole plan and temper of the hymnal shows Methodist, Presbyterian, and other influences. The old German chorales have almost disappeared; only a few of the most popular still survived. Isaac Watts and the Wesley family provided the two most important sources for the hymns, though other English hymnodists like Anne Steele and Doddridge were also represented. Williston used only the English abbreviations of L.M. (long meter), C.M. (common meter), S.M. (short meter), and P.M. (peculiar or particular meter) to indicate which tunes to use. Like Strebeck before him, Williston and his congregation gradually inclined more and more toward the Episcopal Church, and on 10 February 1810 the congregation trustees resolved "that on account of the identity of doctrine, the near alliance of Church discipline subsisting between the Lutheran and Episcopal Churches, the English Lutheran Church do become a parish of the Protestant Episcopal Church, a majority of the congregation coinciding."[14]

Like the publications of both Kunze and Strebeck, Williston's hymnal failed to win general acceptance among the New York congregations. Only five years after its publication, the minutes of the New York Ministerium for the meeting in September 1811 read: "Resolved, that a new Hymnbook & Liturgy in the English language be introduced in the Lutheran churches of this State & others belonging to this Ministerium, & that the Rvd. Presidt., F.W. Geissenheimer & Ph. F. Mayer be a Committee to collect it & cause it to be printed."[15] At this time F.H. Quitman was president and F.W. Geissenheimer secretary of the Ministerium. Two years later at the meeting of the Ministerium in September 1813 it was resolved "that the Committee appointed at the meeting of the Ministerium in the Town of Wurtemberg 1811, for the collection & composition of a new Hymnbook & Liturgy in the English language remain the same."[16] At this time the Ministerium also resolved that the Senior write a preface to the new hymnal recommending it to congregations comprising the New York Ministerium, and that each pastor determine how many hymnals his respective congregation(s) would need. This hymnal was completed in 1814, when it appeared as *A Collection of Hymns, and a Liturgy, for the Use of Evangelical Lutheran Churches; to Which Are Added Prayers for Families and Individuals*.[17] At their annual meeting in 1815 the Ministerium officially accepted the report of the committee charged with editing and publishing the hymnal. The annual meeting then resolved that their president, F.H. Quitman, was to present copies of the new English hymnal to the Lutheran Ministerium of Pennsylvania, and that a copy also be sent to the South Carolina Synod. Unlike its predecessors, this hymnal received wide acceptance in English-language Lutheran churches. Later editions appeared in 1817, 1824, and 1827. In 1834 a new edition had a special supplement, while the editions of 1842 and later incorporated this supplement into the body of the hymnal itself. These editions or reprints continued to appear until 1865.

As was customary, this hymnal contained only the hymn texts. The only indications as to a tune were the use of the standard metric abbreviations of L.M., C.M., S.M., and P.M. In order to locate the music, organists had to use a combination of English-language tunebooks and German chorale books. Thus, the time was ripe for someone to prepare a tunebook specifically for the New York hymnal. Jacob Eckhard, a German Lutheran organist who played for St. Michael's Episcopal Church in Charleston, South Carolina, appears to have been the first person to publish some music for this hymnal, though, as mentioned above, the primary aim of his tunebook was for Episcopal use. Eckhard's *Choral-Book* was published in Boston by James Loring. While there is no date on the title page, the copyright entry is dated 20 May 1816.

Eckhard was born in 1757 at Eschwege in Hessen-Kassel. He came to

America in 1776 as a musician with the Hessian troops. After the Revolution he remained in this country, and on 15 April 1786 St. John's Lutheran Church in Charleston, South Carolina, employed him as schoolmaster-organist. He remained at St. John's until April 1809, when he resigned to become organist at St. Michael's Episcopal Church in Charleston, which had a larger Snetzler organ. However, Eckhard remained active in the Lutheran congregation, and he maintained membership with St. John's until his death on 10 November 1833.[18]

The "Advertisement" or preface which Eckhard wrote for his *Choral-Book* shows that he was clearly aware of the hybrid German and English nature of his collection. Two paragraphs from this preface suffice to indicate his aims:

> The Publisher, having for seven years been employed as an Organist in the Reformed Churches in Germany, and for nearly forty years in Lutheran and Episcopal Churches in this country, thinks he has had an opportunity to judge of the advantages which might arise from a CHORAL BOOK, with appropriate figured basses, and the harmony fully expressed by notes, for those unacquainted with figuration.
>
> Under an impression that this work will be of service not only to the English Lutheran, but also to all the Protestant Churches in America, he has selected many sacred melodies for the particular metres of their several hymn books. The long, common and short metres are a selection of choice tunes, suitable for all congregations.

Eckhard's tunebook contains 77 hymn tunes plus four Anglican chants. Several of these tunes are listed as being by Eckhard himself. The music is written in piano score with figured bass, but the harmonies are fully realized by the right hand in the treble staff. Presumably the music as printed indicates how Eckhard would have realized a figured bass hymn tune. Only the bass line is in the F clef, while the melody and full, triadic harmonies are in the treble. This results in a style where often there is a gap greater than an octave between the lowest treble harmony and the bass. Obviously Eckhard compiled his tunebook for organists and not for singing schools or choirs. This is further shown by his use of the German term *Choral-Book* in the title. Moreover, the great majority of tunes lack any text. The final page of Eckhard's collection contains an index of 66 hymns in particular meter which are found in the 1814 New York hymnal and which may be sung to melodies in his book. Eckhard gives English tune names to some of the German chorale melodies, but he also indicates the German name to avoid confusion. Since Eckhard was able to accommodate the irregular meters of the New York hymnal, his collection could cover the entire hymnal, provided one did not object to using the same tune for several different texts. This somewhat limited number of 77 tunes in respect to 520 texts in the New York hymnal made it necessary for organists to supplement Eckhard's book with other tunebooks. Thus a need still existed for a tunebook that was designed more specifically for the 1814 New York hymnal, and it is here that Peter Erben enters the picture.

ERBEN'S LIFE AND WORK

Appletons' Cyclopedia of American Biography contains the following entry for Erben:[19]

> ERBEN, Peter, organist, b. in Philadelphia, Pa., in 1771; d. in New York city in 1863. After the death of his father, who was one of the early German settlers in Pennsylvania, he removed to New York, where he became an organ-builder, and was also organist in Trinity Parish from 1807 until 1839.

Like Eckhard, therefore, Erben was of German background and undoubtedly was acquainted with German Lutheran and Reformed hymnody and music. While Erben is an uncommon surname, as yet it has not been possible to trace his roots in southeastern Pennsylvania. *Appletons'* is in error in giving 1863 as the year of his death, however, since his death notice in the *New-York Times* for Wednesday, 1 May 1861, reads: "ERBEN. In Brooklyn, on Tuesday, April 30, PETER ERBEN, in the 91st year of his age." The funeral notice in the next day's paper states that his funeral was to be at Trinity Church on Friday, 3 May at 3:30 p.m. The newspaper notices confirm that Erben was born in 1770 or 1771, since he is listed as being in his 91st year.

Erben must have been quite prominent in New York life, for the main item under the heading "General City News" in the *New-York Times* for Saturday, 4 May 1861 was a reference to his funeral. The item refers to his being organist at Trinity for fifty years, whereas he actually worked as organist in the parish from 1807-1839, and Edward Hodges succeeded him in 1840, not 1850. The item from the paper reads:

> An Old Knickerbocker Gone. — The funeral of PETER ERBEN, aged 91, a native of this City, and the last but sixteen of the veritable Knickerbockers surviving, took place at Trinity Church yesterday, and was numerously attended by citizens, as well as by the officers and ministers of the Church, REV. DR. VINTON officiating. The venerable deceased was organist of Trinity Church for *fifty years*,

and was succeeded [*sic*] in 1850 by DR. HODGES. He dined on Christmas last with his descendants of *five* generations, viz. children, grandchildren, great grand and great great grandchildren, and only a few days since was walking the streets with the apparent vigor of a hale man of 70. His son, HENRY ERBEN, is the well-known builder of the largest organs in the country. His grandson, H. ERBEN, Jr., U.S.N., is now doing his duty to his country at Fort Pickens.

Peter Erben first appeared in New York City directories in 1795 and again in 1797, where he is listed as a tanner, while in 1798 and 1799 he is listed as a grocer. From 1800 through 1850, though, Redway's guide[20] indicates variously that he is a "teacher of music," "music teacher," "prof. of music," "musician," and in one case (1843) "organ mnf." He does not appear in any directory after 1850, when he moved to Brooklyn. In his study of the noted organ builder Henry Erben, John Ogasapian observes that no Erben appears in the Philadelphia directories before 1795, though there are early nineteenth-century listings of Erbens, including another Henry Erben.[21] Ogasapian speculates that given the inclination of German families to carry Christian names from generation to generation, a close relationship between Peter in New York and Henry in Philadelphia is likely, and they may have been brothers. Peter Erben was organist at New York's Christ Church in 1800, as a notice in the *Commercial Advertiser* for 29 October 1800 inserted by organ builder John Geib indicates: "JOHN GEIB & CO. — A church organ, in Christ Church, to be disposed of . . . Enquire of the Organ builder as above, or P. Erben, Organist, George-street."[22] In 1806 Erben was organist at the New Dutch Reformed Church, where he replaced James Hewitt, but in 1807 the church "resolved that Mr. Erben our Organist be dismissed and that the Treasurer be directed to pay him the arrears of his salary."[23] Thereupon Erben began his long tenure with Trinity (Episcopal) Parish by becoming organist of St. George's Chapel on Beekman Street, where he remained until moving to St. John's Chapel on Varick Street in 1813. The reasons for Erben's short tenure at the Reformed Church are not known, but there are indications that sometimes he had a rather irascible temperament, and this may have been the reason he was dismissed. In her study of mid-nineteenth-century New York musical life, Vera Brodsky Lawrence refers to Peter Erben as a "peppery Philadelphian of German descent" and also states that his son, Henry Erben, "inherited both his organistic gifts and his contentious nature from his father."[24]

In 1820 Peter Erben became organist at Trinity Church itself, a position which he held until 1839, when the old church building was demolished to prepare for the new Trinity, with a large new organ built by Henry Erben and with Dr. Edward Hodges as organist. In his history of the choir and music at Trinity, A.H. Messiter portrays Erben in a highly critical light. He wrote: "Eighteen years of his incumbency have left no mark upon musical history; but in 1838 . . . there seems to have been a general awakening and a decided movement made to put the music of the Parish on a better footing. In fact, a new era begins here."[25] Messiter's criticism may have been unduly harsh, as Erben probably was conforming to the standards of Episcopal church music of his day. Erben certainly occupied a prominent role in New York musical life, if for no other reason than the positions he held. He was active in arranging special music which St. John's and St. George's chapels regularly sponsored to raise charity funds. For example, here are some advertisements from the *New-York Evening Post* for the years 1815-17. On 3 December 1815 the paper announced a sermon and collection in St. John's Church for the benefit of the Episcopal Charity School, with "a Hymn to be sung by the Charity Children, accompanied with the organ. Music arranged by Mr. P. Erben." A similar announcement ran in the same paper the following week, except that now the sermon, collection, and special music would be in St. George's Church. A year later on 2 December 1816 the *New-York Evening Post* ran a similar advertisement with the statement, "A hymn, set to music by Mr. P. Erben, to be sung by the Charity Children, accompanied with the organ." During the week of 8 December 1817 the *New-York Evening Post* announced the customary benefit sermon and collection, but the wording this time stated that there was to be "an anthem, set to music by Mr. P. Erben, to be sung by the charity children, accompanied with the organ." While it is not clear whether Erben's role was that of director, composer, or arranger, the wording implies that he served in all three capacities.

During the first couple decades of the nineteenth century Erben was active in promoting various societies for the improvement of music. As early as 1800 he had founded The Society for Cultivating Church Music, which was a singing school supported by Trinity Church, and from 1807 for an indefinite number of years he conducted a singing school on Cedar Street "under the patronage of the Bishop and Clergy of the Protestant Episcopal Church, for the improvement of the Church Music adopted by said Church."[26] A notice in the *New-York Evening Post* for 6 January 1817 reads: "The Association for improvement in Sacred Music, under the direction of Peter Erben, will commence on Thursday, the 9th instant, at half past 6 o'clock P.M. and will continue every Monday and Thursday evenings during the season."

Erben appears to have had a close relationship with John Henry Hobart, Trinity's rector and Bishop of New York. On 21 February 1816 Erben wrote a letter to Hobart with comments on the propriety of organ voluntaries and playing during Lent, as well as a list of pieces which Erben considered to be suitable for the season.[27] Among the hymn tunes which he deemed to

America's First Lutheran Tunebook in English 59

be appropriate for Lent were: "Bangor, Burford if Play'd in the Key of D. and Slow, Wilderness Windsor in G., Windham, Crowle Swanwich in G. or A., St. George, St. Ann's, Mear in F. The 139th Ps. Tune, Abridge in D., Little Marlborough, Aylesbury, Peckham in C." He then suggested some voluntaries and some anthems which include several from Handel's *Messiah*. Erben's letter obviously was an answer to a request he had received from Hobart. What is surprising is the fact that Hobart would have asked for such information from Erben at St. John's Chapel and not from his own organist at Trinity Church. It thus appears that Hobart had considerable confidence in Erben's knowledge of church music.

In addition to the many musical activities we have considered, Erben also functioned as an organ builder, though it was his son, Henry, who brought the Erben name to fame as one of America's greatest organ builders. An advertisement in the *New-York Evening Post*, which first appeared on 4 January 1817 and ran for two weeks, contains enough information about Erben's activities to warrant a complete quotation.

> PETER ERBEN informs the public, that having just completed a church organ for Richmond in Virginia, which has received the approbation of the musical professors and amateurs who have heard it, he is encouraged to commence the establishment of a manufactory for church and chamber organs, and assures those gentlemen who may honor him with their commands, that every instrument will be finished in the best manner by experienced workmen in every department, under his immediate inspection. He begs leave also to return his sincere thanks to those who have heretofore employed him as a piano forte teacher, and to assure his present scholars and the public, that his exertions in the profession as a teacher, will be continued with unabated attention. Also, piano fortes, Church and chamber Organs, for sale at his house, No. 66 Mott-street.

Another advertisement in the *New-York Evening Post* for 21 May 1817 first mentions a couple of proposed publications of sacred music and then again mentions Erben's work as an organ builder. It reads:

SACRED MUSIC

> WITH a view to introduce a selection of the best music extant, into the churches, the subscriber offers the following PROPOSALS, for publishing by subscription, a collection of *Church Music*, consisting of a variety of choice psalm tunes, for the use of the different places of public worship in the city and country. The work to contain 116 quarto pages, neatly bound, price $1 50 cents; and no tune will be

inserted but such as are regular in their composition, and all the different parts set in their proper places.

Also, anthems suited for the several festivals throughout the year, selected from works of the first reputation, containing 64 folio pages, price 6 cents per page.

Subscription lists will be left at the several music-stores in this city.

PETER ERBEN

N.B. For sale, at his house, No. 66 Mott-st. 2 chamber Organs, and 1 church Organ, with twelve stops and two rows of keys.

All orders in the organ building line will be punctually attended to.

None of Erben's known tunebooks fit the description of the proposals outlined here, so they may never have been published. However, *A Collection of Church Tunes* for the 1814 New York Lutheran hymnal may well have been an outgrowth of the first proposal, since its publication occurred about this time.

As we can see from this last advertisement, Erben was also active as a music publisher and tunebook compiler in addition to his work as a choirmaster, organist, and organ builder. Richard Wolfe lists a score of publications of piano music, songs, and choral music edited and/or published by Erben during the first two decades of the nineteenth century.[28] Most of these items are piano music and include such works as six sonatas by Muzio Clementi (Wolfe 1888), a collection of favorite airs for beginners on the piano (Wolfe 2697), and a "Grand March & Rondo" by Louis von Esch (Wolfe 2712). He also published songs such as "When Edward Left His Native Plain" by the prolific English songwriter James Hook (Wolfe 4262) or "A Hymn for Whitsunday," which was "composed & published" by Peter Erben (Wolfe 2699).[29]

Erben published at least five books which contain hymn or psalm tunes, chorales, and anthems. His first book was *A Selection of Psalm and Hymn Tunes, for the Use of the Dutch Reformed Churches in the City of New York*.[30] It was published in 1806 during the year that Erben served as organist at the New Dutch Reformed Church. This tunebook opens with a brief rudiments of music and lessons for tuning the voice, after which there are 87 compositions in open score. An "Easter Hymn" and "Easter Anthem" are not in the table of contents and are on unnumbered pages at the back of the book, so they may have been added later. Most of the psalm and hymn tunes have the melody in the top voice, and most are in four-part harmony. There are some tunes for only two or three voices, however, and towards the back of the collection a few have the melody in the third voice. While 32 of the 87 tunes in this book also appear in *A Collection of Church Tunes* for the

1814 New York Lutheran hymnal, a comparison indicates that Erben did not simply copy the music from this book, but frequently he changed the part writing, especially in the inner voices.

While he was organist at St. George's Chapel of Trinity Parish (1807-1813), Erben published three more collections of church music. Not surprisingly, he now turned his attention from Dutch Reformed to Episcopal hymnody, and in 1808 he published *Sacred Music in Two, Three, and Four Parts, Selected from European & American Publications of the Highest Repute. Adapted to the Various Measures and Version of David's Psalms in Use in the Protestant Episcopal Church, of the United States.* While there is no date or publisher on the title page, the endorsement by then Episcopal Bishop Benjamin Moore is dated 12 April 1808. The introduction includes fairly detailed instructions on how Erben believed hymns should be sung in harmony, and one can assume that Erben applied these instructions to all hymn singing regardlesss of the denomination. His instructions read:

> In all regular compositions, the part which is called the TREBLE, contains the air or melody, and ought to be sung by females and boys. The acuteness of the treble renders the air predominant; and although the pitch of the female voice is an octave above that of the male, yet when both sing the same air together, the melody will derive no injury from this interval of sound, because the octave above forms a perfect unison with the octave below. Of right, the treble part belongs exclusively to the female voice, as it is more brilliant, and infinitely better adapted for articulation and expression than that of the other sex.
>
> The TENOR and Counter parts are mere accompaniments to the TREBLE and BASS, calculated only to fill up the harmony, and ought therefore to be sung with a softened male voice, just strong enough to give connection to the several parts, and neither of these ought to assume the character of principals in the tune. Superiority appertains to the treble and bass voices; to the treble voice, because it has the air or melody to perform, and to the bass voice, because it has to support the general harmony of the whole piece; therefore, the bass part ought always to be sung with great judgment, either as to tone, time and tune. The bass voice requires an equal degree of smoothness and fulness [sic], otherwise it will not answer the end of it's [sic] appointment. In sounding the deep notes (octaves below especially) the bass-voice ought to give its full swell; whereas the treble-voice, when ascending to the higher notes of any tune, should progressively be softened, unless they are rendered emphatical by the sense of the words, with which they are connected; and all the parts unitedly ought to sing soft or strong, plaintive or joyful, according to

the import of the words, so that the musical sounds may be an echo to the meaning of the line or verse with which they are connected.

In this collection, some of the tunes have appropriate words placed in connection with the notes, and others are printed without them. The words thus placed may help beginners to acquire some knowledge of the tune, but they tend to divide the learner's attention too much, and not unfrequently to withdraw all regard for the notes, which never fails to retard the proficiency of the learner, and sometimes puts a total stop to future improvement; but with regard to anthems, and long complicated pieces of vocal music, the memory requires the aid of set words, to render the performance more easy.

The main body of this tunebook includes 65 hymn and psalm tunes, of which 39 also appear in Erben's collection for the Lutheran New York hymnal, though not necessarily in the same key or with the same harmonization.

The second of Erben's books from this period is a collection of anthems rather than hymn and psalm tunes. Its title page reads: *Sacred Music Being a Collection of Anthems in Score Selected from European and American Publications, Suitable for Singing Societies and Private Families.* The contents are what one would expect for Episcopal choral music around 1800. It includes 76 pages of anthems and set pieces in open score for two, three, and four voices with keyboard accompaniment. Of its thirteen compositions, Erben attributes two to Mr. Kent, eight to Js. Leach, and one to J. Peene. The engraver was John Will, and this fact plus Erben's reference to his employment at St. George's Chapel enables us to date this publication ca. 1808.[31]

Erben's third book from the 1807-13 period has virtually escaped notice from bibliographers. Like the collection of anthems just cited, it is not dated, but the references both to Erben being at St. George's Chapel and to Hewitt's Musical Repository narrow its publication to the period from 1807 through early 1811. Hewitt moved to Boston in 1811 and did not return to New York until 1816,[32] at which time Erben was no longer at St. George's Chapel. Publication, therefore, must have been ca. 1807-10. The title page to this fifty-page collection reads: *Sacred Music for the Use of Singing Societies and Private Families Selected and Adapted to the Piano Forte.*[33] It contains seventeen compositions with attributions to such composers as J. Beaumont, Milgrove, Dr. Callcot, Leach, and Handel—all of whom represent typical Anglican repertoire of the day. It appears to have been a companion volume to the *Sacred Music* cited immediately above. The only known copy is in the library of the Cooper-Hewitt Museum in New York City, the Smithsonian Institution's National Museum of Design.

A COLLECTION OF CHURCH TUNES

Having published four books of sacred music plus a variety of sheet music, it is not surprising that Erben perceived the opportunity for compiling a tunebook to complement the hymnal published by the Evangelical Lutheran Ministerium of New York in 1814. We have already considered how the somewhat limited scope of Jacob Eckhard's 1816 *Choral-Book* did not fully meet the need for an appropriate tunebook. Thus, Peter Erben jumped into the void with what was to be the largest tunebook of all his publications—*A Collection of Church Tunes*. It is possible that he chose this title so as to complement that of the 1814 Lutheran hymnal, *A Collection of Hymns, and a Liturgy*. Relying upon his extensive knowledge of English hymn and psalm tunes, Erben added some of the more popular German chorale melodies plus several American tunes and a few of his own composition to compile his collection. In some respects Erben's tunebook is a compromise, but it simply reflects the fact that English-speaking American Lutheran worship of the 1800-25 period was itself a compromise between German and English influences. *A Collection of Church Tunes* contains 109 compositions on 104 numbered pages, plus the title page and the index. Since there are 520 texts in the 1814 New York Lutheran hymnal, this meant that most tunes were intended to serve several texts. In some respects it is not a typical tunebook, since it lacks a theoretical introduction. Indeed, it has no introduction or preface of any type. However, one may assume that the introduction to the 1808 *Sacred Music in Two, Three, and Four Parts* written for Episcopal use and cited above could well apply here, since the musical format of the two tunebooks is similar. In *A Collection of Church Tunes* the index immediately follows the title page, and the music in turn begins immediately after the index. The book is in the traditional oblong format and measures 15-1/2 centimeters in height by 24 centimeters in length. The copy used in this study is located in the Krauth Memorial Library of the Evangelical Lutheran Seminary in Philadelphia.[34] While the exact provenance of this particular copy and the date it came to the Krauth Memorial Library are unknown, a hint is found in the fact that the stamp of A.T. Geissenhainer appears on both pages 23 and 41. *The Lutheran Cyclopedia* states that Anastasius T. Geissenhainer was a Lutheran pastor in both New York State and New York City from 1838 to 1851, when he moved to Trenton, New Jersey, and later to Allentown, Pennsylvania.[35] This provides evidence of a direct link between this copy of the tunebook and someone who could have used it in English-language worship in churches associated with the Ministerium of New York.

There is no date on the title page, nor is there any copyright notice. However, the statement, "Engraved and printed by T. Birch, 38 Vesey Street" at the bottom of the title page does provide clues for a date. Thomas

Birch worked as a music engraver in New York starting in 1817, and in 1824 he established a music publishing business which was carried on by him and his descendants until the 1890s.[36] Birch was at the Vesey Street address in 1817 because the *New York Evening Post* for 22 November of that year contains an advertisement for James Hewitt's version of "The Star Spangled Banner" (not today's tune) as well as a song, "This Blooming Rose at Early Dawn," and it gives Birch's address as 38 Vesey Street. Sometime during 1818-19 Birch must have moved to 139 Chamber Street, since that is the address given on the song, "In Sweetest Harmony," listed as number 3358 in Wolfe, *Secular Music in America, 1801-1825*, and dated ca. 1818 because it was "sung by Miss Conrad at several of the oratorio concerts given by the Handel and Haydn Society in New York in June 1818." Redway's *Music Directory of Early New York City* indicates that Birch never returned to Vesey Street, so any music with this address can be dated from 1817 or 1818. Redway's directory does give an 1819 date for Birch being at the Vesey Street address, but this is based upon the fact that "This Blooming Rose at Early Dawn" was registered at the Department of State on 28 May 1819.[37] However, this must have been the same song that was advertised in the newspaper in 1817. Thus, *A Collection of Church Tunes* must have been published in 1817 or as late as 1818, and it appears to have been the first music book to have been engraved by Thomas Birch.

It is possible that Erben had come across Jacob Eckhard's *Choral-Buch* of 1816, and the references which Eckhard made to the New York Lutheran Hymnal may well have inspired Erben to compile a tunebook specifically for this hymnal. Moreover, we know from the advertisement in the *New-York Evening Post* for 21 May 1817 cited above that at this time Erben was seeking a subscription for a new collection of church music, and his Lutheran tunebook may well have been the ultimate result of this effort, though it does not quite fit the proposal as advertised. All the evidence, therefore, points to 1817 or 1818 as being the year when the tunebook appeared.

Considering Peter Erben's long association with Episcopal church music, it is not surprising that this collection is markedly Episcopalian in its orientation. We have already noted that 39 of the 65 melodies in Erben's 1808 Episcopal tunebook are included in *A Collection of Church Tunes*, while of the 87 melodies in his 1806 Reformed tunebook only 32 are included in the Lutheran collection. Further analysis of *A Collection of Church Tunes* indicates that 24 of the 109 compositions are from the core repertory of early American psalmody.[38] Comparison with two major New England tunebooks, both published in 1822, indicates that 48 of the tunes are also in *The Boston Handel and Haydn Society Collection of Church Music*, and 43 are in the tenth edition of *Templi Carmina. Songs of the Temple, or Bridgewater Collection of Sacred Music*. Both these New

England collections are quite large, however, so actually Erben's 1808 Episcopal tunebook has the greatest percentage of its tunes which are also found in his Lutheran collection.

Eleven of the hymns in *A Collection of Church Tunes* have German tune names. While Erben originally may have been of Pennsylvania German background, his knowledge of German must have been minimal, or else he was a very careless proofreader. Here are examples of the "unique" spellings which he gives for some of the German tunes: O EVEGKAET DU DONNER WORD, GOTT SEZ DANK IN ALLER WALT, and ALLE MENCHEN MISSEN STERBEN. One of the German tunes, PRÄCHTIG KOMMT DER HERR, MEIN KÖNIG, may be of American origin. The German text by Philadelphia's Rev. Justus Heinrich Christian Helmuth first appeared in Helmuth's book, *Empfindungen des Herzens in einigen Liedern*, published by Melchior Steiner of Philadelphia in 1781. Early German-American hymnals always list it as having its own tune, which is found in the 1813 *Choral-Buch für die Erbauliche Lieder-Sammlung*.[39] That is the version of the tune which Erben uses, but the text which he suggests is not a translation of Helmuth's German hymn, but instead is "Lord, Dismiss Us with Thy Blessing." The composer of the melody is unknown, but it could have been one of the schoolmaster-organists with whom Helmuth worked, or it might even have been Helmuth himself, since he had some musical background from his studies in Germany before he came to America.

In addition to the eleven tunes with German names, some of the tunes with English names are also of German origin. LUTHER'S JUDGMENT HYMN actually is a variant of NUN FREUT EUCH, LIEBEN CHRISTENGMEIN, usually known in German-American tunebooks as ES IST GEWIßLICH AN DER ZEIT. The tune which Erben calls LAMENTATION actually is the chorale CHRIST, ALLES WAS DICH KRÄNKET, and BRAY or ST. GEORGE'S, a tune in the core repertory of early American psalmody, is related to the chorale LOBT GOTT IHR CHRISTEN. Erben never really tackled the problem of trying to fit German chorale melodies to English translations of their German texts. At that time English hymnody was still awaiting a great poet-translator such as Catherine Winkworth (1829-1878), so whether or not the German tunes were sung to texts which at least paraphrased the originals was hit or miss at best. Of course, this was the basic problem of English-language Lutheran hymnody, and it took most of the next century before American Lutherans began to solve this problem in a satisfactory manner.

A few of the melodies in *A Collection of Church Tunes* appear to be by Erben himself. The initials "P.E." are printed on the tune MANSION, page 85, and as yet it has not been found in any other source. Five other tunes have the initials "P.E." entered in manuscript in an old hand, perhaps by the original owner of the book. In all cases these tunes are otherwise unidentified. These five tunes are ST. STEPHENS (not the STEPHENS or ST. STEPHEN'S found in other tunebooks), POWER, THANKSGIVING (again, not any THANKSGIVING found elsewhere), GRATITUDE, and LIMBETH, which Erben called LAMBETH in his 1806 Reformed tunebook, and which is not the LAMBETH found in other collections. Of these six tunes which may be by Erben, four are written in a German style with fermatas at the end of each line of text. While these melodies may be described as serviceable and competent, they are not especially distinguished—an evaluation confirmed by the fact that later tunebook compilers did not choose to include them in their own collections.

One of the unique features of the format which Erben uses in *A Collection of Church Tunes* is the way in which he assigns each tune to a particular text in the 1814 New York Lutheran hymnal, and he even selects a stanza from that text to illustrate how the music fits the words. In doing this he is following the procedure which he had explained in the introduction to his 1808 Episcopal tunebook, *Sacred Music in Two, Three, and Four Parts*, and which was discussed above. The heading for each tune first gives the number of a text in the Lutheran hymnal followed by its meter, then comes the number of the stanza which is used as an example, the name of the tune, and in a very few cases an attribution to a composer. For example, on page 48 the heading for a tune from the core repertory of early American psalmody reads: "HY: 185—C.M. 3dV. Bangor." This means: "Hymn 185, common meter, third verse, BANGOR." Then follows the music of William Tans'ur's hymn tune, with the text of the hymn's third stanza. Like many persons today, Erben called stanzas "verses," and thus he used the "V" abbreviation. Sometimes he does not indicate which stanza he has set when it is the first stanza. Since Erben never prints more than one of the stanzas, obviously singers would have to learn their parts and then use the hymnbook itself for the other stanzas of text—a practice that seems to be very unwieldy to us today. However, in the introduction to his 1808 Episcopal tunebook Erben had explained that in his view the words divided the learner's attention too much and hindered learning the notes. He stated that singers should add the words only after they had learned their parts.

A majority of the tunes are for four voices in open score, with the melody being in its usual location on the third line immediately above the bass. Erben designated the melody or treble with the abbreviation "Tre:." Some of the tunes are set for three voices, while a few are simply in two parts for melody and bass (without figures). It appears that Erben arranged the parts with organists in mind, since the melody and bass are always bracketed together, and any organist familiar with realizing figured bass could simply play from the two lowest parts. This very practical arrangement is a major reason why many tunebooks which printed the parts in open score continued to put the melody on the line above the bass even

America's First Lutheran Tunebook in English 67

when the practice of assigning the melody to the tenor voice was no longer used. When a tune is scored for four voices, all three upper lines are written in the treble clef. From Erben's comments in the introduction to his 1808 Episcopal tunebook, he recommended that the two highest voices in the treble clef (i.e., the counter on the top line and the tenor on the second line) be sung by male voices, thus dropping their pitch an octave from what was actually written. The melody would then be sung by women and boys. When the tunes are sung in this manner the resulting harmonies and voice leading tend to follow the rules of traditional harmony. For congregational singing the performance probably was similar to that of today, namely, some persons might sing parts, but the emphasis would be on the tune, with the men and women doubling the melody at the octave.

Today when we look back upon Erben's work we find some of the music to be quite dated, though it certainly was in keeping with the standards and tastes of his time. Indeed, hymnodists today find many of the texts in the 1814 New York Lutheran hymnal itself to be of lesser quality, and the translations from the German are often awkward. However, we must not forget that there were no models when it came to providing America's English-speaking Lutherans with a tunebook that reflected both an English-language and a distinctly Lutheran heritage of hymnody and tunes. In this respect Erben was a pathbreaker, and it was to take many more attempts before American Lutheran hymnody was able to establish hymn texts and music that were both American and Lutheran while simultaneously maintaining high standards of both text and music.

CONTENTS OF *A COLLECTION OF CHURCH TUNES*

The following list of the tunes gives the page number, Erben's tune name, and any clarifying comments. References to *"Core"* followed by a number indicate the number of the tune in Crawford, *The Core Repertory of Early American Psalmody*. References to *"Zahn"* give the number in *Die Melodien der deutschen evangelischen Kirchenlieder*,[40] while *"Handel and Haydn"* refers to *The Boston Handel and Haydn Society Collection of Church Music*,[41] and *"Bridgewater"* is the tenth edition of the *Bridgewater Collection of Sacred Music*.[42]

1	OLD HUNDREDTH	*Core* 68
2	ITALY	
4	WINDHAM	*Core* 97
5	WINCHESTER	*Core* 96
5	ST. DENNIS	= ST. DENNIS 'S in Eckhard, *Choral-Book;* not ST. DENYS or ST. DENIS
6	BLENDON	

7 CASTLE STREET
8 ISLINGTON
9 WELLS   Core 94
10 MUSIC
11 PSALM CXXXIX
12 PENITENCE   Not PENITENCE by Lane or Oakley
13 ALFRETON
14 WILDERNESS
15 ST. PAUL'S   = KENT
16 NEW SABBATH
17 FOUNTAIN
18 PORTUGUESE HYMN   = ADESTE FIDELIS; Core 1
19 TALLIS   = TALLIS CANON
20 DUKE STREET
21 HAMILTON   Not *Handel and Haydn* HAMILTON
22 ANGEL'S HYMN   Core 5
23 PERU
24 PORTUGAL   Core 63
25 GERMAN AIR   = MENDON
26 ST. STEPHENS   Has attribution "P.E." in manuscript; Not the common ST. STEPHEN'S.
27 ES EST [sic] DAS HEIL UNS   Zahn 4430
27 O EVEGKAET DU DONNER WORD   = O EWIGKEIT, DU DONNER WORT, Zahn 5820
28 NUN LAßT UNS DEN LEIB   Zahn 352
29 MEAR   Core 49
30 FARRINGDON
32 BETHEL   = PSALM 81 in Erben's 1808 tunebook
33 ABRIDGE
34 HEIGHINGTON   = variant of ABINGTON
35 BRAY   = ST. GEORGE'S; Core 79; variant of LOBT GOTT IHR CHRISTEN, Zahn 198
36 SWANWICK
37 MOUNT PLEASANT
38 JORDAN   Core 38
39 IRISH   Core 36
40 SALEM
41 SEDDON
42 CAMBRIDGE   Is the CAMBRIDGE in C.M.
43 LIVERPOOL

44	BRISTOL	= CHRISTMAS; *Core* 21
45	BURFORD	*Core* 17
46	BEDFORD	*Core* 10
47	BRAINTREE	
48	BANGOR	*Core* 8
49	ABINGDON	= ABINGTON
50	DEVIZES	
51	ROCHESTER	*Core* 75
52	WINDSOR	*Core* 98
53	STEPHENS	
54	HARBOROUGH	= MILES LANE
55	MISSIONARY	= ARISE MY SOUL
56	ROMNEY	Not ROMNEY in *Bridgewater*
57	CRANBROOK	= NORTHAMPTON
58	NEWTON	= SILVER STREET; *Core* 57
59	ALL SAINTS	= ST. BRIDE'S
60	SHIRLAND	
61	DURSLEY	
62	AYLESBURY	*Core* 7
62	LITTLE MARLBOROUGH	*Core* 45
63	PECKHAM	
64	MAJESTY	= AMHERST; *Core* 3
65	WATCHMAN	
66	EGYPT	
67	CONWAY	= MOUNT EPHRAIM
68	MILLER	
69	LAMENTATION	= CHRIST, ALLES WAS DICH KRÄNKET, Zahn 5534
70	CAMBERWELL	
71	LOWELL	
72	ST. THOMAS	*Core* 83
73	CALVARY	Printed attribution to Hill; not the *Handel and Haydn* CALVARY
74	TRIUMPH	= BATH ABBEY
76	POWER	Manuscript attribution "P.E."
77	THANKSGIVING	Manuscript attribution "P.E."
77	GRATITUDE	Manuscript attribution "P.E."
78	MARTIN'S LANE	
79	REJOICE	= EASTER HYMN
80	EAGLE ST.	Printed attribution to I. Smith
81	DIRGE	= INTERMENT; adapted from Handel's *Saul*
82	HOTHAM	*Core* 35

83	PRACHTIG KOMMT DER HERR MEIN KONIG	= PRÄCHTIG KOMMT DER HERR MEIN KÖNIG
84	HELMSLEY	
85	MANSION	Printed attribution to "P.E."
86	PLYELS [*sic*] GERMAN HYMN	
87	GOTT SEZ DANK IN ALLER WALT	= GOTT SEI DANK IN ALLER WELT; Zahn 1230
87	LIMBETH	Manuscript attribution to "P.E." = LAMBETH in Erben's 1806 book; not LAMBETH in *Bridgewater*
88	PLYMOUTH DOCK	
89	WAS GOTT THUT DAS	Zahn 5629
89	VATER UNSER IM HIMMELREICH	Zahn 2561
90	HINTON	Not *Handel and Haydn* HINTON
92	NUN RUHEN ALLE WALDER [*sic*]	= INNSBRUCK; Zahn 2293
93	MACHE DICH MEIN GEIST BEREIT	= STRAF MICH NICHT IN DEINEM ZORN; Zahn 6274
93	HIMEL [*sic*] ERDE LUFT UND MEER	= AUS DER TIEFE RUFE ICH; Zahn 1217
94	ST. MICHAEL'S	= PSALM 149; *Core* 72
95	TAMWORTH	
96	ZION	= DARWELL'S
97	CALVARY	CALVARY in P.M.
98	[No name]	Not identified
98	[No name]	= NUN SICH DER TAG GEENDET HAT; Zahn 212
98	INVITATION	Not INVITATION in later books
99	[No name]	Not identified
99	DOXOLOGY	Same as Samuel Holyoke, *The Columbian Repository of Sacred Harmony* (Exeter, N.H.: Henry Ranlet, [1803]), 423
100	ALLE MENCHEN MISSEN STERBEN	= ALLE MENSCHEN MÜSSEN STERBEN; Zahn 6779
101	AMERICA	Not Billings' nor today's AMERICA
103	LUTHER'S JUDGMENT HYMN	= MONMOUTH; = ES IST GEWIßLICH AN DER ZEIT; variant of Zahn 4429
104	EXALTATION	Not the EXULTATION in later books

[1]*Lutheran Book of Worship* (Minneapolis: Augsburg Publishing House; Philadelphia: Board of Publication, Lutheran Church in America, 1978). This hymnal was prepared by the churches participating in the Inter-Lutheran Commission on Worship, which were the Lutheran Church in America, the American Lutheran Church, the Evangelical Lutheran Church of Canada, and the Lutheran Church—Missouri Synod. Since 1978 the Lutheran Church in America and the American Lutheran Church have merged to form the Evangelical Lutheran Church in America. Likewise, the two publishers of the hymnal have merged to become Augsburg Fortress Press. While the Missouri Synod played an active role in developing the hymnal, doctrinal strife within the Missouri Synod resulted in the Synod's withdrawal from its actual publication, and the Missouri Synod has since published its own hymnal.

[2]Jacob Eckhard, *Choral-Book Containing Psalms, Hymns, Anthems and Chants, Used in the Episcopal Churches of Charleston, South Carolina; and a Collection of Tunes, Adapted to the Metres in the Hymn-Book, Published by Order of the Evangelical Lutheran Synod of the State of New-York. The Whole a Selection for the Service of All Protestant Churches in America* (Boston: James Loring, [1816]).

[3]John Christian Jacobi, *Psalmodia Germanica: or, the German Psalmody. Translated from the High Dutch. Together with Their Proper Tunes, and Thorough Bass* (New York: H. Gaine, 1756).

[4]Theodore G. Tappert and John W. Doberstein, eds., *The Journals of Henry Melchior Muhlenberg*, vol. 1 (Philadelphia: Muhlenberg Press, 1942), 300.

[5]Oscar G.T. Sonneck, *Early Concert Life in America* (Leipzig: Breitkopf und Härtel, 1907; reprint, Wiesbaden: Martin Sändig, 1969), 169 n. 5.

[6]John Christopher Kunze, *A Hymn and Prayer-Book for the Use of Such Lutheran Churches as Use the English Language* (New York: Hurtin and Commardinger, 1795).

[7]George Strebeck, *A Collection of Evangelical Hymns Made from Different Authors and Collections for the English Lutheran Church in New York* (New York: John Tiebout, 1797).

[8]A good account of Strebeck's activities is in Harry J. Kreider, "The English Language Schism in the Lutheran Church in New York City, 1794-1810," *Lutheran Church Quarterly* 21/1(January 1948): 50-60.

[9]Transcript of the Manuscript Protocol of the New York Ministerium, 1786-1806, *Microfilm Corpus of American Lutheranism*, reel 18, part 1 (Princeton: American Theological Library Association Board of Microtext, 1954-), 13.

[10][Lawrence Van Buskirk], *Six Sermons, Preached by the Late Mr.*

Lawrence V. Buskirk, B.A. Candidate for the Holy Ministry (New York: T. Kirk, 1797).

[11] Ibid., iv-vi.

[12] Ralph Williston, *A Choice Selection of Evangelical Hymns* (New York: J. C. Totten, 1806).

[13] *Microfilm Corpus*, reel 18, part 1, 34.

[14] Kreider, "The English Language Schism," 59.

[15] *Microfilm Corpus*, reel 18, part 3, 54.

[16] Ibid., 56.

[17] *A Collection of Hymns, and a Liturgy, for the Use of Evangelical Lutheran Churches; to Which Are Added Prayers for Families and Individuals* (Philadelphia: G. & D. Billmeyer, 1814).

[18] Biographical data on Eckhard is in George W. Williams, *Jacob Eckhard's Choirmaster's Book of 1809* (Columbia: University of South Carolina Press, 1971), xi-xii.

[19] James Grant Wilson and John Fiske, eds., *Appletons' Cyclopedia of American Biography* (1888), s.v. "Erben, Peter."

[20] Virginia Larkin Redway, *Music Directory of Early New York City* (New York: New York Public Library, 1941), 7.

[21] John Ogasapian, *Henry Erben: Portrait of a Nineteenth-Century Organ Builder* (Braintree, Mass.: Organ Literature Foundation, 1980), 1.

[22] Ibid.

[23] Ibid., 2. Erben also apparently served as organist at the Dutch Church for a few weeks in early 1805 before Hewitt was hired. Excerpts from the church minutes for 1805-07 with some references to Erben being employed at an annual salary of $200 are quoted by Peter T. Cameron, "A History of the Organs of the Collegiate Church of New York City, 1727-1861," *The Tracker* 25/1 (Fall 1980): 83.

[24] Vera Brodsky Lawrence, *Strong on Music: Resonances*, vol. 1 (New York: Oxford University Press, 1988), xxxiii and 71.

[25] A. H. Messiter, *A History of the Choir and Music of Trinity Church, New York from Its Organization to the Year 1897* (New York: Edwin S. Gorham, 1906; reprint, New York: AMS Press, 1970), 37-38.

[26] Lawrence, *Strong on Music*, xxxiii.

[27] Morgan Dix, *A History of the Parish of Trinity Church in the City of New York*, 6 vols. (New York: G.P. Putnam's Sons, 1905) 3:124-25. My thanks to John Ogasapian for calling this letter to my attention.

[28] Richard J. Wolfe, *Secular Music in America 1801-1825*, 3 vols. (New York: New York Public Library, 1964).

[29] Facsimile in Richard Jackson, *Democratic Souvenirs: An Historical Anthology of 19th-Century American Music* (New York: C. F. Peters for The New York Public Library, 1988), 159.

[30] [Peter Erben], *A Selection of Psalm and Hymn Tunes, for the Use of the Dutch Reformed Churches in the City of New York. Harmonized by P. Erben. Organist of the New-Dutch Church* (New York: P. Erben; printed by John C. Totten, 1806).

[31] Wolfe, *Secular Music* 3:1175. For an excellent description of this book as well as Erben's 1806 Reformed and 1808 Episcopal tunebooks see Allen P. Britton, Irving Lowens, and Richard Crawford, *American Sacred Music Imprints 1698-1810: A Bibliography* (Worcester: American Antiquarian Society, 1990), 258-61.

[32] *The New Grove Dictionary of American Music* (New York: Grove's Dictionaries, 1986), s.v. "Hewitt, James," by John W. Wagner.

[33] P. Erben, *Sacred Music for the Use of Singing Societies and Private Families Selected and Adapted to the Piano Forte* (New York: Published for the Compiler & Sold at J. Hewitt's Musical Repository, Maiden Lane, n.d.). My thanks to Timothy Sullivan, library assistant at the Cooper-Hewitt Museum, for researching details of this book for me.

[34] My thanks to the Rev. David J. Wartluft, librarian at the Krauth Memorial Library, for making information concerning this book available to me.

[35] Henry Eyster Jacobs and John A.W. Haas, *The Lutheran Cyclopedia* (New York: Charles Scribner's Sons, 1905), 190.

[36] Richard J. Wolfe, *Early American Music Engraving and Printing* (Urbana: University of Illinois Press, 1980), 56.

[37] Redway, *Music Directory*, 27.

[38] Richard A. Crawford, ed., *The Core Repertory of Early American Psalmody* (Madison: A-R Editions, 1984).

[39] See Edward C. Wolf, "America's First Lutheran Chorale Book," *Concordia Historical Institute Quarterly* 46/1 (Spring 1973): 5-17 and Edward C. Wolf, "Justus Henry Christian Helmuth—Hymnodist," *German-American Studies* 5 (1972): 124.

[40] Johannes Zahn, *Die Melodien der deutschen evangelischen Kirchenlieder*, 6 vols. (Gütersloh: C. Bertelsmann, 1889-93).

[41] *The Boston Handel and Haydn Society Collection of Church Music* (Boston: Richardson and Lord, 1822).

[42] *Templi Carmina. Songs of the Temple, or Bridgewater Collection of Sacred Music* (Boston: Richardson & Lord, 1822).

GAETANO CARUSI: FROM SICILY TO THE HALLS OF CONGRESS

James R. Heintze

In 1805 Gaetano Carusi (Caruso), his wife Philippa, and their three young sons, Samuel (Samuele), Nathaniel (Ignazio), and Lewis (Luigi), and a group of musical companions, left Italy and sailed for America.[1] Filled with hopes and aspirations for a better life in a new land, Gaetano, his sons, and the other Italians had enlisted as United States Marine Band musicians. They boarded an American frigate that, to their surprise, was not going directly to America but was on its way to serve in the Tripolian War. Misunderstandings and broken agreements by Marine Corps, Navy, and Army personnel placed the lives of Carusi and his family in peril, and eventually cost him the loss of most of his money and personal belongings. After serving only one-half of his three-year term, Carusi was forced to resign from the Marine Corps. He had not been paid the full amount owed to him for his service. His requests for recompensation from the military services for not meeting their responsibilities in the agreements that were made went unheeded. Unable to speak a word of English, Carusi had been abandoned in a foreign land. Attempts to return to Italy were not successful. In order to support his family, he was forced to seek employment wherever possible.

Frustrated and disappointed by all that happened, Carusi brought several petitions for redress of grievances before Congress. The account that follows is based principally on one such petition he wrote in 1840 in his seventy-sixth year: *Narrative of Gaetano Carusi, in Support of His Claim before the Congress of the United States.*[2] In this unique document, Carusi provides meticulous details about the persons he met and the events that occurred before and during his years in America. The tale he tells is one of sadness, tragedy, and rights that were not protected, but his story is also one of resourcefulness and triumph. He was an accomplished musician who, in the end, achieved success. He contributed to the cultural life in three cities, and his legacy—his children's musical accomplishments as teachers, composers, and impresarios—left its mark on the development of music in early America.

Carusi began his *Narrative* with a summary of his experience in America and why he wanted others to know what happened:

> I, Gaetano Carusi, having been deceived, nay, betrayed and insulted, by persons concerned in the Government of the United States of America, consider it my duty to detail, in as brief a manner as possible, the particulars of my residence in the United States, hoping that Government, or some one interested in its just administration, will take the side of reason; or rather of equity, and see that justice is done me, my losses repaired, and my wants supplied. Besides, my statement may be of service to many who will learn, by my misfortunes, how to regulate themselves under the same circumstances, A.D. 1804.[3]

The events that led to Carusi's decision to come to America began with the creation of the United States Marine Corps Band. On 11 July 1798 an act was passed by Congress that provided for the establishment of the Marine Corps and its first official band of thirty-two fifes and drums. Secretary of the Navy William Benjamin Stoddert had arrived in Washington City on 15 June 1800 and was charged with selecting a new site for the Marine Corps headquarters. By the end of June, Secretary Stoddert sent orders to Lieutenant Colonel Commandant William Ward Burrows in Philadelphia to move the Marine headquarters from that city to temporary quarters in Georgetown. Commandant Burrows stated in a letter he wrote in early July that he planned to "be in the Federal City on the 15th instant." Burrows, who favored the newly established Marine Band, decided to take "nothing but music with him."[4] Not long thereafter, the Band arrived in Washington and began participating in social activities. On 21 August 1800 the Band gave its first public concert in Washington, and Burrows subsequently became one of the managers of the Washington Dancing Assemblies.[5] On 31 August he wrote the following note to Lieutenant Edward Hall in Philadelphia:

> Procure and send with all convenient dispatch the articles hereafter mention . . . 2 French Horns, 2 C. Clarinets, 1 Bassoon. 1 Bass Drum 2 feet & 1/2 long and 2 feet in diameter. Let some reeds be sent for the Clarinets, and Bassoon.[6]

On 3 March 1801 President John Adams approved an appropriation of money for erecting a Marine barracks in Washington. The site selected was the Navy Yard, and according to a letter written by Commandant Burrows to Captain Franklin Wharton in Philadelphia on 31 March 1801, newly-elected President Jefferson had spent an entire morning riding with Burrows "looking for a proper place to fix the Marine Barracks on." Jefferson and Burrows agreed on the new site which was purchased on 21 June 1801.[7]

In late 1803 or early 1804, Burrows issued an order to Captain John Hall to recruit some Italian musicians for enlistment in the Marine Band.[8] At that time, Hall was about to leave for the Mediterranean to join the American fleet under the command of Commodore Samuel Barron.[9] Barron probably knew of Burrows' order and told Captain Hall, who had by now arrived in the Mediterranean, to proceed and "procure a Band of Music for the ship in any part of Cecily."[10]

The first musician Hall contacted was Gaetano Varano, a "professor of music" and "head of the band attached to a regiment in Syracuse, belonging to His Majesty the King of Naples." Hall offered him an enlistment in the Marine Corps which Varano promptly refused. However, Varano recommended Gaetano Carusi, a reputable musician living in Catania, Sicily.[11] Hall located Carusi[12] in 1804 and proposed to him a salary of $12 per month if he would enlist in the Marine Corps.[13] Carusi rejected his offer stating, "I refused, telling him that, without taking the trouble of such a long voyage, I was in possession of the double of that residing as I did quietly at home."[14] However, Hall was persistent and according to Carusi, "For the space of a whole year did this Captain importune me by his letters, making offers which I always rejected as insignificant and pitiful." Finally, Hall "came in person to Catania, to proffer his suit" and was successful in persuading Carusi to change his mind:

> It was in vain for me to state to him that the remuneration he [Hall] offered would not suffice to provide for the necessities of my family, especially in America: he redoubled his entreaties, stating that in America I could not but become rich in the short space of three months. Still I persevered in refusing. Finally, inquiring about my family, and whether any of them were capable of enlisting in the band, I assured him that my boys were able to do justice to their different parts; he then offered them pay; and, upon my still refusing, he at last offered a ration of $6 a month to my wife. *Multa pauca faciun tunum satis.*
>
> Reflecting that, besides these small remunerations, I would be able to gain several others by my individual exertions, we concluded the agreement.[15]

One wonders why Captain Hall was so determined during the course of an entire year to recruit these musicians, especially in light of the importance of his other war-time duties. Perhaps Burrows' order had originated with Jefferson and Captain Hall was aware of that. Jefferson might have had interest in bringing a group of skilled musicians to Washington. His knowledge of music and abilities as an instrumentalist were well known.[16] For example, he began violin studies at at early age and often performed in consort with other competent instrumentalists in Virginia. He was also familiar with the leading European composers and their works and had himself attended all sorts of concerts and operatic performances in France where he served as minister in 1785-88. Moreover, his personal library contained numerous musical compositions by Italian composers, such as Giovanni Battista Pergolesi, Luigi Boccherini, Arcangelo Corelli, and Muzio Clementi.

Presumably, Jefferson had high expectations for cultural life in Washington, for shortly after his arrival in Washington, he began using the Marine Band for special events at the "President's House." On 1 January 1801, for example, the Band gave its debut performance at a reception there in commemoration of the New Year. On 4 July, while reviewing the troops on the grounds surrounding the executive mansion, Jefferson again had the Band perform. After the review was completed, the President and his entourage went inside to the dining room "and the band from an adjacent room played a succession of fine patriotic airs."[17]

While Jefferson did not comment in his writings on his musical expectations of the Marine Band, other contemporary observations appear to indicate that the Band was more than adequate. Margaret Bayard Smith, who was married to the publisher of the *National Intelligencer*, thought the Band was "excellent,"[18] and a notice in her husband's newspaper mentioned the "great precision" and "inspiring animation" of the instrumentalists.[19]

Jefferson's interest in Italian artisans was widely known and provides a possible connection to Carusi and his Italian compatriots.[20] For example, in June of 1803, an "Italian Band of music" was performing in Washington,[21] and Jefferson heard them in January of the following year play a number or pieces, including a work titled "Jefferson's March," at a celebration in honor of the President's purchase of the Louisiana Territory.[22] Not long thereafter, Jefferson had arranged through Filippo Mazzei for a group of forty sculptors to come from Carrara, Italy, to Washington in order to work on the Capitol. The sculptors had come to Washington in October 1805, only a month after Carusi and his friends arrived.

Carusi confirmed the fact that Hall received orders to enlist the Italians from both Burrows and Barron, and stated his belief that those orders came from Jefferson:

> I have discovered that the said Captain John Hall, previous to his departure for the Mediterranean, received orders from Colonel Borrows [sic] to form this band. Captain John Hall, in consequence of this double charge of Colonel Borrows and Commodore Samuel Barron, which, by-the-by, I am better informed originated with President Jefferson, who proposed to Congress a plan for this purpose, which, however, was not adopted, endeavored by every means to meet with some individual not only capable of directing and commanding one band, but calculated likewise to form others.[23]

Gaetano Carusi and his three sons were not the only musicians Hall enlisted. Carusi states:

> As Catania is a small and thinly-peopled city, no sooner did I accept the offer than it was known, and its novelty induced several to unite with me, and, perhaps suspecting some deceit, they were desirous that I should be security to them, respectively, for their miserable pay.[24]

These musicians included Francesco Pulizzi (later appointed first clarinetist), Felice Pulizzi and his son Venerando, Ignazio di Mauro, D. Domenico Guarnaccia, D. Pasquale Loria and his son Frencesco, and Michele, James, and Gaetano Sardo. Counting Gaetano and his three sons, the band totaled fourteen musicians.[25]

The entire group and their families (some of the wives stayed in Italy), were taken aboard the *President*. They signed the following agreement:

> We the underwriters we say we are obliged to serve Captain John Hall, American Captain on Board the United States Frigate President for the space of three years in Rank as musicians, for the formation of a Band, with the pay. The Master of the Band 12 Dollars per Month, the first Clarinet 8 Dollars per Month, and all the others 7 Dollars,—and to be paid at the end of three Months, and with all the rations or Six Dollars or a Month for the rations, and with all the Clothing or without the Clothing 35 Dollars a year, or if pleases the Captain to give the women Six Dollars a month for the rations at the beginning of every month. The Consul of Syracuse is obligated to the Captain to pay the Marrieds Six Dollars a Month

either in Syracuse or Catania while we are in America. And the expiration of our three years the Captain refuse us our seperate [sic] Discharges and he is obligated to the Captain to give us our passage as far as Italy at his own expence. With all the youngest Son of the Master of the Band & the Son of Pasqua Le Loria, & they are to serve and to play on the Triangle, and the other to play the Symbals, and for the pay of those two Boys will oblige the Captain to give them rations and Clothing, or otherways [sic] give them the money for their rations and clothing. And we will be obligated to the Captain when our times will expire to allow each of us Instruments of Music, and withall that the Captn will give to us by his good will a present to each of us of 10 Dollars, and to the Master of the Band 40 Dollars. This 17th day February Catania 1805, [The musicians signatures appear here] I agree to the above, John Hall, Captn. Marines.[26]

In his *Narrative*, Carusi names four musicians not mentioned above—Joseph Papa, S. Antonio and Corrado Signorelli, and Antonio Paterno—as being with him at the time of his arrival in America.[27] It is likely, therefore, that these musicians were enlisted after the agreement was signed by Carusi and the others, and that the band actually consisted of eighteen musicians.[28]

Marine Corps documents provide specific information about the Carusi family. Gaetano Carusi was described at the time of his enlistment as "aged forty-two years, six feet, one inch high, black hair, dark complexion, by trade or occupation a musician"[29] who played the French horn, bassoon, trumpet, and other instruments. He lived in Catania and was well known. His Sicilian friend, Felice Pulizzi, said this about him:

> I hereby certify that I knew and was well acquainted with Mr. G. Carusi (now of Washington City) when he lived in Sicily and do affirm on my own knowledge that he was liberally patronized as a Professor of Music by the citizens of that country before and when he was engaged by the officers of the U. States to come to this country—being always engaged at churches, theatres, concerts and places of public amusements or in giving lessons in music—and that he had always as much as he could attend to. Given under my hand and seal this 19 day of Aug. 1831, Felice Pulizzi[30]

Carusi's "lessons in music" included practically all wind and string instruments. He was also a composer, although there are no extant works from his Italian period. Joseph Carusi, "who was born in Naples about the year 1700, and became famous from having brought out the first opera that was ever presented to the London public," has been cited as Gaetano's father.[31]

Gaetano's eldest son, Samuel, was "born in Sicily" and was ten years of age at the time of his enlistment in February 1805. He was described as having "black hair" and "dark complexion."[32] Nathaniel Carusi, "born in Catania," was nine years old at the time of his enlistment. He also had "black hair, dark complexion."[33] Both Samuel and Nathaniel played the French horn. Lewis Carusi, the youngest of the brothers, was born in 1800,[34] and was five years of age at the time of his brothers' enlistments.

The Carusi family took their most valued possessions, including music and household items, such as the "silk trimmings" from Philippa's bed.[35] They were packed into a large "walnut" or "chestnut" trunk which was secured with "three locks" and marked "Frigate President." Captain Hall later placed the musicians, whom he now referred to as "Marines," and their families aboard "different ships at Syracuse in very excellent order" and left for Palermo where he was to obtain musical instruments for them. He returned to Syracuse on or about 29 February 1805.[36]

Carusi expected to sail immediately thereafter for America but was surprised to learn that the *President* was on its way to the port of Tripoli in order to serve in blockading maneuvers against the so-called Barbary powers (Tripoli, Algeria, Morocco, and Tunisia). He recalled:

> In our bargain there was not a single word said of being obliged to go to the war which was then waging with the Tripolitans; but the fact was, that, as soon as we were enlisted, we were forced to join with the squadron and fight their battles.[37]

On 28 April, the American fleet had taken up positions in the waters surrounding the port of Tripoli. While a battalion of Marines attacked by land, the ships concentrated their cannon fire on the fort.[38] The musicians' families were probably instructed to remain below deck during the barrage. The Italian musicians were now enlisted Marines and, hence, were presumably given specific assignments. What Carusi's orders were is not known. His children, however, were instructed "to hand cartridges to the cannoniers."[39]

The naval bombardment proved successful and by late May or early June 1805 a truce was secured. The *President* subsequently sailed for Malta and arrived there on 3 June. From 7 June to 7 July she was in Syracuse and thereafter returned to Malta.[40] While in Malta, Carusi was offered an enlistment in the British navy. He states, "Admiral Fox of the British Navy offered me at Malta 1000 dollars if I would quit the service of the United States, and remain there to form a Band of 24 musicians."[41] On 13 July, the *President* left Malta for the United States, stopping over at Gibraltar from 27 July to 3 August.[42]

During his months at sea, Carusi began "with great difficulty and trouble" to train his musicians whom he first thought of as "stupid and ignorant." Yet, after hours of practice each day, he was able to "perfect them so they might be enabled to execute well my compositions." Added to the difficulty in training the musicians was the unpleasantness of the voyage itself. Carusi remarked on the "passage from Sicily to America" as a time of "suffering occasioned by hunger, thirst & loss of rest."[43]

While Carusi was at sea, Commandant Burrows had decided to retire due to ill health. Recently-promoted Lieutenant Colonel Franklin Wharton was appointed as his replacement on 17 March 1804. Apparently Burrows had not told Wharton about the newly-enlisted Italian musicians. Captain Hall, who was not aware of that, wrote to Wharton on 28 February and again on 1 April 1805 informing him that he had taken on a group of Italians. His letter of 1 April states:

> I enlisted this Band for the Corps in consequence of an order received from Col. Burrows before I left America, and have engaged them at the same rate as the rest of our music. They will come on with me, and am in hopes you will be pleased with them. As I am now on board of the Congress, cannot forward my different returns to the Staff, but as we go for Malta in a day or two, shall as soon as I join the President forward them by the store ship.[44]

Wharton was not at all pleased about this news and wrote back to him on 29 June:

> I have received your letter from Palermo. . . . That part of it which relates to a band of music, I cannot comprehend. You observe the Commandant [Burrows] had ordered a band procured, it, of course, belongs to the ship [i.e., a Navy matter]. He could not order it for the Corps. You then remark that you have engaged it for the Marine Corps, under the usual enlistment. This must be equally incorrect. I have never given any orders for the collection of a band in the Mediterranean and it will not be mentioned as belonging to the Corps. The expenses already arising from this engagement, I find enormous, by bounty and purchase of instruments, and I am well assured will not be paid. The Secretary of the Navy can never consent to allow two Military Bands for one Corps, and the private fund hitherto used, has been done away.[45]

Apparently Hall never received Wharton's communiqué, for he wrote to Wharton on 10 September: "I have added to my detachment eighteen good musicians which hope you will be pleased with."[46]

On 11 September the *President* arrived in Hampton Roads, Virginia. The ship left six days later and sailed into Washington on 19 September.[47] Just outside of Washington on the Potomac River, she passed Alexandria, Virginia, where a hearty welcome from local residents and an artillery salute was given. Carusi's band responded by playing a patriotic tune on the ship's deck. The event was reported in the local newspaper the following day:

> Alexandria, September 19. The inhabitants of Alexandria had yesterday the pleasure of seeing captain Bainbridge and several of the officers late prisoners at Tripoli, arrive safe and well at Gadsby's tavern. The liberation and restoration of these men to their country, is a circumstance of general felicitation.
>
> It being known that the United States frigate President, Capt. J[ames]. Barron, would pass this town on her way to the navy yard at Washington, a number of our citizens crowded to the wharfs. About eleven o'clock this morning she was nearly opposite to Alexandria, and having the greater part of her sails distended, exhibitted [sic] a very beautiful object—she came up slowly and majestically sailing—the marines on board being drawn up in martial array. When opposite the town she received a federal salute from Capt. Longdon's artillery company, which she returned by firing 16 guns, and immediately after her band struck up Hail Columbia.[48]

Carusi's initial impression of Washington was "a desert, in fact, a place containing some two or three taverns, with a few scattered cottages or log huts." On 20 September, the Italians were asked to provide the music for the celebration of "a great festival in honor of the soldier[s] who had fought against the pirates of Tripoli."[49] A description of the event, its participants, and the music performed was printed in the newspaper:

> Captain Bainbridge was handed by the officers appointed to the seat at the right hand of the chair; and Captain James Barron to that on the left—The other officers present and the citizens of Washington took their seats as convenient, and without distinction. After dinner the following toasts were drank, accompanied by music from the band of the Marine corps, and the elegant Italian band, arrived in the frigate PRESIDENT.
> The President of the United States. Air—Jefferson's March.
> The Vice-President of the United States. Patriotic Air.

The Heads of Departments. Hail Columbia.
The Navy of the United States. Yankee Doodle.
Commodore Samuel Barron. Patriotic Air.
Men in captivity . . . Air—The Galley Slave.
Commodore Rodgers and the officers of the Mediterranean Squadron. Air—Patriotic.
Captivity Triumphant . . . At this toast Captain Bainbridge rose, and in short but appropriate speech, returned thanks to the company in the name of himself and his officers, on which the company gave 3 cheers. Song—The sweet little cherub that sits up aloft to take care of the life of poor Jack. Air—Jemmy's returned from Dover.
Captain Eaton . . . Air—The Battle.
May the powers of Barbary learn . . . Air—the sons of Alknomack.
Lieut. O'Bannon of the Marines, and Midshipman Mann . . . song and air—Hearts of Oak.
Consul Nelson (of Denmark) and cidi Hamet Degese (of Tripoli) . . . Air—Charity.
May we never lose a ship . . . Patriotic Air.
Col. Lear . . . Music.
Mediterranean Laurels . . . Patriotic Air.
The Bashaw of Tripoli . . . Oh Dear! What can the matter be?
No chains but those of love . . . With women and wine we defy every care.

The highest social order prevailed, and benignity dwelt upon every countenance. Several patriotic and other appropriate songs were interspersed with the toasts, and the company broke up at an early hour.[50]

That evening, while the band continued to play (most of the night, according to Carusi), the women and children were taken to the Marine barracks. All of the Italians were tired, hungry, and concerned about locating adequate shelter:

> The band continued playing nearly all night, and the women and children, as well as ourselves, were for thirty hours unable to procure food to satisfy our hunger.
>
> When we had ceased playing for the great festival, we were led to our quarters, where men, women, boys, and children, thirty or more in all, were obliged to bundle together in a single chamber, and sleep upon the bare floor; about eight o'clock next morning bread was distributed among the poor people, who, as famished as wolves in winter, devoured it in an instant. About an hour afterwards the commander of the barracks called me to his presence,

and observed that it was not fit that I should remain with the others, and that a house was prepared for me out of the barracks. This apparent demonstration of respect was not so in reality, but a deception. It would have been nothing if, by chance, a residence could have been obtained in this desert city; but, it is well known that, in 1805, and for many years after, there were no houses for any body at all. After great pains, however, I met with a cabin [on 7 October], which I obtained on paying for it $8 per month.[51]

On 10 October the musicians went before Magistrate Robert Alexander and swore their "allegiance to the United States."[52] Not long after, Col. Wharton ordered the musicians and their families to leave the barracks and find other quarters. The Italians disobeyed the order by pretending either not to hear or understand it. Soldiers were brought in to clear the barracks. With women and children crying, the musicians and their families, who blamed Carusi for getting them into this situation, finally left

in search of some habitable place; but their labors were useless. Signor D. Felice Pulizzi and Signor D. Pasquale Lorio, whose two families amounted to about one dozen souls, set out in search of some cabin, or any thing else that would afford them shelter; but they sought in vain. They found at length a place destined for the shelter of cows, and this they appropriated for their own residence; thence, however, were they driven by order of the Colonel of Marines, the owner having learned with dissatisfaction that men had usurped the resting-place of his cattle.

In this miserable plight they were, through the pity of Signor Augustino Serra,[53] permitted to go into the cellar under his apartment, where, as I before said, they were obliged to lie like dogs upon the bare ground. Signor D. Domenico Guarnaccia and Michael Sardo were more fortunate; for having met with a generous gentleman, they were suffered by him to reside with their families in a little kitchen adjoining his residence, for the sum of $5 a month. All those who had no families were obliged to sleep with the drummers and fifers.[54]

Around 7 January 1806 Carusi received a notice from his landlord, W. Venable, that he owed $24 for three months' rent. Carusi did not read English and was not able to understand the document presented to him. Shortly thereafter, local "constables" appeared and took most of his personal property as security until such time when the debt would be paid. He called on Wharton and Hall for relief but to no avail.[55] In the end, Carusi was forced to sell some personal belongings in order "to pay the rent due to the landlord, as well as the cost of the execution, and redeem the property" which had been taken from him.

Throughout this time, Carusi and his fellow musicians had performed in and around Washington. On 28 December 1805, the Carusi family took part in a concert that included "a display of grand fire works" presented by "Mr. St. Aubin" and a number of other musicians. The program began with a "new march," dedicated to the President of the United States and was followed by a symphony by Mozart, a sonata for "piano forte with violin accompanyments," and other works, concluding with a "Grand Symphony" by Gossec. One of the selections was a "Duet on two Horns By two children [Samuel and Nathaniel Carusi] of 7 and 8 years old."[56] On 6 March 1806, the Carusi band visited Mount Vernon. John Brazier Cannon was present at the event and recorded the following:

> Thursday March 6th At night Mr. Washington returned from the City of Washington. Judge Johnston, W. Hiort [?] and Capt. Hall came with him. Capt. Hall brought part of the Italian band of music with him from the City of Washington. Therefore the remaining part of the evening was musically spent.[57]

Hall and the musicians left after dinner on the following day. On 24 March 1806, they returned to Mount Vernon:

> Before dinner General Eaton[58] Capt. Hall Doct. Davis & his wife Gen. Eaton's niece (Miss Broom) & a Miss Daniels came from Washington City to Mount Vernon, they brought the Band again. Mr. Mae left Mount Vernon this morning and returned to Dinner bringing with him Miss Fanny Fitz [?]. The evening was musically spent.[59]

Carusi's band was well received by Washington socialites. All of the hours of band practice had its rewards. Carusi now boasted, "my band was considered superior to every other in America on account of its well selected music, its good direction and its excellent harmony."[60]

Over a year had passed since Carusi's arrival in Washington and although he lodged many complaints, he had not yet received any payment for his time served in the Marine Corps. Finally, Sargeant Major Forrest[61] offered to pay him $7 per month, not the $12 that was in the enlistment papers. Carusi refused to sign the account[62] and went directly to Robert Smith, Secretary of the Navy, who offered no assistance. Meanwhile Wharton had made up his mind that the Italians had to go. In a letter to Secretary Smith, Wharton stated, "The present establishment of the Marine

Corps and for which appropriations have been made for the last two years will not admit of a greater proportion for it of music than 25 Drummers & 25 Fifers." Further, Smith explained that Marines enlisted while at sea were under the direct authority of the squadron commander and that this matter came under the Navy's jurisdiction.[63] In response, Smith replied that a Naval squadron commander did not have the "authority to increase or add to such detachment without express permission from the Secretary of the Navy." Further, "an increase of the number of music beyond the number authorized by law and as such increased number can not be paid under the authority of law, they will not be paid at all by the Department."[64] Smith agreed to "take measures to prevent a repetition of such irregularities in [the] future," but was not going to get involved with the Italians. Wharton likely interpreted Smith's response as an invitation to get rid of the musicians in an expediant manner.

Wharton ordered Carusi's discharge which he refused to accept:

> The country was unknown to us; we were ignorant of the language, without friends, relations, and without money; some of us burdened with families, and only provided with a profession which in the United States was valueless; and, besides, when we considered our wicked treatment coming from those whose duty it was to protect us, and that we might meet with worse insults and outrages, if mingled with the inhabitants of the country, we determined to suffer in silence until an opportunity offered of returning to our own country.[65]

Wharton, not satisfied with Carusi's reaction, began giving the musicians difficult and burdensome chores and assignments, in addition to the two practice band sessions that Carusi had to conduct each day. At least one musician, Michael Sardo, became ill from digging latrine trenches and was hospitalized for a time. Felix Pulizzi "agreed to pay to a person fifty cents per day, to be excused from doing the filthy work." Wharton became increasingly impatient and presented an ultimatum that all of the musicians had to be out of the compound in forty-eight hours. Hearing that, Carusi and the other musicians proceeded to the Navy Department to address their grievances once again to Secretary Smith. Smith was not there, so the Italians went to the home of James Madison, Secretary of State. Madison decided not to assist them saying "he had nothing to do with the affairs of the Navy." Dolley Madison, however, interceded on behalf of the musicians; she told Carusi that he would find Smith at home.[66] Carusi immediately went to Smith's house and later described the encounter that occurred:

We went accordingly, and found the carriage standing at the door which was to carry him away; I went immediately into the house, followed by all my companions, and the Secretary, Mr. Robert Smith, in great fright, as if the house were attacked by a mob, demanded hurriedly what I wanted, and why all those people had come into his house? I found Commodore [John] Rodgers with him, who interpreted for me in Lingua Franca, and without loss of time, I recounted to the Secretary the insolent message we had received [from Wharton], and our inability to accept our discharge, on account of our present circumstances.[67]

Upon hearing that, Smith ordered Rodgers to have Wharton refrain from harassing the Italians. Wharton, however, did not obey the order. Instead, he made additional threats. He told them that if they did not leave their houses and sleep in the barracks at night, they would be faced with prison. Carusi recounted that

It was necessary now, as he was endeavoring to oppress me, to counteract his intention. So I resolved to send my wife to him, who was to tell him that, if her husband was obliged to lodge in the barracks, she would on the next day go up to Baltimore and lay the case before the Secretary, and inform him at the same time of all we had endured and suffered. She did exactly as I directed, and the gallant Colonel, fearing that my wife would do as she threatened, commissioned Captain J. Hall to speak to me, to do away with the order as regarded myself, but to make it appear as though it had been done through his (Captain Hall's) intercession, that I might be permitted to live in my own house.[68]

Wharton was still intent on getting the musicians out of the compound. He decided to offer all of the Italians furloughs of "two or three months to travel about the country" in order to find work. A few of the musicians accepted and left for Baltimore "but gained nothing by the trip except barely enough to pay their expenses. . . ." Carusi and the others remained.

Not long thereafter, on an evening around 1 August 1806,

Captain J. Hall, together with another marine officer, sent for me to come, with my children, to their quarters, where there were some ladies who wished to hear them (the children) sing; we went, Domenico Guarnaccia, myself, and the children, to amuse a company of little girls with playing and singing; who, when they were done, generously rewarded the children, and sent them away. When the company had broken up, Captain Hall and the other officer began persuading me to accept my discharge, observing that I could make money enough by travelling as a musician over the country. They assured me that it was a great source of annoyance and suffering to them to see the manner in which I was insulted by Colonel Wharton, averring he was an aristocrat, and only fit to command wild beasts.[69]

Two weeks later, on 15 August 1806, Carusi relented. He and some of the other musicians accepted their discharges from the Marine Corps, having served exactly one-half of their three-year terms.

Carusi decided to take his family and his friend Felice Pulizzi to Norfolk to board the frigate *Chesapeake* which was docked awaiting orders for sailing to the Mediterranean. To get there, they boarded a boat on the Potomac that was sailing for Alexandria where, Carusi was told, a ship would be departing for Norfolk. Col. Wharton, on hearing about Carusi's intentions, arrested him and demanded that he return all of the music in his possession.

> I was carried before the Colonel, and he repeated the demand for the books, which I had purchased in Sicily with my own money, the music in which I had copied with my own hand, and composed for the instruction of the band and my own assistance. It was in vain that I averred that the music was my own; that it belonged to me as being the head of the band; and that, moreover, I should be allowed to retain it because I had received no recompense for my labor during my term of actual service. During our altercation a sailor came from the vessel to inform me she was on the eve of departure, and that I must return immediately to secure my passage. The books were in my trunks on board; the sentinels were ordered not to let me pass; I knew not what to do; and, in the hurry of the moment, offered my parol of honor to send the music if permitted to depart; it was refused, and I was obliged to suffer Joseph Sardo to go down to the vessel and rummage over my trunks in search of the books. He returned with them, and I was not even yet permitted to go, until the Drum Major had examined them all.[70]

Carusi purchased his passage to Norfolk for forty dollars, after having sold some of his personal belongings. He arrived in Norfolk and presented a concert on 22 August. The following notice was printed in the newspaper:

> A Great Concert will be performed at Mr. Riffaud's Long Room, well known for the conveniency of such performances. Mr. Riffaud respectfully informs the Ladies and Gentlemen that this evening,

August 22, will be performed by seven Gentlemen, Italian Musicians, just arrived from Naples; among them are two children, the one eleven, the other nine years of age, who blows elegantly the French Horn, and in a manner to astonish the publick; the other are two fine Clarinets, two good Violins, and an excellent bass. The concert will begin as follows:

    1st A grand overture with all the instruments
    2nd The two children will sing an Italian Air
    3rd A duet performed on the French Horns by the two boys
    4th A Grand Symphony
    5th An Italian duet sung by the two boys
    6th A duet on the French Horns
    7th The whole band will play American and Italian Marches.[71]

Not long thereafter, Carusi wrote to Secretary Smith requesting permission to board the frigate *Chesapeake*.[72] On 26 February 1807, Smith wrote back:

> Mr. Gaetano Carusi, Care of Dl. Bedinger Esq.[73] Norfolk Upon delivering the enclosed letter to Capt. James Barron, Commanding Officer of the frigate Chesapeake, he will give you a passage to the Mediterranean in that ship, which may be expected to sail in about six weeks Respy R. Smith

On 14 May 1807, Wharton wrote to Captain Hall, who was in charge of the Marine contingent assigned to the *Chesapeake*:

> For the purpose of sending home the Italians now of the Band, at their request so to go, I have added them to your command as music; you will on reaching that home, as they have been clothed to the 15th of August next, the supposed time necessary there to reach, pay as usual to that period, and give to them the discharges, which will by the adjutant be delivered to you from me.[74]

Carusi looked forward to going back to his homeland. Yet he had no idea as to the dangers that lay ahead. On 15 May Captain Barron received orders from Secretary Smith to proceed immediately to the Mediterranean as soon as the *Chesapeake* was ready.[75] On 16 June Barron reported the ship was ready, however ". . . a strong gale from the North East has prevented our sailing."[76] During this time the Carusi family had boarded the ship:

On hearing of her arrival I went on board to present the Secretary's letter, and the first thing which I recollect to have happened was, that it was thought necessary to deprive me for three days of all necessary sustenance, and, dreading the fate of the marine, was thinking of disembarking, when on the fourth I was justly and properly supplied.[77]

An extract from the log book of Captain Barron records the departure on Sunday, 21 June at 5 p.m. The ship moved up the river where it stayed the night. At 6 a.m. on the following morning, the *Chesapeake* left Hampton Roads and headed for open waters. At 9 a.m. she was in Lin Haven Bay and passed two British Men of War, "their Colours flying and their appearance friendly some time afterwards we observ'd one of the two line of Battle Ships that lay off Cape Henry to get under way and stand to Sea."[78] The ship that got under way and began tracking the *Chesapeake* (36 guns) was the *Leopard* (50 guns). Although Captain Hall reported that "signals were seen passing from the *Belona* to the *Triumph* and from the *Triumph* to the *Leopard*,"[79] no one could determine exactly what the *Leopard*'s intentions were. The *Chesapeake* was not in a state of readiness should an event have called for battle quarters. Some of the ship's cannons were not seated properly in their carriages, powder horns were not filled, and the cartridges brought on board for the Marines were not of the proper size. Moreover, the *Chesapeake*'s decks were littered with provisions, equipment, and personal belongings, including Carusi's baggage. Carusi, who was likely concerned about leaving his large trunk unattended, probably was positioned nearby. At about 3:30 p.m., some twenty miles out in open sea, the *Leopard* came alongside of the American vessel. Lieutenant John Meade, an officer from the British vessel, boarded the *Chesapeake*. In a meeting that lasted over a half-hour, Meade demanded from Barron that he hand over a group of British deserters. Barron refused and Meade returned to the *Leopard*. Although Carusi may not have known right away that the British were looking for deserters, he must have been extremely concerned, for the British had a reputation for impressing foreigners in their navy. Carusi's family and the other Italians decided to go below deck in order to stay out of sight.

In a feeble attempt to prepare his ship for battle, Barron ordered the decks cleared and all baggage, including Carusi's trunk, thrown overboard.[80] Shortly thereafter, the *Leopard* began firing broadsides into the *Chesapeake*. Within twenty minutes, three American sailors had been killed, eighteen others wounded, including Barron. The *Chesapeake* was badly damaged and had over three feet of water in her hold. Barron ordered the ship's colors struck, after which the British immediately came on board to remove the four deserters. The *Chesapeake* was in a state of chaos. William Henry

Allen, Third Lieutenant aboard the American frigate, described the first moments following the event:

> Nothing could equal so horrible a scene as it was, to see so many brave men standing to their quarters among the blood of their butchered and wounded country men and hearing their cries without the means of avenging them.[81]

Carusi also described what he saw:

> In this attack the frigate suffered exceedingly; many were killed and more wounded; the masts shot away and the hull shattered. In a word, she was so much crippled that the Commodore resolved to put back into Norfolk harbor.[82]

The *Chesapeake* arrived in Hampton Roads on 23 June at 3 p.m. With the British threatening to invade, Carusi wanted to leave as soon as possible.

> At this unfortunate prostration of my hopes I left the ship in Hampton Roads, and went to Baltimore, where I passed the time in mournful contemplation of my afflictions; of the disturbed past, the miserable present, and lowering future.[83]

By early fall, Carusi was in Baltimore seeking some means to support his family. General James Wilkinson,[84] "Commander-in-chief of the army of the United States," contacted him requesting that he assist in the formation of a new band for his troops stationed in Carlisle, Pennsylvania. Carusi recounts how good intentions on his part wound up as yet another disappointment:

> I reflected that I was wholly unemployed, and with no expectation of any assistance or countenance, and that starvation, or worse, must be the consequence of the present state of my affairs.
>
> I finally agreed, after many conversations with him, to enter into the following agreement: to receive $200 per month, for five persons, allowance for travelling to and from Baltimore and Carlisle, a house at the General's quarters, rations, &c., and to collect and form, in consequence of said pay, a band of not less than twenty individuals within the space of one year. This agreement was written, signed, and placed in my hands by J. Wilkinson, General-in-chief of the American forces.
>
> I arrived on the following day with my family, and commenced my labors. I soon discovered that the rations dealt out to us were

infamous in quality, and therefore obtained the promise of pecuniary commutation for them. After some time I applied for my salary, and was put off with some excuse, and this repeatedly happened. At the end of about six months, I was called by the commander of the garrison, and informed that General Wilkinson had been sent by order of Government to the Canadian frontier, and would not be back for some time; that he had nothing to do with his contracts with me, and that I was at liberty to do as I chose respecting departure.

Behold me again betrayed! I thought then that the good faith of new States had not only grown old, but had become crippled and without vigor, since not only the word, but a written and signed contract of a general commanding officer was of no avail or power. I, however, persisted in stating my thoughts, and the hardship of my case; but my complaints and mournings were alike useless. In the end, however, they did influence the officers of the garrison to contribute and raise $100; which was intended to be my remuneration, and the release of all the conditions of my agreement. If the conduct of General Wilkinson, in acting as the vilest citizen would not be allowed to act, was bad, I esteem that of the commander of the garrison a great deal worse. I thought, however, that the expedition on the frontier might be a fabricated tale, and sought to gain the truth from Wilkinson's Secretary, whom I introduced into my house, and from whom, by means of various liquors, I discovered that he had in reality gone to the city of Washington. It was now necessary for me to go to the same place, and as it was the last of December or 1st of January, and the weather excessively cold, I thought we should perish from its effects before we reached our destination. Immediately upon my arrival I waited on General Wilkinson, who accosted me in the politest manner, and commenced discoursing of my pretension; asked if I had the contract about me, as he wished to examine the conditions; conditions made and written out by himself! I gave it to him: he read it, and in the presence of his barber, Charles Gallesio, tore it into a thousand pieces; and, turning with a furious look, told me if I had any demand against him I might apply for its liquidation to Congress.[85]

Carusi returned to Baltimore. With the Embargo Act having been passed on 22 December 1807 and trade with Great Britain prohibited,[86] War with England was eminent. Carusi believed, therefore, that it was virtually impossible to obtain safe passage for him and his family to Europe.

Thus I was deprived of the only hope that had cherished me in my suffering, that of returning to my native country. Wherefore I deemed it necessary to abandon all hope, to turn my attention to supporting and educating my family as I might best be able, and to try every means I could devise to support existence. For this purpose I went to Philadelphia.

In a year or two peace was concluded with England, and war against Algiers declared. On the return of a second peace [June 1815], I renewed my solicitations for redress to the Government of the United States; which, however, as before, remained deaf to my supplication.[87]

In November 1810, Carusi was in Baltimore where he placed the following notice in the newspaper there:

Notice is hereby given to the public that Mr. Gaetano Carusi, Italian Master of Music, is arrived in the city of Baltimore—he and his family return thanks for the encouragement he received from his friends and the public in general, and offers his services again, to give Serenades, to play at balls, or for any gentlemen that would wish to have Music played in their houses. Him and his family will attend on to arrange any kind of Music for any sort of Instruments. He also copies music, and tunes Forte Pianos. His residence is No. 56, Market Space.[88]

During that year, he served as a music conductor for the Baltimore circus. His job was to provide background music for the circus acts; some of the works performed were newly composed by Carusi. For example, one piece was a piano arrangement for a set of thirteen "Circus Tunes" performed at the Olympic Theatre and was published by Joseph Carr whose printing establishment at 36 Market Street was close to Carusi's home. Carusi turned over copyright ownership to Carr, possibly in turn for cash or other services.[89] In January 1811, Carusi published a notice regarding his association with the circus and expressed his regrets over his decision to resign due to the less than adequate competence of the other musicians:

Signor Gaetano Carusi, Italian Master and Composer of Music, Informs the ladies and gentlemen of Baltimore and its vicinity, that last year he had the honor to serve the public with general approbation. His compositions which were performed at the circus were highly approved of. This year Signor Carusi has prepared new music for the circus performances in this place, by which he had hoped to gratify public expectation; but not admiring the abilities of the musicians, who are at present engaged from New-York and Philadelphia, he conceived it a duty to himself to refuse his services to the managers of the Circus. Said Signor Carusi offers his services as heretofore, to the ladies and gentlemen of Baltimore and its vicinity, in setting or transposing New Music, for every description of Musical Instruments; and those of himself and family at balls, serenades, or their respective houses. (No. 56, Market-space, Cumberland Row)[90]

In 1812 Carusi met John Pardi, an Italian who was touring America with an unusual instrument called the panharmonicon. It consisted of

> within itself two hundred and fifty different instruments, consisting of flutes, clarionets, hautboys, flagiolets, trumpets, bassoons, french-horns, kettle-drums, large drums, cymbals, triangles, &c &c &c in fine, every instrument to a complete band of music. It performs in full symphony some of the choicest pieces of music of the best composers, such as Hayden, Steibelt, Mozart and others equally celebrated.[91]

Carusi composed a "March and Rondo" (dedicated to Pardi and published by G. Willig in Philadelphia) for piano, based on a tune from the panharmonicon. He assigned copyright ownership to Pardi.[92] The work was advertised in a local newspaper as having been published "in obedience to the desire of several ladies and gentlemen" and available "for sale, at the Coffee House and at the Masonic Hall. . . . The price is 50 cents."[93]

By 1813, Carusi opened a music school in Philadelphia. He described his services as a musician, composer, and instrument repairer:

> Mr. Gaetano Carousi [sic], Italian professor and master of music, begs leave to inform the public of Philadelphia and its environs, that he offers his service and that of his family, to all those who wish to learn the use of any of the military instruments of a band. He teaches the clarionet, French horn, bassoon, German flute, fife and flageolet, etc. as well as every stringed instrument, he also repairs clarionets which are out of tune; tunes the forte piano, and repairs forte pianos which may have any fracture or crevice, he composes music for every kind of instrument and sets the various parts, and copies music correctly and fairly; he repairs fiddles and bows with great care and attention; moreover he offers himself to attend at every public assembly or private party, either at serenade or ball, he has a company of about eight persons who are always ready to attend a summons either by day or night, or any of the above

mentioned occasions. He will attend those which reside in the country, and will afford them a display of his musical powers with his company, by the choicest pieces of music and perfect harmony. Enquire at 38, north Eight Street.[94]

In 1814, Gaetano and his sons participated in a benefit concert for the orphan asylum at St. Augustine's Church. The affair was organized by Benjamin Carr and Rayner Taylor, with a band led by "Mr. Gillingham." The "Messrs. Carusi's" were listed as playing "trumpets" in a number of selections by Haydn (*The Creation*) and Handel (*Messiah*), as well as works by Hasse, Carr, and others.[95]

Also, in 1814, Carusi registered as an alien in compliance with the law that required foreigners to make known their current status. He was described as "age 52 in U.S. since 26 Sept 1809 wife & 3 children, Phil. musician (1-31 Aug. 1814)."[96]

In 1816, Carusi decided once again to leave America. He contacted an acquaintance, Don Luis de Onís, the Spanish Ambassador, requesting his assistance. Ambassador Onís wrote to John Graham of the State Department, who, in turn, contacted Benjamin Homans of the Navy Department. Homans sent the following response to Graham:

> Sir: In compliance with your request of this morning, I have submitted to the Secretary of the Navy, who directs me to inform you that an order will be given for Gaetano Carusi to embark on board the Washington 74 [canons], at Boston, under command of Commodore J.[*sic*][97] Chauncey, who will have him landed at Sicily free of expense.
>
> Carusi, upon presenting himself at this Department, may receive the order and proceed immediately to Boston at his own expense, and repair immediately on board the ship, now ready for sea, and waiting only the return of Commodore Chauncey, who arrived here yesterday.[98]

Carusi, although pleased at this new prospect, was concerned about travelling at that time of year: "A heavy frost has entirely closed the navigation; the cold is excessive; the only possible communication from place to place is by mail."[99] He decided to stay in Philadelphia that winter. In April he received a letter from Commodore Chauncey stating that the *Washington* would be sailing shortly and, therefore, he should not delay any longer in coming to Boston. The Carusi family left for Boston on 13 April 1816. They arrived a few days later and were surprised to learn that the ship was not sailing directly for the Mediterranean but rather Annapolis.

> We arrived in Boston, and though we lived as cheaply as possible, my expenses were forty dollars per week. I presented myself to Commodore Chauncey, who received me politely and courteously, and who told me he was waiting the arrival of Mr. [Albert] Gallatin,[100] who was sent as minister to Naples, to settle the differences existing between the two countries. After some time, however, the vessel was ordered to go to Annapolis, the seat of government of Maryland, to receive on board Mr. [William] Pinkney, who was sent to Naples for the same purpose. In a few days I was ordered to be ready to return home to my own country.[101]

The *Washington* left Boston on 8 May.[102]

> We left Boston and arrived at Annapolis, where the Commodore was informed that Mr. Pinkney was engaged in trying a most important case, and could not go until it was determined.[103]
>
> Commodore Chauncey had on board his wife and sister-in-law, and determined to go, during his stay, to his own house in New York. He went, and left the ship under the absolute control of Captain [John Orde] Creighton.[104]

Carusi arrived in Annapolis on Thursday evening of 16 May.[105]

The newly-built *Washington* attracted much attention in both Boston and Annapolis due to its size, craftsmanship, and number of cannons. The following description of the ship was reported in Boston on 11 May and later reprinted in Virginia and Maryland newspapers:

> We learn from an officer of the *Independence* who went out several leagues in the Washington, that she sailed very fast, worked with much ease, and bids fair to sustain the reputation of this country for superior ship building.[106]

President Madison and his family, Secretary of the Navy Benjamin Crowninshield, and Commodores John Rodgers and David Porter were all eager to see the ship and went to Annapolis, arriving "at Caton's Hotel in the course of Sunday & Monday last," 19-20 May.[107] The presidential visit to Annapolis caused much excitement along the Atlantic seaboard, and accounts were printed in several newspapers. In Washington it was reported that

> The visit of the Washington Seventy-Four gun ship to Annapolis, makes that place the seat of high attraction at present. Many have been drawn to that place within a few days, by curiosity, business, or to visit their friends on board the ship. Among others the PRESIDENT, the Secretary of the Navy, and their families, are at Annapolis.[108]

Additional details were reported in Baltimore:

> A number of gentlemen from this city, visited the United States Ship Washington, Com. Chauncy, off Annapolis on Saturday last, and were received by the commodore with great politeness; and as far as their short stay permitted, they examined the ship and were highly gratified with this noble specimen of American naval architecture, combining force with elegance with neatness—a crew of about six hundred healthy men, and apparently in a state of perfect happiness, content and discipline, who worked the guns with the facility of a company manaeuvering [sic] their muskets.—The decks were clean, and the mess kids [sic], cans and tin cups were placed in rows with two bibles upon them for each mess, and the whole together formed a subject of the highest gratification to the patriot, the man of science and the curious citizens who made the excursion in one of our steam boats.[109]

A different Baltimore newspaper reported that "General [John?] Mason and lady" and "the gallant General [Winfield] Scott" were there for the occasion and that on Tuesday, 21 May, the President and his entourage had dinner, courtesy of Commodore Chauncey, on board the ship.[110] Yet additional information was recorded in the ship's log:

> His Excellency James Madison the President of the United States and Lady, accompanied by the Secretary and Commissioners of the Navy etc, etc, etc, came on board to visit the Ship, on which occasion the yards were manned and they were saluted with 19 guns and three cheers. On leaving the ship at 5 P.M. the yards were again manned and the national salute fired.[111]

In preparation for the presidential visit, the commandant at Fort McHenry in Baltimore was ordered to send his band to the *Washington* so that they could provide music for the President's review. The commandant, however, was not aware that Carusi and other musicians were already on board the ship. F. Gilldorff, "Master of the Band" at Fort McHenry described the circumstances:

> In the month of May the Commandant of the said fort conducted me with the rest of the Band to assist as President Madison was to visit the Vessel 74 Washington which was then anchored in the Bay near Annapolis Md. When we arrived on board the Washington we found they were provided with a band of which Mr Gaetano Carusi was leader and finding they had no need of our Band our Commandant sent us to Fort Severn in Annapolis. . . .[112]

From the information provided by Gilldorff, it can be assumed that Carusi's band did perform for the President on 21 May. And it is likely that he also provided music for other visiting dignitaries.

As memorable as this event must have been for Carusi, he and his family suffered considerable stress during their several weeks on board the *Washington*, due mainly from the harassment they received from Captain Creighton. Carusi explains:

> There is not one who can compare, in tyranny and despotic violence, with J. O. Creighton. He never, to my knowledge, caused any one to be murdered, but it was only because he had not the power; and the power of which he was possessed he was constantly stretching to the utmost, to gratify his cruel disposition. He even studied to invent punishment for his men, and on one occasion caused nearly the whole of his crew, upwards of six hundred men, to be punished at the same time. It may seem impossible; but so it was, on the 1st June, 1816. The laws of the navy direct that, in port, water shall be dealt without limit to the crew; but this gallant officer took upon himself, on this day, to keep the whole ship's crew from this species of refreshment for the space of fourteen hours, notwithstanding they were suffering indescribable tortures from the heat of the weather, their laborious exertion in unnecessary duty, and their salt food.[113]

Carusi's description of Creighton's character is corroborated through the testimony of several persons. George Nicholas Hollins, a "youngster of 16," who later in his career attained the rank of commodore, was serving on the *Washington* and knew Carusi. Hollins described Creighton as an "old style disciplinarian" who forced his men to fetch water for the ship in intense cold and who restricted them from putting their hands in their pockets while doing so or drinking the water until it was brought back to the ship. About Carusi Hollins states,

We also took back that famous Band of Musicians that had been stolen from Naples by Com McNeal, in 1809. Some of the musicians were the Carusi's [*sic*] who returned to the U.S. & became music teachers & teachers of dancing in Washington & Baltimore.[114]

Creighton's unfortunate conduct was also directed towards Carusi, as well as his students he was teaching in Annapolis:

> He had, in fact, no regard for me, either as a passenger or as a man advanced in years, and no consideration for the respectful manner in which I had been treated by Commodore Chauncey. He was not even grateful; for I did oblige him, whenever he desired it, by playing for him, accompanied by my sons, on our musical instruments. He insulted me most infamously, on every possible occasion. . . . He threatened to have my pupils flogged three days in succession, and then have them immersed in the water, with a heavy weight attached to their legs.

Carusi decided to leave the ship.

> My mental suffering had induced a physical disease, which threatened to bring death in its train; and, had I been drowned, I believe the wretched tyrant would have rejoiced. Commodore Chauncey returned on board, and, without stating the course of conduct pursued by J. O. Creighton, (for where was the use,) [*sic*] I only observed to him that my health demanded that I should leave the ship for that attendance and comfort that was not to be obtained on board.[115]

Carusi's testimony is corroborated by several persons. Giuseppe Sardo was on board the vessel and commented, "Gaetano Carusi with his family were obliged to disembark for not being able to suffer the oppression and brutal manners of John Ordo Creighton captain of said ship under Commodore Chauncey. . . ."[116] Thomas Downey was also on board the *Washington* and stated that

> the said G. Carusi and family disembarked in Annapolis, Maryland, to not suffer the insults, tyranny, oppression and maltreatment from Capt. John Ord Creighton, Capt. of the Washington under the command of Com. Chauncey.[117]

In addition, Gilldorff presumably also witnessed events on board the vessel for he said that "Mr Carusi had disembarked with all his family on account of the bad treatment he received from the Captain J. O. Creighton."[118]

Carusi and his family left the ship in the late afternoon of 4 June.[119] They boarded the steamboat *Chesapeake*, under the command of E. Trippe, that had arrived from Baltimore carrying persons who were there to visit the *Washington*. Trippe placed an advertisement in a Baltimore newspaper regarding the excursion, with a note stating that "A Band of Music will be on board the Chesapeake."[120] Carusi may have paid for his trip by providing music for the passengers.

Carusi described his sentiments about having lost his chance to return to Italy, and consequently, his decision to remain in the United States:

> All this is but a shadow of what befel [*sic*] me on my attempted return home. On the 4th of June, 1816, I returned [i.e., left the ship], sick in body, worn out in mind, and with a loss, since leaving Philadelphia, of about two thousand dollars, besides all that I had brought from Sicily, and with no hope of ever now being able to return. I could have been content, had this been all; but it was mingled with personal insult and suffering inflicted on myself, and (which were more acutely felt than my own) with injuries inflicted upon my family; and, more than all, my career of horror was about to be begun over again.
>
> When I had disembarked, I could not help remembering that, in order to escape from what I had been obliged to suffer on land since my arrival in the United States, I had gone on board the frigate Washington, and that now I was obliged to return to that same land, to escape the (if possible) more horrid treatment I had met with in the ship. No one can imagine, nor can I describe, what was my state of feeling. All the past, however, was cast in oblivion by the dark and ominous clouds which imagination pictured as hanging over the future. . . . Of the two evils, of return and exile, I chose the least. I determined to remain in the United States, and conform myself to the decision of the Supreme Court, hoping that a combination of time and circumstances would unite in effecting something in my favor.[121]

He stayed in Annapolis during the following month giving at least three concerts. On 17 June he hosted "A Concert and Ball" in which he and other musicians presented a varied program of songs and instrumental works, including an "Overture to Adrina" by Haydn, a song "Come Take the Harp" by Stevenson and sung by Samuel Carusi, and other works titled "Harmony Piece," "Jackson's Victory," "Bonaparte Entering Paris" by Kaezkow, "Hope

Told a Flattering Tale," by Haydn, and an excerpt from "Battle of Waterloo," by Warner. Carusi performed his own composition (unlocated), "Quartetto, with Yankee Doodle."[122] On 4 July on the occasion of the "Fortieth Anniversary of American Independence," Carusi's band performed for the "republican citizens" at the Assembly Room. The works presented were "Washington's March," "Hail Columbia," "Madison's March," "Yankee Doodle," "Jackson's March," and other pieces.[123] On 8 July, Carusi and his band accompanied "Mr. Duff" who had lately performed at theatres in Philadelphia and Baltimore in "an entertainment consisting of Songs and Recitations."[124] Shortly thereafter, Carusi decided to leave Annapolis and expressed his appreciation to the residents there for having utilized his services as a musician:

> Signior Carusi, Cannot take leave of the citizens of Annapolis without expressing the high sense of grateful feeling with which he is impressed by their generous and benevolent patronage. Distinguished as Annapolis ever has been as peculiarly the seat of liberal feeling and polished hospitality, the feeble testimony of a stranger could add nothing to its character; but as a grateful acknowledgment of the generosity he has experienced is demanded by his own feelings, he indulges a hope that he will not be considered obstrusive in the public expression of them.
>
> It is the intention of Signior Carusi to return to this city, should he succeed in his attempt to establish a *Musical School*.[125]

Carusi returned to Philadelphia. The city directory of 1816 listed him as a "professor of music" living at "243 Mulberry."[126] That year, Samuel and Nathaniel applied for naturalization at the Court of Common Pleas. The following year, Gaetano also decided to become an American citizen and presented his own declaration of intention.[127]

In March 1818, Carusi was in Alexandria where he opened up a "Musical School." He placed the following notice in the local newspaper there:

> Musical School. seignior Gaetano Carusi and Family consisting of eight performers, inform the ladies and gentlemen of Alexandria and its vicinity, that they intend to establish themselves in this city to open a Musical School, both of vocal and instrumental music, namely, Piano forte, Pedal Harp, Violin, Violincello, Flute, Clarionet, Clarion, Bassoon, French horn, Trumpet, all kinds of Flageolet, etc etc. All persons desirous of becoming scholars are

informed that a subscription paper is left at Mr. Robert Gray's book store, King Street, where terms may be known.[128]

Gaetano, who was still residing in Philadelphia, presumably opened this school in order to provide another place in which he and his sons could teach; Nathaniel, whose name does not appear in Philadelphia records at this time, might have stayed in Alexandria.

In July 1818, Carusi was in Easton, Maryland, where he opened a music store and advertised his services for music and dancing instruction:

> Sigr. Gaetano Carusi & family Have the honor to inform the ladies and gentlemen of Easton and its vicinity, that they have taken the house next door to the Post Office, where they intend to practise the Musical and Dancing professions. They will teach all kinds of stringed and wind Instruments, tune and repair Piano Fortes, and mend Violins and all kinds of Instruments, Violin Strings of the best quality, Music, Music Paper, steel and brass Wire for Piano Fortes, Violin Bows of different kinds, Violin Bridges, refined Rosin. Also, a variety of Goods at moderate prices. They will take in exchange old Instruments for new ones—The celebrated Chinese Puzzle complete.
>
> They will have shortly, a few Piano Fortes of superior quality.[129]

By spring of 1819 in Philadelphia, Carusi had opened a "Music and Fancy Store" located at "No. 31 N. Sixth St." It was at this address where he published a number of his own arrangements of musical works. His "Austrian Retreat, with a Waltz, arranged for the piano forte" was copyrighted on 31 May 1819,[130] and was followed by a "March & Waltz at the Battle of Waterloo, arranged for the piano forte," copyrighted on 19 June 1819.[131]

In early 1820, Gaetano, Samuel, and Lewis Carusi joined the Musical Fund Society of Philadelphia, a group of eighty-five musicians dedicated to the practice and performance of musical works.[132] The Carusi family performed in concert with some of the best instrumentalists in Philadelphia at that time, including Benjamin Carr, J. C. Hommann, Charles Hupfeld, George Schetky, and Rayner Taylor. On 11 and 13 April of that year, Gaetano, Samuel, and Lewis participated in a series of four concerts billed as "The Grand Oratorio for the benefit of the Philadelphia orphans' and widows asylums, and Philadelphia Bible Society" at Washington Hall. Two of the concerts were given on 11 April at 10 a.m. and 7 p.m. with over 130 performers taking part.[133] One month later, a list of expenses for the concerts was printed in the newspaper: Samuel was paid $20 for playing the trumpet and bassoon; Gaetano received $12 for playing the trumpet; and Lewis was paid $12 for playing the horn.[134]

By early summer of 1820, the Carusi family had left Philadelphia to establish residency in Washington. Samuel announced his return from Philadelphia on 3 July 1820 and advertised that he was available to teach singing as well as a variety of instruments.[135] According to another notice printed in October 1820, Samuel and his father Gaetano were living "at the corner of 11th and E, (formerly the residence of Mr. Lenox) where he [Samuel] continues to take scholars in Music, as usual." Gaetano opened up a music store at that address; some of the merchandise he stocked was imported from Italy. Part of that notice reads:

> Sig. GAETANO CARUSI also informs the lovers of Music that he has, at the aforementioned place, a selection of musical instruments which he will dispose of on very moderate terms, for cash, consisting of two grand Piano Fortes, one of which is double-keyed, violins, violincellos [sic], double bass viols, bassoons, guitars, flutes, flagelets [sic], French horns, trumpets; also violin-bows, violin strings, of the very best quality from Naples. He will take in exchange old and broken violins or other instruments, for new ones, on reasonable terms.
>
> Sig. Carusi has, also, for sale, a very choice collection of songs, and musical compositions and pieces, each adapted to the accompaniment of various instruments, military bands, or the full orchestra. Likewise, duettos, trio, quartettos, for all the above instruments. Musical instruments repaired on reasonable terms.[136]

In November 1820, Gaetano advertised various imported liquors consisting of "an assortment of best superfine Rosalio, or cordials, which he has received from Italy, of the celebrated manufactory of Benedetto Faggeolli, at Leghorn."[137]

During this time, the Carusi family began participating in musical performances in Washington. In March 1821, Samuel conducted a "Grand concert, vocal and instrumental," in which "Mr. Kelly[138] aided by the professional characters of the city and Georgetown and gentlemen amateurs," including "Mr. Harrison—piano," appeared in the "Long Room" at Tennison's Hotel.[139]

In June 1821 Carusi purchased the site where the Washington Theatre once stood. The theatre had been destroyed by fire on 19 April 1820;[140] only the foundation and walls were left standing. A year later, the land was put up for sale by auction at Brown's Hotel.[141] Philip Mauro,[142] a well-known auctioneer in Washington, conducted the transaction and announced that the final price would have "to be paid for in seven equal annual instalments [sic]."[143] Carusi believed that this represented an excellent opportunity to construct a building on that site where music instruction, concerts, and other entertainments could take place. By fall 1822, the work was nearing completion and a description—the most detailed extant one that survives—of the building with its elegant ball room was ceremoniously printed:

> Mr. Editor, I am happy to observe, among the many improvements now making in this city, that one of the most important is the rebuilding of the old Theatre (which was destroyed by fire) for the purpose of assemblies, concerts, and elegant and rational amusements generally—and for such occasions it certainly furnishes the most spacious and commodious rooms of any in the District; it is strong and well built, and, though so very extensive in its part, is free from cracks in the walls, (which few houses of the same dimensions in this place are) and proves that it has a good foundation, though built in a very unfavorable place for making one: this excellence is attributable to the skill of the architect who originally designed and built the old Theatre, Mr. GEORGE HADFIELD.
>
> The *basement story* contains a room for dining and supping in, 60 by 47 feet, with eight elegant strong pillars supporting the ball room: the entry is at the south front. There are two flights of stairs; with rooms at the sides for dressing and bar rooms.
>
> The *second story* contains the ball room, 80 by 48 feet, 22 feet high, a circular recess for the orchestra, with 9 large windows.
>
> Adjoining the stair case are dressing rooms for the ladies and the *third story* affords also many convenient rooms for the same purpose.
>
> It is understood that the MESSRS. CARUSIS will have it ready during the next month (October) for the purposes before mentioned. It is with much pleasure I notice that this building, which owes its re-establishment to the enterprise of these gentlemen, will be under the directions of men so eminently qualified by their talents and professional skill to conduct these elegant and fashionable amusements; and I trust they will meet with the liberal support of the generous citizens of this Metropolis. OBSERVER.[144]

As promised in their notice above, Gaetano and Samuel announced the opening of the new Washington Assembly Hall in October with great fanfare:

The Washington Assembly Hall being now prepared for the reception of scholars, Samuel Carusi solicits his friends and the citizens at large, to call and inspect the Hall for themselves, and they will be convinced of the complete adaptation of this room for all species of amusements. The expenses have been severe and grinding, and have involved his father deeply, relying solely upon the generosity of his fellow citizens. He offers gratuitously to the amateurs of music a fine and spacious Hall, where they will find all kinds of instruments and where they may daily resort for practice and pleasure. He offers, on moderate terms, to teach thoroughly the whole theory and ground of music, and, in a short time, insure a sufficient knowledge, so as to enable his pupils to compose. He will teach singing, and instruct on the pianoforte, harp, guitar and all other stringed and wind instruments. Ladies and gentlemen, who are disposed to be made acquainted with various instruments, will find it advantageous to apply immediately at the Hall. The terms for those who take their lessons at the Hall will be lower than if he attended them at their own residences. Samuel Carusi. P.S. Mr. Carusi offers his room to his fellow-citizens on all public calls of the people gratuitously.[145]

For the next forty years, the Washington Assembly Hall, known also as Carusi's Saloon, would have the distinction as one of the most popular places for entertainment in Washington. It was located at the corner of C Street north and 11th Street west, and its spacious and elegant ball room served as the perfect setting for the many concerts and presidential inaugural balls that took place there.

The first inaugural ball presented at the Hall occurred on 4 March 1825 for President John Quincy Adams. The lavish affair required considerable planning on the part of Gaetano. A managers and subscribers meeting was held at the Hall on 26 February. Subscription papers had to be placed at various shops and stores throughout the city, and all those attending had to be given directions for carriage routes and available parking.[146]

Numerous concerts were presented in the following years that featured a host of well-known instrumentalists, including Ole Bull, violinist and Maurice Strakosch, pianist; M'lle Teresa Parodi, vocalist assisted by Henri Vieuxtemps, violinist; Louis Moreau Gottschalk, pianist; Aptommas, harpist; Countess Estvan, Laerre de Lacy from Hungary with Chevalier de Szemeleng, pianist; Paul Julien, violinist, assisted by Signora Martini D'Ormy, contralto, Signor Centuri, baritone, and August Gockel, pianist; M'lle W. de Boye, pianist; Robert Heller, pianist; Madame Rosa De Vries and Signor Morino, vocalists, assisted by Martin Lazare, pianist. Vocal and instrumental groups included the Hutchinson Family, Ossian's Bards, directed by Ossian E. Dodge, members of the Germania Musical Society, Columbia Musical Association, and the Washington Philharmonic Society. There were minstrel troupes, including the Harmoneons, Ethiopian Serenaders, Sable Harmonists, Nightingale Ethiopians, and West and Peal's Old Original Campbell Minstrels. There were theatrical productions, including one given by the celebrated Boon Children, a "galaxy of juvenile genius,"[147] and plays by the Dramatic Association. There were also art exhibitions such as the one presented by George R. West and William Heine on China and Japan, as well as lectures, including "Prof." Schonenberg's presentation on German national literature.[148] There were recitations given by Helen Muzzy and F. Bangs, and balls presented by such groups as the Washington German Yeagers, Washington Associates, Washington Light Infantry, National Greys, and the Good Will Club.

Carusi spent the remainder of his years teaching and managing events at the Hall, and assisted as a performer when needed. In 1830 he advertised his services as a piano teacher:

> Gaetano Carusi respectfully informs the citizens of Washington that he has again resumed his professional business of teaching on the Piano Forte: No recommendations, it is presumed are necessary, as it is well known Mr. G. C. is the teacher of several eminent masters of Music in this country. PRICE OF TUITION:
> By the quarter, containing 24 lessons, two lesson per week,} $18
> By the quarter, containing 12 lessons, at one lesson per week} $10
> By the single lesson, $1. Apply at the Assembly Hall[149]

He continued to host a busy schedule of diverse events at the Hall. For example, on 22 February 1827 there was a festive birthday celebration ball in honor of Washington: "The Saloon will be brilliantly illuminated, and the bar will be furnished with the best of every thing."[150] On 12 May 1836, Carusi donated the Hall for a benefit concert on behalf of "expatriated Poles" who were intent on "forming a settlement on the land conceded to them by the Congress of the United States." Performers who took part in that concert included Signor Fabj, vocalist, Henry Diehlman, violinist and flutist, "Señor Perez," violinist and guitarist, and "Signor Vai," guitarist and mandolin player.[151] In February 1841, Carusi hosted a ball "given by the Franklin Fire Company."[152] In March of that year, Leopold Herwig, a celebrated European violinist, and L. Rakemann, pianist, performed at the Hall.[153] In September 1841, Carusi welcomed "The Four Hungarian

Singers, who have before delighted a Metropolitan audience with their national melodies and extraordinary performances as vocalists" who included "Messrs. Rosen, Kaln, Liebenstein, and Reich," for a "Grand Vocal Concert at Carusi's Saloon this evening." This group had only a few days prior performed "before the President of the United States and his family at the Executive Mansion, and in a manner peculiarly gratifying to the audience."[154]

During this time Carusi's sons had become well-known as musicians, composers, publishers, and instructors of music and dance.[155] Samuel taught various musical instruments and voice (mentioned above) at the Hall and assisted his father in managing events there. By the 1830s, he had taken over Gaetano's music store and relocated it to the "corner of 12th Street and Penn Ave." It was at this address that Samuel started his music publishing business. He also opened a music store in Baltimore; many of his compositions were published there. In the ensuing years, he composed, arranged, and published over two hundred works, mostly for voice, piano, and guitar,[156] and was instrumental in the formation of the Washington Philharmonic Society, an organization devoted to the advancement of vocal and instrumental music.

Nathaniel continued to teach music in Washington and Alexandria. He composed a number of works for piano and voice that were published by his brother Samuel.[157]

Lewis gradually took over full responsibilities for the management of the Hall from his father and brother Samuel. In the 1820s he gave dancing instructions at the Hall and continued to teach in Baltimore, Georgetown, Alexandria, and other places. He enjoyed presenting "Cotillion Parties," which included his annual May Ball. In 1841, Lewis rented out the lower level of the building to the city post office. A notice in the *National Intelligencer* of 30 September 1841 announced the new post office address. Lewis discovered subsequently, however, that William Jones, Postmaster, did not take care of the premises and, apparently, Jones had broken the lease without providing due notice. Lewis and Nathaniel sued Postmaster General C. A. Wickliffe for damages. A letter from Lewis Carusi to Wickliffe, written 6 November 1843, states: ". . . he [Jones] has left the apartments occupied by him in a condition not to be occupied by us without extensive repairs."[158] On 23 September 1843 a notice in the *National Intelligencer* announced the removal of the post office to a new location.

By the 1820s all of the original eighteen members of Carusi's band had either returned to Italy, assumed other vocations, or died. Those that went back to Italy included: "D. Domenico Guarnaccia, D. Pasquale Loria,[159] his wife and family; James Sardo and Gaetano Sardo, Joseph Papa, in Aci; S. Antonio and Corrado Signorelli, in the city of Noto." Those that had died included "Francis Pulizzi, Antonio Paterno, Joseph

Sardo, Salvador Loria, Ignatius di Mauro, and Antonia Pulizzi."[160] Michael Sardo stayed in Washington and opened a "Boarding Establishment" at the "corner of 10th Street, West and Pennsylvania Avenue" for the convenience of the "members of Congress."[161] Felice Pullizzi and his son Venerando, a clarinetist, lived in Washington during the 1820s. The latter continued as a member of the Marine Band and eventually was appointed conductor on 17 October 1816. He served in that position until 9 April 1817 and again from 19 February 1818 to 2 September 1827. After his retirement from the Marine Band, Venerando continued to serve in the Corps as a line sergeant.[162]

The unfortunate events in Gaetano's life were cause for concern among many of his friends. He was encouraged to speak out and ask for compensation from the Congress of the United States:[163]

> Such disasters happened while my residence was in Washington City, the Metropolis of the United States; and, whilst suffering under the increased load of my misfortunes, I was frequently incited, by different individuals, to speak of my unfortunate life in America, and particularly of that portion spent in connexion [sic] with the Marine Corps. One day in February, 1829, an individual, (whom I afterwards discovered to be a member of Congress,) besides promising to present my claims, united to what I had undergone in America, also showed me how to present my petitions, of which I had been hitherto ignorant.
>
> Unacquainted with the English language, I employed, the following year, a lawyer to explain all that I have here written, and lay it before the Government of the United States. The lawyer, however, thought it best only to petition for the execution of those articles of agreement of which there was positive proof, from the contract made in Sicily, and the certificate of persons well acquainted with the affair, and living in America.
>
> I, per force, consented to such a petition, although fifty thousand dollars would have been but a poor equivalent for my various abuses by the different branches of the Government of the United States. I, however, consented, but with the reservation of my right in future to be reimbursed for my losses, and relieved on account of my sufferings and misfortunes, in the manner suggested by a member of Congress, of whose name, however, and district, I was never able to become acquainted.[164]

Carusi wrote to James Barron on 1 September 1830 requesting that he certify that Carusi was indeed on board the *Chesapeake* at the time of her encounter with the British ship. Barron's response was: "I am inclined to the belief that the facts set forth in the written communication by Mr. Carusi are correct."[165]

Carusi described what he expected of Congress:

> The most important relief afforded by Government should be on account of my having been driven, by means of false promises and a worthless contract, from a situation which I enjoyed in Sicily, to come to the United States, and then be subject to all the miseries which I have related above.
>
> I demand, moreover, a recompense for assisting in the war with Tripoli; I was not an American citizen; and if I was foolish enough to risk my life in their battles, it was because I was obliged; also, for the risk and loss on board the Chesapeake, and for prize-money due on vessels taken whilst attached to the fleet.[166]

Carusi submitted a petition to Congress on 16 December 1830. It was a brief two-page handwritten document that was referred to the Committee of Naval Affairs. Carusi asked for "a reasonable sum [one thousand dollars] to enable him to take himself his . . . wife and three sons to Italy."[167] Congress did not act on his petition that year. Carusi's second petition was submitted on 13 December 1831 to the Committee of Naval Affairs and included many more details, as well as the following list of specific remunerations:

18 months clothing for 4 persons at $35 each	$210
18 months rations at $6 per month	540
18 months pay for 3 persons at $7 per month	378
18 months pay for 1 person at $12 per month	216
House rent for myself and family $8 per month	288
Balance of pay reduced from $12 to 7 per month	90
Present to myself	40
Present to my sons	30
For my passage to Europe under the present circumstances I am satisfied with half the sum this government has been accustomed to pay for every person, it has sent to Europe—for 5 persons	$1000
[total]	$2792

It now remains for the government to grant me some compensation for the following reasonable demands. The situations I left in Sicily to enter the service of the United States. The assistance, I as well as my sons gave in the war against the Tripolitans, together with my share of prize money, accruing from vessels taken from the Tripolitans & other Barbarous nations. The vexation suffered in my passage from Sicily to America. The labor bestowed towards forming a band of musicians. The dangers suffered on board the Chesapeake. And a trunk with all my most valuable property thrown overboard.[168]

Carusi submitted a supplement to his petition that included these additional demands:

Musical instruments promise by contract	$200
A large case with three locks was thrown overboard	$2000
Total	$4992[169]

John Anderson, Representative from Maine and a member of the Naval Affairs Committee in the House, asked Carusi to produce the original enlistment contract. On 27 January 1832, Carusi reported back to Anderson by letter that he had located the contract in the State Department.[170] On 31 January, Anderson requested confirmation of that information from the State Department, which he received on 4 February.[171] During the next several months Carusi gathered important letters, copies of enlistment papers, and other significant documents from the Adjutant & Inspector's Office of the Marine Corps and the Navy Department. Although Carusi provided ample evidence supporting his case, Lt. Col. A. Henderson of the Marine Corps was puzzled as to why Carusi chose not to remain on board the *Washington*:

> It appears to me probable that the government felt an obligation to return these men to their country in consequence of having discharged them before the terms of their enlistments expired . . . [and that] a passage was provided for himself and family in the Washington line of battleship in 1816. He [Carusi] declined going out in this form what cause I do not know.[172]

Carusi responded to Henderson's remarks stating:

> The information of Col. Henderson of the Marine Corps says, that my passage with all my family was granted in the year 1816 on board the ship of line Washington, and I declined goin [sic] out in her, from what cause he does not know. The reason I did not continue my passage I never will explain with my own hand writing, because I will not hurt my filling [sic], my honour, and my reputation, but if the Government desires an explanation, I will bind myself to explain in public Congress every cause of my not returning to Europe.[173]

Carusi's case continued to linger on in Congress. On 13 December 1833, he again petitioned Congress hoping that his pleas would be heard:

> To the Honourable the Senate and House of Representatives of the United States. The memorial of Gaetano Carusi humbly sheweth [*sic*]. On account of the shortness of the late session, and the immense mass of business requiring the attention of Congress, my case which has been for three years before it was unavoidably postponed. But as the ensuing session will probably be longer, I hope that some notice will be taken of it. <u>Venter non patitur moram</u>—I am now in my seventy three [*sic*] year, and am no longer able to procure support for myself; I therefore intreat, that my claim be considered, and justice be done to it. I have been told by the members of the Committee on Naval Affairs that, all my demands will not be complied with; and this unexpected announcement obliges me to have recurse [*sic*] to a fresh petition, in order to lay before Congress in their full force, all the arguments in favour of my just pretention.[174]

On 16 December, his petition was referred to the Committee of Claims for their review. But by now Carusi had become frustrated with the system.

> When my petition was drawn up, I gave it the proper direction, according to the rules of Congress. And here I must observe that, if hitherto I had been treated ill by the creatures of the Government, I was now afflicted by the Government itself; and that a most active part was taken against my relief by the honorable Mr. [Josiah Ogden] Hoffman, of the State of New York. This gentleman, on my visiting him at his room, to make him acquainted with my just complaints, felt himself authorized to make such propositions to me as might force me rather to consent to sacrifice my rights than be insulted in my person.[175]

Finally on 15 January 1834, the Committee on Naval Affairs issued Report No. 180 recommending to the House that Carusi be awarded $1000 to settle his claim. The Report accompanied Bill H. R. No. 198:

> Mr. [William John] Grayson, from the Committee on Naval Affairs, made the following REPORT: The Committee on Naval Affairs, to which was referred the petition of Gaetano Carusi, report: That it appears from the statement of the petitioner, and from the documents accompanying it, that he and his three sons were employed, in the year 1805, by the officers of the American

squadron then in the Mediterranean, for the term of three years: the petitioner continued in the service during the time in which the squadron remained abroad, and came with it to America. On his arrival in this country he was dismissed from the service, half the term for which he had been engaged being yet unexpired: he was thus abandoned in a foreign country, without support, although a promise had been made him to send him back to Europe at the expiration of the three years for which he had been employed. The officers of the squadron appear to have acted under a mistake as to their powers in procuring his services, but it was not possible for a foreigner to know that the commander of an armed ship had no power to employ a musician, and it appears therefore one of those cases in which the liberality of the government should not permit an innocent and ignorant foreigner to suffer for having enlisted in its service. The committee recommend, therefore, that the petitioner be paid one thousand dollars, and for that purpose they report a bill.[176]

No action was taken, however. On 6 January 1836, Rep. William John Grayson again submitted the Committee's report to the House,[177] along with the following bill:

For the relief of Gaetano Carusi. *Be it enacted by the Senate and House of Representatives of the United States of America in Congress assembled*, That the Secretary of the Treasury pay to Gaetano Carusi, out of any money not otherwise appropriated, the sum of one thousand dollars, for claims on the United States; the amount to be considered a full compensation for all claims on the United States by said Carusi.[178]

Carusi was dissatisfied with the ruling:

At the end of seven years, the House of Representatives condescended to grant me, as a relief, the sum of one thousand dollars; in which, if they could have supposed that my rights, joined to my sufferings, could have been so miserably satisfied, I would in no manner have sought its acquisition, although most necessary. As it was, I conformed to circumstances, considering that I would, for the future, pursue a different plan with the Government, until it should have well thought over all which I have written here, and would then pursue a juster line of conduct towards me.[179]

The bill was passed by the House on 5 April 1836[180] and sent to the Senate. The following day it was referred to the Committee of Naval

Affairs. The Committee must have had some reservations concerning the House ruling for a reading before the Senate was not presented until 17 February 1837 when Senator William Cabell Rives reported a bill "which was read, and passed to a second reading":

> For the relief of Gaetano Carusi. *Be it enacted by the Senate and House of Representatives of the United States of America in Congress assembled,* That the Secretary of the Navy be, and he is hereby, authorized to settle the account of Gaetano Carusi, for the service of himself and his three sons, upon just and equitable terms, and when the balance is ascertained, the same shall be paid by the Secretary of the Treasury, out of any money in the Treasury not otherwise appropriated.[181]

The fact that the $1000 was not included in the Senate version of this bill probably points to that body's dissatisfaction with Carusi's petition. Carusi responded to the contents of the bill by accusing certain individuals of taking an opposing position, as well as noting a general lack of concern by others:

> As soon as the bill for my relief had passed the lower House, it was sent up to the Senate to be re-examined, and to go through all the former delay. Not that I cared for the acquisition of the paltry sum of one thousand dollars, but that a way might be opened for a future hearing of my case, when, all my reasons and circumstances being well considered, I might obtain what was just and proper.
>
> On the evening of 1st July, 1836, the Senate decided that my demands were unreasonable, and that the public money should not be squandered away at the desire of every one. Such, at least, were the sentiments of the honorable Mr. A[lexander] Porter, of Louisiana, who so expressed himself in the room of the Secretary of the Senate, in the presence of Mr. Hickey.
>
> I have but one question to ask here, which is, whether the honorable Mr. A. Porter, and those who united with him against me, have examined my papers? The documents before the House did not emanate from me entirely: some were afforded by the Navy Department, some by the Marine Corps, and some came from the office of the Secretary of State; many certificates also accompanied them, emanating from individuals who have always lived in this city.
>
> I do believe that the House merely glanced at my papers, and then gave me the one thousand dollars as a piece of mere charity;

for, had they examined them, they must have granted my just demands.[182]

The bill read in the Senate on 17 February was read again on 19 December 1837.[183]

Sometime in 1838-39, with no additional action taken on his petition by the Senate, Carusi decided to prepare another more detailed description of his case. He began work on his *Narrative* which was completed in March 1840. He was seventy-six years of age when he presented that document to the Senate:

> It is necessary, moreover, to remind the Government of the United States that I am a man, and that men do not willingly suffer such outrages as I have here related to have befallen me. I therefore esteem it but just that a much larger appropriation should be made for me to repair in some measure my losses, and make in some sort a reward for my sufferings. And, at all events, if power triumphs and reason is oppressed, I shall content myself with publishing my misfortunes, that every one may learn how I have been treated, and how my labors have been rewarded. I could wish, however, that the United States would inform themselves of the truth of my narration, for their entire satisfaction.[184]

Although Carusi waited patiently for a Senate ruling, time ran out for him. He died 17 June 1843 at the age of eighty-three.[185] His accomplishments were a testament to his musical spirit and loving concern for his family. Coming from a comfortable life in Italy to a new land filled with uncertainties, unable to speak English, unknown in name, and with little money, Carusi successfully came to terms with his new environment and status. He was an enterprising musician who travelled from place to place utilizing his musical skills as a performer, conductor, composer, impresario, and seller and repairer of musical instruments. He contributed to the cultural life of Philadelphia, Baltimore, Washington, and other towns. In Washington Carusi and his sons became one of that city's most significant musical families of the nineteenth century. Descendants of his son Nathaniel became prominent Washington lawyers and civic leaders.[186]

The complications that ensued in Carusi's military life stemmed mainly from officers who made decisions that went beyond their authority. Carusi was well aware of that, yet did not relinquish his persistence in doing what he could to honor the agreements he had made. Further, his disenchantment resulting from events related to his military agreements was directed principally towards what he believed were inequities in the political system. In all other respects Carusi quickly adopted the attitudes and values that embodied the "typical" American immigrant. He became an American citizen and through his initiative and that of his sons contributed to community life and needs. For example, in December 1827, Gaetano "lent his large elegant assembly room" for a benefit concert presented by the Marine Corps Band for an orphan asylum in Washington.[187] His son Lewis also participated in worthwhile community endeavors. In January 1850, for example, he collaborated with the Nightingale Ethiopians in presenting "a grand concert for the benefit of the Washington Monument,"[188] and in July 1855 offered the use of his Hall for a benefit concert for the St. Vincent and St. Joseph's orphan asylums.[189]

Even though Lewis withdrew his father's petition from Congress on 28 March 1844,[190] the honor, esteem, and recognition of Gaetano Carusi was, in the end, acknowledged by Congress. Carusi was buried in Congressional Cemetery alongside of other distinguished persons.[191] At his gravesite is a tall stately white monument which bears the inscription:

Sacred
to the memory of
GAETANO CARUSI
Died June 17, 1843,
in his 83 year,
And of his wife,
PHILIPPA CARUSI
Died June 22, 1846
in her 75 year
And of their youngest Son
LEWIS CARUSI
Died Oct. 19, 1872,
in his 73 year.

---

[1]Special thanks to Bonnie Hedges of the Historical Society of Washington and Elise S. Kirk for their valuable assistance in locating information about the Carusi family. This story has been related in a number of secondary sources, some of which focus on Marine Band history, others on the cultural history of Washington. Most of the articles, however, do not provide full details of the events or primary source citations. John Claggett Proctor published a series of 12 articles containing information on the Carusi family in the *Washington Star* during the 1930s and 40s. Although not detailed nor always accurate, Proctor's information points to the musical significance of the Carusi family in Washington. In "Dancing When the Capital Was Young," 3 December 1933, Proctor gives a synopsis of Gaetano's saga with

quotes from the latter's own account about the unfortunate events, and concludes correctly that Gaetano was "unquestionably very badly treated, though he appears to have done everything he could to make good on his part." In "The U. S. Marine Band," 21 November 1948, Proctor describes the Carusi "recruits from Italy" in the context of the formation of the Band, but omits certain key details. Stuart E. Jones' "The President's Music Men," *National Geographic* (December 1959), 754-60, includes an account of some of the facts and names President Thomas Jefferson as the catalyst for the events that followed. Other brief accounts, which are based on some Marine Corps records, are found in Elise K. Kirk, *Music at the White House* (Urbana: University of Illinois Press, 1986), 30-32 and *Musical Highlights from the White House* (Malabar, Fla: Krieger, 1992), 15-16.

[2] Both his original manuscript (dated 16 March 1840) and twenty-page printed edition, as well as other significant documents regarding the Carusi affair are held in the National Archives, Washington, D.C., in Senate Records, RG 46, 36A-E1, box 15.

[3] *Narrative*, 3.

[4] Joel D. Thacker, "Highlights of U. S. Marine Corps Activities in the District of Columbia," *Records of the Columbia Historical Society* 51 (1955): 78.

[5] Ibid., 79. One such "Dancing Assembly . . . was held at Mr. Stelle's" where "the company consisting of above one hundred ladies and gentlemen, among the latter of whom were several public characters, and members of the federal legislature, assembled." *Washington National Intelligencer*, 26 November 1800.

[6] Karl Schuon, *Home of the Commandants* (Washington, D.C.: Leatherneck Association, 1966), 66.

[7] Thacker, 79-80.

[8] Hall states specifically, in a letter he wrote to Franklin Wharton on 1 April 1805, that "I enlisted this Band for the Corps in consequence of an order received from Col. Burrows before I left America. . . ." National Archives, Senate 36A-E1. The letter is reprinted in *Naval Documents Related to the United States Wars with the Barbary Powers*, 6 vols. (Washington, D.C.: Government Printing Office, 1944) 5:474. It may have been the intention of Burrows that the Italians would form the nucleus of a second Marine Band. There is no truth to the legend that Hall actually kidnapped a group of Italian musicians, as stated in A.B.C. Whipple, *To the Shores of Tripoli* (New York: William Morrow, 1991), 339.

[9] Whipple, 146. Barron was appointed commodore in Spring 1804. The frigates under his command included the *President* (44 guns), *Constellation*

(36 guns), *Constitution* (44 guns), *John Adams* (36 guns), and *Congress* (36 guns), as well as a number of additional gun boats and schooners of lesser size. Ibid., 185.

[10] John Hall, Capt. Marines, to Lieut. Col. F. Wharton, 28 February 1805. National Archives, Senate 36A-E1.

[11] *Narrative*, 1.

[12] Carusi stated in a separate hand-written petition to Congress that he "resided in Company with the American Consul and many other offices attached to the U. S. service." National Archives, Senate 36A-E1.

[13] Pay rates for enlisted men varied. A private was paid $9 per month, a sergeant and corporal of marines, $10 per month, ordinary seaman, $9 per month, and an able seaman, $11 per month. Enlisted men were not entitled to rations. For commissioned and warrant officers the pay was higher. A sailmaker and carpenter, for example, each received $20 per month and two rations a day. William M. Fowler, Jr., *Jack Tars and Commodores* (Boston: Houghton Mifflin, 1984), 29.

[14] *Narrative*, 1.

[15] Ibid., 3-4.

[16] See Helen Cripe, *Thomas Jefferson and Music* (Charlottesville: University Press of Virginia, 1974).

[17] Mrs. Samuel Harrison Smith (Margaret Bayard), *The First Forty Years of Washington Society*, ed. Gaillard Hunt (New York: Scribner's, 1905; reprint, New York: Frederick Ungar, 1965), 30.

[18] Ibid.

[19] *National Intelligencer*, 5 July 1801. Some of the Marines were also vocalists. Elise K. Kirk discusses Captain Thomas Tingey, the Commandant of the Navy Yard who apparently had an excellent baritone voice. *Music at the White House*, 28.

[20] In the spring of 1787, Jefferson made a trip to northern Italy where he saw first hand the achievements of local architects and painters. See George Green Shackelford, "Thomas Jefferson and the Fine Arts of Northern Italy: 'A Peep into Elysium,'" in *America, the Middle Period: Essays in Honor of Bernard Mayo*, ed. John B. Boles (Charlottesville: University Press of Virginia, 1973), 14-35.

[21] *National Intelligencer*, 24 June 1803. The band performed once again on 4 July 1804. Ibid., 6 July 1804.

[22] *National Intelligencer*, 30 January 1804.

[23] *Narrative*, 3.

[24]Ibid., 4. In Carusi's handwritten early draft of a petition to the Committee of Naval Affairs of the House of Representatives dated 13 December 1831, he refers to the musicians as "strangers from other countries." Apparently Captain Hall made the final decisions regarding the enlistment of the musicians, for Carusi mentions in his 1831 petition that "Captain Hall unacquainted with the requisites necessary to constitute a musician engaged persons totally unfit. . . ." National Archives, Senate 36A-E1.

[25]Although the Italians were formally enlisted in Catania, James and Gaetano Sardo might have come from Aci.

[26]Marked "A true copy" made around 1830 of Carusi's original agreement with Captain Hall. National Archives, Senate 36A-E1. Another copy which is worded differently and was translated perhaps from Spanish was originally communicated 2 January 1816 by Carusi's friend, the Spanish envoy to the U. S., Don Luis de Onís, on his behalf is held in the National Archives. This second copy, dated 23 January 1831, is in damaged condition, but seems to indicate that there might have been other signatories on the original. See Senate 36A-E1. In a letter from Capt. John Hall to Lieut. Col. Frank Wharton written from Palermo, 28 February 1805, in Senate 36A-E1, Hall states that he was "obliged to give the leader 50 dollars, and the rest ten dollars bounty, with a ration to eight of their wifes. This sir I was obliged to do or I could not have got a single man." Carusi recalled that his position was "Captain and instructor of the band." "Letter: G. Carusi to Commo. Barron," 1 September 1830, National Archives, 36A-E1.

[27]*Narrative*, 11.

[28]In fact, in a letter dated 10 September 1805 from Hall to Commandant Franklin Wharton, Hall mentions the arrival of "eighteen good musicians" in America. *Naval Documents* 6:277. The total number of musicians, wives, and children numbered over thirty. *Narrative*, 4.

[29]Certified copy of original undated registration of "Gaetano Caruso," Headquarters, Marine Corps. Adjutant & Inspector's Office, Washington, 19 August 1831. National Archives, Senate 36A-E1.

[30]A notarized certificate of 19 August 1831 by Felice Pulizzi by request of G. Carusi. National Archives. Senate 36A-E1. In 1833 Carusi recollected that his "talents as Master and Professor in Music were highly esteemed" and that he "had no need of quitting my country or seeking any other situation than that which I already held." "Petition of Gaetano Carusi to Congress," 13 December 1833. National Archives, Senate 36A-E1.

[31] Ainsworth R. Spofford, *Eminent and Representative Men of Virginia and the District of Columbia of the Nineteenth Century* (Madison, Wis.: Brant & Fuller, 1893), 75. Spofford may have interviewed Eugene Carusi or one of the other grandsons of Gaetano.

[32] Certified copy of original undated registration of "Samuel Caruso," Headquarters, Marine Corps. Adjutant & Inspector's Office, Washington, D.C., 19 August 1831. National Archives, Senate 36A-E1.

[33] Certified copy of original undated registration of "Ignatio Caruso," Headquarters, Marine Corps. Adjutant & Inspector's Office, Washington, D.C., 19 August 1831. National Archives, Senate 36A-E1.

[34] From an obituary of Lewis Carusi printed in the *Washington Evening Star*, 25 October 1872.

[35] *Narrative*, 5.

[36] Hall to Wharton, 28 February 1805. National Archives, Senate 36A-E1. This information is also confirmed in a letter from Hall to Captain Samuel Barron written on 12 March 1805 from Syracuse printed in *Naval Documents* 5:409.

[37] *Narrative*, 4. Since Captain Hall was in Messina on 1 April 1805 (letter from Hall to Wharton), sometime not long thereafter his squadron left for Tripoli.

[38] Fowler, 118.

[39] Gaetano Carusi, petition to Congress.

[40] *Naval Documents* 5:10. An account in the *National Intelligencer* for 25 September 1805 confirms that the *President* was in Syracuse on 29 June 1805 when a "Court of Enquiry" was convened (on board the ship) regarding the conduct of Captain William Bainbridge in the loss of the frigate *Philadelphia*. William Eaton served as "Judge Advocate," and presumably Carusi was introduced to him. They would meet again at Mount Vernon. Information in the *Frederick-Town Herald* of 21 September 1805 confirms 7 July as the date the *President* left Syracuse.

[41] Petition of Gaetano Carusi to Congress, 13 December 1833. National Archives, Senate 36A-E1.

[42] *Naval Documents* 5:10.

[43] Gaetano Carusi petition to Congress. National Archives, Senate 36A-E1.

[44] Messina, 1 April 1805. National Archives, Senate 36A-E1.

[45] Schuon, 68.

[46] *Naval Documents* 6:277.

[47] Ibid., 5:10. The arrival of the *President* was reported in the *Easton Republican Star*, 24 September 1805.

[48] *Maryland Gazette,* 26 September 1805. According to a notice in the *Alexandria Daily Advertiser* for 20 September 1805, the time was ten o'clock. James Barron was the brother of the above-mentioned Samuel Barron.

[49] *Narrative,* 4.

[50] *National Intelligencer,* 25 September 1805 and reprinted in the *Alexandria Daily Advertiser* on 26 September 1805. The dinner was also reported in the *Frederick-Town Herald* on 28 September 1805. In the following December, General Eaton was also honored with a celebration dinner complete with toasts "interspersed with songs and instrumental music. During the entertainment the spirits of the company were highly exhiliarated [sic] by the spirited performance of the marine and Italian bands of music." *National Intelligencer,* 2 December 1805.

[51] *Narrative,* 4. The cabin belonged to W. and Elizabeth Venable. The latter testified by certificate on 29 August 1831 that the facts as stated by Carusi regarding their agreement were correct. National Archives, Senate 36A-E1. A William Venable is listed in *The Washington Directory* (Washington, D.C.: S. A. Elliot, 1827).

[52] *Narrative,* 4. This information is corroborated by Parke G. Howle who prepared a certificate on 19 August 1831 based on the original sworn document signed by "Ingnazio Caruso."

[53] Listed as "Augustin Serra," an "overseer of laborers at navy yard—dw e side 7e near the yard," in Judah Delano, *The Washington Directory* (Washington, D.C.: William Duncan, 1822).

[54] *Narrative,* 5.

[55] Ibid. Hall, who was aware of his obligation to Carusi and the other musicians, wrote the following letter to Captain Samuel Barron on 27 November 1805 from Washington: "Dear Sir As there has been some little difficulty in settling my accounts at the Navy Office respecting the Band I enlisted in Catania, will thank you to write me word if it was not your orders for me to obtain one in Sicily—by you doing this I shall be able to settle my Accts: directly & save me a great many dollars." *Naval Documents* 6:311.

[56] *National Intelligencer,* 27 December 1805. The notice for the concert is reproduced in Thomas Froncek, ed. *The City of Washington* (New York: Alfred A. Knopf, 1977), 99.

[57] Diary of John Brazier Cannon. Library, Mount Vernon, Virginia.

[58] General William Eaton arrived in Washington from Gibraltar on 25 November 1805. *Maryland Gazette,* 28 November 1805. He was honored

in December by Congress for his gallant military achievements during the war with Tripoli. Whipple, 265.

[59]Diary of John Brazier Cannon. Library, Mount Vernon, Virginia. Cannon's diary records a "Band of Music" as having visited Mount Vernon on 15 June 1806.

[60]Carusi, Petition to Congress. National Archives, Senate 36A-E1.

[61]Listed as Alexander Forrest, "Sergeant Major Marine Corps at the barracks," in *The Washington Directory* for 1822.

[62]However, apparently he accepted $126 for 18 months service, as documented in his petition.

[63]Lt. Col. Franklin Wharton to Robert Smith, Secretary of the Navy, 14 May 1806. National Archives, Senate 36A-E1.

[64]Robert Smith, Secretary of the Navy, to Col. F. Wharton, Marine Garrison, 15 May 1806. National Archives, Senate 36A-E1.

[65]*Narrative*, 6.

[66]Dolley loved music and was known to have purchased the first piano for the White House in 1809. Kirk, *Music at the White House*, 36.

[67]*Narrative*, 8.

[68]Ibid.

[69]Ibid., 8-9.

[70]Ibid., 9.

[71]*Norfolk Gazette and Public Ledger*, 22 August 1806.

[72]In his petition to Congress, Carusi stated "During my stay at Norfolk, perceiving from the public journals the unjust proceeding of the English, who pressed into their service, all manner of persons, of every nation & fearing lest this might be added to my many misfortunes I resolved to ask for my passage home. . . ." For an illustration of the *Chesapeake*, see Fowler, following 96.

[73]Daniel Bedinger, Navy agent and Superintendent of the Navy Yard, Norfolk. A certified copy dated 13 November 1830 of Smith's letter to Carusi, as well as a copy of Smith's order to Barron are in National Archives, Senate 36A-E1.

[74]*Naval Documents* 6:569.

[75]Ibid., 6:523.

[76]Ibid., 6:535.

[77]*Narrative*, 10.

[78]*Naval Documents* 6:538-39.

[79] Ibid., 6:541. For a discussion and map depicting the setting of the *Chesapeake-Leopard* affair, see Dumas Malone, *Jefferson the President: Second Term, 1805-1809* (Boston: Little, Brown and Company, 1974), 413-38.

[80] Carusi placed the value of his trunk at $2000. Petition to Congress, 13 December 1831. Felice Pulizzi provided the following certification: "I hereby certify that I was on board the frigate Chesapeake, during the attack of the Leopard and that at the time many thing [sic] were thrown overboard to clear the ship for action and among the rest a very large strong walnut chest with three locks which appartained [sic] to the Signor Gaetano Carusi & family who were at that time on their passage in the said frigate Chesapeake to the Mediterranean." National Archives, Senate 36A-E1.

[81] Edward H. Tatum, Jr. and Marion Tinling, "Letters of William Henry Allen, 1800-1813, Part Two, 1807-1813," *Huntington Library Quarterly* 1/2 (January 1938). See letter of 24 June 1807, 215.

[82] *Narrative*, 11.

[83] Ibid.

[84] For a biography of Wilkinson, see James Ripley Jacobs, *Tarnished Warrior: Major-General James Wilkinson* (New York: Macmillan, 1938).

[85] *Narrative*, 11-12.

[86] Fowler, 155.

[87] *Narrative*, 12-13.

[88] *Baltimore Evening Post*, 17 November 1810. Cited in Kirk, *Music at the White House*, 31.

[89] Copyright was granted to Joseph Carr on 15 November 1811. The work was advertised in the *American & Commercial Daily Advertiser* for sale at 75 cents on 18 December 1811, but on 31 December was reduced to 25 cents. The "Circus Tunes" were also advertised in the *Baltimore Federal Gazette*, 18 November 1811. A copy of the piece is located in the Maryland Historical Society in Baltimore.

[90] *Baltimore Federal Gazette*, 26 January 1811.

[91] *Alexandria Gazette*, 13-16 January, 1813. The instrument was exhibited in Vienna, Petersburg, Paris, Boston, New York, Philadelphia, Baltimore, and Alexandria. An illustration of the instrument is printed in the *New-York Gazette & General Advertiser*, 15 October 1811 and *New-York Evening Post*, 28 October 1811.

[92] The work was originally composed by Marchand. Pardi copyrighted the piece on 30 March 1812. Copies are located in American Antiquarian

Society, Buffalo and Erie County Public Library, Harvard University, Library of Congress, and the New York Public Library.

[93] *Poulson's American Daily Advertiser*, 31 March 1812 and subsequent issues in April.

[94] *Philadelphia Aurora General Advertiser*, 18 February 1813.

[95] *Poulson's American Daily Advertiser*, 13 April 1814.

[96] Kenneth Scott, *British Aliens in the United States during the War of 1812* (Baltimore: Genealogical Publishing Co., 1979), 264.

[97] Isaac Chauncey.

[98] Navy Department, 20 January 1816, reprinted by Carusi in his *Narrative*, 13.

[99] *Narrative*, 13.

[100] According to information reported in the *Maryland Gazette* on 27 June 1816, Gallatin, the U. S. minister to France, sailed for Havre from New York on the sloop *Peacock* under the command of Lt. Com. Rodgers on 11 June.

[101] The trip to Boston cost Carusi $1000. *Narrative*, 14.

[102] *Alexandria Gazette*, 16 May 1816; reported also in the *Baltimore American & Commercial Advertiser*, 16 May 1816 and the *Frederick-Town Herald*, 18 May 1816.

[103] This is confirmed by a note in the *National Intelligencer* on 20 May 1820 that reported the *Washington* was commencing "her first trip to sea. . . . She is destined to the Mediterranean to carry out to Naples Mr. Pinkney the minister to Russia and Naples, and his family, and Mr. King, the Secretary of the legation and will remain at Annapolis until the minister is ready to depart."

[104] *Narrative*, 14. It is possible that the Masi family, which included the Boston organist, composer, and publisher Francesco Masi and his brother Vincent, a dancing master, accompanied Carusi from Boston to Annapolis. An obituary for Nathaniel Carusi published in the *Washington Evening Star* on 22 August 1877 mentions the "Masi's" as being on board "the ship of Commodore Creighton" when it "sailed and brought the party to the city." Francesco had arrived in Boston in 1807, having come from Italy. The Masi names appear in the Washington city directory in 1822. Vincent Masi's dancing lesson notices and cotillion parties are cited in Oliver W. Holmes, "The City Tavern: A Century of Georgetown History, 1796-1898," in *Records of the Columbia Historical Society* 50 (1980), 24-25, and in the *National Intelligencer*, 14 February 1822 and *Washington Gazette*, 19 October 1822. Seraphim Masi announced the opening of a goods store in

Washington "between Dr. Gunton's and Duckworth's Apothecary stores" on Pennsylvania Avenue. *Washington Gazette*, 27 November 1822.

[105]*Maryland Republican*, 18 May 1816 and *National Intelligencer*, 20 May 1816. According to a journal (1816-17) kept by Captain William Joseph Belt, who was on board the *Washington*, the vessel arrived at Annapolis at 4:30 p.m. Belt Collection, ms. 117, Maryland Historical Society, Baltimore.

[106]*Alexandria Gazette*, 16 May 1816 and *Frederick-Town Herald*, 18 May 1816. The *Washington* was commissioned at Portsmouth, N.H. on 26 August 1815. An artist's rendition of the ship is printed in James L. Mooney, ed., *Dictionary of American Naval Fighting Ships*, 8 vols. (Washington, D.C.: Naval Historical Center, Department of the Navy, 1981) 8:123.

[107]*Maryland Gazette*, 23 May 1816.

[108]*National Intelligencer*, 22 May 1816. News had reached Boston several days later where the following was reported: "Baltimore, May 20. We understand that the President of the United States and his Lady, with the Heads of Departments . . . leave Washington this day for Annapolis . . ." to visit the *Washington 74*. *Boston Daily Advertiser*, 27 May 1816. The arrival of the *Washington* was described in Charleston: "The Washington, 74, Commodore Chauncey, arrived at Annapolis yesterday, in six days from Boston. She is to take out Mr. Pinkney to Europe, who is expected to embark in a few days. Vessels that came up the Bay at same time report that she sails astonishingly fast, leaving everything with ease, without the use of her steering sails." *Charleston Courier*, 25 May 1816.

[109]*Baltimore American & Commercial Daily Advertiser*, 21 May 1816. Reprinted in *Frederick-Town Herald*, 25 May 1816. The event was also reported in the *Maryland Gazette*, 23 May 1816.

[110]*Maryland Republican*, 25 May 1816.

[111]U. S. Ship *Washington* Log, 1815-20, 3 vols., RG 24, National Archives. The Log also notes the visit on 29 May of Charles Ridgely, Governor of Maryland, who received a salute of 17 guns and three cheers.

[112]Testimony by F. Gilldorff in National Archives, Senate 36A-E1.

[113]*Narrative*, 14-15.

[114]"Autobiography of Commodore George Nicholas Hollins, C.S.A.," *Maryland Historical Magazine* 34/3 (September 1939): 233-34. There is no evidence to suppose that Carusi ever made it back to Italy. There was some confusion evident in other documents regarding musicians enlisted in Europe at that time and brought over in American frigates. For example, Secretary Smith wrote to Captain Hugh G. Campbell who was serving on the frigate

Constitution on 25 July 1806 about his dissatisfaction that Campbell had "engaged" a "Band of Music." Smith stated they had to be discharged immediately. "The Commanders of publick Vessels must be satisfied with the Music assigned them from this Country—they have no authority to encrease the number placed on board in this Country." Captain Campbell wrote back to Secretary Smith on 20 December suggesting to him that his facts were incorrect. "I beg leave to observe, my presumption is that you alluded to the band engaged by Capt. Rodgers, which band he took home in the *Essex*, since that period we have found among the crew a few men that play on different instruments, which have been purchased for them at private expence; on which they play when duty of more consequence is not required of them, this I hope sir is not an objectionable part of my conduct; if so be assured that no one will be more ready to correct it than myself." *Naval Documents* 6:461 and 492, respectively. The *Essex* arrived in Washington from Gibraltar on 27 July 1806.

[115]*Narrative*, 15. And, in addition, Carusi's old adversary, Colonel Wharton, visited the *Washington* on 1 June. Presumably he informed Captain Creighton about his less than admirable opinion of Carusi. *Washington* Log, National Archives.

[116]Testimony of Giuseppe Sardo written in 1833. National Archives, Senate 36A-E1.

[117]Certificate of T. Downey. National Archives, Senate 36A-E1.

[118]Testimony by F. Gilldorff. National Archives, Senate 36A-E1.

[119]*Washington* Log, National Archives. According to the *Maryland Republican*, 8 June 1816 and *Maryland Gazette*, 13 June 1816, the *Washington* sailed from Annapolis on 7 June.

[120]*Baltimore American & Commercial Daily Advertiser*, 4 June 1816.

[121]*Narrative*, 15.

[122]*Maryland Republican*, 15 June 1816.

[123]*Maryland Republican*, 6 July 1816.

[124]Ibid.

[125]*Maryland Gazette*, 11 July 1816.

[126]James Robinson, *Philadelphia Directory for 1816* (Philadelphia: Printed for the publisher, 1816).

[127]*U. S. Index to Records of Alien's Declaration of Intention and/or Oaths of Allegiance, 1789-1880*. Vol. 2, letter C, 44 and 75. The following extract is found in Michael Tepper, ed., *New World Immigrants* (Baltimore: Genealogical Publishing Co., 1979), 252: "Caruso (Carusi), Gaetano; age '51 years and upwards' in 1817; Nativity, Naples, Italy; Declaration of

Intention, (Court of Common Pleas, Philadelphia), 24 January 1817; Proof of Residence, 30 Dec. 1824; witnesses: Felice Pulizzi, Venenando (Benenando) Pulizzi: naturalization granted 30 Dec. 1824." Lewis, Gaetano's youngest son, was not yet of age and likely was later granted citizenship along with his father.

[128] *Alexandria Gazette*, 3 March 1818.

[129] *Easton Republican Star*, 14 July 1818. A notice citing letters for "G. Carusi" remaining in the Easton post office is printed in the *Republican Star*, 2 and 16 July 1822.

[130] His address is cited on a copy held in the Library of Congress. Edward Whitely's *Philadelphia Directory and Register, for 1820* (Philadelphia: McCarty & Davis, 1820), as well as the directories for 1821 and 1822, confirm that address and refer to Gaetano's store as a "toyshop."

[131] Copies in the Library of Congress and New York Public Library.

[132] *Musical Fund Society of Philadelphia* (Philadelphia: The Society, 1970), 50. Nathaniel Carusi's name does not appear on the list. It is possible, therefore, that he was in Alexandria, Virginia teaching during that time.

[133] *Poulson's American Daily Advertiser*, 11 April 1820.

[134] *Poulson's American Daily Advertiser*, 17 May 1820.

[135] *National Intelligencer*, 3 and 19 July 1820.

[136] *National Intelligencer*, 6 October 1820.

[137] *National Intelligencer*, 18 November 1820.

[138] Possibly Patrick Kelly, "professor of music, 16 N. Liberty," from Baltimore. C. Keenan, *The Baltimore Directory, for 1822 & '23* (Baltimore: Richard J. Matchett, 1822).

[139] *National Intelligencer*, 2 March 1821.

[140] *National Intelligencer*, 20 April 1820.

[141] Probably the Brown's Indian Queen Hotel, known for its having provided lodging for visiting Indian chiefs. For an illustration of the hotel, see Froncek, 165.

[142] This is probably the same Philip Mauro, a pianist, who was active in Washington in 1805 as an instrumentalist and concert manager, and who was in Baltimore in 1811 advertising himself as a "Professor of Music." *National Intelligencer*, 18 January 1805 and *Baltimore American Commercial Daily Advertiser*, 25 September 1811 and *Baltimore Federal Gazette*, 28 September 1811. Mauro is listed in James Lakin, *Baltimore Directory and Register for 1814-15* (Baltimore: J. C. O'Reilly, 1814) and in

the Washington city directory for 1822. No connection has been found between Philip Mauro and Ignazio di Mauro (musician in Carusi's band).

[143] *National Intelligencer*, 12 June 1821.

[144] *Washington Gazette*, 9 September 1822. A photograph of the exterior of the building taken in the 1920s before it was razed is in John Clagett Proctor, ed., *Washington Past and Present: A History*, 4 vols. (New York: Lewis Historical Publishing, 1930) 2:527 and George R. Brown, *Washington: A Not Too Serious History* (Baltimore: Norman Publishing, 1930), 183.

[145] *National Intelligencer*, 22 October 1822.

[146] *National Intelligencer*, 26 and 28 February, 4-5 March 1825.

[147] *Washington Evening Star*, 14 February 1855.

[148] *Washington Evening Star*, 20 March 1857 and 29 March 1854, respectively.

[149] *National Intelligencer*, 21 December 1830.

[150] *National Intelligencer*, 21 February 1827.

[151] *National Intelligencer*, 7 May 1836.

[152] *National Intelligencer*, 22 February 1841.

[153] *National Intelligencer*, 1 March 1841.

[154] *National Intelligencer*, 20 September 1841.

[155] A portrait of Lewis, Samuel, and Nathaniel painted by Gardner in 1870 is printed in Kirk, *Music at the White House*, 33 and in Froncek, 307.

[156] Examples include "Oh! Blame Me Not for Loving. Poetry by C. Geo. Dare, Esq. Music composed and arranged for the piano forte and dedicated to Azile, by Samuel Carusi" (Baltimore: Samuel Carusi, n.d.) and *President Van Buren's Grand March*. "Composed & arranged for the piano forte by Samuel Carusi" (Washington, D.C. : Carusi, c1837).

[157] Examples include his *Blue Bell of Scotland* (Washington, D.C.: Carusi, n.d.) for piano and "A Life on the Ocean" (Baltimore: Saml. Carusi, 1844), for voice and piano. For a comprehensive list of works by the Carusi family, see James R. Heintze and Bonnie Hedges, "The Carusi Family: A Bibliography of Musical Works Composed, Arranged, and Published in Philadelphia, Washington, D.C., and Baltimore." Copy located in the Historical Society of Washington.

[158] Correspondence between the Carusi brothers, Wickliffe, and Jones relating to the city post office is printed in Madison Davis, "A History of the City Post Office," in *Records of the Columbia Historical Society* 6 (1903): 180-84.

[159] Loria moved to Baltimore in 1811 where he advertised his services as a teacher of violin, French horn, and clarinet. He lived at the "lower end of Water Street, opposite the Bake House of Messrs. Lovell, Brown and Sultzer." *Baltimore American Commercial Daily Advertiser*, 28 November 1811. Loria also placed a similar notice in the *Baltimore Federal Gazette*, 27 November 1811.

[160] *Narrative*, 11.

[161] *National Intelligencer*, 6 December 1826.

[162] Information on Venerando is found in Kenneth Carpenter, "A History of the United States Marine Band" (Ph.D., University of Iowa, 1970), 32-33, 43, and 48. Both Felice and Venerando are listed in the Washington city directories for 1822 and 1827. Venerando died on 8 October 1852, "aged 57 years." *National Intelligencer*, 9 October 1852.

[163] Evidence seems to indicate that although monetary compensation was an issue Carusi wanted resolved, the principles as stated in his case were more important to him. By the late 1820s, he seemed to have been financially secure. In 1826, for example, he owned 4 parcels of land worth $7,300, and at the time of his death in 1843, his family owned 5 parcels of land at a total value of $13,502. Tax Assessment Books, Corporation of Washington (District of Columbia), RG 351, 1824-26 and 1843, National Archives.

[164] *Narrative*, 15-16.

[165] National Archives, Senate 36A-E1.

[166] *Narrative*, 16.

[167] National Archives, Senate 36A-E1. At that time, Carusi was probably more interested in visiting rather than returning permanently to Italy.

[168] National Archives, Senate 36A-E1.

[169] "Statement of losses." National Archives, Senate 36A-E1. A second "Supplement of the Petition of Gaetano Carusi" specifically mentions "One pair of French horns" at "$125"; "One Bassoon" at "$35"; and "one pair of Cimbals" at "$40."

[170] National Archives, Senate 36A-E1.

[171] Daniel Brent, Chief Clerk, Department of State, to John Anderson, House of Representatives. National Archives, Senate 36A-E1.

[172] Letter from Lt. Col. Henderson to John Brauch, Secretary of the Navy, 21 January 1831. National Archives, Senate 36A-E1. Archibald Henderson, "colonel marine corps at the barracks, N Yrd.," is listed in *The Washington Directory* for 1822 and was appointed commandant 17 October 1820.

[173]"Supplement of the Petition of Gaetano Carusi," National Archives, Senate 36A-E1.
[174]National Archives, Senate 36A-E1..
[175]*Narrative*, 16.
[176]23rd Congress, 1st Session. Copy in Senate 36A-E1. The reading of the bill was cited in the *National Intelligencer*, 17 January 1834.
[177]24th Congress, 1st Session, Document No. 86. House of Representatives. Noted erroneously in the *National Intelligencer*, 7 January 1836, as "for the relief of Nathaniel Carusi."
[178]24th Congress, 1st Session, H.R. 102, 6 January 1836.
[179]*Narrative*, 16.
[180]According to the *National Intelligencer*, 6 April 1836, the bill was read for the third time.
[181]Bill S. 227, 24th Congress, 2nd Session. Senate 25A-B3, S.44-S.56, National Archives.
[182]*Narrative*, 16-17. According to the *National Intelligencer*, 2 July 1836, the "bill for the relief of Gaetano Carusi *was laid on the table.*"
[183]25th Congress, 2nd Session, S. 54. In this reading, the word "service" was also crossed out and replaced with "claims." Senate 25A-B3, S.44-S.56, National Archives. The reading was cited in the *National Intelligencer*, 22 December 1837.
[184]*Narrative*, 20.
[185]As inscribed on Carusi's tombstone. However, the *National Intelligencer*, 19 June 1843, states Carusi died on "Sunday, the 18th instant . . . in the 81st year of his age." Obituaries were also printed in the *Alexandria Gazette*, 20 June 1843; *Baltimore Sun*, 20 June 1843; *Saturday Visitor*, 24 June 1843. Carusi's wife Philippa died 22 June 1846 at seventy-five years of age. *National Intelligencer*, 23 June 1846. See also *Baltimore Sun*, 25 June 1846.
[186]Nathaniel's son, Eugene, assisted in the reorganization of the law school of National University and served as dean of the school for many years. His sons, Eugene D. and Charles Francis, were both successful lawyers. Charles Francis was also a dean of the law school and president of the Washington City School Board. Proctor, *Washington Past and Present: A History* 3:9-10.
[187]Smith, 209-10.
[188]*National Intelligencer*, 10 January 1850.
[189]*Washington Evening Star*, 10 July 1855.

[190] 25th Congress, 3rd Session. Senate 25A-G1-G2 (folder C-F), National Archives. On 17 December 1857, a new petition presented to Congress by the heirs of Carusi was referred to the Court of Claims. On 1 February 1858, the report submitted to the Court was agreed to but not settled. On 27 January 1860, the heirs submitted yet another "new petition" to Congress. The case was referred to the Court of Claims on 30 January 1860. Apparently the suit was never resolved. National Archives, Senate 36A-E1.

[191] Congressional Cemetery was founded in 1812 by Christ Church Capitol Hill and is located near the Anacostia River. Froncek, 175. For a recent article on Congressional Cemetery, see Abby Arthur Johnson, "The Memory of the Community," in *Washington History* 4/1 (Spring/Summer 1992): 26-45.

EDWARD LITTLE WHITE, PROFESSOR OF MUSIC

Barbara Owen

In 1801 the First Religious Society of Newburyport, Massachusetts, erected a handsome new meeting-house, which still stands in the heart of the city. On 15 April 1802, at the "1st Meeting in the New House," the vote was recorded in the proprietors' book "that Gilman White, Andrew Frothingham junior and Nathaniel Knap be a Committee to agree with an Organist and to take care of the Organ." White served on this early church music committee until 1809, when in the meeting of 24 March the proprietors voted to extend their thanks to its members, and "particularly to Maj. Gilman White."

Gilman White (1766-1846) was a distinguished citizen of the thriving seaport of Newburyport. In addition to his church activities, he served the town as Selectman in 1795, 1804, and 1805, and as Constable in 1817.[1] Like many of the town's more prosperous residents, he was a merchant, owning half interest in the brig *Mars* and the brig *Betsey* between 1799 and 1802.[2]

The latter vessel was probably named for Gilman's wife, Elizabeth (Betsy) Brown, whom he married in 1791. Of this union were born nine children. Some of them, inevitably, were shortlived, among these sixteen-year-old Phillips, who died at sea on the brig *New Leader*. Of those who reached adulthood, at least three inherited their father's interest in music: Thomas Brown (1795-1873), the eldest; Mary Ann (b. 1805); and seventh child Edward Little (1809-1851).

On 5 November 1830, the following notice appeared in the *Newburyport Herald*:

> MR. E. L. WHITE, proposing to tarry a few months in this town, will give lessons on the PIANO FORTE and ORGAN, provided immediate applications are made to him at his father's residence.

Terms $10 per quarter.

E. L. White was but twenty-one years old, and where he had been tarrying during his educational years is unknown, although it would appear that his formal studies had included music. His father's address in that period is given as "opposite the head of Market Street," indicating a location at the corner of Market and upper Green Street, near the center of town.

At about this same time Edward became organist of his family's church, the First Religious Society (more commonly known at the time as the Pleasant Street Church). According to a later account, his older brother Thomas B. White directed the choir there during the same period, "and instructed the Sunday school children in singing," while his sister Mary Ann, described as a "magnificent singer," sang in the choir.[3] The organ at the time was a large one-manual instrument built in 1794 by Josiah Leavitt of Boston for an earlier church building on Market Square, and moved to the newer one in 1801.[4]

The musical activities of the two White brothers were not confined to church music and teaching, however. In the fall of 1831 advertisements began to appear in the local newspapers for a new store on State Street operated by T. B. and E. L. White, where books and sheet music could be purchased. Before long the stock had been expanded to include musical instruments, and from 8 November to 30 December the following advertisement appeared in the *Newburyport Herald*:

> T. B. & E. L. WHITE have just received a consignment of
> MUSICAL INSTRUMENTS,
> warranted of the first quality, viz.:
> PIANO FORTES — SPANISH GUITARS —
> CLARIONETS — FLUTES — VIOLINS
> FLAGEOLETS - FIFES — AND
> KENT BUGLES.
> Instruction Books for the above instruments.
> Also, Violin Bows and Bow Hair, and Bridges, Tuning Forks, and
> Hammers. Bassoon and Clarionet Reeds. Together with a large
> assortment of new BOOKS, &c. for the Piano Forte.

The notice goes on to mention their complete assortment of books and stationery, offered "on the most reasonable terms for Cash."

The store on State Street seems to have quickly become a clearinghouse for musical activities. When E. L. Stickney opened a music school in October of 1832, he advertised in the *Herald* that prospective students could sign up at "White's Bookstore." A Mr. Moore placed a similar notice for his dancing school in March of 1832, as did another dancing-master, P. Guignon, a year later.

While secular sheet music probably accounted for much of the Whites' sales, they also sold some of the "oblong" choral collections popular with church choirs. A rather extensive advertisement appearing in the *Herald* on 6 August 1832 sang the praises of Nathaniel Duren Gould's *National Church Harmony*, being sold for "ten dollars a dozen."

Despite its promising beginnings, it would seem that the bookstore was not a success. In the *Newburyport Herald* for 27 August 1833 there is a notice stating that Thomas B. White was "selling off, at a little less than cost, all the stock in the above named store, consisting of Books, Stationery, Paper Hangings, Music and Musical Instruments." Edward L. White appears to have made one last stab at selling instruments, informing the public via the *Herald* of 13 December 1833 "that, having made arrangements with the Piano Forte Manufacturers in Boston and New York, [he] will supply First rate warranted Piano Fortes at the manufacturer's prices, free of expense." This may have meant that he proposed only to take orders for the pianos, although he did have on hand "one fine toned Piano, which has been in use but a short time."

Very little is recorded of the brothers' activities in Newburyport from this time on. It may indeed have been that both were preparing to pull up stakes and move as early as January of 1833, when they advertised their pews in the Pleasant Street Church for sale. One of these, a "front gallery pew," was soon to be removed to make room for a new and larger organ, completed by local organ builder Joseph Alley in the fall of 1834. By this time E. L. White may have left the city, for Daniel A. Cooper of Portsmouth was hired to play the new instrument.[5]

The White family appears to have had some connections (possibly familial) in New Bedford, like Newburyport a thriving seaport in the early nineteenth century. Gilman White's second son, Gilman Jr., was living there as early as 1829, when he married Eleanor Sowle of that town. Possibly Edward had been "tarrying" there himself before his return to Newburyport, for he too married a New Bedford girl. Intentions were published in both Newburyport and New Bedford for his marriage to Hannah Wood on 7 October 1832. Their first child, appropriately named George Frederick, was born a year later but survived only nineteen months. The child's death in May of 1835 was recorded in New Bedford, placing Edward and Hannah there by at least that time.

The first New Bedford city directory was published a year later, in 1836, and E. L. White, "Professor of Music," was listed as boarding at 22 Third Street. In May of that year a daughter, Anna Samson, was born, and by 1838 the Whites had moved to a house at 70 Third Street. The following year Edward moved to Boston, to be replaced in New Bedford by his brother Thomas.

The latter had remained in Newburyport, apparently trying to make a go of the publishing business, for between 1834 and 1836 he had published four of his brother's compositions and a sacred music collection, *Washington Harmony*, on which the two brothers had collaborated, as well as some "orations" by Rev. Thomas Fox, minister of the First Religious Society. If Thomas's hymn tunes and anthems are any indication, he shared Edward's musical gifts, but he opted rather to make a career in banking. His occupation in the year of his arrival in New Bedford is given as "Cashier of Bedford Commercial Bank," and he remained in this position for over thirty years. He never married, although he made a home for his elderly widowed father, who died at his residence in 1846, aged 80. Thomas lived almost as long, dying in 1873 at the age of 78.

Edward seems to have been determined to make his living as an independent "Professor of Music," and he is listed as such in the Boston city directories from 1839 to 1851, the year of his death. He had begun publishing a few songs, piano pieces, and choral collections while in New Bedford, but the twelve years he spent in Boston saw a prodigious output in all three categories.

E. L. White's strong pedagogical inclinations are evident in well-organized drills in the "Rudiments of Music" which appear in a number of his compilations of sacred and secular music. In the preface to *Washington Harmony*, his earliest known collection, he states that

> The Rudiments of music, connected with his collection, will be found to be very simple and comprehensive, and arranged in the modern form of question and answer. The exercises for the learner, especially in time, and modulation, or change of key, will, it is thought, greatly facilitate him in those two very important points.[6]

The "Rudiments" are somewhat more condensed in later publications, such as the *Church Melodist* (1850), but in this and other collections White added several pages of vocal exercises.

Midway through his Boston years White befriended a younger musician, John Edgar Gould (1822-1875), who collaborated with him on nearly half of his choral collections, beginning with the *Modern Harp* (1846), a popular compilation which went into at least six editions. A native of Bangor, Maine, Gould lived briefly in Boston during the 1840s, moving to New York around 1852, where he opened a music store and continued to publish music, later moving the business to Philadelphia. Curiously, his fame rests on a single hymn-tune, "Pilot," written near the

Edward Little White, Professor of Music 137

end of his life. Set to the Rev. Edward Hopper's text, "Jesus, Saviour, pilot me," it is still found in many modern hymnals.[7]

Certain of White's choral collections were occasionally advertised in Boston musical publications of the period, sometimes without mention of the editor's name. White evidently was not as concerned with publicity as were some of his contemporaries, notably Lowell Mason and A. N. Johnson, nor did he feel moved to make literary contributions to the papers. One of the few journalistic references to him concerns a Music Teachers Institute held at Tremont Temple on 13 August 1850. On this occasion White, identified only as "the editor of the Church Melodist," conducted one of the morning church music sessions.[8]

While E. L. White's output of choral collections is impressive, it is dwarfed by the volume of his vocal and piano compositions and arrangements. With the exception of "Prince of Peace" (perhaps written while he was still employed as a church musician in Newburyport), and a Thanksgiving anthem, all of his songs are secular in nature. Most, but not all, are his own compositions, a few others being "arranged" from other composers. Nearly all of these were American, Donizetti being the notable exception.

During the 1840s a musical phenomenon began sweeping New England, the remarkable, melodious, and prolific Hutchinson Family. Their repertoire consisted of folk songs, temperance (and later abolitionist) songs, and many which they composed themselves. Two of the most popular of these were "There's a Good Time Coming" and "The Bridge of Sighs." Thomas Hood's text for the latter had captured the imagination of the Hutchinsons during a tour of famine-stricken Ireland in 1845, and they immediately set it to music and sang it in their next concert.[9] E. L. White apparently knew a good thing when he saw it, for he published his arrangement with "Symphonies and Accompaniment" the following year, along with a similar arrangement of "There's a Good Time Coming." A year later he brought out settings of four more Hutchinson songs. This was, of course, all perfectly legal, copyright laws being quite unknown at the time.

E. L. White's original songs are well crafted in the popular idiom of the time. With the exception of the noted Irish poet Thomas Moore, White chose his texts largely from the works of minor American authors. One such was poet Hannah Flagg Gould (1792-1865) of Newburyport, who may well have been a friend of the White family.

Even greater in number than his songs were White's piano pieces. Many of these are arrangements (often with variations) of popular or operatic songs, including three of his own songs, "The Wrecker's Daughter," "The Home That I Love," and "Smile On." A performing group equally as popular as the Hutchinsons during the 1840s was the Christy Minstrels, white "blackface" singers specializing in "darky" songs, many of them written by Stephen Foster. As with the Hutchinson songs, White was quick to capitalize on their popularity. Foster's "Oh! Susanna" was first published in New York in 1848 and shortly afterward reprinted by Ditson.[10] In the same year Ditson published two piano pieces by White based on the popular tune, a quickstep (which also included the Foster melody "Carry me Back") and a set of variations. Another Foster song published in 1848 was "Old Uncle Ned," and this too served as a theme for two similar White compositions.

Marches, quicksteps, and waltzes were also composed and arranged by White, along with a set of quadrilles which were accompanied by dance directions. Some of White's keyboard pieces are designated as being "for juvenile performers," and may well have been written for his own students. One set of five duets, "The Musical Gift," is dedicated to two sisters, "his pupils Misses Catherine and Pamela H. Robertson."

Although he was a good song writer, it is doubtful whether White ever taught singing; as late as 1850, when *The Boston Melodeon* was published, its author is described on the title page simply as a "Teacher of the Piano Forte and Organ." Certainly the style of his compositions indicates a man who was very much at home with the keyboard conventions of his day—conventions that would very soon be outmoded in the eyes of the younger "professors" who were beginning to study abroad. One of White's most characteristic compositions in this style, the lighthearted variations on "Yankee Doodle," retained its popularity long enough to be reissued in 1857, six years after the composer's death.

Some of the last of White's publications were didactic in nature: *The Seminary Class Book*, *Guitar Without a Master*, *Organ Without a Master*, and his translation of the thoroughbass tutor of Friedrich Schneider, originally published as *Elementarbuch der Harmonie und Tonsetzkunst* in 1820. The *Seminary Class Book* ("designed for Seminaries, High Schools, Private Classes, etc.") was brought out in a "new and enlarged edition" the year following White's death, and advertised by Ditson with the following comments:

> The above work has been before the public only one year, yet has become a universal favorite, and is used in all parts of the Union. During the past year every inquiry has been made in order to ascertain in what way it could be improved and made fully equal to the wants of those for whom it is intended, and from suggestions thus obtained the publisher had been induced to add to and in other ways improve it. It is now pronounced to be exactly what is wanted, and as such it is offered to the public.[11]

The revisor of White's work was T. Bissell, an obscure tune-book compiler known only for his *Boston Sacred Harmony* (1846), also published by Ditson. The *Seminary Class Book* must have remained popular, for Ditson was still advertising it two years later.

White's *Organ Without a Master*, was actually intended for "Melodeon, Seraphine, or Reed Organ" (rather than pipe organ), and was later issued, unaltered, under the title of *Melodeon Without a Master*. The exercises are preceded by some very basic "Elements of Music" in White's favored question-and-answer style, plus a page on "Management of the Instrument" with hints on how to clean silent reeds, and blowing ("press steadily on the pedal in order to produce a smooth and uniform tone"). For pianists learning the melodeon, White lays down but three basic rules (with illustrations): "Hold down one key until the next is actually struck, and no longer," "Never employ the same finger for two consecutive notes," and "Regulate the fingering according to the effect intended to be produced."[12]

Although White worked with a number of publishers, he seems to have been most closely connected to the well-known Oliver Ditson house of Boston, which even re-issued several of his compositions originally published by others. In the year before his death, White may actually have been working for Ditson; either that or he maintained a studio on their premises, for in the Boston City Directory for 1850-51 his home address was on Harrison Ave. while his business address is given as 115 Washington Street—which was also Ditson's address.

E. L. White seems to have been enjoying substantial success as a "professor of music" at the time of his apparently sudden death at the age of only forty-five. His epitaph was penned two years later by his fellow "professor," Nathaniel Duren Gould:

> E. L. WHITE acquired considerable celebrity, both as a teacher and author. He closed his labors on earth, in Boston, in 1851.
>
> White was a native of Newburyport, Mass.; a man of more than ordinary musical talents; commenced teaching in New Bedford; then in Boston, where his labors were incessant as a teacher, writer, and publisher of music, sacred and secular. He was cut down in the midst of life and usefulness, and the hands that used to move the keys of the organ and piano so gracefully are stilled and mouldering in the grave.[13]

Despite Gould's praise of White's keyboard skills, no evidence has been found of his ever having performed in public, and he seems not even to have held a church organist's position after he left Newburyport. But then it is probable that his work as a successful composer, arranger, and teacher precluded such other activities, and that he was happy with the particular niche he had carved for himself. He was survived by his wife, who was recorded as living in his Boston home until 1853.

PUBLISHED WORKS BY E. L. WHITE

The list of E. L. White's published works was compiled from holdings in the following libraries: American Antiquarian Society; Boston Public Library; Essex Institute; Library of Congress; Newburyport (Mass.) Public Library.

Choral Collections

Washington Harmony, A Collection of Sacred Music. With T. B. White. Newburyport: T. B. White, 1834; 2nd ed. 1836.

The Sabbath School Choir. With Wm. Nutting. New Bedford: E. L. White, c1836.

The Sunday School Singing Book. Boston: Wm. Crosby, 1843; 6th ed, Crosby & Nichols, 1851.

The Boston Melodeon, A Collection of . . . Songs, Glees, Catches, etc. Boston: Elias Howe, 1846, 1847; O. Ditson 1850, 1852.

Modern Harp: or Boston Sacred Melodist, A Collection of Church Music. With John E. Gould. Boston: B. B. Mussey, 1846, 5th & 6th eds. 1847, 1848; O. Ditson 1850, 1852; copyright renewed 1874.

The Opera Chorus Book. With J. E. Gould. Boston: B. B. Mussey, 1847 (also O. Ditson).

The Tyrolien Lyre, a Glee Book. With J. E. Gould. Boston: B. B. Mussey, 1847; also O. Ditson, 1848.

The Sabbath School Lute. With J. E. Gould. Boston: B. B. Mussey, 1848 (also O. Ditson).

The Wreath of School Songs. With J. E. Gould. Boston: B. B. Mussey, 1848; O. Ditson, 1850, 1851, 1853, 1854.

The Sacred Chorus Book. With J. E. Gould. Boston: O. Ditson, 1849; B. B. Mussey, 1850.

The Cecilian Glee Book. With A. N. Johnson. Boston: Wilkins, Carter & Co., 1850.

The Seminary Class Book of Music. Boston: O. Ditson, 1850.

White's Church Melodist, A Collection of Sacred Music. Boston: Phillips, Sampson & Co., 1850; O. Ditson, 1851.

Harmonia Sacra, A Collection of Anthems. With J. E. Gould. Boston: O. Ditson, 1851.

The Seminary Class Book of Music, New & Improved Edition. With T. Bissell. Boston: O. Ditson, 1852.

Vocal Music: Songs, Duets, Trios, Quartets

"Prince of Peace." A Sacred Song. [with 4-part chorus] Newburyport: T. B. White, 1834.

"The Ocean." The Words from the *Boston Spectator* [N. Hawthorne]. Philadelphia: George Willig, 1836.

"The Bower of Roses" (Thomas Moore text). Philadelphia: J. Edgar, n.d. (1830's?); George Willig, n.d.

"The Hunted Deer" (Quartet). [title page missing from only known copy; 1830's?]

"The Home I Love So Well" (Thomas Power text). Boston: Parker & Ditson, 1839.

"I'll Think of Thee Still" (Thomas Power text). Boston: C. Bradlee, n.d. (c1840?)

"O Come to Me When Daylight Sets" (Thomas Moore text). Boston: C. Bradlee, n.d. (c1840?)

Evening Melodies. Words by O. W. Withington. [published separately]
    1. "When Twilight Is Stealing" (Duet). Boston: Parker & Ditson, 1840.
    2. "The Music of Thy Song." Boston: C. Bradlee, n.d. (1840?).
    3. "When Voices Breathe a Music Sweet." Boston: C. Bradlee, 1840.
    4. "Ask Not From Me." Boston: Parker & Ditson, 1840.

    5. "Smile On." Boston: Parker & Ditson, 1840.
    6. "The Voice of the Past." Boston: Parker & Ditson, 1840.
    7. "O Touch the Harp." Boston: C. Bradlee, 1840.
    8. "The Hours Tonight." Boston: Parker & Ditson, 1840.
    9. "The Bird of Spring." Boston: Parker & Ditson, 1840.

"The Gloom of Night Is Round My Heart." Ballad. Boston: H. Prentiss, c1841.

"O That I Had Wings" (Trio). Boston: Wm. H. Oakes, 1843.

"When Shall We Meet Again" (Duet). Boston: Wm. H. Oakes, 1843.

"Marion Day." Words & Melody by Mrs. Marion Dix Sullivan, arranged for the Pianoforte. Boston: O. Ditson, 1844.

"The Blue Juniata." Words & Melody by Mrs. Marion Dix Sullivan, arranged for the Pianoforte. Boston: O. Ditson, 1844.

"Thanksgiving Anthem" (Quartet). Boston: A. B. Kidder, 1845; O. Ditson, c1850.

"There's a Good Time Coming." Symphonies and Accompaniment by E. L. W. Boston: O. Ditson, 1846.

"The Bridge of Sighs," Sung by the Hutchinson Family. The Symphonies and Accompaniment by E. L. W. Boston: O. Ditson, 1846.

"The Bridge of Sighs." Arranged as a Quartette. [title page and date missing in only known copy; c1846?]

"Away Down East." Comic Song. Boston: O. Ditson, 1846.

"Billy Boy, A Curious Legend." Arranged for the pianoforte. Boston: O. Ditson, 1847.

Songs of the Hutchinson Family. [published separately]
    1. "The Indian's Lament." Boston: S. W. Marsh, 1847; Ditson, 1853.
    2. "Glide on My Light Canoe." Boston: S. W. Marsh, 1847.
    3. "The Farmer's Daughter." Boston: S. W. Marsh, 1847.
    4. "Old High Rock." Boston: S. W. Marsh, 1847.

"Must Thou Go O'er Moor and Mountain." A Mexican Duet. Boston: Keith's Music Publishing House, 1847.

The Vocal Beauties of Lucia de Lammermuir [six songs], adapted and arranged (trans. J. E. A. Smith). Boston: O. Ditson, 1848.

"The Bird Song" (J. E. A. Smith text). Boston: O. Ditson, 1850.

"The Sachem's Daughter" (J. E. A. Smith text). Boston: Geo. P. Reed, 1850.

"Grave of La Fayette" (Miss H. F. Gould text). New York: J. E. Gould, 1850; Boston: O. Ditson, c1851.

"Sister, Swift the Hours have Fled." Duet written by one of the pupils of the Bradford Female Seminary for their Anniversary, July 16, 1850. Boston: O. Ditson, c1850.

Pianoforte Works

Di Tanti Palpiti. A Favorite Air from *Tancredi* with Variations. Newburyport: T. B. White, 1834.

Boston Quick Step. Newburyport: T. B. White, 1835.

Essex Quick Step. Newburyport: T. B. White, 1836.

Canderbeck's Favorite. Newburyport: T. B. White, c1836

Cottage Waltz. For Juvenile Performers. Boston: C. Bradlee, c1835.

Boundary March and Quick Step. Respectfully dedicated to Gov. Fairfield and defenders of the Territory of Maine. Boston: C. Bradlee, c1836.

Anna's Dance. Boston: C. Bradlee, c1836.

Harrisburg March and Quick Step. For Juvenile Performers. Boston: C. Bradlee, c1836.

New-Bedford Mechanic Riflemen's Quick Step. Boston: C. Bradlee, 1836.

Angelina Waltz. For One or Two Performers. Boston: C. Bradlee, c1839.

Gen. Harrison's Grand March. Boston: C. Bradlee, n.d.

New Bedford Waltz. Boston: C. Bradlee, n.d.

Macomber's Grand March. Boston: W. H. Oakes, c1841.

Phalanx Quick Step, as performed by the Boston brass band. Boston: Wm. H. Oakes, c1841.

The Prima Donna Polka. Dedicated to Signora Benedetti. Boston: O. Ditson, c1841.

The Wreckers Daughter. Quick Step, arranged with variations. Boston: H. Prentiss, c1841.

Yankee Doodle with Variations. Boston: Wm. H. Oakes, 1841; reissued by Russell & Richardson, 1857..

The New Year, or 1842 Grand March. Boston: H. Prentiss, 1842.

The Duke of Reichstadt's Waltz. Boston: H. Prentiss, n.d.

The Musical Gift. A Collection of Popular Melodies arranged for two Performers on one Pianoforte and respectfully dedicated to his pupils Misses Catherine and Pamela H. Robertson.
 1. "The Wrecker's Daughter."
 2. "Cachucha."
 3. "A. B. C." Boston: Wm. H. Oakes, 1843.
 4. "Oak Waltz."
 5. "Cracovienne." Boston: G. P. Reed, 1842. [issued separately].

New Bedford Guards' Quick Step. Boston: G. P. Reed, c1842.

Clay's Quick Step. From a Favorite French Air. Boston: O. Ditson, c1842.

Beauties of the Dance. Arranged for Four Hands.
1. "Pas Espagnol." 2. "El Bolero." 3. "El Jaleo de Xeres." 4. "Tyrolienne." Boston: Wm. H. Oakes, 1843.

Ethiopian Medley. Containing the following Popular Melodies: No. 1: "Jumbo Jum," "De Ole Jaw Bone," "Tell Me Josey Whar You Bin." No. 2:

"Ole Tare River," "Lucy Long," "Jonny Boker," "Settin on a Rail," "Ole Virginny Never Tire." Boston: H. Prentiss, 1843.

Gems from Donizetti's Celebrated Opera Lucia di Lammermoor. Boston: O. Ditson, 1843.

The May Flower Waltzes, arr. for the piano forte. Boston: Henry Prentiss, 1843.

Old Dan Tucker, Quick Step, as played by the Boston bands, arr. by E. L. White. Boston: O. Ditson, 1843.

The Parlour Quadrilles. Boston: Wm. H. Oakes, c1843.

The Village Quick Step, arr. by Ed. L. White. Boston: O. Ditson, c1843.

The Drawing Room. Quadrilles composed and arranged for the Pianoforte [with dance directions]. Boston: H. Prentiss, 1844.

Three Grand Waltzes composed for Pianoforte. Boston: H. Prentiss, 1844.

Smile On, a Favorite Air. Arranged with an Introduction and Variations for the Pianoforte. Boston: H. Prentiss, n.d. (c1844?)

Oh! Poor Miss Lucy Neale! and Dandy Jim. Arranged as a Quick Step. Boston: O. Ditson, 1844.

The Music Box Waltz. Arranged with Variations. Boston: O. Ditson, c1845.

Love Not. Arranged with Variations. Boston: O. Ditson, 1845.

The Home that I Love. Arranged as a Waltz. Boston: O. Ditson, 1846.

Ancelo Waltz. Arranged for the Pianoforte. Boston: O. Ditson, 1846.

The Cochituate Lake Medley. Introducing the airs "Money Musk," "Minuetto a la Marche," and "Fishers Hornpipe with Variations." Boston: Keith's Music Publishing House, 1846.

Grand Triumphal Quick Step. Dedicated to Gen Zachary Taylor. Boston: O. Ditson, 1847.

Verdi's Quick Step. Arranged from the Opera *Ernani.* Boston: O. Ditson, 1847.

Blockley's Beautiful Melody of Love Not. Arranged as a Quick Step for Pianoforte. Boston: O. Ditson, 1847.

Old Zack's Quick Step. Arranged from . . . Rosa Lee. Boston: O. Ditson, 1848.

The Grand French Republican March. Arranged from the popular national Melodies of "Mourir pour la patrie" and "La Parisienne." Boston: O. Ditson, 1848.

Ordway's Collection of Favorite Airs with Variations.
  1. "My Lodging's in the Cold Ground."
  2. "Assalia Waltz" (4 hands).
  3. "German Air."
  4. "Air from *Lucia de Lammermuir.*"
  5. "I'll Pray for Thee."
  6. "Rosa Lee." Boston: A. & J. P. Ordway, 1848 [issued separately]

Linda Quick Step, into which is introduced the beautiful duet from *Linda di Chamounix.* Boston: O. Ditson, 1848.

Oh! Susanna, with Easy Variations. Boston: O. Ditson, 1848.

Oh! Susanna Quick Step. In which are introduced the favorite airs of Oh! Susanna and Oh! Carry Me Back &c. Boston: O. Ditson, 1848.

California Quick Step. Introducing the popular air of Uncle Ned. Boston: O. Ditson, 1849.

Hauser Polka. Arr. for the piano by E. L. White. Boston: O. Ditson, 1850.

Old Uncle Ned, with Variations. Boston: O. Ditson, c1850.

The New Mary Blane. Arranged as a Quick Step. Boston: O. Ditson, 1850 (also C. C. Clapp).

Ricci's Favorite Waltz, arranged in an Easy Manner. Boston: O. Ditson, c1851.

Miscellaneous

The Boston Piano-Forte Instructor: Being an Abridgement of Czerny's Theoretical and Practical Piano Forte School. Boston: E. Howe, c1845.

Guitar Without a Master. Boston: O. Ditson, 1850.

Organ Without a Master. Boston: O. Ditson, 1851.

Melodeon Without a Master. Boston: O. Ditson, 1853. [reprint of above]

Schneider's Treatise on Thorough Bass [translation of Friedrich Schneider's *Harmonie und Tonsetzkunst*]. Boston: O. Ditson, c1851.

---

[1] John J. Currier, *History of Newburyport, Mass., 1764-1909*, 2 vols. (Newburyport: the author, 1909) 2:48, 314.

[2] Stephen W. Phillips, *Ship Registers of the District of Newburyport, 1789-1870* (Salem, Mass.: Essex Institute, 1937).

[3] "Praise Him With Organs," *Newburyport Evening Herald*, 2 February 1889.

[4] Minnie Atkinson, *A History of the First Religious Society in Newburyport, Massachusetts* (Newburyport: News Publishing Co., 1933), 39.

[5] "Praise Him With Organs," op. cit.

[6] "Advertisement" in *Washington Harmony*, 2nd ed. (Newburyport: T. B. White, 1836).

[7] Frank J. Metcalf, *Stories of Hymn Tunes* (New York: Abingdon Press, 1928), 155.

[8] "Boston Music Teachers Institute," *Boston Musical Gazette* 4/23 (1 July 1850): 181.

[9] Carol Brink, *Harps in the Wind* (New York: Macmillan, 1947), 111.

[10] Harry Dichter and Elliott Shapiro, *Handbook of Early American Sheet Music, 1768-1889* (New York: Dover, 1977), 94.

[11] Advertisement in *Dwight's Journal of Music* 1/11 (19 June 1852): 88.

[12] E. L. White, *Organ Without a Master* (Boston: Oliver Ditson, 1851), 12.

[13] Nathaniel D. Gould, *Church Music in America* (Boston: A. N. Johnson, 1853; reprint, New York: AMS Press, 1972), 68.

THE ANTHEM IN SOUTHERN FOUR-SHAPE SHAPE-NOTE TUNEBOOKS, 1816-1860

David W. Music

In 1933, George Pullen Jackson published the first of his six books on American folk hymnody, *White Spirituals in the Southern Uplands*, thereby calling the attention of the musical world to an unusual aspect of American music.[1] Among Jackson's primary sources were a number of four-shape shape-note (fasola) tunebooks published in the southern United States during the early nineteenth century. These volumes and their contents had hitherto gone virtually unnoticed by musical scholars, and Jackson's discovery came as a revelation to many students of American music. Jackson's pioneering work served to stimulate other researchers to further investigation of these tunebooks, resulting in a number of significant studies of the collections and their contents.[2]

Scholarly interest in these compilations has centered mainly on the folk hymns which, in many ways, represent the most distinctive feature of the books. Folk hymns often make up a large proportion of the collections. Furthermore, these volumes contain many first printings of folk hymns, some of which are still sung regularly today.

However, while folk hymns are perhaps the most notable element of the collections, the books also contain many interesting examples of pieces in other forms. Among these are psalm and hymn tunes, fuging tunes, anthems, and set pieces. None of these forms were original to the southern shape-note tradition; all can ultimately be traced to European (primarily English) models. Nevertheless, such pieces often make up a large proportion of the typical southern tunebook, and southern composers occasionally made original contributions in these genres.

This study is concerned with the anthems published in four-shape shape-note tunebooks originating in the southern United States between 1816 and 1860. The primary purpose of the article is to provide a basic list of the anthem repertory found in these books and to determine, insofar as possible, the sources of these anthems, with particular attention given to southern contributions to the repertory.[3]

For the purposes of this study, the "southern United States" is understood to be those states that later formed the Confederate States of America, plus the bordering states of Kentucky and Missouri, both of which were heavily influenced by the musical practices of their southern and eastern neighbors. This limitation takes into account all the major centers of shape-note tunebook production in the South, particularly Virginia, Tennessee, South Carolina, and Georgia. Tunebooks are considered to have "originated" in the South when they were compiled by residents of one of the states falling into the category described above, though many of the collections were published by northern printing establishments, particularly in Cincinnati, Ohio.[4]

The tunebooks which formed the basis for this study are listed in Table 1. The compiler's state of residence is given in brackets at the end of each entry; in a few instances, a question mark appears after the state name, indicating that the information is not certain but is likely, based on the copyright registration of the collection or other data. An abbreviation is given for each tunebook, which will serve to identify it in Table 2 and the succeeding discussion.

TABLE 1

Southern tunebook compilers seem to have generally understood the term "anthem" in the same way as their northern counterparts of the late eighteenth and early nineteenth centuries, that is, as "a through-composed setting of a prose text from Scripture."[5] In addition to their prose texts, anthems in both the northern and southern tunebooks were generally distinguished from other forms by their larger dimensions and greater musical complexity. Anthems tended to include several imitative (or pseudo-imitative) passages and provided textural variety through various groupings of the voice parts or other techniques.

A form that was closely related to the anthem was the set piece. In northern tunebooks of the late eighteenth and early nineteenth centuries, the set piece was "a through-composed setting of a poetic text of more than one stanza." The set piece was often comparable to the anthem in length, and while it was frequently somewhat simpler in style than the anthem, it could also feature imitation, repetition of text, and other devices typical of the anthem.[6] For convenience—and in keeping with the usual southern practice—the term "anthem" will be used in the following discussion to describe both anthems and set pieces.[7] The anthems on which this study is based are listed in Table 2. The table includes the following information:

1. Textual incipit, listed alphabetically.
2. Title of anthem.
3. Tunebooks from Table 1 which contain the anthem, listed chronologically by date of publication. When a piece appears in more than one edition of a tunebook only the earliest is noted here, unless a later printing gives additional information. Composer attributions are given in parentheses following each tunebook in which they appear; where this information is not given it may be assumed that there is no attribution in the tunebook or that a designation such as "unknown" or "anonymous" was used. Variant titles of anthems are also listed after each tunebook where applicable.
4. Other information, including earlier printings of the piece. No attempt has been made to trace all pieces back to their first appearance but merely to indicate an earlier source in northern or English tunebooks.

TABLE 2

The forty-two anthems listed in Table 2 may be conveniently grouped into four categories by their places of origin. The first group consists of pieces by European (mainly English) composers of the eighteenth century. Group two includes anthems by northern and middle United States composers of the late eighteenth and early nineteenth centuries. Works by nineteenth-century southern composers make up the third category, while the fourth contains a group of pieces of uncertain origin.

Seven anthems listed in Table 2 can be securely identified as being of English origin.[8] These works cover nearly a century of parish church composition, ranging from J. Green's "Behold, the Lord is my salvation," first published about 1715, to W. E. Miller's "Our souls by love," issued about 1805. Nearly half of the pieces date from the decade 1760-70.

Perhaps the most influential name associated with the list of English anthems—at lease in terms of the pieces encountered in southern United States fasola tunebooks—is Martin Madan. His popular anthem, "Before Jehovah's awful throne," was the most often printed English work, appearing in nine different fasola tunebooks. Furthermore, as noted in Table 2, Samuel Arnold's "Our Lord is risen from the dead" received its first publication in Madan's "Lock Hospital" collection (1769).

Earlier scholars have demonstrated the importance of English parish anthems in the development of the eighteenth-century "Yankee tunesmith" school of composers.[9] However, by the time the southern fasola collections began to be published, the English model was well established on American shores and an indigenous school of American composers had been created. Southern compilers probably had limited access to English publications, and such English pieces as they saw fit to print were probably derived mainly from reprints in northern tunebooks.

Thus, it is not surprising that English anthems exercised relatively little direct influence on the southern fasola tunebooks. English pieces made up less than seventeen percent of the total number of anthems found in the collections. Furthermore, four of the seven English pieces were printed in but a single tunebook each. Only Madan's "Before Jehovah's awful throne," Harwood's "Vital spark" (DYING CHRISTIAN), and the arrangement of the latter piece by Andrew Law (NEW YORK ANTHEM) achieved multiple printings. And, while the most popular English anthem, "Before Jehovah's awful throne," appeared in over one-fifth of the tunebooks listed in Table 1, it managed only a tie for tenth place among the anthems printed most often in southern fasola tunebooks before the Civil War.

Much more significant in the southern shape-note repertory were anthems written by northern composers of the late eighteenth and early nineteenth centuries. Twenty works—nearly forty-eight percent of the total number—listed in Table 2 can be traced to northern composers or sources.

The northern repertory provided not only the largest number of individual anthems to the southern fasola collections but also the most often printed examples of the form. The popularity of the "Yankee tunesmiths" of the late eighteenth century is of particular interest. Southern compilers demonstrated a marked preference for the works of William Billings, whose "The Lord is risen indeed" (19 printings) and "David the king was grieved" (16 printings) were the two most popular anthems in the four-shape tunebooks. Two other anthems by Billings, "I heard a great voice" (12 printings) and "I am the Rose of Sharon" (11 printings) likewise held important places in the repertory.[10]

The other anthems by northerners that achieved ten or more printings included Jacob French's "I beheld and lo a great multitude" (13) and "My friends, I am going" (10), Justin Morgan's "Hark, ye mortals, hear the trumpet" (11), Jezaniah Sumner's "The morning sun shines from the east" (11), and S. Temple's "Vital spark" (CLAREMONT, 10). The anthems by Billings, French, and Morgan all date from the eighteenth century, while those by the little-known Sumner and Temple were published in the early nineteenth century.

The anthem repertory of the southern fasola tunebooks supports the general impression that the music of the eighteenth-century New England singing-school composers continued to be popular in the South long after it had fallen out of favor in the North. Despite the growing sectionalism that was ultimately to lead to the Civil War, southerners seemingly sang these pieces with relish; many of the singers were probably unaware of their "Yankee" origins. Furthermore, the popular anthems of the Yankee tunesmiths undoubtedly served as models for the anthems of southern composers.

It should be pointed out that after the nine popular northern anthems listed above have been accounted for, the number of anthem publications by northern composers falls off dramatically. Among the remaining eleven northern anthems, only three achieved more than a single printing in the southern tunebooks.[11] Northern anthems received a total of 130 printings in southern fasola tunebooks; the nine anthems that were printed ten or more times each accounted for 113—nearly eighty-seven percent—of these.

It should be further noted that, despite the popularity of pieces by the Yankee tunesmiths in southern shape-note collections, a few anthems by the reformers and "respectable" composers of the early nineteenth century also appeared in some of the southern tunebooks. Lowell Mason, usually seen as the virtual antithesis of both the Yankee tunesmith and southern folk hymn traditions, was represented by one anthem, "Oh praise God in his holiness." Also leaning toward the "respectable" end of the spectrum were John Cole's "O be joyful in the Lord" and C. Meinecke's "O praise the Lord in that blest place." The inclusion of these pieces shows that southern four-shape compilers were not unaware of the more recent trends in anthem composition in the northern states.

The third category of anthems, those written by southern composers, is perhaps the most significant one, for it represents the original contributions of southerners to the anthem repertory. Six anthems can be confidently ascribed to composers whose works appeared for the first time in one of the southern fasola tunebooks. In every case, the composer was connected in some way with the compiling or publication of the book in which the anthem first appeared.

It should come as no surprise that the southern composers generally seem to have approached the writing of an anthem in much the same way they did a folk hymn setting. As in the folk hymns, the principal melody usually appears in the tenor. This melody often has the earmarks of a folk melody or centonization of traditional tunes. The harmonizations are similar to those of the folk hymns, abounding in open fifths, parallel fifths and octaves, brief unison passages between two or more voices, and 6/4 chords at important internal cadence points.[12]

Ananias Davisson's "That awful day will surely come" was both the earliest and the most often printed anthem by a southerner, appearing initially in the first edition of the composer's *Kentucky Harmony* (1816) and subsequently in eight Virginia, Missouri, Tennessee, and South Carolina tunebooks. However, except for its publication in Davisson's own tunebook, the anthem was invariably printed anonymously. Thus, many compilers and singing-school participants may not have been aware of its southern origin.

The lugubrious text of "That awful day will surely come" consists of five stanzas from a hymn by Isaac Watts. Davisson presents the text in a straightforward manner, with no repetition of words or phrases, except for an indicated repeat of the entire last stanza. The anthem contains no changes of meter or key signature, nor did the composer incorporate any fuging sections into his anthem.

Nevertheless, Davisson was obviously aware of the need for varying the texture of the music in a long piece, achieving this by contrasting duets and trios with the full four-part ensemble. The opening stanza of the text is set for four voices. The first half of stanza two begins as a duet for treble and counter voices, changing to treble and tenor for the second half of the stanza. Stanza three likewise starts with a duet, this time for counter and bass, ending with a trio of treble, tenor, and bass. This trio also sings the opening phrase of the fourth stanza; the second line is sung by the full four-part ensemble, which has not been heard since the beginning of the piece. After another counter/bass duet, the four-part ensemble returns to conclude the fourth stanza and sing the entire fifth stanza.

"That awful day will surely come" also illustrates Davisson's seeming predilection for the aeolian mode on A as well as his limited modulatory range—important cadences are all on A, C, or E.[13] There is not a single accidental in the piece, but it should be noted that this was typical of the *Kentucky Harmony* as a whole and "may or may not have reflected the actual practice of the time and place."[14] At any rate, subsequent compilers continued to exclude accidentals from their reprintings of the piece.

The first edition of B. F. White and E. J. King's *Sacred Harp* (1844) contained two anthems, one each by the two principal compilers. Two more anthems, both by White, were added in the 1850 edition. These four pieces continued to appear in subsequent editions of the book, but no new southern anthems were added to the repertory of the *Sacred Harp* before the Civil War.

E. J. King's "Give unto the Lord" is a setting of the King James version of Psalm 96:8-11, 13 but with many omissions from the basic text. The dimensions of the piece are slight, covering only forty-one measures. The music calls for three parts, counter, tenor, and bass, with "choosing notes" on the last chord.

Like Davisson's "That awful day will surely come," King's anthem repeats the last section of text. There is also a brief repetition of the phrase "for he cometh." Another similarity to Davisson's piece is that "Give unto the Lord" does not use fuging technique but relies upon the contrast between brief solo passages, duets, and the full ensemble for textural variety.

Unlike Davisson, however, and despite the shortness of the piece, King incorporated three meter changes, making use of the signatures 6/4, 4/4 (twice), and 2/4. The 6/4 tenor melody that opens the anthem is lyrical, while the 4/4 section is more march-like; the 2/4 passage is marked "Lively." The return to 4/4 for the final two measures probably indicates a *ritard*, an effect which is heightened by the longer note values of these measures. One dynamic indication is given, a "Soft" over the phrase "fear before him, all the earth."

The three anthems by B. F. White represent the largest number of such pieces by a single southern composer. The texts were chosen from a variety of sources. The words of "In those days came John the Baptist" were taken from the King James version of Matthew 3:1-4, with only minor changes. "The Lord spoke unto Moses" is based on selected verses from Exodus 13-15, but these are subjected to considerable alteration and paraphrase; there are also interpolations from other scriptures. Indeed, the text is so loosely tied to the scripture passages that it may almost be considered an original one, probably the work of White himself. "My friends come listen awhile" is a setting of an anonymous prose text, which again was probably by White. Each of the anthems calls for three voice parts.

"In those days came John the Baptist" is the shortest (38 mm.) and simplest of White's anthems. There are no meter or key changes, no fuging sections, and only one brief textual repetition, an echo effect at the words "and saying." This last passage is also the only section of the anthem which calls for fewer than three voices, the texture being otherwise monochromatic. The phrases are short breathed and almost invariably separated by rests. This characteristic, plus the tendency toward cadences on the tonic, gives the work a somewhat choppy effect. The tenor melody begins in an attractive, robust manner but soon becomes stagnant through over-repetition.[15]

In contrast to "In those days came John the Baptist," "The Lord spoke unto Moses" is lengthy (115 mm.) and more varied in technique, employing several different meters (4/4, 2/4, and 6/4), a brief fuging section ("and when he had let them go"), and a short bass solo ("and Pharaoh the king attempted to pursue"). The first 2/4 section is marked "Vivace" and—in the middle of this section—the designation "Piano" occurs. "The Lord spoke unto Moses" is similar to "In those days came John the Baptist" in its use of short phrases separated by rests, as well as its dogged insistence upon cadences on the tonic chord. The tenor melody likewise contains thinly veiled references to earlier material.[16]

"My friends come listen awhile" is of moderate length (65 mm.) and employs many of the same techniques found in "The Lord spoke unto Moses," including two fuging sections and a variety of meters (4/4, 6/8, and 2/4). "My friends come listen awhile" incorporates one feature not found in any of the other southern anthems, a rudimentary modulation from A minor (aeolian) to A major. The purpose of the modulation is unclear, there being no apparent textual reason for using this device. There is also a modest tendency toward longer phrases in certain sections of the anthem as well as occasional cadences on chords other than the tonic. The folk idiom in which White usually worked is evident from the last ten measures of the tenor part, which are strongly reminiscent of "Go tell Aunt Rhody."

In general, White's anthems, though not without their attractive features, reveal his limitations as a composer in the larger form. The attractive melodies which begin each of these anthems soon break down into mere repetitions of the same idea, and there seems to be no overall formal plan for the works. Without a folk melody to guide him, he appears to have been uncertain how to proceed, unable to sustain the forward motion of the music and shape it into a coherent and satisfying whole.

The anthems by White and King appeared too late in the "classic" period of southern fasola tunebook production to exercise much influence on other collections. The two anthems published in the 1844 edition of the *Sacred Harp* achieved currency only in tunebooks associated with the state of Georgia, William Hauser's *Hesperian Harp* (1848) and John G. McCurry's *Social Harp* (1855). The new anthems in the 1850 printing of the *Sacred Harp* do not appear to have been used outside subsequent editions of this book.

The last of the six anthems of certain southern origin, "The breaking waves dashed," received its first—and only—known printing in the second edition of J. W. Steffey's *Valley Harmonist* (1845). This work appears to have been a group project, for the words were attributed to a "Mrs. Hemans," the "air" to her sister, "Miss Browne," and the composition and arrangement of the other parts to "H. T. Wartmann." Nothing is known of Mrs. Hemans or Miss Browne, but from the subject matter of the text (the landing of the Pilgrims in the New World), it is safe to say that they were Americans. H. T. Wartmann was the Harrisonburg, Virginia, publisher who issued Steffey's book; it is likely that Mrs. Hemans and Miss Browne were also southerners.

"The breaking waves dashed" contains no meter or key signature changes and no fuging sections but does include several brief solo and duet passages. Wartmann displayed a dramatic bent by setting a number of phrases for unison voices. The harmony is much more conventional than in the other examples of southern anthems discussed above. Certainly, there are still many open fifths and parallelisms, but the harmonic system is that of the tonal, rather than the modal, system. The piece does not seem to have appeared in any subsequent southern collection.

Why did southern composers make so few contributions to the anthem repertory, especially since many of them were not hesitant to "compose" and arrange new psalm and hymn tunes based on folk hymnody? Three possible answers may be suggested.

First, the anthem itself probably had limited usefulness among southern singers. Most of the fasola tunebooks seem to have been compiled with a dual purpose in mind: to serve as a textbook for singing schools and to be a repository of pieces for use in church. It is the nature of instruction in any subject to move from the short and simple to the long and complex. Developing the skill to successfully sing an anthem like Billings' "The Lord is risen indeed" or "I am the Rose of Sharon" may have been the ultimate goal of a singing school, but it is difficult to imagine that such pieces would be attempted until most of the (easier) psalm, hymn, and fuging tunes had been mastered. Indeed, some singing schools might never have reached that last section of the tunebook. Furthermore, there is little evidence that any of the southern tunebooks ever achieved widespread usage in the church service; even if they had, choirs capable of singing anthems were rather scarce in antebellum southern churches. Thus, anthems were not very "practical" from the standpoint of a southern composer.

Second, the southern four-shape tunebook compilers inherited a rather large body of ready-made material from both English and northern United States composers. Southerners published approximately thirty different English or northern anthems.[17] This number was far more than could be practically included in one tunebook, and yet it was only a small fraction of the hundreds of anthems from these two sources that were available to southern compilers in the early nineteenth century. There was little need for southern composers to add to a repertory that already had ample material.

Finally, the skill level of many southern composers may not have been up to the writing of large works. B. F. White's difficulties with the form have been noted. It was probably a relatively easy matter for a southern composer to transcribe a folk melody—or to centonize a new tune from elements of traditional ones—and harmonize it, though some were obviously more adept at this than others. However, it was quite another thing to set an extended poem or prose passage without reference to a pre-existent melody, and with the added challenge of maintaining musical interest through textural, metrical, and tonal/modal variety, as well as expressing the changing moods of a long text. The southern composers themselves probably realized their own limitations in dealing with a lengthy form, concentrating instead on what was to become their major contribution, the preservation of folk hymns.

The last group of anthems to be considered consists of works whose precise origins are uncertain. Nine pieces from Table 2 fall into this category.

Four of these anthems appear in American tunebooks with attributions to European composers: "And I saw a mighty angel" ("Guiardini"—probably Felice de Giardini), "Grateful notes and numbers bring" (Madan), "Jesus shall reign where'er the sun" (Handel), and "Strike the cymbal" (Pucitta). While there appears to be little reason to question these attributions, none of the pieces have been located in earlier European sources. The pieces ascribed to Giardini, Handel, and Pucitta are almost certainly arrangements from other works, but whether the arrangements were made by Europeans or Americans is not known. The version of "Grateful notes and numbers bring" found in Gillet's *Virginia Sacred Minstrel* was evidently the work of the American Benjamin Carr; the piece had previously been published in America in another—presumably the original—version.

No attribution has been discovered for "Lord, dismiss us with thy blessing" in either its only known southern printing or in northern tunebooks, nor has the work been found in a European source. The piece is probably of English or northern United States origin.

The remaining four anthems are almost certainly of American origin, and some or all of them may very well be by southern composers. The earliest known printings of three of these pieces, "At this unwanted hour," "Behold the changes of the skies," and "Behold the wretch whose lust and wine" (Josiah Moore) occurred in the publications of Ananias Davisson. The text of "Behold the changes of the skies" is attributed to the American Timothy Dwight (1752-1817), suggesting that its composer was probably also an American. The musical style of the three works does not rule out a southern origin. However, the lack of any information about Josiah Moore, the absence of composers' names for the other two pieces, and the possibility that earlier printings might turn up in as yet unexamined European or northern tunebooks suggest that caution is in order in specifying their place of origin.

The only known printing of "Oh how charming" was in the *Sacred Harp* (1844). The folk-like tenor melody, three-part setting, use of meter changes in a short (30 mm.) piece, and harmonic scheme are reminiscent of E. J. King's "Give unto the Lord." This is not to imply that "Oh how charming" was necessarily written by King but to point out that it reflects the stylistic practice of southern composers. Again, the absence of a composer's name leads to circumspection.[18]

The southern four-shape tunebooks will rightly continue to be prized mainly for the corpus of folk hymns which they have preserved for posterity. Nevertheless, these books also contain numerous examples of interesting and significant music in other forms which are worthy of the attention of both scholars and performers. It is hoped that this introductory study will stimulate further investigation into this interesting bit of Americana.[19]

TABLE 1
TUNEBOOKS USED IN THE STUDY

Compiler	Title	Place & Date of Publication	State of Compiler's Residence	Abbreviation
Boyd, James M.	*The Virginia Sacred Musical Repository*	Winchester, 1818	Virginia	VSMR
Caldwell, William	*Union Harmony*	Maryville, 1837	Tennessee	UH
Carden, Allen D.	*The Missouri Harmony*	Cincinnati, 1820; other eds.: 1825, 1835, 1836, 1837, 1838, 1850, 1857	Tennessee	MOH
Carden, Allen D.	*United States Harmony*	Nashville, 1829	Tennessee	USH
Carden, Allen D.; S. J. Rogers, F. Moore, and J. Green	*The Western Harmony*	Nashville, 1824	Tennessee	WES
Clayton, David L. and James P. Carrell	*The Virginia Harmony*	Winchester, 1831; another ed.: 1836	Virginia	VAH
Davisson, Ananias	*Kentucky Harmony*	Harrisonburg, 1816; other eds.: 1817, 1826	Virginia	KYH
Davisson, Ananias	*A Small Collection of Sacred Music*	Mount Vernon, 1825	Virginia	SC
Davisson, Ananias	*A Supplement to the Kentucky Harmony*	Harrisonburg, 1820; another ed.: 1826	Virginia	SKH
Funk, Joseph	*Die allgemein nuetzlich Choral-Music*	Harrisonburg, 1816	Virginia	CM
Funk, Joseph	*A Compilation of Genuine Church Music*, 2nd ed	Winchester, 1835; another ed.: 1842	Virginia	GCM
Gillet, W.	*The Virginia Sacred Minstrel*	Winchester, 1817	Virginia	VSM
Henrickson, George	*The Union Harmony*	Mountain Valley, VA, 1848	Virginia	HUH
Hauser, William	*The Hesperian Harp*	Philadelphia, 1848	Georgia	HES

Compiler	Title	Place & Date of Publication	State of Compiler's Residence	Abbreviation
Jackson, John B.	*The Knoxville Harmony*	Madisonville, 1838	Tennessee	KNH
Johnson, Alexander	*Johnson's Tennessee Harmony*	Cincinnati, 1818; other eds.: 1821, 1824	Tennessee	TH
Johnson, Andrew W.	*The American Harmony*, 2nd ed.	Nashville, 1839	Tennessee	AMH
McCollum, J. D. and J. P. Campbell	*The Cumberland Harmony*, 2nd ed.	Nashville, 1834	Tennessee?	CUH
McCurry, John G.	*The Social Harp*	Philadelphia, 1855	Georgia	SOC
Metcalf, Samuel	*The Kentucky Harmonist*	Cincinnati, 1826	Kentucky	MKH
Moore, William	*Columbian Harmony*	Cincinnati, 1825	Tennessee?	COH
Seat, John B.	*The St. Louis Harmony*	Cincinnati, 1831	Tennessee?	STH
Shaw, Benjamin and Charles H. Spilman	*Columbian Harmony*	Cincinnati, 1839	Kentucky?	SCO
Steffey, J. W.	*The Valley Harmonist*, 2nd ed.	Harrisonburg, 1845	Virginia	VH
Walker, William	*The Southern and Western Pocket Harmonist*	Philadelphia, 1846	South Carolina	SWP
Walker, William	*The Southern Harmony*	Philadelphia, 1847; another ed.: 1854	South Carolina	SOH
White, B. F. and E. J. King	*The Sacred Harp*	Philadelphia, 1844; another ed.: 1860	Georgia	SAH

TABLE 2
ANTHEMS FOUND IN SOUTHERN FOUR-SHAPE TUNEBOOKS

Text Incipit	Title	Printings in Southern Four-Shape Tunebooks	Earlier printings and other information
"And I saw a mighty angel"	ANTHEM FROM REVELATIONS 5TH. CH.	SKH26 ("Guiardini")	Jacob French, *Psalmodist's Companion* (1793)
"At this unwanted hour"	AN ODE FOR CHRISTMAS	SKH26	
"Before Jehovah's awful throne"	DENMARK	KYH16 ("Madan"); VSMR18; MOH20; WES24; COH25 ("Madan"); USH29 ("Madan"); SCO29; VAH31 ("Dr. Madan"); GCM42	By Martin Madan, English composer; 1st pr: Madan, *Collection of Psalm and Hymn Tunes*, 1769 (Crawford, *Law*, p. [349]).
"Behold I bring you glad tidings"	ANTHEM FROM LUKE	KYH16 ("Stephenson")	By Joseph Stephenson, English composer; 1st pr.: Stephenson, *Church Harmony*, 3rd ed, 1760 (Temperley, p. 191).
"Behold the changes of the skies"	THE SEASONS MORALIZED	SKH26	The text of this set piece is by Timothy Dwight (1752-1817); thus, the music is probably of American origin.
"Behold the Lord is my salvation"	ANTHEM, ISAIAH, CHAP. 12	VSM17	By John or James Green, English composer; 1st pr. J. Green, *Collection of Choice Psalm Tunes*, 3rd ed, 1715 (Temperley, p. 166).

Text Incipit	Title	Printings in Southern Four-Shape Tunebooks	Earlier printings and other information
"Behold the wretch whose lust and wine"	PRODIGAL SON	KYH16 ("Josiah Moore"); MOH20; COH25 ("Josiah Moore"); HES48	
"David the king was grieved"	DAVID'S LAMENTATION	KYH16 ("W. Billings"); TH18 ("Billings"); VSMR18; MOH20; WES24 ("Billings"); COH25 ("W. Billings"); USH29 ("Billings"); STL31; UH37 ("W. Billings"); KNH38; AMH39; SAH44 ("Billings"); SOH47 ("Billings"); HES48; HUH48; SOC55 ("Billings")	By William Billings, northern composer; 1st pr: Billings, *Singing-Master's Assistant*, 1778 (Barbour, p. 147).
"Farewell, a sad, a long farewell"	FUNERAL DIRGE	VSM17 ("Holyoke")	By Samuel Holyoke, northern composer; Holyoke, *Harmonia Americana*, 1791.
"Give unto the Lord the glory due"	REVERENTIAL ANTHEM	SAH44 ("E. J. King"); HES48 ("E. J. King")	By E. J. King, southern composer; 1st pr.: SAH44.

The Anthem in Southern Four-Shape Shape-Note Tunebooks 163

Text Incipit	Title	Printings in Southern Four-Shape Tunebooks	Earlier printings and other information
"Grateful notes and numbers bring"	GRATEFUL NOTES	VSM17	Oliver Holden, *Worcester Collection*, 6th ed., 1797 (MAGDALENE ODE; "Madan"; 1st line of text: "Grateful notes of numbers bring". This piece does not appear in Madan, "Lock Hospital"); the printing in VSM17 differs in a number of respects from that of Holden's collection; the version in VSM17 appeared in Benjamin Carr, *Masses, Vespers, Litanies*, 1805 (GRATEFUL NOTES, no attr.)
"Hark hark glad tidings charm our ears"	REDEMPTION ANTHEM	KYH16 (KYH17: "Stephenson"); COH25 ("Stephenson"); SOH47 (REDEMPTION; "A. Benham"; an abridgement of the set piece as found in KYH and COH)	Asahel Benham, *Social Harmony*, 1798 (REDEMPTION).
"Hark ye mortals hear the trumpet"	JUDGMENT ANTHEM	KYH16 ("Morgan"); VSMR18; MOH20; WES24; COH25 ("Morgan"); SCO29; UH37 ("Mr. Morgan"); KHY38; GCM42App; SOH47 ("Morgan"); HES48	By Justin Morgan, northern composer; 1st pr.: Asahel Benham, *Federal Harmony*, 1790 (Daniel, p. 127).
"I am the rose of Sharon"	ROSE OF SHARON	KYH16 ("W. Billings"); MOH20; WES24 ("Billings"); COH25; USH29 ("Billings"); GCM42App; SAH44 ("Billings"); VH45; SOH47 ("Billings"); HES48 ("Billings"); SOC55 ("Billings")	By William Billings, northern composer; 1st pr.: Billings, *Singing-Master's Assistant*, 1778 (Barbour, p. 147).

Text Incipit	Title	Printings in Southern Four-Shape Tunebooks	Earlier printings and other information
"I beheld and lo a great multitude"	HEAVENLY VISION	KYH16 ("French"); TH18 ("French"); MOH20; COH25 ("French"); SCO29; VAH31 ("French"); CUH34; KNH38; GCM42; SAH44 ("Billings"); VH45; SOH47 ("Billings"); HES48 ("French")	By Jacob French, northern composer; 1st pr.: *Worcester Collection*, 1786 (Daniel, p. 122).
"I heard a great voice"	FUNERAL ANTHEM	KYH16 (KYH17: "W. Billings"); MOH20; WES24 ("Billings"); COH25 ("W. Billings"); USH29 ("Billings"); SCO29; STL31; VAH31 ("W. Billings"); CUH34; SOH47 ("Billings"); HES48 ("Billings"); SOC55 ("Billings")	By William Billings; 1st pr.: Billings, *Singing Master's Assistant*, 1778 (Barbour, p. 148).
"In those days came John the Baptist"	BAPTISMAL ANTHEM	SAH44 ("B. F. White"); HES48 (JOHN THE BAPTIST; "B. F. White"); SOC55 ("B. F. White")	By B. F. White, southern composer; 1st pr.: SAH44.
"Jesus our triumphant head"	ASCENSION ANTHEM	COH25; GCM35 (ASCENSION)	*Worcester Collection*, 1788, (ASCENSION, "Wood")
"Jesus shall reign where'er the sun"	JOHN-STREET, OR, 148TH PSALM	GCM42	*Methodist Harmonist*, New York, 1829 ("Handel")
"Lord dismiss us with thy blessing"	DISMISSION ANTHEM	GCM42App	Samuel Dyer, *Dyer's Third Edition*, [1835] (DISMISSION)
"My drowsy powers why"	ANIMATION	SKH20 (SKH26: "Sherman")	Daniel L. Peck, *Valuable Selection of Sacred Music*, 1810.
"My friends come listen"	ANTHEM ON THE SAVIOUR	SAH50 ("B. F. White")	By B. F. White, southern composer; 1st pr.: SAH50.

The Anthem in Southern Four-Shape Shape-Note Tunebooks 165

Text Incipit	Title	Printings in Southern Four-Shape Tunebooks	Earlier printings and other information
"My friends I am going a long"	FAREWELL ANTHEM	KYH16 ("French"); WES24, COH25 ("Billings"); USH27; STL31; KNH38; SAH44; SOH47, HUH48, HES48 ("French")	By Jacob French, northern composer; 1st pr: French, *New American Melody*, 1789 (Britton/Lowens/ Crawford, p. 209).
"My God my king thy various praise"	RONDEAU	VSM17 ("T. Olmsted")	By T. Olmsted, northern composer; 1st pr: Olmsted, *Musical Olio*, 1805 (Britton/Lowens/ Crawford, p. 482).
"No I'll repine"	RESURRECTION	USH29 ("Ely")	By Seth Ely, northern composer; S. Ely, *Sacred Music* (Cincinnati, 1822).
"O be joyful in the Lord"	ANTHEM FROM PSALM 100TH	VSM17 ("J. Cole")	John Cole, *Devotional Harmony*, [1814].
"Oh how charming"	CHRISTMAS ANTHEM	SAH44	
"Oh praise God in his holiness"	ANTHEM OF PRAISE	HES48	By Lowell Mason, northern composer; Mason, *Boston Handel and Haydn Society Collection*, 1832.
"O praise the Lord in that blest place"	ANTHEM	MOH35 ("C. Meinecke")	By Ch[ristopher?] Meinecke, northern composer; Samuel Dyer, *Dyer's Third Edition*, [1835] (according to this source, Meinecke's "O praise the Lord" was composed "about 1807").

Text Incipit	Title	Printings in Southern Four-Shape Tunebooks	Earlier printings and other information
"Our Lord is risen"	CHESHUNT	MOH20	By Samuel Arnold, English composer; 1st pr.: Martin Madan, *Collection of Psalm and Hymn Tunes*, 1769 (Crawford, *Law*, p. [347]).
"Our souls by love"	WASHINGTON	MOH35	By W. E. Miller, English composer; Edward Miller and W. E. Miller, *David's Harp*, London, ca. 1805 (THE PARTING; "W. E. Miller").
"Sacred to heaven"	MASONIC ODE	MOH20; STL31; SAH44 ("Treble by E. J. King"); SOC55 ("Treble by E. J. King")	Daniel Belknap, *Village Compilation of Sacred Music*, 1806 (A VIEW OF THE TEMPLE--A MASONIC ODE; "Belknap").
"Strike the cymbal sound the timbal"	STRIKE THE CYMBAL	SCO29	*Templi Carmina. Songs of the Temple, or Bridgewater Collection*, Boston, 1828 ("Pucitta").
"That awful day will surely come"	THE LOVER'S LAMENTATION	KYH16 ("A. Davisson"); VSMR18; MOH20; COH25; STL31; UH37; KNH38; AMH39; SOH47	By Ananias Davisson, southern composer; 1st pr.: KYH16.

Text Incipit	Title	Printings in Southern Four-Shape Tunebooks	Earlier printings and other information
"The breaking waves dashed"	PILGRIM FATHERS	VH45 ("Air by . . . Miss Browne, parts composed and arranged by H. T. Wartmann").	
"The Lord is risen indeed"	EASTER ANTHEM	KYH16 ("W. Billings"); TH18 ("Billings"); MOH20; WES24 ("Billings"); COH25 ("Billings"); SC25; USH29 ("Billings"); SCO29; STL31; VAH31; CUH34; GCM35; UH37; KNH38; SAH44 ("Billings"); VH45; SOH47 ("Billings"); HES48 ("Billings"); SOC55 ("Billings")	By William Billings, northern composer; 1st pr.: Billings, "Anthem for Easter," 1787 (Crawford, *Core*, p. xxiv).
"The Lord spoke unto Moses"	RED SEA ANTHEM	SAH50 ("B. F. White")	By B. F. White, southern composer; 1st pr.: SAH50.
"The morning sun shines from the east"	ODE ON SCIENCE	KYH16 (KYH17: "Mr. Sumner"); TH18 ("Sumner"); MOH20; COH25; SCO29; STL31; KNH38; SAH44; SOH47; HUH48; HES48	Jeremiah Ingalls, *Christian Harmony*, 1805 (ODE TO SCIENCE).
"Vital spark of heavenly flame"	CLAREMONT	KYH17: TH18 ("Temple"); VSMR18; MOH20; COH25; UH37; KNH38; SAH44; SOH47; HES48	John Wyeth, *Repository*, 1810 ("Temple & M.").

Text Incipit	Title	Printings in Southern Four-Shape Tunebooks	Earlier printings and other information
"Vital spark of heavenly flame"	DYING CHRISTIAN	SKH26 ("Billings")	By William Billings, northern composer; 1st pr.: Billings, *Psalm-Singer's Amusement*, 1781 (Barbour, p. 150). Not the same piece as the next entry in this listing.
"Vital spark of heavenly flame"	DYING CHRISTIAN	VSM17; WES24 ("Barton"); VAH31 ("Harwood"); VH45	By Edward Harwood, English composer; 1st pr.: Harwood, *Set of Hymns and Psalm Tunes*, ca. 1770 (Crawford, *Core*, p. xxxiv). The next entry in this listing, NEW YORK ANTHEM, is an arrangement of Harwood's DYING CHRISTIAN by Andrew Law.
"Vital spark of heavenly flame"	NEW YORK ANTHEM	MOH20; KYH26 ("Billing" [sic]); SCO29	By Edward Harwood, English composer, arranged by Andrew Law, American compiler; 1st pr. of this arrangement: Law, *Rudiments of Music*, 2nd ed., 1786 (Crawford, *Core*, p. xxxiv). For information on first printing of the original form see the previous entry in this listing.

Note: Bibliographical abbreviations of secondary literature refer to the following works.

"Barbour" = J. Murray Barbour, *The Church Music of William Billings* (East Lansing: Michigan State Unviersity Press, 1960).

"Britton/Lowens/Crawford" = Allen Perdue Britton, Irving Lowens, and Richard Crawford, *American Sacred Music Imprints 1698-1810: A Bibliography* (Worcester: American Antiquarian Society, 1990).

"Crawford, *Core*" = Richard A. Crawford, ed., *The Core Repertory of Early American Psalmody* (Madison: A-R Editions, Inc., 1984).

"Crawford, *Law*" = Richard A. Crawford, *Andrew Law, American Psalmodist* (Evanston: Northwestern University Press, 1968).

"Daniel" = Ralph T. Daniel, *The Anthem in New England before 1800* (Evanston: Northwestern University Press, 1966).

"Temperley" = Nicholas Temperley, *The Music of the English Parish Church* (Cambridge: Cambridge University Press, 1979), vol. 1.

[1] George Pullen Jackson, *White Spirituals in the Southern Uplands* (Chapel Hill: University of North Carolina Press, 1933; reprint, Hatboro, PA.: Folklore Associates, 1964); *Spiritual Folk Songs of Early America* (New York: J. J. Augustin, 1937); *Down-east Spirituals and Others* (New York: J. J. Augustin, 1943); *White and Negro Spirituals* (New York: J. J. Augustin, 1943); *The Story of the Sacred Harp, 1844-1944* (Nashville: Vanderbilt University Press, 1944); and *Another Sheaf of White Spirituals* (Gainesville: University of Florida Press, 1952).

[2] To mention only books and dissertations, the following are especially useful: Harry Lee Eskew, "Shape-Note Hymnody in the Shenandoah Valley, 1816-1860" (Ph.D diss., Tulane University, 1966); Charles Linwood Ellington, "The Sacred Harp Tradition of the South: Its Origin and Evolution" (Ph.D. diss., Florida State University at Tallahassee, 1969); Dorothy D. Horn, *Sing to Me of Heaven: A Study of Folk and Early American Materials in Three Old Harp Books* (Gainesville: University of Florida Press, 1970); Ernst C. Krohn, *Missouri Music* (St. Louis, 1924; reprint, New York: Da Capo Press, 1971); James William Scholten, "The Chapins: A Study of Men and Sacred Music West of the Alleghenies, 1795-1842" (Ed.D. diss., University of Michigan, 1972); Rachel Augusta Brett Harley, "Ananias Davisson: Southern Tune-Book Compiler (1780-1857)" (Ph.D. diss., University of Michigan, 1972); David Lee Crouse, "The Work of Allen D. Carden and Associates in the Shape-Note Tune-Books, "*The Missouri Harmony, Western Harmony* and *United States Harmony*" (D.M.A. diss., Southern Baptist Theological Seminary, 1972); Shirley Ann Bean, "*The Missouri Harmony*, 1820-1858: The Refinement of a Southern Tunebook" (D.M.A. diss., University of Missouri-Kansas City, 1973); Richard J. Stanislaw, "Choral Performance Practice in the Four-Shape Literature of American Frontier Singing Schools" (D.M.A. diss., University of Illinois, 1976); Richard J. Stanislaw, *A Checklist of Four-Shape Shape-Note Tunebooks* (New York: Brooklyn College, Institute for Studies in American Music, 1978); Buell E. Cobb, Jr., *The Sacred Harp: A Tradition and Its Music* (Athens: The University of Georgia Press, 1978).

[3] Very little research has previously been done on this subject, and the present article is in the nature of a preliminary report. It is hoped that this article will stimulate additional study of this genre, as well as others found in the shape-note tunebooks.

[4] A special case is presented by Allen D. Carden's *Missouri Harmony* (1820). Carden was a resident of Tennessee, but is known to have held singing schools in St. Louis, and his *Missouri Harmony* was undoubtedly compiled with a view to its use in these schools. Carden evidently sold or

traded his interest in *Missouri Harmony* after the first edition, and subsequently had little or no influence on the contents of the book (see Bean, "*The Missouri Harmony*, 1820-1858," 68-70). While the contents changed little through the 1834 eighth edition, a supplement of a more urban character "by an amateur" was added to the ninth (1835) and subsequent editions. It is not certain who compiled the supplement — Timothy A. M. Flint, compiler of *The Columbian Harmonist* (Cincinnati, 1816), has been suggested as a possibility (see Stanislaw, *A Checklist of Four-Shape Shape-Note Tunebooks*, 3) — and it may be that by this time *Missouri Harmony* was no longer a "southern" tunebook. However, for the purposes of this study, these later editions will continue to be regarded as southern in origin.

[5] Richard A. Crawford, *Andrew Law, American Psalmodist* (Evanston: Northwestern University Press, 1968; reprint, New York: Da Capo Press, 1981), 14. See also Ralph T. Daniel, *The Anthem in New England before 1800* (Evanston: Northwestern University Press, 1966; reprint, New York: Da Capo Press, 1979), x.

[6] Crawford, *Andrew Law*, 15.

[7] It should be noted that not every composition that sets more than one stanza of a poetic text will be considered in the present study, but only those that represent the longer examples of the genre. Opinions on what represents an "extended setting" of a poetic text will vary, and the inclusion or exclusion of some pieces may be open to debate. In general, when there is a question about an individual piece it is included here. Thus, the following guidelines have been used to determine what constitutes an anthem: (1) the word "anthem" appears in the title of the piece, (2) the music is a setting of a prose text, and (3) the music is an extended, through-composed setting of a metrical text.

[8] All numbers of anthems and percentages given in this study must be considered tentative, due to the presence of the pieces of uncertain origin (discussed below) and the possibility that other anthems may be located in southern fasola collections not examined by the present writer. However, even if a few adjustments should prove to be necessary, these figures still give a fairly reliable picture of the sources of the anthems. "English origin" in this case indicates that the pieces are attributed to an English composer and have been found in English tunebooks antedating their American publication. The pieces are: "Before Jehovah's awful throne" (Madan), "Behold, I bring you glad tidings" (Stephenson), "Behold, the Lord is my salvation" (Green), "Our Lord is risen from the dead" (Arnold), "Our souls by love" (Miller), "Vital spark" (DYING CHRISTIAN, Harwood), and "Vital

spark" (NEW YORK ANTHEM, Harwood/Law). It should be noted that NEW YORK ANTHEM is an arrangement by the American Andrew Law of Harwood's DYING CHRISTIAN.

[9]Ralph T. Daniel, "English Models for the First American Anthems," *Journal of the American Musicological Society* 12/1 (Spring 1959): 49-58.

[10]One other Billings anthem, "Vital spark" (DYING CHRISTIAN) received a single printing.

[11]The three are Belknap's "Sacred to heaven" (4), Benham's "Hark, hark, glad tidings" (2 [or 3, depending on whether or not the printing in Walker's *Southern Harmony* is included]), and Wood's "Jesus, our triumphant head" (2).

[12]Indeed, sections of some of the anthems could easily stand alone as folk hymns; an example is Davisson's "That awful day will surely come" (see below).

[13]See Davisson's IDUMEA (KYH16, p. 25) for another example of this characteristic.

[14]Irving Lowens, "Introduction to the Facsimile Edition," in A. Davisson, *Kentucky Harmony* (1816; reprint, Minneapolis: Augsburg Publishing House, 1976), 6.

[15]Compare mm. 15-19 with mm. 24-27 and mm. 28-32; compare also mm. 20-23 with mm. 29-32. Much of the tenor part seems to be constructed from the "head motive" presented in the first two measures.

[16]To note but one example, mm. 14-21 and 60-64 may be compared.

[17]This figure incorporates some of the pieces of uncertain origin discussed below.

[18]The *Original Sacred Harp* ([Atlanta]: [J. S. James], 1911), 225 attributes this piece to "James Denson, 1844." While the attributions in this source are not always trustworthy, this does lend additional support to the southern origin theory for "Oh how charming."

[19]The author wishes to thank Harry Eskew, Marion Hatchett, William J. Reynolds, and R. Allen Lott for their assistance with this project.

THE 1838-40 AMERICAN CONCERT TOURS OF JANE SHIRREFF AND JOHN WILSON, BRITISH VOCAL STARS

Katherine K. Preston

In committing to paper those events which may occur to so humble an Individual as myself during my absence from England, it is with no view of imitating those Journalists so well known to have visited and depreciated America, but to gratify (or perhaps more properly speaking, satisfy) those kind friends, who have expressed a wish to hear of my daily proceedings. So numerous are those friends, that it would be impossible for me to acquaint them severally of my observations on Men and Manners, therefore I adopt this method of informing them collectively of those circumstances which at so great a distance may seem worthy of notice.

With this rather self-conscious explanatory note, "a Young lady who accompanied Miss Shirreff in her Visit to the United States" commenced her "Journal in America" in early September 1838.[1] Both Mary Blundell (the diarist) and Jane Shirreff (the friend she accompanied) have long since disappeared from history. But their story, as related in part by Blundell and as supplemented with additional information from newspapers, periodicals, and primary materials from Shirreff, should be of much interest to those concerned with the study of American culture of the Jacksonian period and, in particular, with the place of music within that culture.

Blundell's name survives because of her manuscript travelogue, which as a document of social history is an insightful and hitherto-unknown first-hand account of the wonders seen, diversions enjoyed, and difficulties endured by a group of English visitors to the United States between 1838 and 1840. It is one of hundreds of such accounts written by nineteenth-century British visitors to North America. Many of Blundell's observations—the wonders of various natural sights, the sometimes-wretched travel and lodging conditions, the friendliness, unfriendliness, and sundry peculiarities of Americans—are remarkably similar to those made in published accounts by other British travellers in the 1820s and 1830s, including Thomas Hamilton, Captain Frederick Marryat, Charles Murray, Frances Trollope (of the infamous "depreciating" comments), Harriet Martineau, and—slightly later—Charles Dickens.[2] As such, Blundell's account both illustrates American life of the period and confirms the contemporary observations of others. Her travelogue, however, differs from these better-known accounts because of the circumstances of her visit here and—in particular—because of the identity of the friend she accompanied.

Jane Shirreff (1811-1883), an English soprano with a full-toned and powerful voice that was "clear, full, and bird-like," was a star of Covent Garden and Drury Lane.[3] She came to this country to sing opera. During the twenty months she spent performing in North America, Shirreff—with the assistance of the successful Scottish tenor John Wilson (1801-1849), with whom she travelled and performed—created a musical and theatrical furor unmatched here by any English opera star until the mid-1850s.[4] The two singers and their entourage toured up and down the East Coast of North America—as far north as Quebec City and as far south as Savannah—singing in operas and in concerts, to great critical acclaim and at great financial remuneration. As a consequence, Blundell's journal is much more interesting and valuable to the historian of American music than are other similar "observations on Men and Manners" of the period. This document, along with the other materials in the Shirreff Collection, make possible an unprecedented eyewitness account of the American adventures of two British singers during this period. Through Blundell's eyes we can understand more in general about itinerant British musicians who toured and performed in this country during the 1830s and 1840s. And by so doing, we can examine more closely the significant—and for the most part unexplored—influence exerted by early nineteenth-century vocal stars on the development of musical culture in the United States.

Vocal stars who came to this country in the early part of the nineteenth century typically performed in both concerts and in staged productions of operas. True to form, during their stay here Shirreff and Wilson starred in operas during two theatrical seasons (1838-39 and 1839-40) and mounted two different concert tours (summer 1839 and late 1839-early 1840). Blundell's diary contains a wealth of information about both types of performances, but her details of travel are particularly useful for reconstructing the concert tours. For that reason, the principal focus of this article will be the singers' concert tours. First, however, I will commence with some background information about the cultural context of the singers' visit and with a broad summary of their operatic activities.

Shirreff and Wilson—and the bass Edward Sequin (1809-1852), who also sang with them for a time—were lured from London by an offer in 1838 from the National Theatre in New York. English opera by such composers as Thomas Arne, William Shield, and Charles Dibdin had been an essential component of the standard theatrical repertory on the American stage since the eighteenth century; by the late 1830s, American theatre managers had added English-language works by contemporary composers like Henry Rowley Bishop and Michael William Balfe, as well as "Englished" operas (adaptations of continental—and, in particular, *bel canto*—operas).[5] The importance of music in the American theatrical repertory is particularly significant because it greatly influenced concert life: British singers, who were engaged by theatre managers to sing on the stage, also appeared in concerts. Numerous English vocal stars had preceded Wilson, Shirreff, and Seguin to the United States; the most notable were Elizabeth Austin (who visited this country from 1827 through 1835) and Joseph and Mary Anne Paton Wood (who toured the United States in 1834-36 and would return for another tour in 1840-41). These and many others had met with marked artistic and financial success in North America.

What permitted such visits by vocal and theatrical stars was the prevailing theatrical *modus operandi*, the star system. Under this system (which had been introduced to the United States from Britain in the 1790s), dramatic or vocal stars were free agents.[6] They were attached to no particular company and hence were free to travel around the theatrical circuit and make their own contracts for short- or long-term (but non-permanent) engagements with theatre managers.[7] As visiting performers, they typically assumed the major roles in plays or operas; the actors and actresses of the theatre's stock company filled in the supporting roles and made up the chorus, and the theatre's orchestra provided the instrumental accompaniment. Dramatic stars generally toured alone or occasionally in pairs. Vocal stars more often toured as pairs, trios, or sometimes quartets, in order to better insure that all the principal roles in the operas they performed were covered adequately.

As was typical of such vocal-star engagements, Shirreff, Wilson, and Seguin signed a contract with the National to appear there for only two weeks. Their engagement in New York began on 15 October 1838 and was an undeniable success. During their run they mounted performances exclusively of the surprise hit *Amilie; or the Love Test*, by the Irish composer William Michael Rooke.[8] The singers attracted huge audiences and created a theatrical furor, all but eclipsing the offerings at the venerable Park Theatre, arch-rival of the relatively new National. Despite their unbounded success in New York, however, the singers were forced to leave at the end of their brief engagement. Blundell explained the situation in her diary: "the success of the operatic corps has been most decided. The orchestra [is] very good, which is of utmost importance, [and] *Amilie* drew crowded houses during the whole engagement, and would have done so another fortnight but Mr. Wallack had engaged a corps de Ballet, to succeed them."[9] Since the National's manager James Wallack had had no clue that the unknown singers would enjoy such astounding success at his theatre, he had booked them for the standard two-week period, after which another itinerant company (in this case, a ballet troupe) was scheduled to arrive. The British singers, as a consequence, left their home base (the National Theatre) in early November to travel and perform elsewhere on the East Coast. The immutable reality that performers had to leave a theatre at the end of their allotted time—even though they might be at the height of a theatrical triumph—was one of the most obvious failings of the star system.

The trio of vocal stars may have left New York, but they clearly maintained business contact with the manager of the National. James Wallack evidently had a hand in organizing the visiting singers' itinerary during the next several months, for the vocal stars toured with something of an entourage from his National Theatre. Cast lists from playbills of performances in Boston, Philadelphia, Washington, and Baltimore include the names of various actors not in the ranks of the local stock companies, and newspaper advertisements and playbills announce that the visiting stars' performances were supported by chorus members from the National Theatre in New York.[10] Although this type of arrangement was not unheard-of, it was rather unusual for vocal stars of this period. It perhaps is another measure of the singers' success, for Wallack evidently wished to sustain the public's perception that he and the National Theatre were closely associated with this very successful vocal-star troupe.

For the remainder of the 1838-39 theatrical season, the singers travelled to a variety of cities on the East Coast, performing with the stock companies associated with the local theatres. They performed in operas that were both novel and familiar, including among the latter standards from the English comic-opera repertory such as John Davy's *Rob Roy*, Arne's *Love in a Village*, and Bishop's *Clari, or the Maid of Milan* and *Guy Mannering*. For the most part, however, the singers relied on the new *Amilie* and on two well-known works: Vincenzo Bellini's *La Sonnambula* (as adapted by Bishop) and *Fra Diavolo* by Daniel-François-Esprit Auber (as adapted by Michael Rophino Lacy). Other works included Lacy's adaptation of Gioachino Rossini's *La Cenerentola* (retitled *Cinderella; or the Fairy Godmother and the Little Glass Slipper*) and Bishop's adaptation of *The Marriage of Figaro*. Over the course of this season they performed this repertory in the following cities: Boston (5-23 November), Providence (26-30 November), New York (3-21 December), Washington (24-29 December), Baltimore (31 December 1838—12 January 1839), Philadelphia (14 January-9 February), New York (11 February-30 March), and Philadelphia (1-27

April).[11] They finished their season where they had started, with a lengthy engagement at the National in New York (29 April-22 June).

The extent of the company's popularity during this season is indicated by the length of their engagements, particularly in Philadelphia (where they appeared for a total of eight weeks at the Chestnut Street Theatre) and in New York (where they completely dominated the National's season, singing for a total of twenty weeks throughout the year). The singers' success was even more remarkable because of the generally dismal state of American theatricals during this season. In 1838 and early 1839 parts of the Northeast (including New York) were either on the verge, or were already in the midst, of a severe depression that had been looming on the nation's economic horizon ever since the Panic of 1837. Theatres all over the country were encountering difficulties. In retrospect, it is clear that the opera singers did much more than dominate Wallack's season—they kept his theatre open. No other kind of dramatic fare besides opera was attracting theatrical audiences of any size in the winter of 1839. "It would be more characteristic," commented a critic in March of that year, "if [the National] theatre were called the Opera House, for it is to the refined and elevating entertainments which music affords, that it owes all its prosperity."[12] A writer for the *Spirit of the Times* expressed a similar view on 9 March. "The entertainment which is most universal and absorbing in its attractions," he wrote, "is with us [the] Opera." So successful was the opera—and so moribund everything else Wallack tried—that he must have rued the day he allowed his stars to leave for a month-long engagement in Philadelphia during April. When the singers finally returned to the National, a New York critic welcomed them back with open arms. "Most gladly did we read the announcement that the vocalists of the opera [have] returned to us," he wrote. "Another week without them and the National would have been as lifeless as a dead lion. It was pleasant to witness with what alacrity the lovers of music responded to the call, and filled the house on Monday evening."[13]

After spending the summer of 1839 on the concert circuit (about which more below) the singers returned to the East Coast in September and prepared to mount a second operatic season. Considering the extent of their success during 1838-39, Wallack and his vocal stars can be forgiven for expecting another triumph during 1839-40. But this was not to be. The theatrical season that started in September 1839—to the misfortune of Shirreff, Wilson, Wallack, and the rest of the American theatrical community—was an unmitigated disaster. It was, in fact, the beginning of what one theatre historian has called "perhaps the most grievous [period] in the history of the American stage."[14] The depression that had been threatening the nation for several years had caught up with the Northeast by late 1839. Imports were down, currency was scarce, people lost jobs.

Theatres now were not only facing difficulties, they were closing. By 16 November 1839—only two months into the season—the New York *Morning Herald* reported that "theatricals are at a low ebb in this country—[with] every principal theatre losing money, including the Park and National in New York, the Chestnut in Philadelphia, and the Tremont in Boston." Slightly over a month later, on 26 December, a critic writing in the *Spirit* apologized for the dearth of theatrical news and expressed despair about the situation in general. "How all the difficulties of Managers—not in New York alone, but in Philadelphia, Boston, New Orleans, &c.—will terminate," he wrote, "it is impossible to conjecture." He continued, "it cannot be that the taste for pleasures of this kind has suddenly become extinct; but it is very sure that the conduct of a theatre is now the most disastrous business that one can attempt."

To compound matters greatly, in late September 1839 Wallack's National Theatre burned to the ground. Although the manager gamely tried to continue his season in rented quarters at Niblo's Theatre, this attempt failed. With his momentum gone before the season even started, Wallack succumbed to the general theatrical malaise and in mid-November gave up. All the members of his company—and all the visiting artists engaged to appear during the upcoming season—were thrown out of work. Shirreff and Wilson suddenly no longer had a base of operations; worse, their beneficial business affiliation with James Wallack was also terminated. Faced with no work in New York and with the uncertainty of finding theatrical work elsewhere, the two singers abandoned their plans for a second operatic tour of the Northeast. Instead, they decided to mount another concert tour. The plan evidently was to perform in opera where that was feasible but to rely primarily on concert performances.[15]

As a result of this chain of events, the visiting British singers mounted two concert tours during their sojourn in the United States. On the first, which lasted eight weeks (27 June-28 August 1839), they headed north and west, travelling through New York State (they performed in Albany, Troy, Utica, Syracuse, Auburn, Geneva, Canandaigua, Rochester, and Buffalo), northern Ohio (Cleveland), southern Michigan (Detroit), Ontario (Toronto and Kingston), and Quebec. For their second—and lengthier—concertizing tour (which lasted from 31 October 1839 through 13 March 1840), they first went to Connecticut and Massachusetts (where they performed in New Haven, Hartford, Springfield, and Worcester), stopped briefly in New York City and Philadelphia, then headed south to give concerts in Baltimore, Washington, Charleston, Augusta, Savannah, and Norfolk, before returning once again to their home base in New York.[16] (For their itineraries on these two concert expeditions, see Figures 1 and 2.) On both trips Shirreff and Wilson toured with rather a large entourage— John Wilson had the company of his wife Mary, and Jane Shirreff was escorted by her mother, her friend Mary Blundell, and her dog Flint.[17]

The British visitors embarked on their concert tours and made decisions about where they would go in response to a variety of factors. First—and certainly foremost—was the availability of work. It was standard practice for itinerant singers to mount concert tours during the summer, as most American theatres were dark during that period. This, of course, explains the singers' summer concert tour undertaken during July and August 1839. It was also normal for entertainers to embark on concertizing expeditions as a fall-back activity when other plans fell through. This latter explains the second tour by Shirreff and Wilson. Another (although much less important) factor that had an influence on the singers' itinerary was the North American climate. During the hot summer months, the British singers headed north in search of more-temperate weather. For their second (winter) trip, on the other hand, they went south, on the advice of "many persons who . . . told us we should find an English July in a Charleston December."[18] Despite their geographical precautions, however, the English visitors were bitterly disappointed by the weather on both expeditions. In western New York State in July, Shirreff recorded that the weather was "oppressively hot" and further mentioned that at one hotel the "room [was] so warm that [I] could not sleep"; in Kingston, Ontario, a month later it was still "intensely hot."[19] To heap insult upon injury, when the singers headed south from New York in November they left behind their warm clothes, only to run into "such cold weather" as "has not been known . . . in the South for forty years." According to Blundell, they had expected weather appropriate for "Muslins and Parasols" and found a climate in which "Fur and Umbrellas were much more in our request."[20]

FIGURE 1: FIRST CONCERT TOUR OF JANE SHIRREFF AND JOHN WILSON
2 JULY—2 SEPTEMBER 1839

2 July	Albany
8 July	Troy
9 July	Albany
12 July	Utica
13 July	Syracuse
15 July	Auburn
16 July	Syracuse
17 July	Geneva
18 July	Canandaigua
19 July	Rochester

25 July	Buffalo
30 July	Toronto
2 August	Buffalo
5 August	Toronto
8 August	Cleveland
9 August	Cleveland
12 August	Detroit
13 August	Detroit
16 August	Buffalo
19 August	Toronto
23 August	Kingston
28 August	Montreal
2 Sept.	Montreal

The final motivational force influencing the singers' concert itinerary was a desire by the Britons to see as much of the United States as possible. That they were mixing pleasure with work on their travels is apparent from Blundell's journal, for her account clearly illustrates that the party made a point to seek out natural and man-made curiosities and attractions wherever they went. Blundell describes sight-seeing activities during both tours, but evidently this factor was much more important for the summer excursion (which Blundell refers to as a "tour of pleasure") than it was for the (last-minute) winter one.[21] It is also clear that although the singers were disappointed in the weather they encountered on these two journeys, they were delighted with their sight-seeing activities. During the summer the group visited a Shaker village near Albany, salt works close to Syracuse, and a prison at Auburn, New York.[22] At Troy, New York, they undertook "a charming walk up to Mount Ida, where there are very beautiful views of the City and River, and also a very picturesque fall" and also made a point to visit Cohoes Falls, "being fully aware [that] all these minor ones should be seen previously to Niagara."[23] From Utica they made a day trip to Trenton Hill to view Trenton Falls Gorge (near modern Berneveld, N. Y.); Shirreff was delighted by the "splendid sight" and Blundell waxed rhapsodic, gushing "what a romantic place [this] is!"[24] Several days later, Shirreff noted her delight with the "very beautiful scenery" around Geneva, New York, which is located at the top of Seneca Lake, one of the Finger Lakes.[25] The sight-seeing high point of that trip, however, was obviously Niagara Falls. At her first glimpse of the cataracts, Blundell reacted with joy, astonishment, and "many other feelings, which seem impossible to occupy ones mind in almost a moment's space." These feelings "were so overwhelming, that I felt nothing would be so salutary as a flood of tears." She later wrote that her first impression had been "fear and awe at beholding and closely approaching such a marvellous work of Omnipotence," and concluded that "no language can describe nor can the mind at once embody so much grandeur, such an expanse of awful magnificence."[26]

FIGURE 2: SHIRREFF AND WILSON'S ITINERARY SEPTEMBER 1839—MAY 1840

16-28 Sept. 1839	Philadelphia (Chestnut St. Theatre)
	12 opera performances
30 Sept.—7 Oct.	Baltimore (Holliday St. Theatre)
	7 opera performances
14-26 Oct.	New York (National Theatre/Niblo's)
	12 opera performances
31 Oct.	New Haven (concert)
1 Nov.	New Haven (concert)
2 Nov.	Hartford (concert)
4 Nov.	Hartford (concert)
5 Nov.	Springfield, Mass. (concert)
6 Nov.	Worcester (concert)
11 Nov.	New York City (concert)
15 Nov.	New York City (concert)
21 Nov.	New York City (concert)
25 Nov.	New York City (concert)
27 Nov.	Philadelphia (concert)
29 Nov.	Philadelphia (concert)
2 Dec.	Philadelphia (concert)
4 Dec.	Baltimore (concert)
14-27 Dec.	Charleston (Charleston Theatre)
	10 opera performances
30 Dec.	Augusta (concert)
1 Jan. 1840	Augusta (concert)
3 Jan.	Augusta (concert)
6 Jan.	Savannah (concert)
7 Jan.	Savannah (concert)
8 Jan.	Savannah (concert)
9 Jan.	Savannah (concert)
10 Jan.	Savannah (concert)
11 Jan.	Savannah (concert)
18 Jan.	Charleston (concert)
22 Jan.	Norfolk (concert)
? Jan.	Norfolk (concert)
28 Jan.	Baltimore (concert)
29 Jan.	Washington, D. C. (concert)

30 Jan.	Baltimore (concert)
31 Jan.	Washington, D. C. (concert)
1 Feb.	Baltimore (concert)
7 Feb.	Philadelphia (concert)
10 Feb.	Philadelphia (concert)
11 Feb.?	Philadelphia (concert)
18 Feb.	New York City (concert)
21 Feb.	New York City (concert)
26 Feb.	New York City (concert)
2 March	New York City (concert)
6 March	New York City (concert)
13 March	New York City (concert)
30 Mar.—13 Apr.	New York City (Park Theatre) 11 opera performances
20 Apr—2 May	Philadelphia (Chestnut St. Theatre) 12 opera performances
22 May	New York City (Park Theatre) One opera performance. Farewell appearance (by Shirreff): final American performance

Despite the pleasurable sight-seeing activities in which the travellers engaged, the principal focus of each tour was the performance of concerts by Wilson and Shirreff. Even so, the two singers apparently did not set up a definite performance-driven itinerary for either of their concert tours before leaving New York City. This was probably typical of concert tours mounted by vocal stars in the 1830s and 1840s. The schedules of both trips were somewhat flexible, so concerts could be repeated in towns where bad weather had interfered with a good turn-out, or when it looked as though a second performance might draw a large crowd. After their first concert appearance in Syracuse on 13 July 1839, for example, Shirreff noted in her diary that they had been "persuaded to return on Tuesday to give another [concert]."[27] This lack of prior planning also had its drawbacks, for when the two singers arrived in Boston for a concert they had planned to give on 7 November, they were unable to secure a hall and had to leave the city without a performance.[28]

Sometimes the impromptu nature of concert giving by one or another touring troupe worked to the detriment of other travelling performers, for Shirreff and Wilson experienced competition from at least one other British concert-giving group. During the same summer months that Shirreff and Wilson were concertizing, the English bass Edward Seguin and his wife Anne (a soprano), along with W. H. Latham (a popular buffo singer) likewise took to the road.[29] They performed in a number of the same cities as Shirreff and Wilson, sometimes within a week of their competitors' concerts.[30] The two concert troupes actually crossed paths in Quebec City on the last weekend in August, much to the consternation of Shirreff. When the Shirreff/Wilson party arrived in Quebec the morning of Friday, 30 August, the singers discovered that—without their permission—their scheduled concert had been postponed from Friday to Saturday because the Seguins (who were singing in the same hall) had changed their night from Thursday to Friday. Before they had left Montreal for Quebec, however, Shirreff and Wilson had scheduled a concert in the former city for Monday, 2 September; there was no transportation available between the two cities on Sunday, and as a consequence Shirreff and Wilson were forced to cancel their concert in Quebec and leave the city without having performed. The soprano was understandably miffed. She and Wilson ran into the Seguins in the hotel lobby on Saturday morning, and Anne Seguin "had the arrogance," Shirreff recorded in her diary, "to speak to me as tho' nothing had happened—bah!"[31]

Whether or not the singers' itinerary was carefully arranged ahead of time, someone had to do a certain amount of advance work. In particular, a suitable hall had to be rented, a competent accompanist engaged, and the concert advertised. Wilson probably managed both tours; the older singer apparently regarded the soprano as his protégée or even his ward, for he looked after her interests and managed her affairs during their entire American visit.[32] Furthermore, neither Shirreff nor Blundell were bothered by such managerial details and neither mentions such information in her diary. Wilson probably travelled a day or so ahead of Shirreff and the rest of the group in order to take care of arrangements; in fact, on several occasions Shirreff mentions in her diary that Wilson had departed prior to the rest of the entourage, or had arrived from elsewhere "late at night."[33] It was also possible that Wilson could have hired someone by mail to see to the necessary details. Extant correspondence between performers and theatre managers during this period suggests that the latter was an accepted *modus operandi*.[34]

Publicity for upcoming concerts never appeared in newspapers more than several days in advance, which also suggests that the singers were not working from a firm itinerary. In many towns the vocalists did not announce their concert in the newspaper at all, for in small towns during the antebellum period most publicity for public performances was accomplished by the posting of handbills.[35] Someone had to have the handbills printed and distributed, however; again, either Wilson made such arrangements by mail or he travelled to the town beforehand to take care of the task himself. Occasionally the entourage arrived several days in advance of their planned concert date (sometimes in order to accommodate sight-seeing activity) or left to give a concert in a nearby town and then returned to the first location for a second or third performance; in either of these cases the singers had plenty of time to publicize an upcoming appearance.

Despite the nascent and growing economic depression, the popular pair of singers drew (relatively) large crowds to their concerts. Even in the tiny towns of upper New York State—Utica, Syracuse, Geneva, Canandaigua, and Rochester—the vocalists regularly attracted between fifty and one hundred paid auditors for each of their concerts.[36] Concerts given in large urban areas, according to available information, drew huge crowds—especially those given in New York and Philadelphia in the fall of 1839. According to Shirreff's financial records, the vocalists grossed a total of $2190 for their four New York performances and $1927 for the three in Philadelphia in November and December 1839; since the price of admission to their concerts was $1.00, these figures translate into audiences that averaged 550 in the former and 640 in the latter city (not taking into account the inevitable—and often quite numerous—deadheads, complimentary admissions, members of the press, and so forth). Other information, in fact, suggests that these average crowd figures may be conservative. For their concert on 11 November, for example, the New York *Morning Herald* reported the next day that "at least 1500 persons were there, and about 500 went away, unable to obtain admittance." Shirreff herself confirms their success. "Our first concert in New York," she wrote on 11 November, attracted "an overflowing house and [a] most delighted and delightful audience—numbers [were] turned away and many could neither see nor hear—I never sang better. A glorious triumph and gratification." The other three concerts held in Manhattan drew a "splendid room," "very good rooms," and a "very fine room—immensely crowded," according to Shirreff. It was "certainly most gratifying," she wrote, "that our four concerts should have been so splendidly successful"; this was particularly so because of the disappointment connected with the singers' recently cancelled opera tour.[37] The public response was similar when the singers travelled to Philadelphia the last week in November, for they attracted large crowds to each of their three concerts in that city. The first, which undoubtedly was the most successful, drew (according to Shirreff) a "tremendous room—between 2 & 3,000 people! The effect was splendidly beautiful."[38] The monetary figures that Shirreff recorded in her financial ledger confirm the singers' success in New York and Philadelphia. For these seven concerts the two vocalists earned (after paying expenses) a total of $2875 (in 1992 dollars, approximately $37,634); Shirreff's half came to $1437 ($18,817).[39]

The vocalists attracted these large crowds with concert repertory that was a mixture of operatic arias and popular and Scotch ballads. Their programs generally included almost equal proportions of ballads and selections from the musical stage, either English or translated Italian or French operas. A typical program—from the singers' final concert at

Niblo's Grand Saloon in New York City on 25 November 1839—appeared in the New York *Morning Herald* on the day of the concert:

PART I

Duett, "Love like a shadow flies" (Parry) ....Shirreff/Wilson
Song, "Who hath not mark'd?" (Rooke) ....Wilson
Polacca, "Trifler, forbear" (Bishop) ....Shirreff
Song, "The Flowers of the Forest" (Old Scotch Melody) ..Wilson
Song, "Meet me in the Willow Glen" (A. Lee) ....Shirreff
"The Meeting of the Waters" (Irish Melody). Harmonized
    for three voices by Maeder ....Wilson/Shirreff/Maeder
"Savourneen Deelish" (Irish Ballad, S. Lover) ....Wilson
Rondo, "The Rapture Dwelling" (Balfe) ....Shirreff
Irish Song, "Rory O'Moore" (Lover) ....Wilson
Duett, "Birks of Aberfeldie" (Old Scotch Melodie
    harmonized by Mr. Wilson) ....Wilson/Shirreff

PART II

Scena--From the Opera of Fra Diavolo,
    descriptive of the life of a Brigand (Auber) ....Wilson
        Recitative, "My Companions are Warn'd"
        Air, "Proudly and Wide My Standard Flies"
        Recitative, "Now a poor and simple maid appears"
        Cantabile, "We never aught demand from the fair"
        Allegro, "Then since time flies so fast away"
Scotch Song, "I'm ouer young to marry yet" ....Shirreff
Song, "The land far away" (Maeder) ....Wilson
Song, "Bid me discourse" (Bishop) ....Shirreff
Scotch ballad, "My Boy Tammie" ....Wilson
Scotch song, "The bonnie briar bush" ....Shirreff
Trio, "The Last Rose Summer"
    (Maeder) ....Wilson/Shirreff/Maeder
Scotch Song, "John Anderson, My Joe" ....Wilson
Scotch Song, "Oh whistle and I'll come to you my lad" ...Shirreff
Old Scotch Ballad, "Tak yer auld cloak about ye" ....Wilson
Duett, "Though I leave now in sorrow"
    (Scotch melody) ....Wilson/Shirreff

Of the twenty-five selections on this concert program, nine—or over one-third—are from operas: "Who Hath Not Mark'd" from *Amilie*, "Trifler, Forbear," a recitative and polacca from Henry Bishop's comic opera *The*

Farmer's Wife, "The Rapture Dwelling" from Michael Balfe's *The Maid of Artois*, "Bid Me Discourse" from *Twelfth Night*, also by Bishop, and the lengthy scena from Auber's *Fra Diavolo*. Three compositions, "Meet Me in the Willow Glen" by George Alexander Lee, "Love Like a Shadow Flies" by John Parry, and James G. Maeder's "The Land Far Away" are the only nonoperatic composed songs on the program. The other thirteen are contemporary arrangements of traditional songs, mostly Scotch or Irish. The British composers Samuel Lover and George Alexander Lee, and the Bohemian Leopold Kozeluch, arranged four of the songs: "Savourneen Deelish" and "Rory O'Moore" (Lover), "I'm O'er Young to Marry Yet" (Lee), and "Flowers of the Forest" (Kozeluch); for the remainder the singers probably used arrangements by John Wilson or those by James Maeder, who was their accompanist for this and their other New York concerts.[40] Six of the songs later appeared in John Wilson's *Edition of the Songs of Scotland* (although with slightly altered titles): "The Birks of Aberfeldy," "My Boy Tammy," "The Bonnie Briar Bush," "John Anderson, My Jo," "Whistle and I'll Come to Ye, My Lad," and "Tak' Yer Auld Cloak Aboot Ye."[41] Maeder already had published an arrangement of Parry's "Love Like a Shadow Flies" (in 1833), and his arrangements of the two traditional melodies "The Meeting of the Waters" and "The Last Rose of Summer" would be published in 1840 in a collection titled *Six Irish Melodies by Thomas Moore Esq As Sung by . . . Miss Shirreff, Mr. Wilson & Mr. Maeder, Harmonized for Three Voices . . . by James G. Maeder*.[42] The predominance of the Scotch and Irish melodies on this program—and their ready availability in sheet-music publications—is further evidence of early nineteenth-century Americans' well-documented love for such traditional tunes. The exceedingly popular songs of Thomas Moore had been introduced to Americans by the vocal star Thomas Philipps when he visited the United States in the late 'teens and early 'twenties.[43]

All twenty-five of the selections on this concert program are vocal works, which is rather atypical of standard concert fare of the time. Wilson and Shirreff included instrumental compositions in their concerts only when they were accompanied by an orchestra, which usually occurred when the concert was in conjunction with an operatic performance. Occasionally the singers hired a band to accompany them in concert (in Toronto, for example, Shirreff noted that they "had the band of the 32nd" for their concert on 5 August), but for a vast majority of their concert appearances their accompanist was a local pianist. Presumably the singers had little choice in this matter and had to make do with what was available; as might be expected, the pianist sometimes was skilled and sometimes was not. In Albany, for example, the local newspaper highly praised the accompanist, identifying her as "Miss Jackson, a resident teacher of rare skill"; in contrast, after a concert in Baltimore in December, Shirreff wrote with disgust in her diary, "Such an accompanist, ye Gods! defend me!"[44] Regardless of his or her level of skill, however, the accompanist almost never performed a solo instrumental work as part of the program.

Although concert selections changed from town to town, the relative percentages of opera, traditional, and non-operatic non-traditional songs on this program are typical. The singers also occasionally chose operatic selections by other composers, such as Rossini ("Rapture Fills My Joyful Heart," from *La Gazza Ladra* and "Let Thine Eyes on Mine Mildly Beaming" from *Cinderella*), Balfe ("Well if I Must Speak My Mind," from *The Siege of Rochelle*, "O'er Shepherd Pipe & Rustic Dell" from *Joan of Arc*, and "Oh Hasten, Dearest Lady," from *Diadeste*), Bellini ("Goodnight, Love" from *La Sonnambula*), Donizetti ("Barcarole" from *Marino Faliero*), Adam ("Romance" and "Pastoral Aria" from *Postillion of Longjumeau*), and Hérold ("Lovely Lady Mine," from *La Pré Aux Clercs*).[45] This list includes a fair sample of Italian composers; by far, however, the majority of operatic selections included in the Shirreff and Wilson concerts were from works by Balfe, Rooke (especially from *Amilie*), and Auber (*Fra Diavolo*). A large number of the songs on this and similar concert programs were published in sheet music form in the United States in the late 1830s and early 1840s. Many of them, as was usual, have tags like "As Sung by Miss Shirreff & Mr. Seguin," "As Sung with Enthusiastic Applause by Mr. Wilson," and "As Sung by Mr. Wilson in the Opera of Fra Diavolo."[46] Although most of the publications are not dated, their release undoubtedly coincided with the singers' highly successful performances and constitute further evidence of their renown in this country.

The vocalists' mixed bag of concert repertory met with audience approval in most places; in only one city did newspaper reports indicate otherwise. In the winter of 1840 Shirreff and Wilson gave a series of six concerts in Savannah, Georgia, which at first were not well patronized. The repertory of the first two concerts was similar to the program quoted above, and after the second one the reviewer from the *Savannah Republican* scolded his fellow citizens for their poor showing. He also expressed distress that "none of the pieces were much applauded, except some of the popular street ballads."[47] Wilson and Shirreff knew how to gauge the taste of their public, however, and henceforth gave the Savannah audiences a slightly larger dose of ballads—and attracted larger audiences. On 10 January the two vocalists evidently decided that most people in Savannah preferred ballads and popular tunes to operatic selections, so they offered a concert comprised entirely of the former. (Apparently no program from this concert survives.) The local critic was mortified. "We regret the selection of pieces for tonight," he wrote.

That Mr. Wilson and Miss Shirreff are better appreciated now, than at first, is entirely owing to the influence of those who have taste enough to discriminate in such matters. When [the size of the audience is] obviously in a state of improvement, why select a whole bill of popular ballads? However, the plan will no doubt fill the house, for these ballads have been all the go, at previous concerts, and if these distinguished strangers cannot give us the delightful strains of Rooke, Bellini, and Auber, then we are content to take such songs as Lover's 'Rory O'More.' The many-headed monster has decreed it, and it is sovereign in this country, but this same democracy is a horrid tyrant in all matters of polite accomplishments. For ourselves, we would rather hear Miss Shirreff and Mr. Wilson in their operatic selections, than all the ballads that were ever sung.[48]

Whether musical tastes in Savannah were different from those around the country is unknown. In no other cities where Shirreff and Wilson gave concerts were such sentiments expressed in print; in no other cities, however, did they offer such unusual concert fare. For most of their concerts in the Northeast the singers performed the usual mixture of repertory, and attracted audiences that were "large and fashionable," or "very numerous and fashionable"; in New York and Philadelphia, as we have seen, the singers had no trouble whatsoever attracting "most crowded" houses and "immense numbers of persons."[49] All of these audiences—made up of residents of both large cities and small towns—were attracted by programs that regularly included both operatic airs and ballads.

For the most part, the singers travelled by steamboat, stage coach, and rail. On their summer trip their route took them from New York City up the Hudson by steamer to Albany and Troy, then to Utica by rail, then by canal to Syracuse and Auburn. After returning to Syracuse from Auburn they continued west, mostly by stage but in part by rail; the remainder of the summer trip was accomplished primarily by steamship or railroad. The travellers' tour of the South was likewise made by rail, steamer, or stage. Although Blundell's comments about scenery viewed from the bridge of steamboats (especially en route up the Hudson) usually indicate a pleasant passage, the travellers' steamer trip south from Baltimore was marred by overcrowding and by noisy and ill-behaved children. Furthermore, stage travel was generally hot, dusty, crowded, and fatiguing. Both Blundell and Shirreff complain frequently of the difficulties of this mode of travel in the United States. Blundell grumbled that "riding 84 miles in a stage coach here is as fatiguing as 164 in England." She eventually concluded that there was "no one thing in which our country so far excels [the United States], as in the stage and the coach" and that stage travel was "perhaps . . . the only business which is not done on a 'go a head' style here, where everything is done with such expedition."[50]

Blundell's numerous comments about travel conditions are often amusing; more important, they help to recreate a clear picture of many of the now-forgotten daily difficulties encountered by itinerant musicians. Travel during the summer was not nearly so difficult as it was in the winter, but even so Blundell's graphic descriptions are vivid and provide a valuable sense of immediacy. In mid-July, for example, after Shirreff and Wilson gave a concert performance at Utica, their party hired a private stage for their sight-seeing trip to Trenton Falls Gorge. They took very little luggage for this overnight trip, and, according to Blundell, this "added to the inconveniences of the bad road, for the four horses finding less weight than usual, kept up a brisk pace, which almost shook out our teeth. It was dangerous to talk," she continued,

> for if a word with th occurred, you were in certain danger of severely biting your tongue. We were like so many india rubberballs, for the circumstances of feeling the seat, was a certain signal of instantly rebounding either against each other, or sending your head to the roof of the coach.[51]

Several days later, when en route to Niagara Falls from Rochester, she wrote that "the sides of the Stages [were] made open nearly to the seat," because it was an "excessively warm day." This innovation, according to Blundell, not only admitted "air into the coaches," but also allowed "six pairs of legs to dangle out of them." The effect, she points out, "was amusing."[52]

Blundell's accounts of the travel conditions encountered by the singers on their winter concert tour, in contrast, are more horrifying than amusing. She vividly describes some of the privations she and the other members of her party endured on that trip to the American South. One wonders what must have been going through the minds of these British sophisticates, accustomed as they were to living conditions in London, or to modes of travel around Great Britain, as they suffered through their trip to Charleston, South Carolina. It is illuminating to recount some of the horrors of their journey.

After travelling from Baltimore to Portsmouth, Virginia, on the steamer *Alabama*, the singers elected to journey overland to Charleston. They had sent their luggage (including music and costumes for a brief opera season at the Charleston Theatre) by steamer but chose themselves to travel overland, surely because of the dangers of an ocean passage around Cape Hatteras during northeaster season. Jane Shirreff's brief (but emphatic) comments provide the general outline of their (mis)adventures:

> Arrived in Portsmouth at 6 o'clock. Breakfasted! Ye Gods!—left by

rail cars at 8 o'clock—dined at 2 o'clock on the road—Oh mercy what dirt!—left by cars again till 6 o'clock [p.m.]—then into coaches—such roads—supped on the road at 1 o'clock [a.m.]—bah! At 3 o'clock [a.m.] took railcars—stopped to breakfast at 4 o'clock—the dirt & filth cannot be described. Left by cars again and arrived at Boat—Wilmington—at 2 o'clock.[53]

Blundell's account fills in some of the grim details. From Portsmouth the group headed south by railroad into Virginia's Great Dismal Swamp. "The Woods on each side," Blundell wrote, "were two or three feet deep in water, from which we were protected by the track being elevated on trees placed across the road." She continued:

> At two o'clock we halted to dine at an obscure looking place called Weldon, the hovel (for that is a more appropriate name than hotel) showed symptoms of recent attack upon the windows, for many a frame had given place to a blanket, stuffed into the frame. To approach this House, we must have walked over very wet turf, had it not been for a pavement which was more kindly than ingeniously contrived, small trees had been split through the middle, and laid down with the flat side uppermost, which required something of a tight rope dancers' ingenuity to keep your balance.
>
> The table was covered with a great variety, the only resemblance one dish had to another was in its being equally nasty. There was one, which to my mind surpassed them all, it was barbecue pig [but] I would like to exchange the word for barbarous. After the pork is roasted, it is covered with vinegar. The only beverage besides water was apple jack, a very green spirit distilled from apples.[54]

By 6 o'clock in the evening, the train reached the terminus of the tracks, and all the passengers disembarked to find stage coaches waiting for them. When all were accommodated, they set off—into the twilight—and onto a corduroy road (which Blundell described as "formed of trees placed across, and not being very particular about their being of equal size"). She continued:

> To add to the danger . . . we soon discovered that the greater part of the road was under water, therefore what ever derangement there might be in the corduroy, the driver was prevented from avoiding it, and consequently no limit can be given to our uprisings and down-fallings; and for this portion you must call forth your notions of peril; for the ridiculous, facing us in total darkness, so tossed about,

that we came in constant collision, and long ere you had time to apologize for the intrusion, you would meet with the retort courteous, and to liquidate the debt on that score.

Although it was impossible to help laughing at the various ridiculous situations into which we were constantly thrown, we were generally checked by some awfully dangerous plunge, with a prospect of an immediate upset, with the additional horror of its being in water. To thoroughly feel for our various situations of terror, you must possess a large share of compassion. . . . You will perhaps conjecture that we were proceeding at a rapid pace, but it was far otherwise, being that of three miles and a half an hour.

After seven hours of this, the travellers stopped for a dinner, about which Blundell wrote, "of all the disgusting sights that hungry mortals ever witnessed, the repast we were ushered into must I think exceed them . . . [it was] composed of the refuse of some other meal, every little dish containing little black lumps swimming in fat." After this interlude, they all clambered back into the coaches to finish the rest of the stage leg of their trip. This, according to Blundell, "terminated about three o'clock in the morning, in a wild unfrequented part of the road, without a house or shed of any description to receive and shelter you if bad weather." Here the travellers had to stand around for an hour in a darkness that was lit only by a "large log fire on the ground . . . [that created] a most curious and wild effect," while they waited for the arrival of the other stages (one of which had met with a serious mishap). The passengers were all finally able to board a train that conveyed them to Wilmington, North Carolina, from whence they caught a steamship to Charleston.[55]

When the singers finally reached South Carolina, they discovered that their costumes and baggage had not arrived—the steamer on which they had been shipped was in the Atlantic outside Charleston harbor, unable to make land for almost a week because of dense fog. This delay necessitated cancellation of five scheduled opera performances at the Charleston Theatre. The conditions that the singers endured en route to the South and the ill-luck with their baggage once they arrived there were portends of a southern tour that would be uncomfortable and fraught with inconveniences and irritations. The theatre audiences in Charleston, according to Shirreff, were not only meagre, they were also the "dull[est] and most uninteresting and disagreeable . . . I have ever played to in America."[56] Shirreff's complaints on this trip, in fact, are endless. The hotel in Augusta, Georgia, was "cheerless, cold and comfortless," the climate in the South was "unhealthy," the weather cold, rainy, or just plain "cold and wretched in the extreme."[57] Furthermore, as we have seen, the singers had to vary their usual concert repertory in order to attract sufficiently large audiences to their concerts in Savannah. Blundell's diary entries during this trip indicate that despite adversity (and regardless of numerous complaints), she maintained her generally cheerful outlook. This cannot be said about Jane Shirreff, however; by the winter of 1840 the soprano was clearly ready to go back to England. The novelty of travel and of sight-seeing had been supplanted by the pressures of constant performances, the inconveniences of travel, and homesickness. "Oh how I long for my . . . dear home," she wrote in her diary on 20 December; ten days later she echoed the sentiment: "Every day makes me more anxious to get to my own home."

Shirreff and Wilson concluded their stay in the United States as they had begun it, with opera performances in Philadelphia (at the Chestnut Street Theatre) and in New York (now at the Park Theatre). Over the course of twenty months the singers had appeared in concert and in operas in eleven states, two Canadian provinces, and the District of Columbia. With their companions they had covered approximately 9,000 miles on their travels around North America, appearing in approximately two hundred and fifty opera performances and seventy concerts.[58] During their visit, the two singers were immensely successful, both financially and artistically.

The extent of their fiscal triumph is easy to document, thanks to the information recorded in Shirreff's financial ledger. For her twenty months' work in the United States, Jane Shirreff earned (after expenses) the remarkable sum of $21,748 (approximately $284,678 in 1992 currency); presumably John Wilson, who had missed no performances because of illness, earned even more. To put this into a clearer perspective: during the 1830s unskilled American workers made approximately $2.50 or $3.00 per week, and skilled workers (such as craftsmen and skilled factory workers) earned a maximum of $4.50-$5.00 per week; as late as the 1850s shoemakers in Massachusetts were earning between $15 and $20 per week. During his tenure (1837-41) as the nation's eighth president, Martin van Buren was paid an annual salary of $25,000.[59]

Of this total amount of $21,748, the majority was for opera performances.[60] During the 1838-39 season, Shirreff sang in 172 operas and gave at least three concerts. In this eight-and-one-half month period she recorded earning $13,098—roughly $171,450 in 1992 dollars. Her income for the next eleven months—during which time she and Wilson mounted their two concert tours—came to $3,975 ($52,032) for appearances in 65 operas and $4,675 ($61,196) in 63 concerts, for a total of $8,650 ($113,228). Her earnings for 1838-39 were greater than for 1839-40, but work in the earlier period had been steadier: 175 performances over the course of eight and one-half months, compared with 128 appearances over eleven months. Perhaps a more useful way of looking at the information from the latter season, however, is a comparison between the amount she earned from concerts and the amount she was paid for singing in operas. In

1839-40 the number of concert performances (63) was almost precisely the same as the number of operatic appearances (65). Her income from concerts, however, was $700 (approximately $9,150) higher than was her income from operas. In effect, she earned $74 (approximately $970) for every concert performance and $61 (approximately $800) for every appearance in opera. This indicates clearly that although work on the theatrical circuit was a more-reliable source of income for itinerant performers, concerts—at least on the average—were more profitable. This difference is easily explained, of course: concerts were a much less complicated and less expensive performing mode; furthermore, there were fewer people with whom to share profits. In any case, singers who came to this country to perform during this period had two viable performance venues: in operas with the assistance of stock companies or in concerts with the assistance only of an accompanist.

The singers' pecuniary success clearly demonstrates their popularity in North America. Their continued celebrity here over the course of twenty months—especially in the face of an economic recession—seems also to indicate concomitant artistic success. But the issue of the singers' artistic triumph and their long-term impact on the development of musical life in the United States is a question somewhat more difficult to resolve than is the matter of their financial success. A clear-cut answer to this question is all the more elusive because of the scarcity of contemporary observations about the impact of vocal stars on American musical life in general. The occasional pertinent remarks that do surface, however, suggest clearly that British vocal stars who visited this country in the 1830s and 1840s—of whom Jane Shirreff and John Wilson are excellent prototypes—had an extremely important role in the development of musical culture here.

To understand this impact, we must briefly summarize the influence of the vocal stars who preceded Shirreff and Wilson to the United States. Starting with Elizabeth Austin in the mid-1820s, American audiences—especially those on the East Coast—were exposed to more and more music from English and "Englished" operas, through either stage productions or concert performances. Austin's artistic and financial success encouraged visits by even higher-calibre singers, such as Joseph and Mary Anne Paton Wood, who came in the mid-1830s. The appearance of singers of increasingly higher calibre on the theatrical and concert circuits in America meant that performance quality gradually improved. And improved performances brought about an increase in the expectations of American audiences. Heightened audience expectations, in turn, added to the pressure on theatre managers to recruit even better singers. This pattern continued through the 1830s and well into the 1840s. In fact, as early as the mid-thirties, according to one theatre manager, the practice of importing British vocal stars had become so entrenched here that opera had become "essential to the success of a theatrical season."[61] During this period, itinerant singers—recruited from England by America's theatre managers—introduced to Americans large numbers of English operas as well as Italian operas in translation; as a result, Americans' taste for opera in general (and *bel canto* opera in particular) grew apace. Perhaps more important for our purposes, however, is the fact that Americans' level of expectations also grew; by the late 1830s Americans were no longer satisfied with performances—either in concert or on the stage—by mediocre or low-calibre singers. One contemporary critic, writing in 1847, neatly summed up his perception of the important role that vocal stars had played in the development of music in America when he wrote that they had "made the citizens of these United States [fall] in love with music."[62]

It would be tempting to conclude from commentary of this nature that the impact made by vocal stars was felt almost exclusively in urban areas of the Northeast, for most print criticism about vocal stars (like that quoted above) is in reference to appearances by singers in staged productions of operas. Operatic performances, by their very nature, required the services of a stock company at an established theatre, and established theatres thrive in large urban centers. And despite the fact that theatre audiences during this time—even those in attendance at performances of opera—were comprised of a wide range of Americans of mixed social and economic backgrounds, they were, for the most part, urban-dwellers. But all of these vocal stars concertized widely, and those Americans who attended concerts—especially those attracted to concerts like those that Shirreff and Wilson presented during much of their 1839 summer tour—were often residents of small towns, villages, or even the countryside. One could argue, then, that visiting singers like Shirreff and Wilson had a greater—or at least as significant an—impact on the development of American musical culture from their activities on the concert circuit than from their performances in theatres, for the former were given, for the most part, *away* from large urban areas. Furthermore, those concerts given in places like New York, Philadelphia, and Boston attracted audiences more diverse than those typically in attendance at the theatre. Many individuals, for example, preferred the increased variety available in concert performances; others—of a religious persuasion—were cut off from theatrical performances entirely because of moral objections. As a consequence, even in urban areas the singers—by giving the occasional concert—were able to reach and influence an audience larger than that possible by means of theatrical performances alone.

Vocal stars also had an impact on the development of American musical culture through means besides their performances. For example, countless Americans—urban- and rural-dwellers alike—learned operatic music by purchasing sheet music publications of operatic arias "as sung by" celebrities such as Jane Shirreff or John Wilson. Furthermore—and perhaps more important in the long run—singers like Austin, the Woods, Shirreff, and Wilson helped to attract many good instrumental performers to the United States by creating a demand for better theatre orchestras to accompany their operatic performances. One critic, writing in 1835, suggested that the musical profession in general—and the orchestra of New York's Park Theatre in particular—was indebted to Elizabeth Austin, for these instrumentalists owed to her the fact that they were "being paid full salaries during the whole season." Furthermore, the critic continued, "through her means have managers of the principal theatres found out the necessity of maintaining full bands."[63] By helping to create an environment in which higher-calibre instrumentalists were valued—and sometimes even actively recruited by theatre managers—vocal stars helped to attract these instrumentalists to the United States. And the presence of these musicians in theatre orchestras, of course, had a major impact on the communities in which they came to live and work, for theatre musicians were also teachers of music, composers, performers, and organizers of concert series.

Jane Shirreff and John Wilson, as singers who followed in the paths of Austin, the Woods, and others, were part of a thriving vocal-star tradition; even more important, perhaps, they encouraged the continuation of the tradition by their very success. Surely the numbers of Americans who witnessed their operatic and concert performances, the media publicity generated by their tours, and—last but hardly least—the immense financial success they enjoyed in North America encouraged other British musicians to try their luck on American audiences during the 1840s and 1850s. Because of a wealth of primary-source materials (including Mary Blundell's detailed journal), the experiences of Jane Shirreff and John Wilson in this country are easier to document than are the experiences of other vocal stars. It is important to remember, however, that these two were far from alone. Other vocal stars had experiences similar to theirs in the 1820s, 1830s, and well into the 1840s. The success of any of these British singers helped to increase the number of professional musicians—instrumental and vocal, visiting or immigrant—in the United States during the 1840s. And the many concerts and operatic performances in which singers participated during their visits to this continent acquainted many Americans with much unfamiliar vocal music: traditional ballads, composed songs, and works from the operatic stages of Europe.

---

[1] The journal by Mary Blundell is part of the Jane Shirreff Collection, housed in the Billy Rose Theatre Collection of The New York Public Library. The Shirreff Collection also includes volumes of playbills from Shirreff's London career in addition to documents pertinent to her American

tour—such as her financial ledger, a pocket diary, playbills, and clippings. The library is unable to supply any information concerning the provenance of the collection.

This article is based in part on a chapter from my book, *Opera on the Road: Traveling Opera Troupes in the United States, 1825-60* (Urbana: University of Illinois Press, 1993).

[2] For excerpts from many of these published works, and for a very useful discussion of them, see Allan Nevins, ed., *American Social History as Recorded by British Travellers* (New York: Henry Holt and Company, 1923).

[3] *Knickerbocker* (November 1838): 470. For additional information about Shirreff, see Harold Rosenthal, *Two Centuries of Opera at Covent Garden* (London: Putnam, 1958), 40, 42, 46-50; W. H. Husk, "Jane Shirreff," *A Dictionary of Music and Musicians*, ed. Sir George Grove (London: Macmillan, 1898); Stephen S. Stratton and James D. Brown, *British Musical Biography: A Dictionary of Musical Artists, Authors, and Composers Born in Britain and Its Colonies* (Birmingham: Stratton, 1897; reprint, New York: Da Capo, 1971); and Preston, *Opera on the Road.*

[4] According to theatre historian Joseph N. Ireland, writing in the mid-1860s, Jane Shirreff was America's "most admired English prima donna between the days of Mrs. Wood and those of Louisa Pyne." The latter singer, the immensely successful star of the Pyne and Harrison Opera troupe, toured the United States from 1854-56; Pyne was also quite an influential force in an attempt to establish English opera in London in the late 1850s and 1860s. Joseph N. Ireland, *Records of the New York Stage from 1750 to 1860*, 2 vols. (New York:T. H. Morrell, 1866-67; reprint, New York: Burt Franklin, 1968) 2:276.

[5] For information about American musical-theatrical repertory in the 18th and early 19th centuries, see Julian Mates, *The American Musical Stage Before 1800* (New Brunswick, N.J.: Rutgers University Press, 1962) and *America's Musical Stage: Two Hundred Years of Musical Theatre* (Westport, Conn.: Greenwood Press, 1985); Susan L. Porter, *With an Air Debonair. Musical Theatre in America, 1785-1815* (Washington, D. C.: Smithsonian Institution Press, 1991); and Preston, *Opera on the Road.*

[6] George C. D. Odell, *Annals of the New York Stage*, 15 vols. (New York: Columbia University Press, 1927-1949; reprint, New York: AMS Press, 1970) 2:348.

[7] In the 1830s and 1840s there were two dominant theatrical centers in the United States: New York and New Orleans. Both cities had their own spheres of influence (for New Orleans, this included Mobile and Baton Rouge—and slightly later, Nashville and St. Louis; in New York's sphere

were Philadelphia, Boston, and Baltimore) and itinerant performers visited each. In the late 1830s the two circuits still were fairly independent of each other. Only in the early 1840s did travelling actors and singers begin to include both cities on their tours on a regular basis. It was not until the 1850s that visits to each became expected; this occurred in the later decade only after such long-distance tours were made economically feasible by the construction of a viable transportation system and the establishment of permanent theatres in towns and cities along the Ohio/Mississippi River network.

[8]Rooke (1794-1847), an Irish composer and violinist, is best known as the teacher of the British opera composer Michael William Balfe (1808-1870). Rooke was a well-known theatre musician first in Dublin and later in London; he served as chorus master at Drury Lane and orchestra leader under Bishop at Vauxhall Gardens in the 1830s. *Amilie*, Rooke's first opera, had been composed in 1818, so it was not new at the time of its London premiere, which took place on 9 December 1837. See *The New Grove Dictionary of Music and Musicians* (London: Macmillan, 1980), s.v. "Rooke, William Michael," by H. W. Husk and W. H. Grattan Flood. See also, the *Athenaeum* (9 December 1837): 900.

[9]Blundell diary, 40.

[10]Information about casts is gleaned from a variety of sources, including playbills in the Shirreff Collection and advertisements in numerous newspapers, including the following: *Boston Evening Transcript* and *Morning Post* (5-23 November 1838); *Baltimore American & Commercial Advertiser* and *Daily Advertiser* (31 December 1838—13 January 1839); *The Pennsylvanian, North American,* and *Philadelphia Gazette* (14 January—9 February 1839); *Washington National Intelligencer* (24-29 December 1839). Information on the 1838-39 stock companies of the New York and Philadelphia theatres is from Ireland, 2:274; Odell, 4:334 (National Theatre); and Arthur Herman Wilson, *A History of the Philadelphia Theatre, 1835-1855* (Philadelphia: University of Pennsylvania Press, 1935), 103 (Chestnut St. Theatre).

[11]The North American premiere of *La Sonnambula* (in Bishop's adaptation) was presented by the Woods in New York on 13 November 1835. *Fra Diavolo* was first seen here in an adaptation by Thomas Reynoldson (starring Elizabeth Austin, in New York in June 1833); the North American premiere of the Lacy adaptation was given by the Woods, also in New York on 19 November 1833 (Odell, 6:661). The Lacy/Rossini *Cinderella* was first performed here by Elizabeth Austin at the Park Theatre on 24 January 1831. All three of these operas—and, in particular, *Cinderella* and *La Sonnambula*—continued to be very popular on the American stage until

well after the Civil War. In fact, according to Charles Hamm, *Cinderella* was "one of the most popular works of musical theatre in the history of the American stage." *Yesterdays: Popular Song in America* (New York: Norton, 1979), 71-72.

During their 20 months in this country Shirreff and Wilson performed in twenty-three operas. In addition to those already mentioned, the most frequently performed were Adolph Adam's *The Postillion of Longjumeau*, John Barnett's *The Mountain Sylph*, and Auber's *Gustavus III*. For more information on operatic repertory and on the singers' operatic activities in general, see Preston, *Opera on the Road*.

[12]*The Corsair* (23 March 1839): 30.

[13]*The Corsair* (4 May 1839): 123.

[14]William G. Carson, *Managers in Distress: The St. Louis Stage, 1840-1844* (St. Louis: St. Louis Historical Documents Foundation, 1949), 15.

[15]During 1839-40 Shirreff and Wilson sang in 65 operatic performances, as follows: twelve in Philadelphia (16-28 September), seven in Baltimore (30 September—7 October), twelve in New York (14-26 October), ten in Charleston (14-27 December), twelve in New York at the Park Theatre (30 March—13 April and 22 May), and twelve in Philadelphia (20 April—2 May).

[16]Instead of concerts, they sang in a brief operatic season in Charleston.

[17]Blundell mentions several times in her diary that their group numbered six; the identity of the additional individual, however, is unknown.

It was not unusual for singers and other performers to travel with other members of their families; as Michael Baker points out in his study of nineteenth-century actors, "While the stock system predominated, acting was essentially a family affair. The family unit was central to almost all companies, large and small; indeed among the smallest troupes a single family might comprise . . . the whole company" (quoted in Arthur W. Bloom, "The Jefferson Company, 1830-1845," *Theatre Survey. The American Journal of Theatre History* 27/1-2: 93-94). The same could be said for itinerant musical performers. Sometimes two performers who travelled together were husband and wife (such as the vocal stars Anne and Edward Seguin and the actress Charlotte Cushman and the musician James Maeder); sometimes they were father and daughter (such as the actor Peter Richings and his soprano daughter Caroline). It was likewise not unusual for non-theatrical family members—spouses, parents, siblings, children—to travel with itinerant performers, although this information is almost never mentioned in the print media of the early nineteenth century. Barring a handful of chance references, one would assume that itinerant performers did not have families, or that they were tucked away back home somewhere, safe and sound. Published references to Shirreff's mother, for example, are limited to the list of passengers who arrived on the steamer *Great Western* from London in September 1838. Information about such travelling companions must be ferreted out from other (usually rare) sources, such as the diaries kept by Blundell and Shirreff.

[18] Blundell diary, 204.
[19] Shirreff diary, 20 July and 21 August 1839.
[20] Blundell diary, 204.
[21] Blundell diary, 131.
[22] Blundell diary, 136-44, 150-54.
[23] Blundell diary, 144.
[24] Shirreff diary, 11 July 1839; Blundell diary, 146.
[25] Shirreff diary, 17 July 1839.
[26] Blundell diary, 162, 166, 164-65.
[27] Shirreff diary, 13 July 1839.
[28] Shirreff diary, 7 November 1839.
[29] Latham was a singing actor who performed widely with the stock companies of both the Park and National theatres. The Seguins had come to the United States at the same time as Shirreff and Wilson; Edward Seguin performed with the other two vocal stars for all of the 1838-39 season, and Anne Seguin joined the troupe in February.

After the Seguins concluded their various engagements with James Wallack following 1840, they formed the Seguin Opera Company, a well-travelled vocal-star troupe that performed English opera in the United States until shortly before Edward Seguin's death in 1852. The Seguins played an important role in the cultivation of English opera in this country during the 1840s; it would be easy to argue, in fact, that they were the most important proponents of opera in English in this country throughout the entire decade. For more information about their later careers, see Preston, *Opera on the Road*, chapter 5 and *The New Grove Dictionary of American Music* (New York: Grove's Dictionaries, 1986), s.v. "Seguin," by Nicholas Tawa.

[30] For example, the Seguins gave "Grand Vocal Concerts" in Montreal on 21 and 23 August, the week before Shirreff and Wilson were to appear in that city (*Montreal Gazette*, 20, 22 August 1839).
[31] Shirreff diary, 31 August 1839.
[32] John Curtis, "One Hundred Years of Grand Opera in Philadelphia," n.d., typescript, p. 249, The Historical Society of Pennsylvania, Philadelphia.
[33] Shirreff diary, 5 and 15 July 1839.
[34] Extant correspondence between performers and managers active during the

antebellum period suggests that although some engagements (especially at the more prominent theatres) were set up months in advance, it was certainly possible to make last-minute arrangements. See, for example, Peter Richings (manager of the soprano Caroline Richings) to Henry Warren (the manager of theatres in Buffalo and Rochester), 4 November 1856, in the William James Davis Collection, Manuscript Division, Chicago Historical Society; Nicholas Bochsa (manager of the soprano Anna Bishop) to Messrs. Peters and Field of the Music House, Cincinnati, 19 June 1848 in the Manuscript Division, Chicago Historical Society; and Correspondence, John T. Ford Theatre Collection, Manuscript Division, Library of Congress.

[35] Bloom, "The Jefferson Company, 1830-1845," 91.

[36] Shirreff financial ledger.

[37] Shirreff diary, 25 November 1839.

[38] Shirreff diary, 27 November 1839.

[39] Gary Greene, "Understanding Past Currency in Modern Terms," *The Sonneck Society Bulletin* (Summer 1987): 48.

[40] James G. Maeder (1809-1876), an Irish-born theatre musician, composer, and vocal coach, had come to the United States in 1833 with the Woods and had travelled with them on their 1833-34 tour around this country. He and his wife, the well-known actress and singer Clara Fisher, travelled widely in North America. Maeder was an active and highly visible musician in the antebellum period; he led theatre orchestras, wrote and arranged music, and coached and accompanied singers. His association with Shirreff and Wilson is reported in the *Morning Herald*, 11 and 21 November 1839. For more information on Maeder, see *The New Grove Dictionary of American Music*, s.v. "Maeder, James G.," by William Brooks.

[41] John Wilson, *Wilson's Edition of the Songs of Scotland* (London: Printed for Mr. Wilson, 47 Gower Street, n.d.).

[42] Copies of these compositions can be found in the collection of the Music Division, Library of Congress.

[43] See Preston, *Opera on the Road*, Prologue. For a discussion of the American popularity of Thomas Moore's *Irish Melodies*, see Hamm, *Yesterdays: Popular Song in America*, chapter 3.

[44] *Albany Argus*, 9 July 1839; Shirreff diary, 4 December 1839.

[45] The dates on which these selections were performed were as follows: Rossini: Albany, 8 July 1839 and Baltimore, 30 January 1840; Balfe: Albany, 8 July 1839; Baltimore, 27 January 1840; and New York City, 15 November 1839; Bellini: Albany, 1 July 1839; Donizetti: Baltimore, 1 February 1840; Adam: Baltimore, 1 February 1840; and Hérold: New York City, 15 November 1839.

[46] The quotations are taken from the following pieces of sheet music, all from the collection of the Music Division of the Library of Congress: "The Rapture Dwelling" (New York: Atwill, 184-?), "The Flowers of the Forest" (New York: Millett Music Saloon, n.d.), and "Proudly and Wide" (New York: Atwill, n.d.). These publications are typical.

[47] *Savannah Republican*, 8 January 1840.

[48] *Savannah Republican*, 10 January 1840.

[49] These quotations are taken from the following newspapers: *Hartford Courant*, 5 November 1839; *Montreal Gazette*, 29 August 1839; *New York Morning Herald*, 12 November 1839; *Philadelphia National Gazette*, 28 November 1839.

[50] Blundell diary, 160-61.

[51] Blundell diary, 145-46.

[52] Blundell diary, 160.

[53] Shirreff diary, 6-7 December 1839.

[54] Blundell diary, 186-87.

[55] Blundell diary, 188-90.

[56] Shirreff diary, 16 December 1839.

[57] Shirreff diary, 30, 23, and 31 December 1839.

[58] Jane Shirreff was ill for several weeks in early 1839 and missed sixteen opera performances in Philadelphia and New York; her total opera appearances during this visit was 237; Wilson appeared in 253 productions.

[59] Information on salaries paid to Americans during this period is exceedingly difficult to find. The information cited is from Daniel Preston, "Market and Mill Town: Hamilton, Ohio, 1795-1860" (Ph.D. diss., University of Maryland, 1987) and Alan Dawley, *Class and Community. The Industrial Revolution in Lynn* (Cambridge: Harvard University Press, 1976), 53-54. Information on van Buren's salary is from Richard B. Morris, ed., *Encyclopedia of American History* (New York: Harper and Row, 1976), 299.

[60] Although the financial information available is from Shirreff's account book, her earnings presumably also reflect those of John Wilson.

[61] Francis C. Wemyss, *Twenty-Six Years of the Life of an Actor and Manager* (New York: Burgess, Stringer & Co., 1847), 236.

[62] Ibid., 236.

[63] *American Musical Journal* (April 1835): 115.

CATHOLIC CHURCH MUSIC IN THE MIDWEST BEFORE THE CIVIL WAR: THE FIRM OF W. C. PETERS & SONS

Richard D. Wetzel

INTRODUCTION

The number of Roman Catholics living in America during the Colonial period was small, especially in the Midwest, which was populated largely by Methodists, Baptists and Presbyterians. As late as the first decade of the nineteenth century, there were fewer than 100,000 Catholics outside Louisiana; and a single diocese, Baltimore, served all the Roman Catholics in the country.

The first Catholic Bishop in America, the remarkable John Carroll (1735-1815), was consecrated Bishop of Baltimore in 1790. American-born but educated in Belgium by Jesuits, he survived the suppression of his order by Pope Clement XIV in 1773. Upon returning to America he distinguished himself as an able administrator and educator and was elevated to Archbishop of Baltimore in 1808, the year in which his diocese was divided and four other dioceses were created (Boston, Philadelphia, New York, and Bardstown—later Louisville).

Under subsequent bishops, among them John England, Francis Patrick, Martin Spalding, John Hughes, John Purcell, Simon Brute, and Benedict Flaget, the Catholic Church grew rapidly. By 1840, Baltimore, now an archiepiscopal see, presided over fifteen suffragan sees. In addition to those cited above, the following were added: Charleston and Richmond (1820); Cincinnati (1821); St. Louis and New Orleans (1826); Mobile (1829); Detroit (1833); Vincennes (1834); Dubuque, Nashville and Natchez (1837). By 1852 there were six provinces: Baltimore, Oregon City, St. Louis, New York, Cincinnati, and New Orleans.[1]

The initial increase in the number of American Catholics resulted from the large influx of Irish Catholics in the 1820s. Catholic Church historian, Thomas Bokenkotter states that ". . . because of Irish immigrants, the number of Catholics jumped from about 500,000 (out of a population of 12 million) in 1830 to 3,103,000 in 1860 (out of a population of 31.5 million)—an increase of over 800 percent. . . ."[2]

German immigration added to the numbers in the 1840s and 1850s, and German parishes were so numerous in Milwaukee, Cincinnati, and St. Louis that the area between them came to be called the "German Triangle." "So large was the increase in members that by 1850, Roman Catholicism, which at the birth of the nation was nearly invisible in terms of numbers, had now become the nation's largest religious denomination."[3]

But the liturgy in most parishes was in disarray, and views about Church polity and liturgy were far from uniform. Catholic Church music was not distinctive; published liturgical music and the musicians needed to perform it were in short supply. Benedict J. Fenwick, Bishop of Boston from 1833 to 1836, estimated that in the first half of the nineteenth century there was "no singing at all in two thirds of the Catholic churches of America."[4]

There were several reasons for this condition. First, newly arrived immigrants were from divergent cultural backgrounds, and many were musically and liturgically illiterate. Most came from countries where Catholicism had been suppressed, and they had forgotten the liturgy. Second, even among clergy and musicians, there were few who knew the history and subtleties of the music of the Mass and Office, and an enormous pedagogical challenge confronted those who did. Third, as the number of Catholic immigrants increased, the reception given them upon their arrival in America became less hospitable; this had an inhibiting effect upon the composition and publication of liturgical music.

Evidence of religious intolerance is abundant. Hostilities between Catholics and Protestants were especially virulent between 1830 and 1860, and in some cases culminated in the burning of churches and convents.[5] Religious prejudice and bigotry were kept alive by clergy and laymen on both sides, and efforts to both promote and combat them were made in sermons, pamphlets, books, and sectarian newspapers. Among the latter was *The Catholic Advocate and Journal of Useful Literature and General Intelligence* (hereafter *The Catholic Advocate*), published at Bardstown, Kentucky, in the 1830s and 1840s. The first editor of this paper appears to have been B. J. Webb, a noted music publisher, musician, and entrepreneur in the Bardstown (Louisville) area. From the following, which Webb included on the first page of each issue of *The Catholic Advocate*, one can infer the major criticisms leveled at Catholics at that time.

> Catholics abhor from their hearts all kinds of idolatry; they adore no images, nor the saints, nor any other creature: they adore one true

living God, and no more; they give no money to the Priests or the Pope for Absolutions or Indulgences; it is not an article of Catholic faith that the Pope is personally infallible or impeccable; Catholics sincerely believe the whole of God's word, and that faith is to be kept with all men, of every creed and nation, and that due allegiance and just taxes are to be paid to their country, whether native or adopted.

In the issue of 10 February 1838, Webb states that he is entering upon his "3rd year of . . . Editorial Labors." Some of the issue is taken up with an account of the Presbyterians, ". . . who lately met at Columbia, Pennsylvania, for the purpose of declaring war against the Catholic church." But Webb now devotes more space to the activities of the numerous "academies" and "seminaries" (the first designated schools for girls, the second those for boys) then being established throughout Kentucky, Illinois, and Ohio. "By 1840 there were at least two hundred parochial schools in operation, half of them west of the Alleghenies. They formed the nucleus of what was to become the largest system of private schools in the world."[6]

The quality of Catholic schools was soon widely known, and music was a significant element in their curricula. By 1850, it was not uncommon to find children of well-to-do Protestant families enrolled in Catholic schools. Enmity among the general population, however, did not subside appreciably until the beginning of the Civil War.

But education would not bring order to the liturgy, let alone create the distinctive American Catholic liturgy which many desired. The traditional liturgy had its roots in European countries, and the Pope remained the ultimate figure of authority in the church.[7] Even among Catholics, allegiance to a foreign monarch, albeit a religious one, was an idea in conflict with the prevailing democratic attitude. Americans, generally, saw religion as a wholly individual affair and held "that there should be as few intermediaries as possible between the believer and his God. . . ."[8] Some American Catholics not only rejected the idea of a European papacy but believed that the Church hierarchy should not own the property of the parishes. Throughout the Colonial period and well into the nineteenth century, Catholic clergy were understandably more concerned with the survival of the church than with music and the correctness of the liturgy.

This was especially true on the American frontier, where social decorum and politeness were often held in contempt. Curiously, this fiercely independent frontier spirit found expression in an act which frustrated clergy and civic leaders, appalled visiting Europeans (who consistently referred to it in their travel diaries), and is documented in numerous contemporary sources which describe American's early governmental, cultural, and religious life: it was the habit of chewing tobacco and spitting. The following are excerpted from a column titled "Eleven Rules for a Gentleman at Church," which appeared in *The Catholic Advocate*, 10 March 1838:

> No. 6. Never thinks of defiling the House of God with tobacco spittle, or annoying those who sit near him by chewing that nauseous weed in Church.
>
> No. 9. Does not whisper, or laugh, or eat fruit in the house of God, or lounge in that holy place.
>
> No. 10. Does not rush out of the Church like a trampling horse, the moment the benediction is pronounced.

Bringing unbridled and rebellious Americans to acceptable social behavior would be difficult enough; teaching them to appreciate the symbolism and theological subtleties of the Roman rite, especially in its music, would be a monumental task.

But a formidable obstacle to the cultivation of liturgical music in American Catholicism was inherent in the Church itself. Even those few American clergy and musicians who had the requisite training and resources to look to Europe for models for liturgical music, found centuries of confusion and disagreement. Through the proliferation of imperfect editions of chant and through the incursion of operatic and theatrical performance manners, plainchant—the life blood of the liturgy—had all but disappeared by the close of the eighteenth century.[9]

Eighteenth-century papal edicts and encyclicals against the use of popular and theater music in the church had had little effect, and some suggest a wavering papal attitude. Pope Benedict XIII addressed the awarding of "singing benefices" in 1725, stating that ". . . those are to be preferred who know the Gregorian chant. . . ."[10] That any who did not know chant should be considered for such awards seems incredulous.

The same Pope, however, took a harder line in 1727 when he chastised a monastic order for its music which was causing "great harm" and similarly criticized the nuns of a convent at Milan for their use of "figured music" and musical instruments. The reprimand of the latter was especially harsh:

> Never more, and at no time in the future may anyone for any reason, cause, or . . . make use of figured music, or dare to introduce musical instruments into the Church and choir. . . . Anyone who might . . . dare to disobey this edict will suffer the punishment of interdict of the Church. . . .[11]

That monophonic chant was in decline, however, is seen clearly in the encyclical *Annus qui* (1749) of Pope Benedict XIV. Under the heading "Divine Office," he wrote:

> The third thing of which we desired to warn you is the musical chant. It has now been introduced into the churches and is commonly accompanied by the organ and other musical instruments. Let it be executed in such a way as not to appear profane, worldly or theatrical.[12]

In the same encyclical, Pope Benedict XIV attempted to make a distinction between sacred or liturgical music and theater music and theatrical performance practices:

> ... All the authors whom we have quoted above as being favorable to figurative chant [also referred to as "harmonic chant"] and the use of musical instruments in churches, clearly say and testify that they have always meant and wished by their writings to exclude the chant and that music proper to the platform [concert hall] and to theaters, because they, like others, condemn and despise such chant and music.[13]

But operatic elements continued to be assimilated into church music throughout the eighteenth and nineteenth centuries and contrafacta (especially Marian texts) on opera arias were numerous. Further, instrumental music was increasingly used in Mass and Office, and the leading church musicians were also successful composers of concertos, sonatas, and operas. Meanwhile, singers who understood Gregorian chant became fewer in number, and as the Roman Catholic church in America was in its first great era of expansion (1820-60), the status of chant was at an all-time nadir.

The first efforts to publish Catholic music in North America were made by Protestants in the cities of the East. John Aitken's *Compilation of the Litanies and Vespers, Hymns and Anthems as they are sung in the Catholic Church, adapted for Voice and Organ* (Philadelphia, 1787), appears to have been the earliest of its kind.[14] Aitken's compilation included Protestant hymns, Catholic hymns, and two masses, all in two-part settings. John Cheverus, Bishop of Boston, issued *Anthems, Hymns, etc., Usually Sung at the Catholick [sic] Church in Boston* in 1800. While its compiler was Catholic, the collection borrowed heavily from Protestant repertories, and neither of these collections was especially distinctive.

The earliest important Catholic music composed in the United States was that of Benjamin Carr (1768-1831), who over a period of some thirty years, served as organist at four Philadelphia churches: St. Augustine's Roman Catholic; St. Mary's Roman Catholic; St. Joseph's Roman Catholic; and St. Peter's Protestant Episcopal. In 1805 he published *A New Edition with an Appendix of Masses, Vespers, Litanies, Hymns, Psalms, Anthems & Motets. Composed, Selected and Arranged for the Use of the Catholic Churches in the United States of America & Respectfully Dedicated by permission of the Right Rev. John Carrol D. D. Bishop of Baltimore, By Benjamin Carr.*[15] While designed for use in the East, this, and other works by Carr, had a profound influence on the publishing of liturgical music in the Midwest, to which we now turn our attention.

THE SACRED MUSIC CATALOGS OF W. C. PETERS & SONS, CINCINNATI

Two catalogs of sacred music issued by the firm of W. C. Peters & Sons, Cincinnati, suggest that this company was possibly the earliest, and from 1845 to 1865, the leading publisher of liturgical music in the Midwest. Further, W. C. Peters' own sacred music shows a dedication to liturgical reform that is unique for the time and place. Some background on this patriarch of what was a virtual music publishing dynasty in the Ohio Valley will be helpful before focusing upon the catalogs.

William Cumming Peters was born in Devonshire, England, in 1805. Around 1820, he reportedly immigrated to Canada with his father, two brothers, and a sister. (There is no mention of a mother, although accounts of Peters and his family at this period are secondary and largely anecdotal.)

Around 1827 Peters was in Pittsburgh, where he established a "Musical Repository," selling pianos and sheet music and giving instruction in piano. From 1827 to 1831, he was associated with the musicians of a German religious commune, Georg Rapp's Harmonie Gesellschaft, for whom he composed a Symphony in D, possibly the earliest work of its kind composed West of the Alleghenies.[16] He also gave public concerts in Pittsburgh and was organist at Trinity Episcopal Church. Peters left Pittsburgh for Louisville in 1832 and in that year was listed in the city directory as "Professor of Music."

For a time he operated a private school and circulating library, assisted by his brothers Henry and John. In the 1830s and 1840s he became famous as a composer of songs and piano pieces which were published in the East by J. L. Hewitt (New York); George Willig (Philadelphia and Baltimore); and Firth, Hall, and Pond (New York), among others. Peters was also active as a publisher in the late 1830s and by 1844 had issued about ninety titles through his companies "W. C. Peters, Louisville" and "Peters and Co., Cincinnati." With profits made from publishing songs by Stephen C.

Foster and through his consistently astute business practices, he founded or was affiliated with about a dozen publishing companies. Among his many partners were his brother Henry, F. J. Webster, Joel Field, his sons William, Alfred, and John, and B. J. Webb, the editor of *The Catholic Advocate*.

Peters was appointed organist at Louisville's St. Louis Cathedral no later than 1844 and presumably became a Roman Catholic about the same time. He left Louisville in 1849 and moved to Baltimore but remained there for only one year. In 1851, he moved to Cincinnati and established the firm W. C. Peters & Sons which became the largest publishing house and music and musical instrument dealership in the Midwest.

Peters was choirmaster at St. Peter's Cathedral in Cincinnati and devoted much of his later life to composing, compiling, and publishing music for the Roman Catholic Church. He was a towering figure in the publishing industry, a charter member of the Board of Music Trade of the United States of America (1855), and his activities and interests touched every facet of musical life in the Midwest before the Civil War.

1856 Catalog

Around 1856, the firm of W. C. Peters and Sons issued a song sheet with a back-page catalog titled *Select Sacred Music Suitable for the Catholic Church Service*....[17] This catalog and a subsequent one issued by the same company in 1863 provide information about music used in American Catholic Churches at this time and document the achievements of a remarkable man.

The catalog lists 137 titles of pieces and collections, by fifty-one composers, and gives the plate numbers of the items and the voices for which they are written or arranged. The plate numbers range from number 49, a number consistent with secular pieces issued by W. C. Peters around 1844, to number 2638, *Adoremus Te* by Lambillotte, which Peters deposited for copyright 26 June 1856.[18]

The contents of the catalog are given below in complete but condensed format. Each title is given once. The title is followed by the names of the composers who set the text, the plate number of the title, and the vocal arrangement of each setting as given in the catalog. For most entries, the catalog gives only the last names of the composers, and some titles appear without the composers' names. The latter are shown below with the symbol (nn) before the plate number. Where no setting is given in the catalog, the symbol (ns) is inserted. All other parenthetical insertions are found in the catalog.

Adeste Fideles and **Respones** [*sic*]: (nn) 1059 (ns).
Agnus Dei: Marcello: 2216-Duett for Bassi.
Adoremus: Lambillotte: 2638-4 voices.
Alma Redemptoris: Pleyel: 120-4 voices; Stadler: 1701-4 voices; Lambillotte: 2370-4 voices; Zimmers: 1772-2 voices.
A solis ortus, and **Litany B.V.**: (nn): 1704-(ns).
Asperges: Himmel: 1762-4 voices; Zimmers: 1763-3 voices; Himmel: 1764-4 voices; Himmel: 1765-4 voices; Novello: 1766-3 voices; Cross: 1768 (ns) (See **Laudate**).
Audi Benigna, and **Lucis Creator**: (nn) 1691 (ns).
Ave Maris Stella: Donizetti: 1653-3 voices.
Ave Maria: Onslow: 75-4 voices; Schwing: 1434-Solo; Winter: 1965-3 voices; Italian: 1737-Solo.
Ave Maria: or **O Queen**: Marlianai: 1738-Solo.
Ave Maria: or **Ave Regina**: Cherubini: 1741-Solo.
Ave Regina: Novello: 2626-Solo and Chorus.
Ave Regina: or **Gaude Virgo**: Novello: 1740 (ns).
Ave Regina; and **Ave Maria**: Mercadante: 1742 (ns).
Ave Verum: Novello: 1757-Solo; Himmel: 1758-Solo; Mozart: 1700-4 voices; King & Cook: 1759-Solo; Rossini: 1825-4 voices.
Catholic Harmonist: A Collection of Masses, Hymns, Vespers, etc., for the Principal Feasts of the Year. . . .: Peters: 2633 (ns).
Credo (Semi chant): (nn): 2237-4 voices.
Domine Exaudi: Schwing: 1684-Beautiful Sop. Solo.
Ecce Panis: Himmel: 1729-Solo; Herold: 1730-Solo; Himmel: 1731-Duett; D'Hollander: 1697-Duett; D'Hollander: 1702-Duett; Donizetti: 1854-Duett; Verhayden: 1486-Solo and Chorus.
Gaude Virgo: Novello: 1740 (ns).
Hail to the Lord's Annointed: (nn): 67-Solo and Chorus.
Hymns for Easter: Schwing: 1445-4 voices.
Hymn to B.V. (See **Ave**): Schwing: 1434-Solo.
Inclina Domine: Scheidermeyer: 1695-4 voices.
In violata: (**Who can Compare**) Colliere: 2214 (ns).
Iste Confessor: (nn): 1703-3 voices.
Jesu dulic memoria: Baumgarten: 1699-Bass Solo.
Jesu Fili Dei: Winter: 1124-3 voices.
Jesu Mater Ave: Mozart: 1675-Solo and Chorus.
Laudate Dominum: Cross: 1768 (ns); Himmel: 1735-4 voices.
Magnificat: Mozart: 2164 (ns); Loder: 2629 (ns).
Mass: Carr: 1654-(Chant Mass); Carr: 1656-3 voices (For Low Mass); Scheidermeyer: 1376-in C-4 voices; Buhler: 2325-in E

Flat-4 voices; Stark: 1667-3 voices (easy); Knitze: 1607-**Pastoral in G**-4 voices; Dietsch: 1607-3 voices. Selected; Gregorian: 2631-for one voice in D; (nn) 2632-3 voices. Selected; Ohnewald: 1644-**Requiem** for 3 or 4 voices.
Memorare: Lambillotte: 74-Solo and Chorus.
Miserere nostri: Martini: 1732-Duett.
Miserere: 1773-Gregorian Chant.
Newland's Collection of Sacred Music, containing No. 1-**Alma** by Webbe; No.2-**Ave** by Carr; No. 3-**Ave** No. 2 by Carr; No. 4-**Regina Coeli**, by Purcell; No. 5-**Salve Regina**, by Handel: 1649 (ns).
O Benigna (Bless'd be thou): Novello: 952 (ns).
O Cor Amoris: (nn): 1626-Solo, Duett and Chorus.
O Gloriosa Domina: Lambillotte: 1777-4 voices.
O Maria; or **Ave Maria**: (nn): 1733-Duett.
O Quam dilecta: Lambillotte: 1487-Solo and Chorus.
O Salutaris: D'Hollander: 1115-Duett; D'Hollander: 1696-Duett; (nn) 1753-Treble Solo; (nn) 1754-Trio; (nn) 1755-Solo; Dufort: 1652 (ns); Stradella: 2215-Solo.
Parce Domine, and Misere: Schwartz: 1448 (ns).
Pastores (See **Christmas H.**): Lambillotte: 2361 (ns).
Prayer for the Commonwealth: Taylor 1648 (ns).
Quid Retribuam: Lambillotte: 1375-Solo and Chorus.
Regina Coeli: Lambillotte: 2202-Duett and Chorus; Gansbacher: 1438-4 voices; Winter; 2627-3 voices; Herold: 1743-Solo and chorus; Stark: 1687 (ns).
Riposa in Pace: Martini: 1769-Duett.
Salve Regina: Baumgartner: 1693- 4 voices; Himmel: 1744 Solo; Manners: 1745-Solo; Cooke: 1746-Solo; Loder: 2628-Trio.
Sancta Maria: Buhler: 2635-Solo and Chorus.
Stabat Mater: Baini: 1686-3 voices.
Stabat. Jerusalem and **Miserere**: (nn): 1761-(ns).
Tantum Ergo: Novello:; 1747-3 voices; Cooke: 1748-3 voices; Winter: 1749-3 voices; Giardini: 1750-3 voices; Carusi: 1751-3 voices; Schwartz: 1451-4 voices; Terziani: 1689-4 voices; Stark: 1698-4 voices; Lambillotte: 2334-(grand) 4 voices; Lambillotte: 1966-5 voices.
Te Deum: Newland: 1645-3 voices; B. Carr: 1647-3 voices.
There Were Shepherds: B. Carr: 1647 (ns).
Thirteen Hymns for Vespers: Loder: 1771 (ns).
Tu Rex Gloriae: Novello: 1734-Bass Solo.

Veni Creator: Sofge 2162-4 voices; (nn): 1690 (ns); Himmel: 1855-Solo and Chorus.
Veni Sancte Spiritus: Handel: 1736-Solo; Dietsch: 1933-4 voices.
Veni Filii: Baini: 1694-3 voices.
Vesper Hymn to B.V.: (nn): 49- Solo and Chorus.
Vesper Hymn to the Assumption: W. C. Peters: 112 (ns).
Vespers with **O Salutaris**: Loder: 2630 (ns).
Vespers and **Magnificat**: Novello: 1770 (ns).
Vespers (10 Setts for various F'ts): Newland 1655 (ns).
Vidi Aquam: Novello: 1767-3 voices.
Young Catholic's Vocal Class Book: (nn) 2634 (ns).

The catalog does not classify the items by type, nor does it indicate where they fit in the Mass or Office. Most are identifiable as psalms, antiphons, hymns, single parts of the Ordinary, canticles, anthems with English texts, collections of hymns, and complete masses.

The hymn *Tantum Ergo*, a text ascribed to St. Thomas Aquinas, and generally sung before the Benediction in the Mass, appears eleven times, outnumbering all other single items.

The popularity of Marian texts is apparent. The four major Marian Antiphons are represented with four settings of *Alma Redemptoris*, sung from Advent to the first of February; four of *Ave Regina*, sung from the second of February (Purification of the Virgin Mary) to Wednesday of Holy Week; five of *Regina Caeli* sung from Easter to the Friday after Pentecost; and five of *Salve Regina*, sung from the Feast of the Trinity until the Saturday before the first Sunday in Advent. The catalog, then, offers settings of these to cover the entire Liturgical Year. Additional settings of some of these are also found in *Newland's Collection*.

Among the other antiphons are *Adoremus* (let us adore forever the most Holy Sacrament), generally coupled with the psalm *Laudate Dominum* and sung at the close of the service; and *Asperges*, sung as a "prelude" to the Mass.

The greater number of antiphons and hymns are those used at the Office of Vespers. Among these are *A solis ortus*, antiphon for the Second Vespers of the Holy Name of Jesus; *Audi benigna*, hymn for Vespers during Lent; *Ave Maris Stella*, Vesper hymn; *Ave Maria*, antiphon for Second Vespers of the seventh of October; *Iste Confessor*, hymn for Second Vespers of a Confessor Bishop; *Jesu dulci Memoria*, hymn for Vespers during Christmastide; *quid Retribuam*, antiphon for First Vespers of the Feast of the Most Sacred Heart of Jesus; and *Veni Creator*, hymn for the Second Vespers of Whit Sunday. In addition, there are five presumably complete

Catholic Church Music in the Midwest 213

"Vespers," combined with *O Salutaris, Magnificat,* and *10 Setts for Various F'sts* [sic].

Five settings of *Ave Verum* and seven of *O Salutaris* are provided for use at the Elevation, while Canticles are represented by two settings of the *Magnificat* and one of *Miserere Nostri.*

Sequences include *Ecce Panis*, an alternative verse for the sequence, *Lauda Sion salvatorem* originating in the Sarum Rite; *Gaude [Maria?] Virgo*, for the octave of Christmas; *In Violata*, from the "litany of Loretto"; *Stabat Mater*, from the Mass of the Seven Sorrows of the Blessed Virgin Mary; and *Veni Sancte Spiritus,* for Whit Sunday Mass.

Peters issued these pieces over a twelve-year period, in three cities with significant numbers of Roman Catholics: Louisville, Baltimore, and Cincinnati. The times when they were issued and the composers he selected give perspective to his efforts. While copies of some of the titles have not been found, when some of the sheets were issued can be determined by comparing their plate numbers to related ones found on published sheets bearing copyright dates. The following chronological table has been created using this procedure.

YEARS	PLATE NUMBER	TOTAL ISSUED
1844-45	49; 67; 74; 75	4
1846-49	107; 112; 120; 952; 1059; 1115	6
1850-53	1124; 1375-76; 1434; 1438; 1445; 1448; 1451; 1486-87; 1607; 1625-26; 1644-1650; 1652-1656; 1667; 1675; 1684; 1686-87; 1689; 1690-91; 1693-1699; 1700-04; 1729; 1730-1738; 1740-1749; 1750-55; 1757-59; 1760-69; 1770-73; 1777; 1825; 1854-55; 1933; 1965-66	95
1854-56	2162; 2164; 2202; 2214-2217; 2237; 2325; 2334, 2361; 2370; 2626-2635; 2638	23

Unfortunately, this procedure does not guarantee complete accuracy. While unlikely in view of other considerations, it is possible that some sheets not located were never issued. Also, the plate numbers of the various Peters companies interlock, although irregularly, so that reconstructing an accurate plate number and copyright date table would require the collecting of a large amount of music issued by no fewer than ten companies. Further, a study of several hundred song sheets, as well as copyright ledgers in the Library of Congress, shows that some plate numbers were skipped and used at a later time; some were registered for copyright twice; and it is possible that some were never used.[19] A few samples illustrate these problems.

A secular piece, number 1955 ("Bridal Waltz") was registered for copyright in 1854; but a sheet numbered 1965 (*Ave Maria* by Winter) was registered with other pieces, 17 June 1853. Also in this group was sheet number 1777 (Lambillotte's *O Glorioso Domina*), but the sheet numbered 1780 ("Answer to Ben Bolt") had been entered for copyright almost one year earlier, 12 August 1852. The table above shows that widely separated numbers were used between 1850 and 1853 in what appears to be random order. The sheet numbered 1675 was registered 13 January 1853, and again, 17 June 1853.

While there are 137 titles in the catalog, there are only 128 plate numbers because nine pieces are given under two titles. For example, *Ave Maria*, by Schwing, plate number 1434, is also listed as "Hymn to B.V."[20] Further, some pieces were intended for use in Protestant and Catholic services and as parlor songs. While the author and composer are not given in the catalog, "Hail to the Lord's Annointed" (No. 67) is a setting by Peters of a text by the Reverend John H. Hopkins, who was Rector of Trinity Episcopal Church in Pittsburgh while Peters was organist there in the late 1820s. Similarly, Rayner Taylor's "Prayer for the Commonwealth," and Weisenthal's "Fading, Still Fading" appear designed for use in the Anglican Church and home parlor, respectively. Peters' "Vesper Hymn to the Blessed Virgin" (No. 49), has a Roman Catholic text but is in form and style (solo and chorus) similar to the numerous parlor songs he was then writing for Hewitt and Jaques and other publishers in the East.[21] Most of the later titles, however, are distinctively Roman Catholic and liturgical.

Peters issued more than half of the pieces on this catalog between 1851 and 1854, and he must have spent considerable time preparing the editions during his residence in Baltimore (1850) and his first two years in Cincinnati (1851-52). Endorsements in *Peters' Catholic Harp* show that he received encouragement to publish liturgical music from Catholic Church officials, and it appears that the encouragement came from Cincinnati rather than Baltimore.[22]

While in Baltimore, he was largely occupied with the *Baltimore Olio and American Musical Gazette*, the monthly music magazine he published there in 1850, and he was also active compiling pedagogical music at that time. Plate numbers for W. C. Peters & Sons would exceed the number 3000 by the end of the decade, and sacred pieces, while much fewer in quantity than secular ones, would comprise the most enduring part of the total production.

Peters' emphasis on music for the Catholic Church intensified after 1850. While undoubtedly concerned about making a financial profit, he was dedicated to initiating improvements in the music of the liturgy and educating musicians and clergy in its use. He often included responses which preceded or followed a piece in the Mass or Offices and added or altered accompaniments and texts to make them more accessible. An example is *Ave Regina* & *Ave Maria* "arranged from Cherubini" (No. 1741). Peters' edition is for soprano solo and keyboard and has two texts: the *Ave Regina* is set inside the vocal staff, and the *Ave Maria* above it. At the end of the setting Peters includes the following with the chant pitches, shown here with letters above the text.

```
          a'
PR: Dignare me laudare [te virgo sacrata]

     a'                        a'g'  g'f#'
CH: Da mihi virtutem contra hostes tu - os.
```

Only the incipit of the verse is given, followed by an ellipsis, and Peters takes the precaution to show that it is to be sung by the Priest, while the Response is to be sung by the choir. These texts are found in the First Vespers of the Feast of the Blessed Virgin Mary, and in Vespers after the Purification, respectively. The *Ave Maria* was popular as a prayer offered before the sermon during Mass, among other places, and Peters combined it here with the equally popular *Ave Regina*.

The style of this piece, like most by Italian composers in the catalog, has a florid melody with numerous appogiaturas, turns and trills, rapid scale passages and expressive leaps. The accompaniment is full-textured and rhythmic, and Alberti and arpeggiated figures support the operatic vocal line.

1862 Catalog

In 1862, A. C. Peters and Bro. (Alfred C. and John L.), who had taken over the company of W. C. Peters & Sons, registered for copyright in Ohio a catalog titled *Catholic Music With Latin Words . . . Arranged With an Accompaniment For the Piano or Organ*.[23] While divided into two parts and issued on two separate sheets, titled *Catalogue No. 1* and *Catalogue No.*

2, it is a continuous listing of titles in alphabetical order and was published as part of *Jubilate Deo* by A. Diabelli (No. 3575), which was registered for copyright by the Peters brothers in 1863.

Catalogue No. 1 lists titles beginning with the letters A through M; *Catalogue No. 2* resumes titles beginning with the letter M and extends through those beginning with the letter Y. The first contains 106 titles; the second contains 127, making a total of 233 titles. Of these, 31 in *Catalog No. 1* are new, and 45 are new in *Catalog No. 2*, making a total of 76 new titles issued between 1856 and 1862. The remainder are repeated from the 1856 catalog.[24]

Entries in *Catalogue No. 1* with plate numbers above 2638 (not in the Catalog of 1856) are given below (that is, titles on the 1856 Catalog are not repeated here) and the items are shown here exactly as given in the catalog.

Peters now gives the plate number, the key (in parentheses), the voices required, exactly where in the service the piece is to be used, and the composer's name for each item. [Where the composer's name or vocal setting is lacking, I again use the symbols (nn) and (ns). When a key is not given, I insert the symbol (nk). Brackets are used to show editorial additions, but all other parenthetical items are shown as they appear in the catalog. Peters' spelling (e.g., "base" for bass) is retained throughout.]

Catalogue No. 1

1756: **Adoremus** (G) (Sop., Ten., Alt., and Base) For Benediction or Offertory. Gregorian.
1739: **Alma Redemptoris** (F) Solo (Sop. or Ten.) Advent to Purification. Novello.
3007: **Alma Redemptoris** (D) Solo (Sop.) Duo (2 Sop.) and Cho. Advent to Purification. Webbe.
2970: **Alma Virgo** (F) & Eng. "Thou Art Our Father." Solo (Sop.) & Cho. For Offertory. Hummel.
3387: **Anima Christi** (D) Solo (Mez. Sop. or Base) & Chor For Offertory. Peters.
2971: **Asperges**, No. 7 (G) (2 Sop., T. & Base). Peters; [Combined with] Asperges, No. 8 (E) 4 v. (Sop., Alt., Ten. & Base) Sung before Mass. Bissell.
1692: **Audi Benigna** (A Minor) 4 v. (Sop., Alt., Ten., and Base) also **Lucis Creator** (Alt. & Base) Vesper Hymns. Witzka.

Catholic Church Music in the Midwest 217

2974: **Ave Maria** (G) 4 v. (2 Sop., Ten. and Base) For Offertory. Zingarelli.
2198: **Ave Maria** (nk) Solo Eng. and Ger. words. Kuchen.
3320: **Ave Maria** (F) (Sop. & Ten. Solo, with Cho.) For Offertory. Haydn.
2972: **Ave Maris Stella** (A) 4 v. (2 Sop., Ten. and Base) for Offertory or Benediction. Schubert.
3018: **Ave Maris Stella** (A) 4 v. (2 Sop., Ten., & Base). For Offertory or Benediction. Schmid.
3299: **Ave Maris Stella** (C) 4 v. (Sop., Alt., Ten. & Base) For Offertory or Benediction. Lambillotte.
3009: **Ave Regina** (G) 4 v. (sop., Alt., Ten., & Base) Purification until Easter. Van Bree.
3019: **Ave Verum** (A Flat) Solos (Sop., Alt., Ten., & Base) with Cho. Offertory or Benediction. Newkomn. [*sic*]
3014: **Ave Verum** (F) and **Ecce Panis** (G) 4 v. (2 Sop., Ten., & Base). Offertory or Benediction. German.
3218: **Beatus Vir** (D) 4 v. (Sop., Alt., Ten., and Base) Vesper Anthem. Haydn.
3296: **Bone Paster, Panis Vere** (G) Solo (Base), Duo (Ten. and Base) and Cho ad lib. Offertory or Benediction. W. C. Peters.
(nn): Peters' *Catholic Harp* (Bound) a new School Book, containing instructions in Singing Hymns, etc. Prepared expressly for Catholic Schools. W. C. Peters.
3355: **Choral Mass**. See **Mass in F**. Carl Greith.
3320: **Confitebor Tibi Domine** (D) Psalm 110. Solo (Base) Vesper Psalm. Haydn.
2337: **Credo** (D) Semi Chant 4 v. (2 Sop., Ten., & Base) Peters.
2975: **Evening Service** (Peters) Bound. A collection of Motetts, Hymns, Chants and Pieces for Benediction. (ns) W. C. Peters.
3235: **Gaude Virgo** (C) duo (Sop. & Base) with Cho. For offertory or Benediction. Haydn.
3368: **Gaudeamus** (B Flat) Solos (Base & Sop.) and Cho. For Offertory. Diabelli.
2944: **Gloria Patri** (C) 4 v. (2 Sop., Ten., & Base) From Magnificat, by Emerig.
2982: **Grosser Gott** (G) See Spirit Creator. 4 v. (Sop., Alt., Ten., & Base) Before Service. (nn)
3361: **Lauda Sion** (D) Grand Chorus (Sop., Alt., Ten., & Base). For Offertory. Labillotte.

3219: **Laudate Dominum** (C) Solo (Sop.) and Cho. Vesper Service or Offertory. Haydn.
2930: **Laudate Pueri Dominum** (C) Solo (Sop.) and Cho. For Offertory. Zingarelli.
1692: **Lucis Creator**, See **Audi Benigna** (A Minor) Vesper Hymns. Witzka.
3017: **Lucis Creator** (C) and **0 Jesu Fili Maria** (F) 4 v. (2 Sop., Ten., and Base). **Vesper Hymns** Winter and Novello.
3221: **Magnificat** (C) Grand 4 v. (Sop., Alt., Ten., and Base) for Vesper Service. Lambillotte.
2944: **Magnificat** (C) Grand No. 3, 4 v. (2 Sop., Ten., and Base) with Base Solo (or Mez., Sop., or Alt. Solo) Vespers. Emerig.

Catalogue No. 2

2743: **Mass in C** Bound. (2 Sop., Ten., and Base) Drobisch.
3352: **Mass for the Dead in F**. Bound. (1 v.) with Cho. in unison ad lib. Peters.
2632: **Mass in G. Selected**. Bound. 2 v. (Sop. and Base) (Can also be sung by T & B or 2 Sop.) Peters.
3355: **Mass in F**. Choral Mass. Bound. 4 v. (2 Sop., Ten. and Base) Carl Greith.
3360: **Mass in C**. Bound (2 Sop., and Base ad lib) De Monti.
3354: **Mass in Plain Chant. Missa de Angelus** (C) Bound. (1 v.) with Cho. in unison ad lib. Peters.
2744: **Mass of the Holy Trinity** (D) Bound. 4 v. (2 Sop., Ten., and Base) Peters.
3353: **Mass of the Holy Guardian Angels** (G) Bound. (2 Sop., with Alt. or Base ad lib) Peters.
3351: **Mass of the Annunciation** (D minor) Bound. (2 Sop., with Alt. or Base ad lib) Peters.
2633: **Mass in C**. (Sop., Alt., Ten. and Base) by Tauman. See **Peters' Catholic Harmonist**. Peters.
3236: **O Gloriosa Virginum** (A) Sop., Ten. and Base with Cho. For Offertory. Haydn.
3017: **O Jesu Fili, Maria Lucis Creator** (C) (ns) Vespers. Winter and Novello.
3376: **O Salutaris** (B flat) Ten. and Base, Solo and Trio. Beethoven.

3434:	**O Salutaris** (D) (Sop., Alt., Ten. and Base) Lambillotte.
3300:	**O Salutaris** (E flat) Duo (2 Sop. or 2 Ten.) Lambillotte.
3360:	**O Salutaris** (E flat) Solo (Sop. or Ten.) and **Ave Verum** (F) 4 v. (2 Sop., Ten. and Base) Benediction. Himmel and Novello.
3374:	**O Salutaris** (D) Solo (Sop. or Ten.) Proch.
2977:	**O Salutaris** (G) Solo (Base) Duo, Trio & Cho. for Benediction. Rossini.
3016:	**O Salutaris** (F) Duo (Sop., or Ten., and Base). **O Salutaris** (G) 4 v. (2 Sop., Ten. and Base) for Benediction. Webbe and Gregorian.
3015:	**O Salutaris** (G) 4 v. (2 Sop., Ten. and Base). **O Salutaris** (G) 4 v. (2 Sop., Ten. and Base). German.
2978:	**O Sanctissima** (F) and **Tantum Ergo** (G) 4 v. (2 Sop., Ten., and Base). Benediction. Schmid.
2976:	**Panis Agelicus** (G) Hymn of St. Thomas Aquina. Trio (Sop., Alt. and Base) Offertory or Benediction. Peters.
2984:	**Quem Adinodum** (D) 4 v. (Sop., Alt., Ten., and Base) Choral Motet for Festivals of Rejoicing. Romberg.
2979:	**Regina Coeli** (A) Solo (sop) Duo (Sop and Base) and Cho. Easter to Trinity Eve. Beethoven.
2720:	**Regina Coeli** (F) 4 v. (2 Sop., Ten. and Base) Weninger.
2676:	Services Trinity Eve to Advent. Weninger.
3139:	**Salve Regina** (E flat) 4 v. (2 Sop., Ten. and Base) Spoth.
3011:	**Salve Regina** (G) Sop. and Ten., Solo and Cho. Carr.
2981:	**Salve Regina** (C Minor) (2 Sop., Ten. and Base) Lambillotte.
2982:	**Spirit Creator of Mankind** and **Grosser Gott** (G) 4 v. (Sop., Ten. Alt., and Base) Before Service. (nn)
3318:	**Super Flumina Babylonis** (A minor) (Sop., Ten., Alt., and Base) Offertory for Feast of the Ascension. Lambillotte.
3298:	**Tantum Ergo** (E flat) 5 v. (Sop. or Ten., Solo, with Chorus) For Benediction. Lambillotte.
2070:	**Tantum Ergo** (F) (Sop. and Base), with Cho ad lib. Rossi.
2983:	**Tantum Ergo** (G) Alto, Solo and Quartette. Evans.
3012:	**Tantum Ergo** (F) (2 Sop., Ten. and Base) Webbe [with] **Tantum Ergo** (G) (Sop., Ten. and Base) Meineke.

3013:	**Tantum Ergo** (D) (2 Sop., Ten. and Base) [and] **Tantum Ergo** (G) (Sop., Ten. and Base) Noeren.
3317:	**Te Deum**, Grand (D) 1st and 2nd Sop., Ten., and Base and Sop. Solo. Lambillotte.
2984:	**Te Deum**, Grand (D) (Sop., Alto, Ten. and Base) Romberg.
2985:	**Veni Creator** (F) Russian Hymn (Sop., Solo with Quart. and Cho.) Before Service. (nn)
2986:	**Veni Creator** (C) (2 Sop., Ten. and Base) Lambillotte.
3359:	**Veni Creator** (D) Quartette and Cho. (2 Sop., Ten. and Base) Before Service. Lambillotte.
2987:	**Veni Sancte Spiritus** (A) 4 v. (2 Sop., Ten. and Base) Before Service. Vogler.
3238:	**Vespers** (G) Gregorian and....[word missing; Catalog page torn]

The 1862 catalog offers additional hymns, psalms, and anthems for Mass and Vespers. Added texts include *Lauda Sion*, a sequence set for "grand chorus" by Lambillotte; *Confitibor Tibi Domine*, Psalm 110 (also classified as a canticle) set for bass solo by Haydn; *Super Flumina Babylonis*, Psalm 136, by Lambillotte; and the Thomas Aquinas hymn, *Panis Angelicus*, set by Peters. The largest increase is seen in the number of complete masses, and especially significant are the seven by Peters. (There are eight mass titles by Peters listed but the *Mass in Plain Chant* is also listed with the title *Missa de Angelus*.)

Many of the new works are in the prevailing late Classic and early Romantic styles: soloists alternate with chorus (the word "grand" is used to describe some); the alto voice is used more frequently (although the earlier vocal combinations for S.S.B. and S.S.T.B. are not abandoned) and the cover sheet to the catalog lists an additional fourteen pieces (described as "just published" and apparently issued after the catalog was printed), seven of which are offered with orchestral parts.

In conclusion, we focus upon two aspects of the catalogs: the composers and the musical traditions they represent; and Peters' specific efforts to teach the Roman Catholic liturgy through his *Catholic Harp*, registered for copyright in 1863. The composers of both catalogs (1856 and 1862) are given in alphabetical order on the chart below, along with the number of compositions by each published by Peters, and the approximate years in which they were published. (Numbers in parentheses indicate works attributed to two composers.)

Name	1844-45	1846-49	1850-53	1854-56	1857-62
Baini			2		

Catholic Church Music in the Midwest

Baumgarten			2		
Beethoven					2
Bissel					1
Buhler				1	
Carr			6		1
Carusi			1		
Cherubini			1		
Colliere				1	
Cook			(1)		
Cooke			2		
Cross		1			
D'Hollander		1	2		
DeMonti					1
Diabelli					1
Dietsch			1	1	
Donizetti			1		
Drobish					1
Dufort			1		
Emerig					1
Evans					1
Gansbacher		1			
Giardini			1		
Greith					1
Handel			1		
Haydn					6
Herold			2		
Himmel			9		1
Hummel					2
King			(1)		
Knitze			1		
Kuchen					1
Lambillotte	1	2	2	5	12
Loder			1	4	
Manners			1		
Marcello				1	
Marliani			1		
Martini			2		
Meineke					1
Mercandante			1		

Mendelssohn					1
Mozart		2	1		
Newkomn[sic]					1
Newland			3		
Noeren					1
Novello		1	7	1	3
Ohnewald			1		
Onslow	1				
Peters	2	2		1	14
Pleyel		1			
Purcell			(1)		
Proch					1
Romberg					2
Rossi					1
Rossini					1
Scheidermayer			1	1	
Schmid					3
Schubert					1
Schwartz			1		
Schwing			4		
Sofge				1	
Spoth					1
Stadler			2		
Stark			3		
Stradella				1	
Tauman				(1)	
Taylor			1		
Terziani			1		
Van Bree					1
Verhayn			1		
Vogler					1
Webbe			1		2
Weisenthal			1		
Weninger					2
Winter		1	1	1	1
Witzka					1
Zimmers			2		
Zingarelli					2
[Anon.]		1	12	4	8

The composers in the catalogs represent dissimilar musical traditions, all in use at the same time. The most significant tradition is represented by the music and editions of Vincent Novello (1781-1861). Peters included no fewer than twelve pieces by Novello, and these and others by Haydn, Samuel Webbe (1740-1816), J. N. Hummel (1778-1837), and Beethoven came from Novello's numerous compilations, the best-known of which was *A Collection of Sacred Music*, 2 vols.(London (?), 1811). In his own *Catholic Harp*, Peters states: "The model adopted in the arrangement of the Vespers for Sundays, is taken from *Novello's Cantica Vespers*."[25]

While explaining the chanting of Psalms, Peters quotes Novello:

> ... After the Tone has been simply played through on the organ, the first verse is sung by the cantor alone, and the remaining verses, by all the choir in *unison* and by the congregation alternately. This antiphonal effect may be obtained by the choir arranging themselves on opposite sides, and singing alternate verses, but still in *unison*, and a very grand variety is produced by their suddenly bursting into full harmony at the Gloria Patri and other verses printed in Capitals — if this however be attempted, care should be taken to learn the proper harmonies perfectly; thereby avoiding the barbarous custom, of each person inventing his own.[26]

The Anglican tradition in America is well represented by the music of Benjamin Carr (1768-1831) and his pupil Benjamin Carr Cross (1786-1859), as well as by Carr's friend Rayner Taylor (1742-1825) — all of Philadelphia. Together they account for more than a dozen pieces in Peters' inventory. It is likely that Peters knew Carr's *Masses, Vespers, Litanies* (1805), for it was the source of the latter's *Mass in Three Parts*, which Peters issued. In his own *Mass of the Holy Ghost*, Peters followed Carr's procedure of giving explicit directions and rubrics for the priest as well as the choir throughout the mass. The style of Peters' masses, especially the predominantly homophonic SSB texture, is similar to Carr's although Peters generally places the melody in the top rather than the middle voice.

Newland's Collection of Sacred Music (probably William A. Newland, fl. c1840), which contains two pieces by Carr and one each by Purcell, Webbe, and Handel, is also modeled upon Carr's earlier publication. Peters traveled East regularly, visiting Philadelphia and New York, and was acquainted with Eastern publishers and musicians. Before 1850, the American music publishing and piano manufacturing industries were dominated by English immigrants, and English sacred and secular music arriving by Eastern seaports was quickly sold — or edited and reprinted — and through entrepreneurs like Peters was eventually made available in the Midwest.

Peters' work as a liturgical pedagogue is best seen in his *Catholic Harp*, in which he explains the "Modes and Tones," and presents the "Gregorian Melodies" in both square and round notes. The *Mass of the Holy Ghost*, given in this oblong volume, illustrates his attention to liturgical detail. While it is largely the Anglican tradition which shaped its musical style, the specific liturgical instructions show his familiarity with the Roman mass and, equally important, his recognition that many musicians and clergy would need such guidance.

Texts and music for both the Proper and Ordinary items are given and each is marked "Priest" or "Choir." The following appears after the Credo: "The Credo being finished, the Priest kisses the altar, and, turning to the people, says, V/Dominus Vobiscum R/Et cum spiritu tuo. . . ." Before the Sanctus, he states: "When the Bell rings at the termination of the Preface, the Choir will commence the Sanctus." Generally, the material of the *Catholic Harp* is designed to enable the musician with little experience or knowledge of the liturgy to perform the music of the mass.

It is not clear where or when Peters first committed himself to improving the condition of music in the Roman Catholic Church. The reform efforts of the Monks of Solesmes were begun in France in the early 1830s, but the results of their work were not felt in America until late in the century. Peters seems to have been unaware of their work. Nor did he become active in the St. Cecilia Society, which was founded in Cincinnati under the direction of Father Martin Henni, at Holy Trinity Church, 22 November 1838. A second society was formed in Cincinnati in 1856 under the direction of Frederick Ritter, the well-known music historian. Both Henni and Ritter were German Americans, as were many of the participants in the Cecelian movement in the Midwest. No records have been found to show that Peters communicated with either Henni or Ritter, and while some pieces in the catalogs are given with optional German texts, these do not form a large part of Peters' sacred music inventory.

But the inclusion in the catalog of pieces by Giuseppi Baini (1775-1844), Pietro Terziani (fl. 1840), and Louis Lambillotte (1796-1855) suggests that Peters was aware of other reform movements in church music. Baini was Director of the Papal Chapel and he and Terziani were appointed to a commission, the leader of which was the composer Gasparo Spontini (1774-1851), which made recommendations for reform in sacred music in Rome in the late 1830s.[27]

In 1839, Spontini wrote to the *Primicerio* and congregation and academy of St. Cecilia in Rome on the "condition of Music in the churches of Rome," stating that "the House of God has been invaded by a horde of plagiarists." He then cites specific contrafacta: "One brings into the Church the *Gerusalem* of Zingarelli, an opera produced in a theater but here adapted to the words of the *Gloria*. Another introduces the *Orassi*, and the *Curiasii* of Cimerosa, another theatrical work disguised as a mass. One the *Eliza* and *Claudio* of Mercadante, set to a Vesper . . ., the *finali* and duets of Rossini's *Gazza Ladra* and *Armida*, sung to the solemn and sacred words of the *Tantum Ergo*."[28]

Spontini's criticisms were rather belated and somewhat hypocritical. The Statutes for the Roman Society of St. Cecilia had already been approved in 1830, and his own efforts at reform were exerted quite close to the end of his sharply declining career as an opera composer. Nevertheless, he was awarded the rank *Conte de Sant Andrea* by the Pope in 1844. Peters did not publish sacred music by Spontini, but ironically, G. Mercadante (1795-1870) and Nicolo Zingarelli (1752-1837) are both represented in the inventory, and Peters issued other pieces by Mercadante which are not listed in the catalogs.

Peters issued liturgical pieces by Louis Lambillotte (1796-1855) consistently from 1844 through 1862, and the catalogs give twenty-two titles by this composer, four more than by Peters himself. Lambillote was a scholar and expert on Gregorian chant, and he published studies on its transcription and interpretation, a widely known example being his *Antiphonaire de Saint Gregaire* (Brussels, 1851). Lambillotte's compositions, like those by Peters, were re-issued by Oliver Ditson after the latter bought the Peters inventory from John L. Peters.[29]

The predominance of opera composers of all nationalities is apparent. F. H. Himmel (1765-1814), notorious for his insobriety but a prolific composer of operas and sacred music, has 10 titles. Other masters of opera include Alessandro Stradella (1644-1682), Gaetano Donizetti (1797-1848), and Gioacchino Rossini (1792-1868).

Peters seems to have acquired the music of Anton Diabelli (1781-1858), Joseph Haydn, Gioacchino Rossini, Sigismund Neukomm (1778-1858), Abbe G. J. Stadler (1749-1814), Abbe Vogler (1749-1814) and pieces by the early Romantics Franz Schubert and Felix Mendelssohn, relatively late in his publishing career. But he issued pieces by the Mannheim composer Peter Winter (1754-1825) regularly from 1846 to 1862; and the *Regina Coeli* by Johann Gansbacher (1778-1844), Kapellmeister of the Cathedral at Vienna, and former pupil of Vogler and friend of Weber, Meyerbeer, and Beethoven, was among Peters' early publications of sacred music.

These, and others in the catalogs, indicate that Roman Catholic Church music in Midwest America just before the Civil War was vital and grounded in the strongest European traditions. Not all names in the catalogs can be identified, however. For example, the most popular and enduring of Peters' own masses was his *Mass in C Major* "from Tauman," which was published in Louisville in 1848 as part of *Peters' Catholic Harmonist*.

"Tauman," if indeed that was his name, remains unidentified, and the name, like some others on Peters' lists, may be misspelled.[30]

Finally, Peters' sacred music catalogs show his interest in American composers and give credence to the call for a distinctly "American Music" which he expressed in the columns of the *Baltimore Olio*. Among the Americans is Henry D. Sofge, whose songs were issued by W. C. Peters in Baltimore and Cincinnati.[31] Sofge was a close friend of the Peters family. His *Cincinnati Polka* bears the dedication: "Composed and inscribed to Wm. M. Peters by his friend Henry D. Sofge."[32] William M. Peters was the eldest son of W. C. Peters and his first wife, Charlotte. Further, Sofge's *Baltimore Olio Waltz*[33] appears to be a tribute to W. C. Peters' monthly music magazine. Sofge's one piece on Peters' first list, is a setting of the text *Veni Creator*.

Samuel Carusi (b. 1795) produced numerous guitar arrangements which were issued by Peters, Webb & Co.,[34] and was himself a publisher in Baltimore and Washington.[35] His father, Gaetano Carusi (c1762-1843), was a composer, instrumentalist, publisher, and member of the "Italian Marine Band" contingent of the U. S. Marine Corps.[36] Carusi's one piece in the catalogs is a three-voice *Tantum Ergo*.

H. Proch was the composer of the popular song, "Oh! Think Not Less I Love Thee," which W. C. Peters registered for copyright in Ohio in 1847. His *O Salutaris* bears a high number in the catalog (3374). J. M. Noeren's *Midnight March* (plate number 3074) was issued by W .C. Peters & Sons in 1859. His setting of *Tantum Ergo* and the setting of the same text by Baltimore organist, Charles Meineke (1782-1850) have adjacent numbers in the catalog (3013 and 3012).

Among the other Americans or composers living in America, are L. Coradie Colliere (fl. 1855); Friedrich Kuchen (fl. 1853); E. J. Loder (1813-1865); Edward Spoth (fl. 1859) and Thomas Van Dyke Wiesenthal (fl. 1850).[37] Wiesenthal dedicated his *Fading, Still Fading*, to the "Sisters of St. Joseph."[38] This is among the few pieces in the catalogs intended "for use in church and parlor." Colliere and Sofge had a common friend in J. T. Stoddard, a noted piano manufacturer in Baltimore, and each dedicated a piece of sacred music to him.

While some titles in the catalogs described above were issued after the commencement of the hostilities of the Civil War, and while Peters remained active as a composer and editor through the year 1865, his national reputation in American music was established well before the war began. Because few primary sources about W. C. Peters are extant, the catalogs provide a valuable summary of his achievements in what was to him a genre of particular importance.

His own compilations show that he envisioned a flowing, dignified liturgy with smooth coordination between priest and choir. The latter was to consist of singers capable of performing both chant and polyphony, and accompaniments, while not virtuosic, were idiomatic, and some were clearly intended to be performed on the organ.

Peters knew and published the works of the best European and American composers of sacred music, and while he severely edited some to make them more practical for the singers and accompanists, his modifications preserved the integrity of both text and music. He published and promoted settings of liturgical texts in the popular Classic and Romantic operatic aria styles as well as complete "concert" masses, but he also labored for the revival of Gregorian plainsong as he knew it. In the latter case, he seems to stand as a lone figure in the Midwest before the Civil War. Peters' contributions as composer, pedagogue, and editor of music for the Roman Catholic Church in America deserve broader recognition.

---

[1] Thomas Bokenkotter, *A Concise History of the Catholic Church.* Expanded edition (New York: Doubleday, 1990), 330. See also Robert Lacour-Gayet, *Everyday Life in the United States Before the Civil War: 1830-1860* (New York: Ungar Publishing Company, 1969), 210.

[2] Bokenkotter, 332.

[3] Ibid.

[4] Robert F. Hayburn, "The Reform at Solesmes," *Pastoral Music* (Dec.-Jan. 1991): 41.

[5] Lacour-Gayet, 211. In 1831 the Church of St. Mary in New York was burned down, and in 1834 the Convent of the Ursulines of Boston suffered the same fate. In 1850 the "Secret Order of the Star Spangled Banner" was formed to "defend the Republic against Roman agitators." Anti-Catholic sentiments appeared in politics with the formation of the Know-Nothing Party which was especially strong during the 34th Congress (1855), controlling five senators, forty-three representatives, and about seventy additional political leaders including former President Millard Fillmore. In Louisville, in August 1855, a riot instigated by the Know-Nothings left twenty-two dead.

[6] Bokenkotter, 334.

[7] *The New Grove Dictionary of American Music* (New York: Grove's Dictionaries, 1986), s.v. "Roman Catholic Church, Music of the," by John Grady.

[8] Lacour-Gayet, 198.

[9] Hayburn, "The Reform at Solesmes," 41.

[10]Robert F. Hayburn, *Papal Legislation on Sacred Music: 95 A.D. to 1977 A.D.* (Collegeville, Minn.: Liturgical Press, 1979), 87.

[11]Ibid., 90.

[12]Ibid., 95.

[13]Ibid., 99.

[14]J. Vincent Higginson, "John Aitken's Compilations—1787 and 1791," *The Hymn* 27/3 (1976), 68-75. See also, Leonard Ellinwood, *History of American Church Music* (New York: Morehouse-Gorham Company, 1953; reprint, New York: Da Capo, 1970), 38-40. See also, *New Grove Dictionary of American Music*, s.v. "Aitken, John," by Richard Crawford.

[15]For a comprehensive study of Carr's music see Ronnie L. Smith, "The Church Music of Benjamin Carr (1768-1831)" (Diss., Southwestern Baptist Theological Seminary, 1969).

[16]Peters' Pittsburgh years are discussed in Richard D. Wetzel, *Frontier Musicians on the Connoquenessing, Wabash, and Ohio* (Athens: Ohio University Press, 1976). See also Richard D. Wetzel, "The Search for William Cumming Peters," *American Music* 1/4 (Winter, 1983), 27-41 and Karl J. R. Arndt and Richard D. Wetzel, "Harmonist Music and Pittsburgh Musicians in Early Economy," *The Western Pennsylvania Historical Magazine* 54/2-4 (1971).

[17]Copy in Gaylord Library, Washington University, St. Louis.

[18]Library of Congress Copyright Ledger, vol. 4, p. 38.

[19]*Jesu, Mater Ave*, by Mozart (No. 1675) was registered for copyright by W. C. Peters, January 13, 1853, and again June 17, 1853. Peters' own *Vesper Hymn to the Blessed Virgin* (No. 49) is listed on the back-cover of his *Ashland Quadrilles* (No. 76) issued in 1844, but he registered it again in Baltimore in 1851. The same is true of *Memorae* (No. 74).

[20]The plate numbers with two titles are: 1434, 1646, 1647, 1654, 1656, 1740, 1768, 2361, and 2630.

[21]Nicholas Tawa, *Sweet Songs for Gentle Americans: The Parlor Song in America, 1790-1860* (Bowling Green, Ohio: Bowling Green University Popular Press, 1980), 29, describes the use of parlor songs in church. Peters published the following advertisement in *The Catholic Advocate*, 2 November 1844: "Hail to the Lord's Annoited [sic]." W. C. Peters has just published a piece of Sacred Music as above named, being the third number of a series entitled "A Collection of Airs for One, Two, Three and Four Voices, with an Accompaniment for the Pianoforte or Organ. The piece is arranged in such a manner as to be suited to the Church or the Parlor."

[22]J. B. Purcell, Archbishop of Cincinnati, gave the following endorsement which Peters included in the *Catholic Harp*. ". . . I am happy to acknowledge that I know of no English speaking composer or publisher who has labored so long, so zealously and so successfully in this department as you have done: I therefore cheerfully add my approbation to that of Rt. Rev. Dr. Rosecrans, of Peters' *Catholic Harp*."

[23]The imprint reads: "A. C. Peters & Bro., 94 West 4th Street, Cincinnati, O., J. L. Peters & Bro., 49 North 5th Street, St. Louis, MO. Sole agents for the Sale of W. C. Peters' Catalogue of Sacred Music."

[24]Some of the new titles have plate numbers *below* the highest number of the 1856 catalog (2638). They are: 1449; 1692; 1702; 1756; and 1739. These may have been "left open" for sacred pieces. Fifteen pieces on the 1856 catalog are not repeated on the 1862 lists: 1736; 1744-52; 1760; 1767; 1769; and 1770-71. The new plate numbers on Catalog 1 are 2930; 2944; 2970-72; 2974-75; 2982; 3007-09; 3014; 3017-19; 3218-19; 3221; 3235; 3296; 3299; 3320; 3355; 3361; 3368; 3375; and 3387.

[25]W. C. Peters, *Peter's Catholic Harp: A Collection of Sacred Music Designed for the Use of Choirs, Schools and Musical Associations, Containing Morning and Evening Services, Consisting of the Mass, Motets, Offertories, Litanies, Hymns for the Benediction, Vespers for Sundays, and Vespers for the Various Feasts of the Blessed Virgin* (Cincinnati: A. C. Peters & Bro., 1863), 9.

[26]Ibid., 10.

[27]Hayburn, *Papal Legislation*, 39.

[28]Ibid.

[29]The firm John L. Peters, New York, was the last of the Peters companies. It was the successor to W. C. Peters & Sons, Cincinnati, A. C. Peters & Bro., Cincinnati, and J. L. Peters & Bro., St. Louis. Most of the titles of the 1856 and 1862 catalogs were continued by John L. Peters and are found under the heading "Latin Songs" in the *Complete Catalogue of Sheet Music and Musical Works, 1870* (Board of Music Trade, 1871; reprint, New York: Da Capo, 1973), 175-78. Peters' publications in this list are designated with the number 5.

[30]"Scheidermayer," for example, is Joseph Bernhard Schiedermeyer (1779-1840), Cathedral organist at Linz. A *Mass in C* by Schiedermeyer was registered for copyright by Peters in 1855.

[31]*The Egeria Waltz*, registered for copyright by W. C. Peters, Baltimore, 13 October 1847.

[32]*Cincinnati Polka*, registered for copyright by W. C. Peters in Ohio, 1848.

[33] *Baltimore Olio Waltz*, registered for copyright by Peters, Webb and Co., [Louisville, Ky.] 1850.

[34] An example is "Oh! Soon Return." Ballad. Music arranged for the guitar by Samuel Carusi. Louisville: Peters, Webb & Co, (n.d.). Plate number 1657-2.

[35] An example is "When Stars are in the Quiet Skies," registered for copyright by S. Carusi, District Court of Maryland, 1841. Copy in the Center for Popular Music, Middle Tennessee State University.

[36] Elise K. Kirk, *Music at the White House* (Urbana: University of Illinois Press, 1986), 32.

[37] Biographical information about many American song composers of this period is scant, and the understanding of the state and progress of music in America in the nineteenth century will not be complete until the numerous small collections and holdings of printed sheet music throughout the U.S.— many not yet identified—are cataloged and studied. Two outstanding achievements in this area are George Russell Keck, "Pre-1875 American Imprint Sheet Music in the Ernest C. Krohn Special Collections, Gaylord Music Library, Washington University, St. Louis, Missouri: A Catalog and Descriptive Study" (Ph.D. diss., University of Iowa, 1982) and Marion Korda, *Louisville Music Publications of the 19th Century, Dwight Anderson Music Library, University of Louisville* (Louisville: Published by the Author, 1991).

[38] "Fading, Still Fading," registered for copyright by W. C. Peters, Baltimore, 1851. See also Nicholas Tawa, ed., *American Solo Song Through 1865*, vol. 1 of *Three Centuries of American Music: A Collection of American Sacred and Secular Music* (Boston: G. K. Hall, 1989).

THE ORIGINS OF MUSIC JOURNALISM IN CHICAGO: CRITICISM AS A REFLECTION OF MUSICAL LIFE

James A. Deaville

Chicago of the mid-1830s, a period during which it had grown from 350 inhabitants in 1833, the year of incorporation as a town, to 3800 inhabitants in 1837, the year of incorporation as a city,[1] was described at the time with the following words:

> Rival cities called Chicago a mudhole, a pigsty, a sinkhole of vice and gambling. John Hankins, leader of the Washingtonians, a Temperance movement, roared in to declare Chicago the vilest city he had seen, "a universal grogshop." . . . Even the American Temperance House had a bartender. . . . Saloons and brothels stretched along Wells Street. . . . It is true that Chicago was a mudhole and many of the lots sold to outsiders were under water most of the year.[2]

A mere thirty-five years later, on the eve of the Great Fire, Chicago numbered almost 300,000 citizens and had made so much progress as a city to warrant the following portrayal:

> Chicago, in 1871, could not be other than a great and powerful city, her wealth filling capacious warehouses and stores, lining scores of miles of streets, her merchants and manufacturers princes in the land, residing in palaces that found few equals in the old world, and surrounded by every luxury that genius could invent or art supply. . . .[3]

Musical developments kept apace with this growth of Chicago as a city. Music was in its infancy in Chicago of the 1830s: the first piano arrived in 1834, the first sheet music was sold in 1835, the first instrument dealer set up shop in 1836, and the first concert society gave performances (four in number) during the 1835-36 season.[4] By 1871, according to the opinion of contemporaries,

> the city really stood forth prominently in the United States [as a musical center]. . . . Pease, as a pianist, and a hundred and fifty other professional musicians, without counting teachers, many of them ranking with the best performers of Europe, not to speak of vocal talent of no mean order–these flourished in the city where more than two thousand pianos were sold annually, with thousands of other instruments, and many tons of sheet music, much of which was written by home composers. It is no wonder that opera singers and concertists looked for the verdict of such a wide-spread musical culture with as much anxiety as for that of the seaboard cities.[5]

The main thesis of this paper is that music criticism in Chicago not only kept pace with but also reflected that development of music in Chicago just described. Immediately, however, a problem presents itself: Mary Ann Feldman sets 1855 as the date for the first music criticism in Chicago in two reputable publications,[6] which in reality excludes twenty years of critical activity (and musical development) in that city.[7] Her date is based on a very narrow definition of music criticism, which views it as being practiced by a trained musician who is impartial and whose views are borne out by posterity. She used George P. Upton to define criticism, which led her to dismiss the previous stage of music criticism as being "in a crude state" because of the "abysmal ignorance" of the critics.[8]

Although a full-scale study of the true character of music criticism would take the present study too far afield, it is essential to clear up Feldman's misconceptions, since they reflect a not uncommon jaundiced and inaccurate view of the early stages of music criticism.[9] Certain aspects of the body of writings in question undoubtedly led Feldman to her conclusions. That music criticism in its incipient stages also served a promotional function clearly contributed to her perceptions. While it is true that much of the early writing did not transcend the level of reportage, especially considering the nature of American criticism and the fact that the authors usually were editors without any musical experience,[10] many of the writings in question nevertheless do conform to widely accepted definitions of music criticism. Winton Dean calls criticism "current discussion, in the daily and periodical press, of contemporary musical trends."[11] According to that definition, the following excerpt, taken from a Chicago newspaper of 1843, would qualify as music criticism:

> Signior Martinez. —The audience last evening were highly gratified with this gentleman's performance on the guitar, & c. We doubt whether as a player upon this instrument he has his equal. He may be justly termed the Paganini of the guitar. His imitations upon it of the bugle, trumpet and French horn, were complete. It will be seen by reference to his advertisement that he will play tomorrow evening upon two guitars at the same time, holding one in each hand, a feat of no ordinary character.[12]

The view may be biased toward the positive; the review may even have been paid for by the artist, but it is no less criticism than that which appears in many a paper today.

Having corrected the misconceptions about the nature of music criticism, we can proceed to trace it in Chicago back to its origins. A review in the *Chicago American* pushes the first music criticism in Chicago chronologically back by twenty years, from Feldman's year of 1855 to 19 December 1835, a mere two years after Chicago's incorporation as a town and one year after the establishment of the first newspaper (*Chicago Democrat*). This remarkable document merits closer examination, which is presented here in its entirety:

> The Concert given by the Harmonic Society at the Presbyterian Church on Friday evening of last week, afforded a fine treat to a crowded audience of intelligence, beauty, and fashion. The performance, on the whole, exhibited the skill and good taste of the players. The chief objection, if we may venture to allege one, was to the selection and arrangement of the sacred pieces—not that the sacred pieces were sung—but that they were such and so arranged as to seem less interesting than they really are, by being performed between the livelier airs of the more fascinating glees. All who were there, we think, will believe with us, in calling it an agreeable entertainment. A Down-Easter remarked the other night in coming out of the church, after listening to a powerful and thrilling sermon, that there was some talent in Chicago. We presume if he had been at the entertainment on Friday evening he would think there is some music here also.[13]

The review has all the features of a modern criticism: opening description of the concert, evaluation of the performance with some favorable and unfavorable comments, and an interesting, humorous closing section. The complaint against the juxtaposition of sacred and secular pieces shows discernment on the part of the critic. This early concert brought forth the first music criticism in the emerging city—music criticism serving in response to and as a reflection of musical life.

Thus, criticism was alive and well in Chicago even during the first stage of its musical development. Much of the criticism during these first two decades of the city's existence tended to be brief and largely positive in tone, as in the following example:

> *Daily Democratic Press*, 5 January 1853 [excerpts].
>
> The public rehearsal of the Chicago Philharmonic Society, on Monday evening last, was very satisfactory to the audience in attendance.... The pieces were well adapted for the occasion, and were generally executed with neatness, taste and spirit. We occasionally discovered a little halting with regard to time, here and there a note of discord, and some passages performed with little or no expression; but these will disappear with practice, and crudeness will give place to pleasing harmony. Of one fact we were well satisfied—that when a forte passage was performed, allowing the members of the Society to join in full chorus upon open notes and common chords, there was sound sufficient to rival a young Niagara, and give listeners some idea of the "voice of many waters."
>
> The quartettes were well done, and two solos, by a lady, would have produced a much more pleasing effect, had there been a more distinct enunciation. She has a good voice, which is full of richness and melody—but a clearness in the delivery of the words was wanting in the execution of her pieces. Let this be remedied, and we think her solos will be listened to with pleasure.
>
> The "Hailstone Chorus" was much better performed than on the Thursday evening previous. A more correct and distinct expression was observable, thus bringing out to better advantage the beauties of the piece....

The relatively infrequent articles, which appeared in the various papers presented in Table 1,[14] document a musical life dominated by the occasional visits of traveling artists like the Scottish singer William Dempster in 1839 and the guitarist Martinez in 1843.[15] Local ensembles during this period were generally short lived (Table 2), due in part to the economic depression that extended from 1837 to 1843.[16]

The performance of an amateur ensemble called the Chicago Brass Band in November of 1844 not only evoked the first substantial, detailed evaluation of a concert in Chicago (in the *Gem of the Prairie*) but also was the cause of the first music-critical battle between Chicago newspapers (the *Gem* and the *Chicago Daily News*). As is evident in the following excerpt, James Campbell (editor of the *Gem* and author of the review) had clear ideas about correct performance and had the courage to express them:

> The lovers of good music had a rich treat in the Saloon on last Thursday evening. We are glad to be thus able to testify to the rapid progress which the Chicago Brass Band is making; and we are also glad, that their efforts are appreciated by our citizens generally.
> The performance was very creditable to the members of the Band; and the different pieces were executed in a style far exceeding our most sanguine anticipations. If we take it upon us to make a few remarks on the music, we do so with the desire that they may be taken as they are meant, kindly, and that the performers may know there are those who take interest in their efforts, and who are desirous that the Band may improve.
> "Oft in the busy throng." Miss M. Lewis' voice, apparently from want of confidence, was flat. This appeared to be so, as in subsequent efforts she sang in good time and taste. . . .
> "Hindoo Girl." This was sung in perfect time by Miss R. Lewis, who has, in our opinion, a soft sweet voice which needs only a little more cultivation to make it perfectly beautiful. . . .
> The Brass Band played well, the only fault was in the tongueing. This can only be remedied by practice.
> The attendance was good. We hope that the company will soon favor us with another concert.[17]

Note that, after some opening laudatory remarks, Campbell felt compelled to present his rationale behind exercising critical judgment, and then he launched into a series of perceptive observations about problems in intonation, tempo, and ensemble. This remarkable critical accomplishment drew some opposition from a fellow critic—Campbell's response provides a unique insight into early music criticism in Chicago, especially regarding the qualifications of critics:

> In our article on the concert, we inadvertently used the word "embrasure" instead of "embouchure," which is more proper. This mistake has been the theme of a very uncourteous article in the Daily News. . . .
> We feel above a petty cavil, and have a pleasure in correcting the mistake.
> It was however slight, and did not affect the intrinsic merit of our criticism. . . .

Besides, an editor cannot responsibly be expected to be acquainted with the technicalities of every department of science. His province is to observe what is going on around him, and to show that he takes an interest in every praiseworthy object.

And when he makes his suggestions modestly, and in a cordial spirit, (as we assure our readers that ours will ever be made,) no man who possesses enough intelligence and liberality to understand the duties of the press will be disposed to find fault. . . .[18]

The year 1850 marked a turning point in the musical history of Chicago. In that year, Chicago coincidentally experienced both its first performance of opera (Bellini's *La Sonnambula* on 29 July) and its first symphonic concert (under Julius Dyhrenfurth on 24 October).[19] Both events heralded a new age of musical activity in Chicago, which would be further fed by visits of internationally known virtuosi and by the creation of a professional chorus and orchestra,[20] and which in turn—in conjunction with the establishment of a music publishing industry in Chicago[21]—would inspire the founding of music journals in the city. This golden age of music, which would continuously unfold and develop until 1871,[22] also helped foster the development of music criticism in the daily press, especially after Upton's arrival in Chicago in 1855.

This article individually examines the development of each of the Chicago musical institutions reported and reviewed in the daily press between 1850 and 1871. Because of his unique position in Chicago musical and literary life, Upton will be treated separately.

Opera did not immediately find a foothold in Chicago. Unfortunately, on the night after the first performance in 1850, the McVickers Theater burned down, which put an end to the operatic season.[23] The second set of operatic performances followed in October of 1853,[24] the third set in September and October of 1858.[25] After 1858, short visits by touring opera companies became annual events in Chicago—however, the city would not have its own opera company until 1910.[26] Nevertheless, between 1850 and 1871, Chicago audiences heard "433 operatic presentations in thirty-six opera engagements or seasons. . . . *Martha* was given twenty-eight times; *Il Trovatore*, twenty-seven; *Faust*, twenty-one; *The Bohemian Girl*, nineteen; and *Norma*, seventeen."[27]

How did the local newspapers respond to this new and in large part unfamiliar genre? While these unnamed reviewers generally accepted without comment the standard Italian repertory of the touring companies,[28] they showed discrimination in the treatment of the vocal performance. For example, the anonymous critic for the *Chicago Daily Journal*, in the only review of the *Sonnambula* presentation in 1850, describes Messrs. Manvers and Guibeli as possessing

> voices of admirable tone, power and cultivation, [who] with Miss Brienti and Miss Matthews make melody and harmony, that Apollo would not hesitate to accompany upon his ocean-tuned harp.[29]

For the 1858 and successive seasons, Upton became the leading figure for opera reviewing in the local press. Nevertheless, an anonymous review in the *Chicago Daily Tribune*, dated 28 September 1858, shows how critical some of Upton's contemporaries could be:

> The performance [of *La Sonnambula*] was not of a character to endure sharp and vigorous criticism; but as it is the nearest approach to Opera that Chicago has ever been permitted to enjoy, it must, like a gift horse, be accepted without complaint. We could point out grievous defects, but the task would be ungracious. . . .

It stands to reason that the critics in the newspapers of Chicago would encourage the emergence of indigenous performing organizations. Preeminent among these ensembles were the Philharmonic Society, founded in 1850 by Dyhrenfurth and taken over in 1860 by Hans Balatka, and the Germania Männerchor, a touring chorus that was "adopted" by Chicago and eventually became resident there in 1869.

The Philharmonic Society, initially consisting of local amateurs, had a rather insecure early history.[30] Although the musical press outdid itself in expressing support for the new ensemble, through frequent, lengthy reviews filled with encouraging remarks,[31] the interest in its continuing existence moved the critics to give free vent to their concerns. For example, the anonymous *Chicago Daily Journal* review of the first concert in 1850 noted how Dyhrenfurth "might improve his programme by giving more play to the vocal powers of the 'Song Union'."[32] After an open rehearsal of the Society on 3 January 1853, an unnamed perceptive critic for the *Daily Democratic Press* made the following trenchant remarks:

> The pieces were . . . generally executed with neatness, taste and spirit. We occasionally discovered a little halting with regard to time, here and there a note of discord, and some passages performed with little or no expression; but these will disappear with practice, and crudeness will give place to pleasing harmony.[33]

A major media event for the Society was Hans Balatka's appointment as director in 1860. Balatka came from Milwaukee, where he had founded and directed the eminently successful Musikverein.[34] The anonymous review of his first concert on 19 November illustrates the goodwill of the press toward the conductor and ensemble:

> The whole performance went off admirably and without any faults that any reasonable critic should notice, when considering the comparatively short time in which the orchestra and chorus were organised.[35]

Balatka became a favorite of the Chicago critics, and especially of Upton,[36] but his popularity could not keep the Society and its short-lived successor, the Orchestral Union, from disbanding in 1868.[37]

Unlike the Philharmonic Society, the Germania Männerchor received the undivided praise of the critics, by virtue of the ensemble's excellence.[38] The local newspapers followed every concert, activity, and organizational development of the choir and, by keeping it in the forefront of attention, contributed to its success—published letters of gratitude from the Germania in the papers substantiate this observation of the power of the musical press in Chicago. One example from the *Daily Democratic Press* of 16 April 1854, suffices to reveal not only the high esteem accorded the ensemble but also the refined methods of the critic to promote the Männerchor, also at the expense of the Philharmonic Society:

> Local Matters—. The Germania Song Union realized from their late concert the handsome sum of one hundred and eight dollars. This will materially aid them in their design of purchasing instruments. The society consists of about thirty male members, all performers and amateurs. In chorus their voices are of great compass and power. They executed the choruses at their last concert with such energy and spirit as to call out the most rapturous applause. We were particularly pleased with the "Hunter's Song," the "Battle Song," and "Die freien Geister." We could understand but a word or two of the poetry and yet the music spoke a language thrilled out listening soul. The gem of the evening was a duett from *Norma*, executed by the Misses Zenzius, accompanied on the piano by Mr. Zenzius. We were delighted with the perfect tones that came ringing full and clear upon the ear from the Alpine summits of A and B flat. It reminded us of the lark singing more clearly and more sweetly the higher it ascends towards Heaven. The Chicago Philharmonic Society will have to look after its laurels or they will be lost. We would suggest that the two societies unite at some convenient season and give a joint concert. We would think that it would be a capital idea, and one that would "draw."

The Origins of Music Journalism in Chicago 239

The concise description and evaluation of the performance, the vivid verbal imagery reflect a sophistication that, while not operating at the level of Upton's ability, further puts to rest Feldman's assertion about the "abysmal ignorance" of early music criticism in Chicago.

As the fame of musical guests to Chicago rose during the 1850s and 1860s, so did the accompanying efforts of the music critics in the newspapers. During those two decades, the singers Adelina and Carlotta Patti, Christina Nilsson and Karl Formes, violinists Ole Bull and Camilla d'Urso, and the pianist Louis Moreau Gottschalk numbered among the distinguished performers greeted by public and press in Chicago.[39] Bull's visit in April of 1853 was the city's first truly important media event in the realm of music—the extent and type of coverage in the local newspapers typifies the press' response to traveling virtuosi over the next two decades. Notice of Bull's visit was given two weeks in advance of his date of arrival.[40] The three leading newspapers (*Daily Chicago Journal*, *Chicago Daily Tribune*, and *Daily Democratic Press*) generated excitement over the impending event by previewing the concerts,[41] initially emphasizing the fact that he would give only two concerts.[42] The scarcity of seats was stressed in all pre-concert notices. If Bull followed traditional nineteenth-century practices, he would have visited the various critics before the concert and might also have offered some type of bribe,[43] although an artist of his stature probably would not have needed to use such measures to ensure himself of a favorable reception in the press. While the reviews did indeed reflect the overwhelming popular success of the Bull concerts, especially in the critics' rapturous encomia,[44] there are adequate examples of weighed reflection and perceptive observations to speak of a musical press well on its way to maturity in response to a blossoming musical life. Note, for example, the insightful comparisons of repertory and performing conditions, coupled with an effective, highly descriptive use of images, in the following anonymous review:

> We have perhaps never enjoyed as great a musical treat in our city, as Ole Bull's Concerts have given us; and the overflowing houses, the many bursts of applause, from a delighted audience, are but a poor tribute to the wonderful powers unfolded by the prince of living violinists, the magical sounds he so often draws from his instrument will ever be remembered. Time cannot efface the impression of those plaintive tones, which in the fullness of our ecstasy brought tears to our relief. The second evening's performance of Ole Bull, we especially refer to; the choice of his pieces was better, (with the exception of one encore, a nameless something). He seemed to us more in communion with his instrument, and the bad weather [*sic*] had not effected the strings as

on the first evening, when the windows of the hall were open. Nothing then to interrupt the flow of his mind, he seemed to pour out the fullness of his soul in his adagios. . . . His execution throughout the evening was faultless, extraordinary, and inimitable. May he long wield his sceptre.[45]

All it took was a person of true literary genius and critical perspicacity to bring music criticism in Chicago to a state of full maturity.

This person is the previously mentioned George P. Upton (1834-1919), who arrived in the city on 27 October 1855.[46] He came to the city of 50,000 inhabitants at the age of twenty-one, after having received the A.M. degree from Brown University.[47] Despite Feldman's references to the *Chicago Evening Journal*, Upton's first important journalistic work was for the *Chicago Daily Journal*, where he served as a local reporter. His first music reviews of substance appeared anonymously in 1858—already these early writings reveal Upton's "incisive wit and uncompromising standards,"[48] as is evident in the review of *Il Trovatore* from 1858:

> Last evening, we attended McVicker's, at the rendition of the glorious Il Trovatore at the hands of the Opera Troupe, performing there. We listened for anything which might remind us of our old favorite. To be sure, the anvils seemed natural, and the orchestra played something, which sounded like the anvil chorus, but otherwise, Il Trovatore was shrieked, screamed, groaned and killed. The whole performance was below mediocrity. The properties were miserable, the action tame, the music inharmonious, false and discordant. Miss Durant labored under such a cold that her voice was entirely unmanageable and painful to hear. Il Trovatore is far beyond the capabilities of the troupe and we trust that they will not again allow the charge of murder to rest upon them.[49]

As he became more sure of himself as critic, Upton's reviews became more expansive and polished in style, also increasing in musical insight.

It is not coincidental that Upton's ascendancy in the late 1850s and early 1860s corresponded with the dramatic rise of operatic and orchestral music during those years.[50] Above all, the Philharmonic Society of Balatka, whose endeavors Upton enthusiastically supported, provided the critic with opportunities to write at length and in detail.[51] He was similarly inspired by his favorite conductor, Theodore Thomas, in the decades after 1870.[52] In those promotional activities, it appears that Upton's first priority was to see the orchestral tradition firmly established and subsequently fully developed in Chicago.

As Feldman writes, "in November, 1861, Upton joined the staff of the *Chicago Daily Tribune*, with which he would be identified for the rest of his life."[53] Already at that time, the *Tribune* was the pre-eminent newspaper in Chicago, the organ for the better-educated citizens, and a publication of considerable influence in the country at large.[54] At first as city editor and then as associate editor, Upton could wield tremendous authority among the musical audiences of the city, since he also continued to write reviews.[55]

He stood out from the fellow newspaper critics working in Chicago by virtue of his "graceful pen and trenchant wit,"[56] his abilities as a "polished writer, a man of keen discrimination and a student of musical history and literature."[57] Two examples from his mature *Tribune* criticisms of the 1860s suffice to reveal these characteristics.

Upton conducted his own media campaign in the spring of 1862 on behalf of Balatka's impending performance of Mendelssohn's *Elijah*, which culminated in a generous eighteen-column-inch review on 27 May:

> Chicago may be said to have arrived at the third stage in its musical experience. It is within the recollection of all when audiences were satisfied with the ballad; and Baker families, Rainer families, Hutchinson families, Alleghenians, Dodge, Dempster and such were the rage. Then came the operatic stage, its success doubtful at first, but so complete at last that impresarios always put down Chicago in their memoranda as the city west of New York to line their pockets. The season now closing has witnessed another step upward. Beethoven's symphonies have been produced, appreciated and received with a sincere enthusiasm, and last night, Elijah—the first thoroughly public representation of Mendelssohn's genius in this city— . . . was successfully performed and appreciatively received by one of the largest and finest audiences ever assembled in Chicago.
>
> Mr. Lumbard undertook the laborious part of the "Prophet," but in his hands it proved an unwieldy material from over-effort. The part so full of dramatic element was rendered with too much uniformity of expression. . . . His declamation was the same throughout. We advise him to husband his vocal powers, great as they undoubtedly are, more carefully. . . . He sang, considering the extreme difficulty of his part, remarkably well in tune, the exact contrary of which usually obtains with the powerful bassos, and apart from the fault we have mentioned, is entitled to credit for his effort to sustain the laborious part. . . .
>
> The chorus was not as powerful as the number of singers led us to expect, and was at times drowned out by the orchestra. It

showed, however, careful training, and we are inclined to ascribe short-comings in time and precision to mere carelessness. . . .

We have thus pointed out what we conceive to be the faults as well as the merits of the performance last evening. The faults can be easily remedied, and undoubtedly, this evening, the Oratorio will be represented in much better style. . . .[58]

In the first paragraph, he remarks on the evolution of musical life in Chicago, noting with a certain pride the state of accomplishment of the era about which he was reporting as critic.[59] Despite his subsequent detailed praise of most singers, critical comments are not lacking in the insightful discussions of the tenor and the chorus. Upton summarizes his balance sheet of pros and cons near the end of the review and then concludes with a portentous comment about the condition of musical taste in Chicago:

Elijah is probably one of the most severe musical tests for an audience, and it was a problematical matter with many musical people whether a Chicago audience would appreciate this highest class of music, and whether they would have the patience to sit out its hearing. Last evening proved, however, that the Oratorio was appreciated, and thoroughly appreciated, and that there is a genuine and sincere love of legitimate music among our concert-goers.

Later in the decade, between the years 1867 and 1869, "Upton published as a regular weekly feature his widely-read 'Letters of Peregrine Pickle' (named after the Smollett character), which functioned partly as a column of arts news and criticism while masquerading as provocative essays on Chicago society. . . . The tone was gently satirical . . . and the observations were keen."[60] In these essays, Upton anticipates the witty feuilletonistic style that George Bernard Shaw would adopt in his Corno di Bassetto articles of the early 1890s.[61]

The following excerpts taken from a "Peregrine Pickle" essay in the *Tribune* of 17 April 1869, typify the style of these essays:

. . . The tenor, I take to be the happiest man in the world, or at least he ought to be. If he be a tenor di grazia, lovely women will sigh for him; if a tenor robusto, lovely women will die for him, or wish that Heaven had made her such a man. The amateur tenor enjoys the same advantages as the operatic tenor, on a small scale . . . .

The basso, on the other hand, is the personification of vocal misery, and he knows it. If a cavalier, he is some dilapidated old duke, with a young and pretty wife, just packing up preparatory to elopement with the tenor....[62]

It is interesting to observe how, as the sophistication of the concert life and audience increased, so rose the level of the accompanying music journalism in the local daily press.

The Great Fire of 1871 put a temporary halt to musical activities and the concomitant reviews and criticisms in the newspapers.[63] It ended a period of tremendous expansion in the concert and operatic life of the city and in the music journalism of the newspapers. However, the daily press was not the only literary vehicle for writings about music during the pre-Fire era.

The city also developed a burgeoning music periodical press during the course of the 1850s and 1860s,[64] largely as a product of the phenomenal growth in the music publishing industry. In fact, the decade prior to the Fire could be considered as the Golden Age of music publishing in Chicago. For that industry, the losses were devastating—as Dena Epstein notes, "Chicago's music publishing never regained the leading position it had assumed during the Civil War."[65]

At least eight discrete music publishers plied their trade in Chicago at various times during the pre-Fire years.[66] The most important and successful of them, including Root & Cady and Lyon & Healy, issued their own periodicals, which as house organs would often almost exclusively devote themselves to the company's music either in publication or in performance.[67] All together, nine music periodicals appeared in Chicago prior to 1871 (see Table 3). The total of 45 music journals published there between 1845 and 1900 makes Chicago second only to New York City for number of music periodicals published in an American city during the nineteenth century.[68]

Although they appeared in Chicago, the journals concerned themselves less with local musical matters than did the newspapers, except when their own publishing house and its activities were concerned. The explanation is simple: the journals could not survive alone on subscriptions from the Chicago area, and thus they had to cater to broader interests by extensively reporting on music in Europe and the East-Coast cities.[69] Nevertheless, the periodicals do provide valuable insights into the state of music publishing in Chicago and into the city's leading musical literary figures (who served as journal editors and contributors) and also occasional glimpses of local musical activities through the eyes of critics.

The first music journal of consequence published in Chicago for which copies can still be found is *The Song Messenger of the North-West*, which began monthly publication in August 1863 under the editorship of the noted songwriter Henry C. Work.[70] The longest surviving of the pre-Fire music journals in Chicago (it attained an age of twelve years), the *Song Messenger* succeeded by virtue of the talent of editors and contributors (above all, Work and George F. Root) and the perspicaciousness and tenacity of its publishing company. Work, who edited the journal only until November of 1863 but remained an occasional correspondent afterward, and Root were probably the most talented pre-Fire writers on music besides Upton.[71] The following excerpt typifies the humorous, bantering style of the publication, which provides a parallel with Upton's own literary style, especially in the "Peregrine Pickle" articles for the *Tribune*:

> People usually attend concerts to gratify their ears rather than their eyes. Yet it adds much to one's pleasure, to secure a good view of the performance. . . . For this reason, at a late concert in Bryan Hall, we chose a seat in the gallery. . . . While congratulating ourselves on this wise selection of seats, we noticed a peculiar phenomenon. The center of the stage . . . suddenly became invisible to us. We gazed on an immense blank. Scrutinizing it carefully, it assumed form.—. . . It was—no!—yes! It was a bonnet!
>
> Now, we are not usually very observing with regard to the style of bonnets worn. But, gazing on this as we did for two long hours, its form is indelibly fixed in our memory.
>
> It was one of those steep-roofed species, built according to the latest principles of millinerie architecture. . . . What we heard at the concert—the sweet solos, the grand choruses—we shall not here describe; but this is what we saw.[72]

As a house organ for Chicago's most important music publisher, Root & Cady, the *Song Messenger* almost exclusively concerned itself with the company's publications, concerts, and related activities. Its pages reflect how Root and Cady were able to take advantage of local Civil War sympathies to become the pre-eminent music publishers in Chicago.[73] With sales of 875,000 copies for the publishers' five most popular Civil War songs between 1862 and 1865 (a total weight of 33 tons of music, according to the *Song Messenger*), it is not surprising that the company would turn to the musical press and its own two most popular composers to make its products known, not only in Chicago but throughout the West. This media manipulation, which included such tactics as printing favorable criticisms of the company's recent publications and positively reviewing concerts and institutes in which the publishers had some hand,[74] helped bring the journal success, which however occurred at the cost of Chicago. As Work himself remarked in the first issue,

Chicago . . . is comparatively but a small point in our great field. We do not propose therefore to occupy much space with our own musical matters, unless they possess more than a merely local interest.[75]

More informative about musical life in Chicago, albeit primarily in its first issues, was the *Chicago Musical Review* of 1866-67, edited by music publisher Hiram Murray Higgins.[76] Higgins' company served as the major pre-fire competitor for Root & Cady in Chicago, although it did not offer a very extensive or distinguished catalogue.[77] Despite his aforementioned intention of providing accounts of all worthy news from the field of music,[78] Higgins did publish articles of local interest.[79] Most valuable as a reflection of Chicago musical life during the 1866-67 season was the column "At Home,"[80] in which Higgins reviewed performances by undistinguished traveling virtuosi and the following local institutions: the Germania Männerchor, the Philharmonic Society, and four Chicago church choirs. The reviews of the Männerchor performances document the ensemble's high performance standards and esteem in the community:

> The summer nights' festival at the Rink, given immediately after the issue of our last number, was one of the most pleasant musical occasions we remember. . . . The programme was very carefully chosen, embracing songs from Mendelssohn, Abt, Storck, and the modern German composers, with a quartette from the Prophet, and a handful of overtures for the orchestra. . . . A worse place to sing in than the Rink cannot well be found, and the Maennerchor sang therefore at a disadvantage, but they acquitted themselves admirably. Mr. Schultze, who took the melody in the quartette from the Prophet, was encored, although the air, full of high and sustained tones, was very trying to him. The Maennerchor made their debut under the best of auspices, and we hope to hear more of them in the coming season.[81]

Less partial, more critical than the *Song Messenger*, the *Chicago Musical Review* attempted to have a positive effect on the city's musical life, through its obvious concern over and frequent encouragement of the indigenous performing ensembles. Although Higgins could not compare as a stylist with Upton, his writings also reveal a level of musical sophistication and judgment that places him in the forefront of music critics working in Chicago before 1871.

The third significant pre-Fire music journal in Chicago was *The Musical Independent*, the house organ for publisher Lyon & Healy.[82] In its five years of existence (1868 through 1873),[83] the journal distinguished itself by virtue of the literary talent, musical insight, and local orientation of its editor, the organist W. S. B. Mathews, who would become a leading literary figure in Chicago's musical scene after the Fire.[84] Of the three music journals surveyed, *The Musical Independent* provides the fullest and most authoritative picture of music in Chicago at the time, perhaps because of what appears to be an autonomy granted to the editor by the publisher.[85] Prior to 1871, the journal documented such important musical events as the first Thomas concert (November 1869) and the first performance of Haydn's *Creation* (May 1869), evaluated the progress of Balatka's subscription orchestral series and the Mendelssohn Quintette Club, and reviewed traveling opera troupes and virtuosi, including violinist Ole Bull and pianist Alida Topp.[86] Table 4 presents an overview of the rich repertory of one season, 1868-69, as covered in *The Musical Independent*—the listing in the journal is ample proof of how far the city had musically developed since the first concert in 1835. Despite his progressive musical inclinations, which led him to criticize Balatka's orchestral matinees for the lack of new works,[87] Mathews had some difficulty in the acceptance of works by Liszt and Wagner, as is evident in two excerpts:

> CHICAGO.—The second Symphony concert came off Dec. 22, at Library Hall. . . . The Liszt piece [Tasso] was played for the first time here. Of course it would be hardly fair to judge it from one hearing. But our impression is that in real melodic wealth it is not [at] all to be compared with the works of Mendelssohn, or Schubert, far less with those of Mozart and Beethoven. Its excellencies consist chiefly in the expert management of the various tone-colors of the orchestra so as to obtain a variety of interesting and unique effects. No doubt the work does possess great unity, as Mr. Balatka kindly informed us in our programmes, but it is rather "unity of origin," (the unity that arises from constructing an entire work on one motive), than the "unity of membership," which consists in such an invention of parts as that though intrinsically unlike, each completes or complements the other. . . .[88]

> CHICAGO.—Balatka's Fifth Symphony Concert came off April 26, at Farwell Hall. . . . The Wagner overture [Tannhäuser] went well, and seemed to be understood better, both by conductor and players. It is fearfully noisy in some places, and we do sincerely wish Mr. Wagner could be coaxed to "draw it a little milder." But the "Pilgrim Chorus" air, which opens the overture, went splendidly.[89]

These attempts to obtain to an unbiased, truly critical evaluation of music and performance typify Mathews' writing and his editorial policies for reviews, as noted in July 1869:

> From the beginning of this journal it must have been apparent to our readers that it was no part of the Music Reviewer's intention to deal chiefly in white-wash and soap.[90]

The Musical Independent points to a new age of criticism in Chicago music journals, perhaps in keeping with the two musical developments it anticipated and advocated: subscription orchestral concerts under Thomas and a full season of opera performed by an indigenous company.

The burgeoning musical life in Chicago not only supported the development of a local music criticism and music journalism, intended for consumption by readers in Chicago but also encouraged the emergence of an interest in the Chicago musical scene within the national and international musical press. It is of more than passing interest that some of the more talented and perceptive reviews of music in Chicago during the 1860s, those published by Upton and Root in the local press notwithstanding, appeared in the extremely influential Boston publication entitled *Dwight's Journal of Music*, which had a national scope and readership.[91] Regular correspondence reports from Chicago began in 1858, although the first letter had already appeared in 1853.[92]

The coverage of music in Chicago provided by *Dwight's Journal of Music* paralleled the development of musical life in the city. The first concerts of the Philharmonic Society under Balatka and the establishment of yearly operatic seasons coincided with the publication of the first regular correspondence reports from Chicago. Other topics of reviews include virtuoso concerts, organs, and the activities of local chamber ensembles.[93] Although neither column space nor frequency for correspondence reports from Chicago could compare with the coverage offered for Boston and New York City, Chicago occupied third place among the North American cities reported on in *Dwight's*. The following comment from the issue of 14 November 1863 reflects the importance attributed to Chicago in the journal: "Boston is the Athens of the East, while influential and far-seeing men strive to make Chicago the centre of the West, in Commerce, Education and Music."[94]

The Chicago correspondents for *Dwight's Journal* did not identify themselves other than through initials or fictitious names.[95] However, it is clear from other sources that the critic named "Der Freyschutz" was actually W. S. B. Mathews, aforementioned editor of *The Musical Independent*. The first "Freyschutz" review appeared in November of 1867 and brought

Chicago into the national spotlight, since it was detailed and well written.[96] Here is a typical passage from one of the "Freyschutz" correspondence reports:

> CHICAGO, FEB. 6 . . .
> Ole Bull gave three or four concerts, but they were not well attended. Of his playing different opinions are expressed. Camilla Urso was here with Gilmore, and played at his promenade concerts. I think the general opinion of the connoisseurs places her quite above Ole Bull as an artist. The reed and wind effects of Gilmore's band were quite novel here, where it is so unusual to find more than the smallest possible assortment of instruments in the orchestra. So our people curiously enough "went out to see" and hear "reeds shaken in the wind."
> Just now we are having Italian Opera by a troupe compounded from those of Grover and Maretzek. The operas for the week are Ernani, Crispino e la Comare, Romeo and Juliet (Gounod's), Trovatore, Fra Diavolo, Lucrezia Borgia, and Faust. Both orchestra and chorus are better than we usually have here, which is saying little to their credit. Moreover, Mr. Maretzek contrives to keep them well together without pounding, or stamping, or making any undue fuss. And that is a great relief, for the labors of Strakosch's director were so onerous and after all so ineffective, as to make one positively uncomfortable to see him waste so much hard work.
> Last night Romeo and Juliet was performed for the first time here. In the case of an opera concerning which the doctors so widely disagree, it is scarcely becoming the writer to speak confidently; yet certain facts became apparent as the work progressed. Among them, these: —The instrumentation is exceedingly pleasant, appropriate, and consequently varied. The accompaniments, both in the score and in performance, were so in the best sense of the word. The real meaning of the work was brought out better by them, and the voices were never covered up or drowned out by brass. The melodies were pleasing and not especially commonplace. But the solo singing was "no better than it should be." . . .[97]

Note the ease and wit of style, as evident in the comments about Strakosch's director, and the frankness and perceptiveness in the specific evaluations of the music and performance. Mathews not only revealed to the nation the richness of musical life in Chicago during this vibrant period of its history but also showed how that environment fostered the development of a sophisticated music criticism.[98]

This article has attempted to prove that, by the time of the Great Fire of 1871, Chicago could boast of an active and informed music criticism in its newspapers and music journals and in local reports for national journals. This development did not take place in a vacuum but rather as a response to the tremendous growth of the city's musical life. Furthermore, contrary to prior opinion, this critical "awakening" was not the result of one man's efforts, beginning in the mid 1850s, but instead represents the culmination of thirty-five years of activity in papers and journals on the part of countless unnamed individuals who had the most varied backgrounds. However, despite these critics' frequent lack of qualifications, the writing from this early stage of criticism in Chicago offers many a surprise in the areas of literary talent and musical perceptivity. Chicago has nothing to be ashamed of in the first stages of its music criticism, just as its early musical activity cannot be viewed as being "primitive." As Bessie Louise Pierce has remarked,

> although circumstances attending the development of the [musical] art [in Chicago] may not always have been happy [during its first stages], they were, nonetheless, the basis of a later leadership in the Middle West.[99]

TABLE 1. Chicago Newspapers, 1833-71

1833- *Chicago Democrat* (Weekly), becomes *Weekly Chicago Democrat* in 1846. In 1861 merges with *Chicago Daily Tribune* (s.v.).

1835- *Chicago American* (Weekly), becomes *Chicago Daily Democrat* in 1839. In 1842 ceases publication.

1840- *Chicago Democrat* (Daily), becomes *Chicago Daily Democrat* in 1849. In 1861 merges with *Chicago Daily Tribune* (s.v.).

1842- *Chicago Express* (Daily), becomes *Chicago Daily Journal* in 1844. Becomes *Daily Chicago Journal* in 1853. In 1855 becomes *Chicago Daily Journal* which becomes *Chicago Evening Journal* (Daily) in 1861.

1844- *Gem of The Prairie* (Weekly), merges with *Chicago Daily Tribune* (s.v.) in 1852.

1844- *Chicago Weekly Journal*.

1847- *Chicago Daily Tribune*, merges with *Gem of The Prairie* in 1852. In 1858 merges with *Chicago Daily Press* (s.v.) and becomes *Chicago Press and Tribune* (Daily). In 1860 becomes *Chicago Daily Tribune*, which merges with *Weekly Chicago Democrat* (s.v)

and *Chicago Daily Democrat* (s.v.) in 1861. In 1864 becomes *Chicago Tribune* (Daily).
1852- *Daily Democratic Press*, becomes *Chicago Daily Democratic Press/Chicago Daily Press* in 1857. In 1858 merges with *Chicago Daily Tribune* (s.v.) and becomes *Chicago Press and Tribune*.
1854- *Chicago Daily Times*, merges with *Chicago Daily Herald* (s.v.) in 1860 and becomes *Daily Times and Herald/Daily Chicago Times*. In 1861 becomes *Chicago Times* (Daily), which becomes *Times* (Daily) in 1866. In 1871 becomes *Chicago Times* (Daily).
1854- *Chicago Times* (Weekly).
1857- *Chicago Daily Herald*, merges with *Chicago Daily Times* (s.v.) in 1860.
1860- *Chicago Post/Chicago Morning Post* (Daily), becomes *Chicago Daily Republican* in 1865.

TABLE 2. Important Musical Events in Chicago, 1833-71

1833	Projected series of monthly concerts by Charles Butler; first newspaper established (*Chicago Democrat*)
1834	First piano brought to Chicago (Jean B. Beaubien)
1835	First sheet music sold by booksellers Russell and Clift; school of music inaugurated by Samuel Lewis
1835-36	Concert season of the Chicago Harmonic Society
1836	Establishment of instrument dealer Osbourn and Strail
1837	First season of theater
1839	First concert of guest artist (tenor William Dempster)
1842	Music introduced into public school curriculum
1846	Choral Union established
1849	Mozart Society established
1850	Tremont Music Hall opened; first opera performance (Bellini's *La Sonnambula*) on 30 July; first orchestra concert (Dyhrenfurth's Philharmonic Society) on 24 October
1850-68	Philharmonic Society of Dyhrenfurth (1850-60) and Balatka (1860-68) (with some interruptions)
1853	Concerts of Patti and Ole Bull in April; first complete symphony performed in Chicago on 11 June; second season of opera begins in October
1855	Arrival of George P. Upton on 27 October

1856 First music journal in Chicago (*Western Journal of Music*)
1856-58 Orchestra of Henry Ahner
1858 Third season of opera, September-October
1858-66 Musical Union
1860 Arrival of Hans Balatka (conductor of Philharmonic Society)
1865 Opening of Crosby's Opera House on 20 April
1867 Florence Ziegfeld founds Chicago Academy of Music
1868-71 Oratorio Society
1869 First concert of Theodore Thomas on 27 November

TABLE 3. Music Journals Published in Chicago Prior to the Great Fire of 1871

WESTERN JOURNAL OF MUSIC
    May 1856-?; biweekly
    Published by R. G. Green; edited by W. H. Currie

THE FLOWER-QUEEN (later *CHICAGO MUSICAL REVIEW AND FLOWER-QUEEN*)
    May-November 1856; monthly
    Published by Higgins Brothers; edited by W. C. Webster, C. M. Cady

THE SONG MESSENGER OF THE NORTH-WEST (later *THE SONG MESSENGER*)
    April 1863-October 1875 (vol. 1-13, no. 9); monthly
    Published by Root & Cady; edited by H. C. Work, J. R. Murray, W. S. B. Mathews, G. F. Root

MUSICAL MISCELLANY (published in Kalamazoo and Chicago)
    August (?), 1863-1864 (?); monthly
    Publisher and editor unknown

THE SEVEN SOUNDS: A MUSICAL MAGAZINE DEVOTED TO THE YOUTH
    March 1865-October 1865 (vol. 1, nos. 1-3); quarterly
    Published by Merrill and Brennan; edited by H. T. Merrill

THE CONCORDIA
   January 1866-December 1867 (vols. 1-2); monthly
   Published and edited by H. R. Palmer

CHICAGO MUSICAL REVIEW (later *HIGGINS MUSICAL REVIEW*)
   September 1866-May 1867 (vol. 1, nos. 1-9); monthly
   Published and edited by H. M. Higgins

THE MUSICAL INDEPENDENT
   7 November 1868-March 1873 (vols. 1-4); monthly
   Published by Lyon & Healy; edited by W. S. B. Mathews

CHICAGO MAGAZINE OF FASHION, MUSIC, AND HOME READING
   April 1870-1876 (vols. 1-6); monthly
   Published by R. R. Donnelley; edited by M. L. Rayne

TABLE 4. Repertory of 1868-1869 Season Covered in the *Musical Independent* ("The Good Music of Last Year's Programmes" 1 [October 1869]: 353)

A. Orchestral

Symphonies.—Mendelssohn's in A minor; Liszt's *Tasso*; Beethoven's Fifth; Haydn's in E; "Romance" from Schumann's Symphony in D minor; "Andante" from Ulrich's *Triumphal Symphony*; Symphony in C major, F. Schubert.

Overtures.—*Loreley and Lurline*, Wallace; *Midsummer-Night's Dream* and Trumpet Overtures, Mendelssohn; *Zampa*, Herold; *Max Robespierre*, Litolff; *Night in Grenada*, Kreutzer; *William Tell*, Rossini; *Der Freyschutz* and *Oberon*, Von Weber; *Massaniello*, Auber; *Tannhauser*, Wagner.

Concerto.—Mendelssohn's for violin.

Transcriptions.—*Theme and Variations*, Onslow; Chopin's *Funeral March*.

B. Oratorio

The *Creation*. (Twice.)

C. Opera

Trovatore (3); *Ernani* (2); *Don Giovanni*; *Barber of Seville*; *Sicilian Vespers* (2); *Faust*; *Fidelio* (2); *Martha* (given also in English, 4); *Fra Diavolo* (2); *Czar and Zimmerman*; *Norma*; *Bohemian Girl*; *Cobbler and the Fairy*; *Crown Diamonds* (2); *Traviata*; *Sonnambula*; *Cantata Erl King*, *Gade*; *La Grande Duchesse*; *Genevieve*; *La Vie Parisienne*; *Orpheus aux Enfers*; and two or three other French operas which we do not recall....

---

[1] Population statistics are taken from Marianne Kozlowski, "Music in Chicago: 1830 to 1850" (M.M. thesis, University of Illinois at Urbana-Champaign, 1977), 3. The most comprehensive single source for these figures and the standard authority on the city's history is Bessie Louise Pierce, *A History of Chicago*, 3 vols. (New York: Alfred A. Knopf, 1937-57).

[2] Unidentified author, cited in Herman Kogan and Lloyd Wendt, *Chicago: A Pictorial History* (New York: Bonanza Books, 1958), 78-79.

[3] Elias Colbert and Everett Chamberlin, *Chicago and the Great Conflagration* (Cincinnati: C.F. Vent, 1872; reprint, New York: Viking Press, 1971), 173-74.

[4] Pierce 1:303-04 and Dena J. Epstein, *Music Publishing in Chicago Before 1871: The Firm of Root & Cady, 1858-1871* (Detroit: Information Coordinators, 1969), 3. In the absence of an authoritative history of music in Chicago, Epstein's book provides one of the best available pictures of musical life in the city during the nineteenth century.

[5] Colbert and Chamberlin, 182.

[6] Mary Ann Feldman, "George P. Upton: Journalist, Music Critic and Mentor to Early Chicago" (Ph.D. diss., University of Minnesota, 1983), 47 and 102, and *The New Grove Dictionary of American Music* (New York: Grove's Dictionaries, 1986), s.v. "Upton, George P.," by Mary Ann Feldman.

[7] See below for a discussion of the earliest music criticisms and musical life of the city.

[8] Feldman, "George P. Upton: Journalist, Music Critic and Mentor to Early Chicago," 42 and 47, respectively.

[9] For example, John Beckwith all but dismisses Canadian music criticism of the nineteenth century in his entry "Criticism" in Helmut Kallmann, Gilles Potvin, and Kenneth Winters, eds., *Encyclopedia of Music in Canada* (Toronto: University of Toronto Press, 1981), when he notes that "the late

19th century was in fact not entirely devoid of informed and impassioned criticism" (p. 243).

[10] As Edward Downes has pointed out in the article "Criticism" in *New Grove Dictionary of American Music*, "the character of American music criticism, which differs sharply from that of European, is derived primarily from a historical development in which the news element of criticism has played an important part."

[11] *The New Grove Dictionary of Music and Musicians* (London: Macmillan, 1980), s.v. "Criticism," by Winton Dean.

[12] *Chicago Express*, 19 January 1843.

[13] *Chicago American*, 19 December 1835.

[14] Tables are located at the end of the article.

[15] Dempster was the first musical celebrity in the press—as Kozlowski notes (p. 8), "the *Chicago American* ran ten articles over a period of twelve days on him—unheard-of coverage of any artist, local or visiting, for years to come." Martinez received a similar response: eight items over 23 days in the *Chicago Express*, for three concerts.

[16] Kozlowski, 11.

[17] [James Campbell], "The Concert," *Gem of the Prairie*, 30 November 1844.

[18] [James Campbell], "Embouchure," *Gem of the Prairie*, 7 December 1844.

[19] For a discussion of the early history of opera in Chicago, see Edward C. Moore, *Forty Years of Opera in Chicago* (New York: Horace Liveright, 1930; reprint, New York: Arno Press, 1977) and Ronald L. Davis, *Opera in Chicago* (New York: Appleton-Century, 1966). Symphonic music prior to the founding of the Chicago Symphony Orchestra in 1891 is not really covered in any single monograph, although sources like Feldman and Epstein certainly address the situation.

[20] The ranks of virtuosi included such figures as Adelina and Carlotta Patti, Christina Nilsson, Karl Formes, Ole Bull, Camilla d'Urso, and Louis Moreau Gottschalk. The chorus was the Germania Männerchor, the orchestra, the Philharmonic Society.

[21] Epstein outlines the earliest phase of the music-publishing industry in Chicago on pp. 3-39 of her study.

[22] Of course, the year of the Great Fire must be seen as an important juncture in the musical development of the city. See below for a discussion of its ramifications.

[23] Curiously, the *Chicago Daily Journal* (9/117) did not carry a report on the fire, even though it favorably reviewed opening night. For some unknown

reason, only one review of the event was published in the Chicago daily press.

[24] The second season featured performances of Donizetti's *Lucia di Lammermoor* and Bellini's *Norma* and *La Sonnambula*, performed by the so-called "New York Italian Opera Company."

[25] Again, *La Sonnambula* figured prominently in the repertoire of the third "season," staged by the English Opera Troupe at the new McVickers Theater. However, Verdi's *Il Trovatore* also was performed, for the benefit of the prima donna Rosalia Durand.

[26] The first company called itself the Chicago Grand Opera, relying initially on singers from New York. It went out of business in 1932. See *The New Grove Dictionary of American Music*, s.v."Chicago," by Annette Fern.

[27] Pierce 2:424.

[28] While certain non-Italian works like Balfe's *Bohemian Girl* were quite popular, the bulk of the repertories consisted of Rossini, Bellini, and Donizetti operas. Charles Hamm deals with the dissemination of Italian opera in nineteenth-century America in *Yesterdays: Popular Song in America* (New York: Norton, 1979), 62-88.

[29] *Chicago Daily Journal* 9/117 (30 July 1850). A very insightful review of opera anonymously appeared in the *Chicago Daily Tribune* on 31 October 1853, after a performance of *Norma*. Though fully positive in tone, the half-column review analyzes the singing and performance of each character, dwelling at length on the accomplishment of the prima donna Mad. Rosa de Vries, and also evaluates the conducting of Maestro Arditi.

[30] Feldman notes that the early Philharmonic consisted "partly of hired hands from the conductor's farm who also happened to play instruments" and "lasted two seasons before being wiped out financially." "George P. Upton: Journalist, Music Critic and Mentor to Early Chicago," 100.

[31] Among the relevant favorable items dating from the Society's first stage of existence were a promotional ad in the *Chicago Daily Democrat* (14 October 1850) and an anonymous review in the *Chicago Daily Journal* (25 October 1850). Later coverage included lengthy reviews from January 1853 in the *Daily Democratic Press* and briefer notices in the *Chicago Daily Tribune* from that month. Eagerly anticipated by the critics, and heavily promoted in the newspapers, was the first performance of a symphony in Chicago, Beethoven's Symphony no. 2 as presented by the Society on 11 June 1853. Unfortunately, other news items had to take precedence in the following days, so that no full review appeared.

[32] *Chicago Daily Journal* 9/191 (25 October 1850). The overall assessment was that "the entertainment was excellent and the music exquisite."

33The program for this concert of the Philharmonic Society, on 3 January 1853, is as follows:

> Part I
> 1. Glee—Hail! Hail! Happy Day—Benedict
> 2. Quartet—Voices of the Night—Glover
> 3. Duet
> 4. Grand Chorus—Praise Ye the Lord—Naumann
> 5. Glee—Adieu to Home—A Swiss Melody
> 6. Solo
> 7. Piano Forte—On the Mountain's Airy Summit—Ka[ü]cken
>
> Part II
> 1. Song with Vocal Accompaniment—My Mountain Home—Wetmore
> 2. Solo—Dara's Vale—Bayley
> 3. Quartet—Where Are the Bowers, O Canaan—Rossini
> 4. Glee—Come Live with Me—Lee
> 5. Solo
> 6. Glee—Ha! Ha! We've Stemmed the Stream—Verdi
> 7. Quartet & Grand Double Chorus—He Gave Them Hailstones for Rain—Handel

Example 1 (see p. 234 above) provides further excerpts from the review in the *Daily Democratic Press*, 5 January 1853, which substantiate the insightfulness of this noteworthy reviewer.

34See an article in the Chicago-based *Song Messenger of the North-West* ("Sketches of Musical Celebrities of the North-West: No. 1—Hans Balatka," 1/10 [January 1864]), 146, for a contemporary discussion of Balatka's life and activities.

35*Chicago Tribune*, 23 November 1860.

36Feldman, "George P. Upton: Journalist, Music Critic and Mentor to Early Chicago," 142-46, treats Upton's relationship with Balatka and the Society.

37The stage was set for Theodore Thomas, who—with his orchestra—made two visits to Chicago during the pre-fire era: in November 1869 and in 1871, on the very eve of the conflagration.

38The chorus was especially prominent through its performance of larger choral and vocal pieces, many of which were being presented to the inhabitants of Chicago for the first time. These performances often took place with the collaboration of the Philharmonic Society. In fact, it was on a concert of the Germania that the first performance of a symphony in Chicago took place (*Chicago Daily Tribune*, 11 June 1853). That the newspapers engaged in superlatives in their reportage of the choir is evident from a review of 7 June 1853 in the *Daily Democratic Press*: "We could speak of every single piece in the programme, but our words would only be repetitious. *Criticism* we call our notice, but what is there to criticise, when every thing is perfect?"

[39]This list is by no means exhaustive, especially with regard to singers and pianists. The level of accomplishment for the travelling virtuosi certainly had climbed since the 1830s and 1840s, although itinerant artists of more popular taste also provided entertainment, with the Swiss Bell Ringers and the Druids or Ox Horn Players prominently figuring among them. See Pierce 2:426.

[40]The announcements took the form of feature ads that most prominently featured Bull's name and included a tentative program.

[41]Typical is the promotional announcement in the *Daily Chicago Journal* of 21 April 1853, the day of Bull's first concert: "OLE BULL'S CONCERT—To-night the world renowned OLE BULL appears for the first time before an audience in Chicago. His fame, world wide as it is, is sufficient without endorsement by us, to call forth all with music in their souls to witness the magic power he practices over the violin."

[42]He ultimately nevertheless gave three additional final concerts.

[43]Arthur Loesser, *Men, Women and Pianos: A Social History* (New York: Simon and Schuster, 1954; reprint, with a new foreword by Edward Rothstein and a preface by Jacques Barzun, New York: Dover Publications, 1990), 483.

[44]For example, in the *Daily Democratic Press* of 25 April 1853, the anonymous reviewer used such phrases as "highest genius," "complete success," and "true artistic excellence."

[45]"City Matters: Ole Bull's Concerts," *Daily Chicago Journal*, 26 April 1853.

[46]The standard study is Feldman's dissertation, which--despite her distortion of musical history through the exaggeration of Upton's role— reveals much solid research in uncovering the sources that document his life. Upton's autobiographical *Musical Memories: My Recollections of Celebrities of the Half Century, 1850-1900* (Chicago: A. C. McClurg & Co., 1908) is an invaluable source about music and journalism in Chicago during the second half of the nineteenth century. The most important body of unpublished materials is in the McClurg Collection of the Newberry Library, which contains various letters and contracts. Other significant

collections of items relating to Upton can be found among the holdings of the Chicago Historical Society and the Library of Congress.

[47] Feldman, "George P. Upton: Journalist, Music Critic and Mentor to Early Chicago," 96.

[48] Ibid., 103.

[49] [George P. Upton], "Il Trovatore at McVicker's," *Chicago Daily Journal*, 9 October 1858.

[50] Opera finally became an annual occurrence in 1858 and Balatka's arrival in 1860 heralded an intensification of concert activity in Chicago.

[51] Balatka's eight-year tenure as director of the Philharmonic Society introduced the city to virtually all of Beethoven's symphonies, for example. Upton fondly recalled his contributions to the orchestral scene in Chicago in *Musical Memories*, 263. Feldman keenly observed the critic's typical tactics in promoting the conductor's work: he would first list a full program, then provide a program note a few days before the concert, and finally after the concert engage in "puffery," although Upton would not spare criticism when warranted. "George P. Upton: Journalist, Music Critic and Mentor to Early Chicago," 141-42.

[52] It is interesting to note how rumors accused Upton of killing Balatka's Philharmonic Society, since he unequivocally championed the superior Theodore Thomas and his orchestra when they came to Chicago in the late 1860s. See Feldman, "George P. Upton: Journalist, Music Critic and Mentor to Early Chicago," 183-90, for a discussion of Upton's early support of Thomas.

[53] Ibid., 104.

[54] Beside Upton's own *Musical Memories*, several publications provide accurate historical information about the newspaper: *Tribune: A Century of Tribune Editorials, 1847-1947* (Chicago: Tribune Company, 1947); Philip Kinsley, *The Chicago Tribune: Its First Hundred Years* (New York: Alfred A. Knopf, 1943), 3 vols.; and "The Chicago Tribune," *Graphic* (9 January 1892): 29-33.

[55] The periods of Upton's critical and editorial activities at the *Chicago Tribune* overlapped: he was music critic from 1863 to 1881 and associate editor from 1872 to 1905. *The New Grove Dictionary of American Music*, s.v. "Upton, George P.," by Feldman.

[56] Feldman, "George P. Upton: Journalist, Music Critic and Mentor to Early Chicago," 111.

[57] George B. Armstrong, "The Musical Journalist," *Music* 4 (August 1893): 379.

[58][George P. Upton], "The Oratorio of Elijah," *Chicago Tribune*, 27 May 1862.

[59]The replacement of popular traveling acts with "high-brow" entertainment is a development not only observed by Upton but probably also ushered in by his columns. The three-stage view of early Chicago musical history is interesting—most historians would, however, exchange the second for third periods, since opera really did not have a firm foothold in Chicago until the twentieth century.

[60]Feldman, "George P. Upton: Journalist, Music Critic and Mentor to Early Chicago," 109.

[61]According to Feldman, Upton could have made the same boast as Shaw did, when the latter claimed that "he could make a deaf stockbroker read his column." "George P. Upton: Journalist, Music Critic and Mentor to Early Chicago," 154. Whether there were any mutual influences between the two critics remains to be determined, through stylistic analysis and study of their letters. Upton did have some local models for a higher literary style, including Frank B. Wilkie at the *Chicago Times* and Benjamin Taylor at the *Chicago Journal*, albeit not at the same level of inspiration as his work.

[62]Peregrine Pickle [George P. Upton], "The World of Amusement," *Chicago Tribune*, 17 April 1869.

[63]The Fire itself however spawned a number of popular histories and "documentary" accounts of the conflagration and the city prior to that disaster, including the aforementioned Colbert and Chamberlin book, as well as Edgar Johnson Goodspeed, *History of the Great Fires in Chicago and the West* (New York: H. S. Goodspeed & Co., 1871) and James W. Sheahan and George P. Upton, *The Great Conflagration. Chicago: Its Past, Present and Future* (Chicago: Union Publishing Co., 1872).

[64]Research into American music periodicals has tended to focus on major publications, like *Dwight's Journal of Music*, that were based in New York City or Boston. Typical studies resulting from such research are dissertations by Marcia Wilson Lebow, "A Systematic Examination of the *Journal of Music and Art* Edited by John Sullivan Dwight: 1852-1881, Boston, Massachusetts" (Ph.D. diss., University of California at Los Angeles, 1969) and Calvin Bernard Grimes, "American Musical Periodicals, 1819-1852: Music Theory and Musical Thought in the United States" (Ph.D. diss., University of Iowa, 1974). Good places to begin research into specific American periodicals of the nineteenth century are the following bibliographic studies: William J. Weichlein, *A Check-List of American Music Periodicals, 1850-1900* (Detroit: Information Coordinators, 1970) and M. Veronica Davison, "American Music Periodicals, 1853-1899" (Ph.D.

diss., University of Minnesota, 1973). The most complete list of American journals is *New Grove Dictionary of American Music*, s.v. "Periodicals," by Imogen Fellinger and John Shepard. The international indexing project RIPM (*Répertoire international de la presse musicale*) will be of assistance to scholars of American music, although no Chicago-based periodical is on the list of publications for indexing.

[65] Epstein, 3. Epstein furnishes by far the most complete, detailed picture of music publishing in Chicago—and indeed, in any American city—during the nineteenth century.

[66] The following publishers were prominent in Chicago prior to the Great Fire: H. M. Brainard, B. K. Mould, R. G. Greene, Higgins Brothers, Root & Cady, Lyon & Healy, H. T. Merrill, and Molter & Wurlitzer.

[67] This practice was not unique to Chicago. In fact, the earliest and most significant German music periodicals of the nineteenth century were associated with specific publishing houses: the *Allgemeine Musikalische Zeitung* with Breitkopf und Härtel, *Cäcilia* with Schott, and *Signale für die musikalische Welt* with Bartholf Senff. In the United States, the *Message Bird* was publication organ for publisher Richard Storrs Willis, Ditson and Co.'s *Musical Record* for Oliver Ditson Company. It is interesting to note that the leading nineteenth-century journals in Germany and the United States (respectively, Schumann's *Neue Zeitschrift für Musik* and *Dwight's Journal of Music*) were edited and produced independently, i.e., not as house organs for music publishers.

[68] Nineteenth-century New York could boast the publication of 82 music journals. These statistics are based upon information presented in Weichlein (q.v.).

[69] As H. M. Higgins noted in the first issue of the *Chicago Musical Review* (September 1866): "Each issue will contain . . . well digested accounts of what is going on in musical circles, not only in Chicago, but in all the prominent musical localities, and, in general, give to the reader a bird's eye view of all that is transpiring in the musical field worthy of note."

[70] Epstein discusses Work's brief editorship of the *Song Messenger* on pp. 49-50. Concerning Work's other activities, see Richard Hill, "The Mysterious Chord of Henry Clay Work," *Notes* 10/2 (March 1952): 211-25 and 10/3 (June 1853): 367-90, and *New Grove Dictionary of American Music*, s.v. "Work, Henry Clay," by Dale Cockrell.

[71] Work edited the journal only until November of 1863 but remained an occasional correspondent afterward. It would appear that James Murray, a frequent contributor to the journal, took over editorship by volume 5. (Editorship is difficult to determine, since neither the masthead nor the body

of the issues contained references to editors.) This position of Murray is confirmed in an article by George Root: "To Friends and Acquaintances," 5/9 (December 1867): 142.

[72][Henry C. Work], "What We Saw at the Concert," *The Song Messenger of the North-West* 1 (April 1863): 8.

[73]Their first and decisive successes came with publication in 1862 of Work's song "The Kingdom Has Come" and Root's patriotic song "The Battle Cry of Freedom," the former with a print run of 75,000 copies, the latter totaling 350,000 copies in both sheet and book form. Epstein provides a detailed account of the company's Civil-War publishing on pp. 48-50.

[74]At times the self-promoting activities of the publishers in their journal were quite blatant, such as in the column entitled "New Publications" and signed "Root & Cady": "A new song, by Geo. F. Root, titled 'Will you come to meet me, darling,' just published, is creating considerable interest in musical circles in Chicago. It is, as a composition, rather in advance of the musical education of the masses, and yet, like the beautiful productions of Schubert, of which it reminds us, it possesses a popular vein, and will win its way to the popular heart." *The Song Messenger of the North-West* 1/9 (December 1863): 137.

[75]George F. Root, "Musical Intelligence," *Song Messenger of the North-West* 1/1 (April 1863): 14. An examination of the journal itself reveals how, as time passed, it reported progressively fewer events and publications from Chicago, despite an auspicious start in volume 1 with such articles as "Concerts in Chicago," "Musical Matters in Chicago," and "Sketches of Musical Celebrities of the North-West: No. 1—Hans Balatka."

[76]The question of title for the *Chicago Musical Review* is as problematic as for some of the Chicago newspapers. It is not to be confused with the *Chicago Musical Review and Flower-Queen*, edited by the Higgins Brothers in 1856. After number 3 (November 1866) of the *Chicago Musical Review*, the title became *Higgins Musical Review*.

[77]A discussion of this company can be found in Epstein, 8-10. With its emphasis on musical instruments, particularly pianos and organs, the *Chicago Musical Review* reflected the company's own specialization.

[78]See footnote 69 of this study.

[79]The journal contains the following articles of local interest: H. M. Higgins, "The Review"; "The Music Department of Clark Seminary, Aurora, Ill."; "The Iowa Normal Musical Academy"; "At Home" (a monthly feature); "Board of Music Trade"; "To Music Teachers"; "To Music Dealers"; "An Organ for Chicago"; "Dearth of Pianos"; "The Opera Campaign"; "The

Northwest"; "Col. Wood's Museum and Gallery of Fine Arts"; H. M. Higgins, "To the Public"; "Obituary" [Charles Ansorge]; "Our Choirs"; "Musical Convention"; "The Rockford Convention"; "The Star of Hope"; "Our Choirs." It may be safely presumed that the unsigned articles were by Hiram M. Higgins as well, since there is no evidence of other contributors within the pages of the journal itself.

[80]"At Home" was a feature of all nine issues of the journal that appeared.

[81][H. M. Higgins], "At Home," *Chicago Musical Review* 1 (October 1866): 18.

[82]Mentioned by Epstein, 12. The first volumes of the journal itself make no reference to the subtitle indicated by Weichlein (p. 54) as applying to the complete run: "A Monthly Review of the News, Literature, and Science of Music."

[83]The first issue appeared on 7 November 1868, the last in March 1872. Publication was suspended for one year due to the effects of the Fire.

[84]He founded the journal *Music* in 1891, the *Journal of School Music* in 1908, and contributed to *The Etude* (1884-1911). During the 1870s and 1880s, Mathews wrote for at least three newspapers in Chicago. Books that he wrote include *How to Understand Music* (New York: T. MacCoun, 1885; reprint, New York: AMS Press, 1970); *A Hundred Years of Music in America* (Chicago: G.L. Howe, 1889; reprint, New York: AMS Press, 1972); *A Popular History of the Art of Music from the Earliest Times Until the Present* (Philadelphia: T. Presser, 1891; revised ed., 1906); *Music, Its Ideals and Methods* (Philadelphia: T. Presser, 1897; reprint, New York: AMS Press, 1972); *The Masters and their Music* (Philadelphia: T. Presser, 1898); and *The Great in Music* (Chicago: Music Magazine Publishing Co., 1900). Detailed studies of his life and literary activities are provided by Robert W. Groves, "The Life and Work of W. S. B. Mathews" (Ph.D. diss., University of Iowa, 1981) and James W. Clarke, "Prof. W. S. B. Mathews (1837-1912): Self-Made Musician of the Gilded Age (Illinois)" (Ph.D. diss., University of Minnesota, 1983).

[85]Unlike either the *Song Messenger* or the *Chicago Musical Review*, *The Musical Independent* was not edited by one of the owners of the publishing house.

[86]Noteworthy, for example, is the article "Our Symphony Concerts" 1/4 (February 1869): 102-03, in which Mathews (?) admonishes the public to use the symphony concerts of Balatka as a type of school of music, for the advancement of their musical knowledge and taste.

[87]". . . We must admit, that in fineness of finish the kind of playing of the orchestra is by no means what we could desire, nor in the matter of new

works do the programmes exhibit quite the enterprise that Chicago is wont to show in all other directions." "Monthly Summary of Musical Doings," 1/7 (May 1869): 211.

88[W. S. B. Mathews], "Monthly Summary of Musical Doings," *The Musical Independent* 1 (February 1869): 121.

89Ibid., 1 (June 1869): 243.

90"Our Musical Reviews," *The Musical Independent* 1/ 9 (July 1869), 256.

91See footnote 64 for a reference to the most recent bibliography about Dwight's publication. From the start, commentators have recognized the importance of Dwight and his journal. The list of such studies includes George Willis Cooke, *John Sullivan Dwight: Brook-farmer, Editor, and Critic of Music* (Boston: Small, Maynard, 1898; reprint, New York: Da Capo Press, 1969) and Edward Waters, "John Sullivan Dwight, First American Critic of Music," *Musical Quarterly* 21/1 (January 1935): 69-88.

92The first article was entitled "Musical Intelligence: Chicago Philharmonic Society," 2/16 (22 January 1853): 126. These reports were quite sporadic until mid-1858, when a series of correspondence reviews appeared under various pseudonyms.

93See, for example, the discussion of Morgan's organ concerts in "Musical Correspondence: Chicago," 25/12 (2 September 1865): 96, and the report on the testimonial benefit of the Mendelssohn Quintette Club in "Musical Correspondence: Chicago, March 25," 30/2 (9 April 1870): 221-22.

94"Musical Correspondence: Chicago, Ill., Oct. 10," 23/17: 128.

95The practice was not really much different from the anonymity in the newspapers. Nineteenth-century American music critics in general preferred to remain anonymous, but Dwight's preference for pseudonyms was a practice associated with publications of higher literary pretensions.

96This first review concerned performances of the Strakosch Opera Troupe, the Chicago Art School, and Robert Goldbeck's piano recital. Most interesting is the concluding paragraph, which criticizes the condescending attitude of traveling virtuosi from the East.

97[W. S. B. Mathews], "Musical Correspondence," *Dwight's Journal of Music* 27 (15 February 1868): 189.

98After the Fire, other journals built upon the success of the publications of Mathews and his colleagues. This proliferation of music magazines in the city not only had a number of smaller journals as a result, such as the *Musical Bulletin* (1879-83), *Chicago Musical Times* (1881-1907), *Presto* (1884-1937), and *Musical Critic* (1897-1900), but also brought forth several widely read and respected publications, including Mathews' own *Music*

(1891-1902), *The Music Review* of publisher Clayton F. Summy (1891-94) and the long-lived *Musical Leader and Concert-Goer* (1895-).
[99]Pierce 1:307.

AN AMERICAN MUSE LEARNS TO WALK: THE FIRST AMERICAN-MUSIC GROUP

Richard Jackson

In all probability, the New York American-Music Association, born in 1856, died in 1858, was the first group devoted to the performance of concert music composed in this country.[1] If there was an earlier one that fact has not been preserved by the historians of American music. Fifty years passed before another such group appeared: Arthur Farwell's American Music Society of Boston, created in 1905.[2]

Many will say that it should be no surprise that the first American-music concert group was founded as late as 1856. After all, they might say, there was only a small amount of the native product around before this. But more original compositions may exist at any time in someone's desk or organ bench or computer than anyone perhaps suspects.

Frequency of performance or publication by establishment organizations are surely not accurate gauges. A look at the pioneering NYA-MA might open a few eyes to the kinds of American musical compositions around five years before the Civil War. And the professions of the composers connected with the NYA-MA are wide ranging. We will meet a physician, a wealthy patron of the arts, two journalists, school teachers, students, singers, a violinist, assorted pianists and organists, besides the expected full-time composer like American-visitor William Vincent Wallace. (Only one United States-born full-time professional composer existed at the time in this country: Stephen Collins Foster.) In other words, as in later years, composers were where you found them.

THE NEW YORK MUSICAL CLIMATE OF 1856

At a time when the former English colonies, just eighty years old, yearned for cultural respectability in the eyes of the Old World, performing groups like the New York Philharmonic had little inclination to program American compositions. They reasoned, perhaps correctly for the goal, that the way to gain Europe's acceptance of American musical culture as mature was to perform mainly European music. If their aim had been to stimulate American musical culture, they would have encouraged American composers by performing American compositions. Journalists such as Boston's John Sullivan Dwight (1813-1893) and a host of New York critics believed the European music-in-America cause was a just one and aided it at every opportunity.

Hence, New York *circa* 1856 was musically rather like it would be *circa* 1956, except, of course, there was more of everything in 1956: there were good European-music chamber series (in 1856 New York, one run by the German-American Theodore Eisfeld (1816-1882) started in 1851, the other by the American William Mason, who patterned his series after that of Franz Liszt at Weimar, started in November 1855); there were choral societies, the Philharmonic, lots of Italian opera, glamourous visiting European soloists (both vocal and instrumental), and all manner of lighter musical fare. The critical emphasis was on the performance, not on the composer.

American audiences came quickly to want the repetition of certain works—be they operas, oratorios, church anthems, symphonies, songs, or chamber pieces. We should always remember, after all, that those were the days before reproduced sound. The only way to hear a piece of music was through live performance. And there was some justification in wanting to hear for the second time in, say, five years a symphony by Beethoven instead of an unknown piece by an unknown composer. Precious performance time was usually devoted to the well-tried work or the known composer. American "novelties" were kept to a minimum.[3]

A few American works were, of course, performed, thanks to the persistence of such men as George Frederick Bristow, William Henry Fry, and Jerome Hopkins. Lest we get carried away with altruism, however, as some commentators seem to have,[4] we should realize that most of them were hard-nosed individuals (as revealed in their writings and actions) whose motives were perhaps similar to those of American composers in later years, who worked doggedly to get their compositions performed by a phalanx of indifferent conductors and soloists. "Perform American music!" the older composers cried in their public rhetoric, and may have added privately, "and me first."

Most of the articles I have listed as "Sources of Background Information," deal not so much with the NYA-MA itself as with the musical climate in New York in the mid-1850s that had a direct bearing on its formation. Importantly, they cite the public letters written to Richard Storrs Willis, influential editor of the *Musical World and Times*, by George

Frederick Bristow in the wake of that editor's long exchange of public letters with William Henry Fry. The Willis-Fry debate arose when Willis criticized Fry's *Santa Claus Symphony* as a good but slight musical work. Fry, apparently defensive to an almost clinical degree, himself a music critic, fired off a rebuttal staunchly maintaining the greatness and seriousness of his *Santa Claus*. Rather than treat this answer as simply that of another highly sensitive, disgruntled composer and end the matter, Willis allowed and encouraged the scholarly "feud" to continue, as magazine editors always do (gleefully aware that such continuing sagas are good for business).

Somehow the argument turned to the topic of the New York Philharmonic's slighting of American composers, and just when the public debate seemed over, Philharmonic-violinist and active-composer Bristow got into the act. In a letter dated 27 February 1854 beginning "Dear Sir: I have observed that my name is used several times in the discussion just concluded between yourself and Mr. Fry" (I),[5] Bristow expressed complaints about the Philharmonic that lasted another month or so. With passionate righteous indignation he asked rhetorically if there was a Philharmonic Society somewhere in Germany "for the encouragement solely of American music?" (I), and made his famous statement that the "Philharmonic Society has been as anti-American as if it had been located in London during the revolutionary war and composed of native born English Tories" (I). There were outraged answers from the Philharmonic and from a writer for *Dwight's Journal of Music*, but they were no match for Bristow's injured eloquence. The writer from *Dwight's Journal*, signing himself or herself "Pegan," made an interesting and sharp statement, however, amidst the otherwise dim prose: "The present audience of the Philharmonic . . . has been indebted for its musical culture to that society, and its taste formed upon its models" (VI). (Yes, and that taste was largely Germanic even in 1854.)

In a letter defending the Philharmonic Society signed by Henry C. Timm, then its President, the following statement was made: "At the regular meeting of the Society on Saturday, March 11th [1854] . . . Mr. B[ristow]'s resignation as one of the Board of Directors and as performing member of the society was accepted" (III, 122). In another letter, Bristow also announced his resignation and added grandly, "I considered such a course to my own dignity, and the dignity of my country, decidedly necessary. I will neither see my country nor myself continually kept in the background by those who should cherish its best efforts in Art" (V, 153). (So Bristow considered his artistic efforts among the best!) When he calmed down, however, he rejoined the Society—the very next season.

What does this feud have to do with the NYA-MA? A great deal. In the same letter that he announced his retirement from the Philharmonic Society, Bristow wrote: "I am happy to inform all interested parties that measures are on foot for the establishment of The American Philharmonic Society, which I trust will be free from all *cliques*, and whose aim will be to promote and cultivate the Divine Art regardless of any national prejudices" (V, 153). (Well, none except that the "Divine Art" be mostly of the American variety.) Such a society never came about, as far as we know, but apparently not long after the Philharmonic-Bristow exchange in the *Musical World*, Jerome Hopkins came to New York City.

JEROME HOPKINS

The exact circumstances surrounding the formation of the NYA-MA are unknown to me (perhaps they were never recorded). But (with council from Bristow?) it was the brainchild of Charles Jerome Hopkins (1836-1898), or C. Jerome or Jerome, as he apparently wished to be known (certainly not the totally incorrect Edward, as mystifyingly he would be referred to later by some, John Tasker Howard among them).[6] A study of the programs of the NYA-MA reveal the prominence of Bristow's participation and the involvement of all the "right" people, including Willis, Fry, Gottschalk, and even Henry C. Timm (see the program of 27 February 1857).

Jerome Hopkins—naive, maddening, brilliant, fiery, goofy, stubborn, warm-hearted (he started free music schools for poor boys in 1861, and his obituary in the *New York Times* tells us he spent the last ten or fifteen years of his life travelling the country to train children's choirs). Maybe he was a genius. Maybe he was deranged. He definitely was one of thirteen children of John Henry Hopkins, Sr., the Episcopal Bishop of Vermont, his own life an ideal subject for a soap opera or romantic novel, seeing as how he left law practice to found his own school, to become assistant organist at an Episcopal church in Pittsburgh and then at the church's request its priest, finally Bishop of Vermont (see his entry in the *Dictionary of American Biography*). Among John Henry Hopkins, Sr.'s, other children was John Henry Hopkins, Jr., also an Episcopal cleric (he came to be known as Deacon Hopkins), editor of New York's *Church Journal* from 1853 to 1868, and composer of the Christmas carol *We Three Kings of Orient.* One of John Henry Hopkins, Sr.'s grandchildren was the famous pianist and writer Amy Fay, who was close to her uncle Jerome Hopkins in his later years (Hopkins' obituary in the *New York Times* says that Amy Fay's sister, Mrs. Pierce, arrived at Hopkins' house in Athenia, New Jersey, a half hour after he died). Hopkins bequeathed his manuscripts to Amy Fay; they are now at Harvard University.

Jerome Hopkins was born in Burlington, Vermont, and attended the University of Vermont, where he studied chemistry. His obituary in the

Times also tells us that he did not graduate from the University but came to New York City at age seventeen (1853—*AmeriGrove* says 1856), left the study of chemistry, and took up music. Richard Storrs Willis would write in 1857 that he believed there were always "two antagonistic biases" in Hopkins—"chemistry and music." He added, perhaps wickedly: "We advised him, some time since to strike the tag of his inclinations to chemistry; but he would not heed us" (EE, 355).

In any case, this young man in his early twenties, a beginning and enthusiastic composer, made something of a mark for himself in the New York music world by starting the NYA-MA. He probably founded the Society for this very reason as well as to get his compositions and those of his fellow composers performed. I say Hopkins was a "beginning" composer in 1856 though his *Times* obituary tells us that at the age of five he composed a "chant" that was performed at home by his family. At the time he formed the NYA-MA, Hopkins made a meager living as organist of St. John's church in Yonkers. Willis wrote in 1857 that Hopkins had been taught music informally at home and by one T. E. Miguel, "who died a few weeks ago in the greatest penury" (FF, 355). Willis also wrote that Hopkins played the viola, trombone, and cello (FF, 355).

After Jerome Hopkins started the NYA-MA, he immersed himself in its activities. Willis wrote that young Hopkins was not only

> President of the Society, but also Vice-President, Financier, all the Directors, Agent, and almost Door-keeper and type-setter of the programmes—in short, he is the Society itself. He started it, keeps it in a state of active vitality, lives in it and for it, in very close sense is engaged to it, and one of these days, for aught we see to prevent it, will marry it (EE, 355).

STRUCTURE AND PUBLICIZED OBJECT OF THE ASSOCIATION

Ten days before the second season of the NYA-MA commenced, Boston's *Dwight's Journal of Music* finally acknowledged the organization's existence with a now-valuable article, or rather a portion of its section titled "Musical Correspondence." The report is so important to this study, that it will be quoted in full:

> New York, Dec. 16 [1856]. There has recently been organized in this city a new Musical Association, which, though as yet small in numbers and of limited influence, promises in time to become a mighty lever in raising the standard of musical appreciation in this

country. It is called the "American Music Association," and its fundamental principle is the fostering of native talent and the production of native musical works. This object is more explicitly expressed in the first article of its constitution, which says: the object of this Society shall be to further the interest of musical composers residing among us, by having their works effectively presented to the public, in order that they may be fairly criticized and impartially judged. By this it will be seen that, though intended as an American society, and as such presenting special claims to public regard, it is by no means proscriptive in its regulations. Any resident composer has a right to present his works for public presentation by the Society, on the payment of a fee of $5.00, and the Society already enjoys unusual facilities for a proper presentation of such works. There are a body of chorus singers and a vocal quartet, for the production of vocal compositions, and a string quartet for the production of symphonic works, George Bristow, the composer, being one of the members.

At a recent meeting of the Society, Charles J. Hopkins, a talented young musician and organist of this city, through whose indomitable perseverance and energy the Society has been organized, was elected President, and T. J. Cook, a Broadway music-publisher, Vice President. The consulting committee includes the well-known names of Richard Storrs Willis, of the *Musical World*, Geo. F. Bristow, and George H. Curtis.

As yet this Society is in its infancy, and the experiment may fail, and will unless a lively interest is taken in it by musical men. Strange to say, though many worthy musicians give it their hearty co-operation, a still greater number treat the project with contempt, while others, ladies especially, think it quite beneath their dignity to look favorably upon the day of small things. Among those who have, however, agreed to give it their hearty co-operation are Gottschalk, Dr. Hodges [of Trinity Church], and other eminent American musicians [VIII].

Apart from telling us something about the workings of the group and its officers, this piece is valuable for the light it shines on the concert-public's attitude toward the NYA-MA. Clearly, the Society was treated with contempt by the majority, though it is not clear whether it was the NYA-MA itself or American music by relatively unknown composers that was among "small things." Despite the contempt, Hopkins was apparently proud of his group, even boasting repeatedly in its concert advertisements: "This Association has for its particular object the development of the science of musical composition among native Americans, and is the first EVER started with that object in view" (H).

We can add to the known officers the name of the secretary, William H. Walter, a young organist, learned from advertisements for the Association's concert of 30 April 1858 (SS, TT) and that of F. A. Stuart, treasurer, as listed in the surviving printed program of the last season's second concert.

Not all of those connected with the NYA-MA approved the manner of its operation. With justification, Willis grumbled about the five-dollar fee and suggested a subscription policy. He went public with his reservations in the 25 April 1857 issue of his journal:

> We venture to suggest a different mode of permanently sustaining the pecunary resources of this young Society than that now partially adopted by them. A musical association should make its appeal by subscription to those who are able to pay, and not by exactions upon composers, who are not, ordinarily, blessed with an abundance of this world's goods. A composition that is fit to be performed ought not to be subjected to the ordeal of being pitted against its decided inferior simply because the latter has been whistled in to the tune of $5. The temptation to supply funds in this way is strong, but . . . the burden comes upon those who are least able to bear it (AA).

A year earlier Willis had given the NYA-MA public advice on the front page of his *New York Musical World*:

> We trust the American-Music Association will go on. But they should have a regular organization; regular practice; tickets for performing and non-performing members; in short, they should be constituted like the Philharmonic and like Eisfeld's Quartette. Above all, should they secure an attractive and suitable place for their performances (G). . . .

Also in Willis's journal, "G. H. C.," probably George Henry Curtis, a work of whose was performed by the NYA-MA on 12 November 1857, wrote that the Society was "impractical." He pointed out that

> at this last concert [that of 27 February 1857] we had music by native American composers, by foreigners naturalized and unnaturalized, and one piece [Liszt's *Les Preludes!*] by a European who has never visited these shores. Is it not time that the Name of

the Society, as well as one or two objectionable by-laws of the constitution be changed? (U, 148)

(The curious presence of *Les Preludes*, published 1856, on this program was no doubt through the influence of William Mason, Liszt's American student and friend, who had seen him as recently as 1854. The work was performed on two pianos by Mason and the young pianist Candido Berti, probably in its American premiere.)

One startling and no doubt weakening aspect of the Society's operation was that performers were not paid; the services of apparently all were voluntary. This may be the largest single cause of the group's demise after so short a life. The volunteerism is revealed early on, in the *New York Times* review of the first concert:

> At the next *soiree* of the Association we hope to hear better instrumental music and see the names of some distinguished volunteers. There are a few eminent American musicians in New York who should be associated with this movement (B).

Willis also mentions the volunteerism in the course of a brief notice of the group's approaching concert on 21 May 1857. After listing some of those scheduled to appear, he wrote:

> The *voluntary* cooperation of such performers as these proves the interest entertained by some of our best artists for the objects of this Association (CC).

Indeed, that young unknown Hopkins was able to secure *gratis* the appearances of older contemporary "stars" as Gottschalk, William Mason, Theodore Thomas, and many others is nothing short of miraculous (more of this later). To be sure, some of the performers were more famous later, but, at the very least, they were busy, well-known professional musicians.

Before the start of the second season, Hopkins was perhaps worried about getting performers to donate their time and talent, especially the "eminent American musicians" alluded to by the *New York Times*. Perhaps he had had trouble getting performers during the first season. Whatever the reason, he felt it necessary to have several key performers sign a simple handwritten document promising to volunteer. To our great good fortune, that document survived and is in the Music Division of The New York Public Library for the Performing Arts (classmark: *MNY-Amer.). It is a crudely cropped light-blue lined note page approximately 7 1/4 inches wide by 6 1/2 inches long, pasted at the top to a white cardboard embossed with the initials "J. H." and reads:

Dec. 30, 1856

We the undersigned do hereby promise and consent to take part as artists in the concerts of American music to be given in this City of New York during the Winter Season of 1856-57 under the name of "the concerts of the New York American-Music Association," or "Society for the encouragement of Native Art."

[signed]

L. M. Gottschalk
Candido Berti
Emma G. Bostwick
Geo. F. Bristow
T. J. Cook
Wm. Mason

Since the document is pasted to the board only at the top, it swings free to reveal signatures, presumably of chorus members, on the verso. The signatures of Gottschalk, Bristow, and Cook are, as an autograph dealer might say, "bold;" those of Berti and Mason less so; that of Mrs. Bostwick is small and "feminine." This document is valuable both commercially and historically.[7] It is only one of two known handwritten documents relating to the NYA-MA. The other item is a letter from the important, shadowy Philadelphia composer Charles Hommann to Jerome Hopkins. (For more on this letter, see below in the section "The Three Concert Seasons.")

TRINITY CHURCH AND THE NYA-MA

From the spring of 1856 to the spring of 1858, Jerome Hopkins must have been perpetually nagged by the need to secure free performers for his struggling Association. Securing musical scores was apparently no problem. Willis announced in his journal early on his willingness to accept scores and cash at the journal's address. After reviewing the first concert he wrote:

> The *Musical World* would announce to all American composers . . . wishing to take part . . . that on the remittance of $5 any person will become a member of the association and will have the liberty of sending compositions for examination to be subsequently performed if deemed worthy. Remittances of music or the fee of membership may be made to the *N. Y. Musical World* office (D).

The following events may not be connected at all. Perhaps I have assumed relationships that did not exist. The key factor that leads me to believe they are not merely circumstantial is that Jerome Hopkins' father, Bishop John Henry Hopkins, Sr., was visiting New York and attending Trinity Church from March until some time in May 1856.[8] Maybe it was his desire to help his young son that resulted in musicians at Trinity becoming importantly involved with the NYA-MA in its second concert season (1856-57) and its third (1857-58).

The opening work of the second concert of the second season was a composition apparently billed as *Consecration Anthem* by Trinity's august English-born organist-music director Dr. Edward Hodges, who usually was never associated with secular concerts. Not only were three members of the solo quartet (required for the anthem) from Trinity Church choir, but Dr. Hodges himself was there to conduct and to accompany on the piano (there being no organ). The work was either from Hodges' *Consecration Service*, composed in 1846, published by subscription in 1865, or more likely *I Was Glad* (Psalms 91 and 22), a twenty-minute piece he composed for the consecration of Trinity Chapel in 1855.

Altogether, eight—maybe nine—Trinity singers participated in NYA-MA concerts until its last one on 30 April 1858. Compositions by two Hodges pupils were also heard, those by the organists William Henry Walter and Samuel Parkman Tuckerman. It was Walter who got Hodges' *Consecration Service* copyrighted and published, and Tuckerman who was named to succeed Hodges at Trinity.

The strains of family and Episcopal Church are combined in the person of Jerome Hopkins' brother, Rev. John Henry Hopkins, Jr., then living in New York City, one of whose Christmas hymns was performed at the first concert of the second season. It was not his hit *We Three Kings of Orient*, but *The Shepherds of Bethlehem*, the composer credited in the printed program only as "Jr." Willis, who happened to have the music, knew the composer's identity and revealed it in his review.

Hodges also reaped benefits from the Episcopal arrival among NYA-MA ranks. One of the Association's leading singers, the bass Dr. Charles A. Guilmette, became an occasional soloist at Trinity, and Hodges became a contributing editor to Willis's journal in 1857. (Emma G. Bostwick, a NYA-MA soprano soloist, and her husband had been volunteers in the Trinity Church choir for some years.)

SELECTED MUSIC CRITICS AND THE NYA-MA

I have examined five period sources for advertisements, notices, and reviews of the NYA-MA: the newspapers *New York Daily Tribune*

(William Henry Fry, music critic) and *New York Daily Times* (widely available on microfilm in the twentieth century); and the periodicals *Dwight's Journal of Music*, the *New York Musical World and Times* (Richard Storrs Willis, editor; usually referred to as the *Musical World*), and *New York Musical Review and Gazette* (William Mason's two brothers, editors; usually referred to as the *Gazette*).

With the exception of the one important article quoted above, *Dwight's Journal of Music* was least helpful of the periodicals since reviews of NYA-MA concerts were frequently reprints of those in the *Musical World*; *Dwight's* also quoted the *Tribune*. With a few exceptions, the Mason brothers' *Gazette* generally ran comparatively short reviews of NYA-MA concerts, reviews that seemed mostly to botch personal names and fret about the group's structure (was this a reflection of William Mason's attitude?).

The *Musical World* was the best all-round source. Its reviews tended to be fairly detailed as to who and what was performed. But all of them were important in their day: in the aggregate, the leading source of American musical opinion of the time. They would have been a significant force in influencing public thinking about music. For a twentieth-century commentator on the subject—and what must have been ambrosia for the Association at the time—it is of no small interest to find that in the mid-1850s they all were generally supportive of the new American-music organization. (One might wonder if the leading print sources at the threshold of the twenty-first century would even notice a new, probably amateurish group dedicated to the performance of contemporary American music?) The *Times* before the first concert:

> We suggest that an investment of fifty cents [the cost of admission] may be profitably made in what we believe to be a deserving undertaking. . . . We do not know whether American music is better or worse than what we have been hearing. It is but right, therefore, that all of us should judge for ourselves. . . . When we are riding the stormy billows of the Atlantic, we should not forget that the oak-ribbed vessel which gives us security owes its being to a few unconsidered acorns dropped in a kindly soil. Let us hope that in some future day when the American Music Association shall have become flourishing and strong, we shall not have to upbraid ourselves with the early neglect of the little germ planted in hope and good faith tonight (A).

From the *Times'* revealing review of the first concert:

> The evil that we see in the present state of music in New York is that Americans do not work together.... Every man goes on his own hook. There is no cooperation. The consequence is that the Germans who do cooperate with each other have command of all the avenues that lead to the public. An American finds it difficult to obtain a hearing for his works. He must spend a lifetime in negotiating with committees. He must submit to the ill will of executants. He must have the maw of an ostrich to digest all the harsh and stupid things that will be said of him. But when he has reached the public he will find no lack of sympathy. We are anxious to see the American Music Association prosper, in order that fresh facilities may be extended to young composers.... It will not injure foreign music but will do good to that of native origin (B).

From the *Tribune*'s review of the first concert: "This pleasant soiree, the first of a series, has no doubt won for them the favorable opinions which their excellent experiment deserves" (C). And two months later in the *Tribune*:

> Due concientious attention on the part of the public and it will be discovered that as good compositions can be rendered here as in Europe. It is a settled fact already that we have some as good American performers as are in Europe (E).

Willis' journal (in a review probably not written by Willis) at the start of the second season:

> Every school must have a beginning, and we heard fully enough to convince us that the American school of composition has taken vast strides since the days when Billings was looked upon as the grand musical authority of New England (O).

The New York City correspondent of *Dwight's Journal of Music* before the second concert of the second season: "It is, in my opinion, the most deserving of success of any of our musical associations" (Z). The *Gazette* at the start of the third season: "There is one thing certain about the Association: it strives hard to advance the cause it advocates, and each of its members seems to be anxious to do something for the good of music" (JJ). Willis at the beginning of the third season:

> We trust that this young society, which shows signs of decided vigor, will prove itself a permanent institution of this city. The

President, Mr. Hopkins, has energy enough for several such musical enterprises, and if in perseverance and musical assiduity lie a promise of success, the association will succeed (KK).

The *Gazette* after the second concert of the third season: "They offer to American composers the only chance to make such of their works known as have not as yet attained a high degree of excellence and finish" (VV).

One critical complaint, however, concerned the very name of the organization. "G. H. C." (George Henry Curtis, as suggested earlier) wrote in the *Musical World*:

> The name given to the Association covers an area geographically bounded by four oceans. The cabalistic seal of the Society [it can be seen on the surviving printed program] would lead one to suppose that that portion of the Western hemisphere denominated by North America is the one which freedom's eagle delights to watch over. . . . But then Canada and Mexico would naturally come in for a share of musical glory. . . . We incline to the belief that the word American has been adopted not so much to express a grand national sentiment, as to carry out . . . certain political and religious abstractions. The prefix *New York*, is very garish and wants originality. . . . A better name for this can easily be supplied (U, 148).

This was probably the first complaint about the use of a form of the word "America" instead of "United States," as in *The New Grove Dictionary of American Music* and the title of this article.

Occasionally the critics encouraged support in terms of duty and patriotism (purposely?). The *Tribune* in the first season: "We commend it emphatically to all who feel an interest in national art" (E). The *Tribune* in the third season: "We repeat our earnest commendation of this young patriotic art association" (MM). They could be condescending, especially Willis. Here he is on 10 January 1857: "The concert itself proved a very creditable affair, all things considered. We do not yet expect 'American Music' to rival the productions of the great masters of Europe" (O). And on 8 May 1858:

> We requested a friend to listen for us at the last concert, and report upon the music. But we are rather disconcerted with the result of this arrangement—our friend speaking his mind rather freely as to the music performed, and not in as complimentary terms as would best have met our hopes (WW).

However, Willis did proceed then to print the "result" of his "arrangement," which seems a mild enough assessment, though it does contain a sentiment that was perhaps not unique among supporters of the organization:

> While we wish to see the native music of America advanced in this community, we think that the director might find better compositions to bring before the public . . . while we have such *good* native composers among us as G. F. Bristow, Wm. H. Fry, and others (WW). . . .

Willis answered this immediately: "To this we must say that the Association would doubtless have been happy to perform any thing of Fry's or Bristow's if they had been supplied by these gentlemen with any thing to perform" (WW). (The magic of a celebrated name, even in the New York concert world of the mid-1850s! Always the hunt for masterpieces!)

A complaint somewhat similar to that of Willis's "friend" had appeared in the Mason brothers' *Gazette* the previous season: "If the results can not often satisfy a really artistic taste and experience, we must consider that not every competent native composer is an active member of the Society" (JJ).

The critics also offered advice, especially the *Gazette*. Here it was during the second season:

> We do not understand too strict observance of the rule that the programme[s] shall be entirely an exhibition of native and resident art and execution. . . . If the programmes of this young Association have only three numbers by natives done in an artistically satisfactory manner, while the rest of the music is the best of old and modern masters performed by able foreigners . . . we think the object of encouragement will be better attained than in the other way (EE).

During the last season, when the NYA-MA was struggling just to keep afloat, it changed its policy about performing only compositions created in the United States, saying this would contribute to the performance proficiency of Americans and, oh yes, "add interest to the concerts" (QQ). The *Gazette* responded: "The Directors have at last taken a step in the right direction, from which their Association will, after a while, derive the full benefits. If they will only adhere to this new arrangement we will get good sound music (QQ). . . ." And later in the same review after mentioning that this concert was apparently the Association's last, noted in an "I-told-you-so" manner: "Had they adopted the policy which we always advocated . . . they would have not been compelled to close for want of patronage" (QQ).

Questionable is the critical participation of William Henry Fry throughout the NYA-MA's brief existence. Inexplicable for this so-called champion of American music, Fry and the *Tribune* were not a major source of reviews. The paper was kind to the organization but generally detached. It might be imagined that Fry's reticence stemmed from his participation in the Society as a composer (works by him were performed on 30 May 1856 and on 27 February 1857). Yet, the same situation did not prevent Willis from publicizing the Society in many issues of his journal throughout the group's existence. (Two songs by Willis were performed 3 April 1856.)

The only time Fry devoted an extensive review in the *Tribune* to the NYA-MA was after its concert of 11 February 1858, rumored to be its last.[9] And that review was devoted mainly to a discussion of the performance of the English violinist Henry C. Cooper and of the English-American pianist Richard Hoffman. Unbelievable as it might seem later, Fry began the review by cruelly parodying a passage in the *Times*' supportive editorial that appeared on the day of the NYA-MA's first concert: "Tall streams from tiny acorns grow, large oaks from little fountains flow—someone has said" (OO).

Fry used much space in that review to deny the NYA-MA's allegation that American music was unappreciated by audiences. He countered with an allegation of his own, one that has become an "old chestnut," namely that Americans might not know a lot about art, but they knew what they liked. He stated that American compositions sometimes won their hearer's hearts when those by European masters did not. He argued, with justification, that American compositions simply were not performed often enough. "Let a new man, like a Verdi, for example, write as they like," Fry wrote, "and the audience care[s] nothing for the reputation. . . . Why not make this American Music Association the base for such a spirit and action?" (OO). This last remark was good for the Association, to be sure, but apparently it came too late to have much of an impact. The next concert, an occurrence that was a surprise to many, proved to be the NYA-MA's last.

THE THREE CONCERT SEASONS

In the issue of 16 February 1858 the *Daily Times* lamented the supposed passing of the NYA-MA (it presented one more concert):

> It is to be deplored [it stated] that a society which was beginning to do so much good for native music should die because the very musicians whose good it contemplated thought themselves too important to lend a helping hand to the sinking little craft (LL).

So much good for native music that it had been hailed earlier by *Dwight's Journal of Music* as the possible nucleus of an "American Conservatory of Music, that will in a few years be an honor to the country" (Y).

The beginnings were quiet. We know for certain only the date and place of the first concert: 16 February 1856 at the rooms of the Mendelssohn Society, Clinton Hall, and that of the nine compositions performed, two were the first movement (or first two movements) of Jerome Hopkins' symphony "Life," and two others were an *adagio* and a *scherzo* from Sonata for Violin and Piano by Charles Hommann. For anyone paying attention, Hopkins established here the self-serving nature of the enterprise with the presence of a truly altruistic strain. Hommann was unknown to New York concert audiences: Hopkins' championship of his music in the concerts of the NYA-MA is dramatic evidence of his belief in Hommann's music. (Hopkins' performance of his own compositions, a greater number of times than he performed Hommann's (5), is dramatic evidence of his personal sense of self-worth.)[10]

At least three of Hommann's works had been published by 1856 in Philadelphia—a *Te Deum*, a song, and a piano piece—but others are extant without publication dates and may have appeared before 1856. None of the larger instrumental works presented by Hopkins was ever published.

Hommann's E-flat symphony, also never published, "composed in the early 1830s or early 1840s" and "dedicated to the Philharmonic society of Bethlehem, Penn." may be "the earliest symphony by a native composer,"[11] a copy of which is in the Fleisher Collection, Free Library of Philadelphia. Aside from the violin sonata excerpts in the first concert and a movement from it on the 30 May 1856 concert, his String Quartet in D minor was played at the Hopkins concerts, along with his String Quintet, movements either divided between the concerts of 16 February 1856 and 3 April 1856 or played entire at the first and repeated at the second, and a *scherzo* and *finale* from his violin sonata at the last concert on 30 April 1858 (was the *scherzo* a repeat from the concert of 16 February 1856?).

A letter (mentioned earlier) from Hommann to Hopkins exists in The New York Public Library for the Performing Arts, Music Division (classmark: *MNY-Amer.). It is dated "Philadelphia, April 8th, 1856," and is unremarkable except that it proves contact between the two men and tells us the source of the performance materials used by the NYA-MA (Hommann). It also proves that the two men were not on intimate terms. Hommann begins, "My dear sir," and concludes, "Respectfully yours."

What *is* remarkable about the communication is that Hommann, out of gratitude, one suspects, appends to the letter an unpublished manuscript composition for piano which he refers to as a *Notturno*, "a trifle," he writes, "which you are at liberty to do with what you like." Hopkins had apparently written to Hommann immediately after the second (3 April 1856) concert. "I congratulate you," Hommann's letter continues, "on getting through with the 2 Soiree, which I hope was successful."

"Not widely advertised," as the *Tribune* labelled this first concert (C), it apparently caught some critics off guard, even those probably not drawn to one of the concert's rival attractions, the appearance of Kit Carson, "the backwoodsman."[12] Willis wrote in the *Musical World*: "We regretted exceedingly that we were not present—the sudden arrival of friends at the moment having made me oblivious of all else" (D).

The second concert (3 April 1856) also was not advertised in either the *Times* or *Tribune*, but Hopkins gave a New York concert audience another dose of music by Hommann, this time all or part of his Quintet for Strings. The critics did not share what apparently was a personal conviction of Hopkins; nevertheless, he programmed Hommann's music three more times before the Association's end. The *Times*' review was rather noncommittal on the piece: "It is a work correctly and classically written, and was performed in a highly creditable manner, having had but four rehearsals" (F). Willis's comments about the work were a little fuller but hardly enthusiastic:

> Mr. Hommann's Quintette was conceeded [sic] by those who can well judge of this style of composition to be exceedingly creditable to him. The instruments are well employed, none lying idle and listless during the momentary prominence of others.... There was altogether considerable *swing* to the composition, showing that Mr. Hommann has got beyond the first hesitating A, B, C of the art (G).

This second concert was the only one at which Gottschalk personally appeared. Willis deplored the acoustics of the concert's location, Stuyvesant Hall, but noted:

> Mr. Gottschalk at this moment appeared [near the end of the concert?] and accompanied Mrs. Brinkerhoff in an original song of his entitled *Alone* [Philadelphia: Hatch, 1902], a piece we would rather call a duet between piano and voice, inasmuch as both talk so very expressively to each other (G).

The *Times*' review tells us what happened at the end of the concert:

> At the close of the performances Mr. Gottschalk appeared in response to reiterated calls to end the evening pleasantly with one of his bewitching melodies "The Last Hope" [New York: William Hall & Son, 1856] (F).

Having a star introduce a new song and play one of his popular piano pieces must have delighted Hopkins. This was just what his new organization needed. As the last printed item on the program, Hopkins had shrewdly placed a piece by the then-publicized William Mason, a vocal quartet titled *Gondolier's Serenade* (*The Social Glee Book*, Boston: Wilkins, Carter, and Co., 1847), but *The Last Hope* was perhaps more than he had dared wish for. (Incidently, Willis called the Mason piece "rich" and mentioned that it was encored (G).)

Of the three Gottschalk piano pieces scheduled on the NYA-MA concerts, all performed by Candido Berti, two titles are not familiar: *Galop di Bravura* (played 30 April 1856) and *Valse di Bravura* (17 April 1857). Doyle speculates that the first is *Tournament Galop* (New York: Horace Waters, 1854), Gottschalk's uncredited "free transcription"[13] of *Mazeppa*, op. 21, by Alfred Quidant (1815-1893), and that the second may be the piano duet *Radieuse, Grand Valse de Concert*, published under the pseudonym "Seven Octaves" (Boston: Ditson, 1865). If Doyle is correct about the latter item, it was, of course, played by Berti in a solo version. Ditson published another solo version posthumously in 1878.

Another composer on that concert was the just-then busy pianist T. Franklin Bassford. The *Times* and *Tribune* both had advertised that day Bassford's "First Piano-forte soiree," one of four, for the next evening, 4 April 1856.[14] Bassford was surely better known as a pianist than as a composer,[15] although at his piano concert the advertisement promised that Candido Berti would join him at a second piano to play the *Triumphal Fantasy* by Bassford, and that the English baritone Allen Irving would sing "Thou gazest deep and earnest" from Bassford's unpublished opera *Phantom Ship*.

The opening work of the third concert (30 May 1856) of NYA-MA's first season was again by Hommann, a continuation or repeat of his Quintet for Strings. Willis thought it "well written and evincing talent," adding that its performance was "measureably perfect" (K). The *Tribune* directly contradicted this last part, saying that while the NYA-MA required "a good deal of kindness, generosity, magnanimity, and tenderness on the part of the public," in general, this quintet was "not adequately rehearsed . . . so much so that no adequate opinion of it could be formed" (J).

Later in the concert, Hopkins continued his promotion of Hommann by performing with violinist Julius E. Meyer the *andante* movement of Hommann's D-flat violin sonata, a continuation from the 16 February concert. The sonata presumably would be completed on the last concert (30 April 1858). The movement received no critical attention in the sources consulted, although Willis thought that even alone it was "sufficiently long" (K).

Other than an excerpt for baritone sung by C. W. Wooster from Bristow's opera *Rip Van Winkle* (1855), barely a year old,[16] and a vocal quartet by Fry,[17] this concert was notable for its introduction to a New York audience of the estimable Baltimore composer James Monroe Deems. His virtuoso song "Switzerland! My Switzerland" (Baltimore: Miller & Beecham, 1855) was sung by the Bassini pupil Miss K. V. Comstock. Introduction and finale, that is, for music by this relatively important American composer was featured in no other New York concert known to me outside the NYA-MA series. He would have three other works performed by the Hopkins group.

The "star turns" on this concert were provided by cornet virtuoso Allen Dodworth and by William Mason, playing his already-popular piano solo *Silver Spring* (1856), whose encore was "inevitable," wrote Willis (K).

The second season of the NYA-MA was perhaps its most satisfying artistically and commercially. Reviews were more plentiful, houses were good (to judge from the critics), and four concerts were given instead of the first and third seasons' three. The arrival of Dr. Hodges and the other musicians from Trinity Church must have considerably boosted the company's morale, especially that of Jerome Hopkins.

The arrival of another musician among the NYA-MA's ranks at this time was also notable: this was the British-born (?) singer Dr. Charles A. Guilmette, who was probably recruited by Bristow from the Pyne-Harrison opera company. Bristow was conductor of the company's opera in English during the summer of 1855 at Niblo's Garden. It was on 27 September 1855 that Bristow's *Rip Van Winkle* received its premiere by the Pyne-Harrison troupe. Guilmette was not in the original cast but left the company around this time and settled in New York City, a fact noted by the *Tribune* in the issue of 3 March 1857 (R).

Guilmette joined the Hopkins group ostensibly as conductor of the chorus.[18] At the first concert of the second season, however, he sang songs by Bristow and Jerome Hopkins; later, among other things, he would perform an excerpt from *Rip Van Winkle* and participate in Hodges' *Consecration Anthem*.

From advertisements for this concert, we learn that the Bohemian-American composer-pianist J. N. Pychowski was scheduled to take part. If he did, it was not mentioned by the critics—an unlikely happening. We do know that he was represented as composer on the second and third concerts of that season with, respectively, the *Duetto Dramatico*, for clarinet and piano, and an *Allegro de Concert*, for piano. On the first concert of the third season, Pychowski played all or part of his own Violin Sonata with violinist Theodore Thomas.

The last concert of the season featured ten works, ending with an excerpt from Deems's opera *Esther*, sung by Dr. Guilmette and Miss Simons.[19]

The third season began with three excerpts from the Deems oratorio *Nebuchadnezzar*. The organization's probable demise was "mentioned at the second concert of the season" (VV), though this was not stated by Fry in his long review (OO) as it was by the *Times* (NN).[20] For this concert Hopkins not only managed to secure *gratis* the services of the violinist Henry C. Cooper, "the head of the English school" (OO), as Fry called him, but he also performed a "Drinking Chorus with two soprani obligati" by the prominent Dr. Thomas Ward, a wealthy physician who dabbled in poetry and music. Maybe the chorus was from Ward's operetta *Flora, or The Gypsy's Frolic*, "libretto and music both his own" (RR), the libretto published apparently at Ward's own expense in 1858 and at least four full musical excerpts published as sheet music in 1858-59. The operetta received its premiere the previous 30 July at Ward's country estate "Land's End," in Huntington, Long Island, "Mr. Timm presiding at the piano" (RR). (Was the programming of Dr. Ward's work mainly a ploy by Hopkins for financial help?)

"We think it extremely creditable," Willis gushed, "that a gentleman of means and leisure like Dr. Ward should persue so beautiful an Art to such issues — where the tendency of fast New York is so decidedly different in the employment of money and leisure" (RR). He added that "the chorus was so inadequately rendered from lack of drilling that one really could form but little idea of its real merits" (RR). Fry also found Dr. Ward's piece "badly executed and of which we could not form an opinion" (OO).

At the end of its review of this concert, the *Gazette* stated: "Since writing the above, we regret to learn that the Directors have concluded to disband the Society, and that this was their final concert" (QQ). *Dwight's Journal of Music* stated: "The American Music Association, established some three years ago in New York, for the encouragement of American composers, has disbanded" (PP). With a sureness that was proved wrong, the *Times* wrote: "We are assured that [the Society] is permanently and emphatically dead" (NN). It elaborated:

> At a time when music appears to be really popular and remunerative, it is a little hard that our only native society languishes and dies in cold neglect. Yet this is actually the case. After struggling for three years under all sorts of oppressive difficulties, the New-York American Music Association gave its final soiree on Thursday of last week; decently yielding up the ghost amid the religious odors of Hope Chapel (NN).

The announcement occasioned some eloquent and philosophical remarks from the *Times*. It continued:

> The American musician unfortunately is wholly indifferent to nationality in art. As a general thing he is nothing but a superfluous appendage to the skirts of Germany; he sings German songs, plays German music, and drinks German lager beer. . . . He distrusts himself. . . . It is very foolish for a man to think that he can do everything better than another, but it is deplorable to find a man who thinks that others can do everything better than he (NN).

Somehow, Hopkins rallied his forces for one more concert on 30 April 1858. "Up starts the American Music eagle and spreads its wings again," wrote Willis after this concert (WW). The program, not reviewed by the *Tribune*, seemed sprightly enough, reflecting the organization's new policy of performing foreign compositions, as well as those created in the United States. Hattie Andem, a promising newcomer, sang a Donizetti aria, and a song and vocal quartet by Mendelssohn were performed. The popular harpist Aptommas played a solo, and the popular tenor George Simpson sang a recitative and aria from "the American opera" (VV) *The Peri, or The Enchanted Fountain* by James G. Maeder.[21]

The well-known, eccentric pianist-composer Gustave Satter was scheduled to appear at what was the actual last concert, but "at the moment a letter was received announcing that he was unable to fulfill his engagement; a few hisses were scored up to the account of the eminent pianist" (UU).

What killed the NYA-MA? Was it the *Gazette*'s reason: "lack of patronage" (QQ)? Was it the *Times*' reason: "the very musicians whose good it contemplated thought themselves too important" to perform free regularly (LL)? Probably something of both. Especially the latter. The largest part of the blame, however, must be laid at the feet of the group's young, inexperienced, visionary founder. Hopkins apparently could not effectively organize and operate such a complex and difficult undertaking.

The *Times* could write after the 11 February 1858 concert: "There are few men in the City who will sacrifice so much of their time, or earnestly contend with the weak foibles of artists as did Mr. Hopkins" (NN). Perhaps. But enthusiasm, dedication, and tact were not enough. Hopkins' unwise policies resulted in repeated performer cancellations and lack of rehearsal time.

Building a concert series on the performance of works by unknown composers—as important as it is to expose the works—may be the kiss of death. A twentieth-century organization, Composers' Forum of New York, which gave its first concert as part of the Works Progress Administration in 1935, learned the truth of this. The group performed works by young and unknown composers. After decades of dwindling audiences and critical coverage, the group changed its policy to one of fewer concerts with the works of well-known American composers mixed with those of unknowns.

Precisely when the NYA-MA came to an end we do not know, except in the issue of 6 November 1858 of the *Musical World* (without Hodges listed on the magazine's masthead, incidentally—he left Trinity that year), Willis would refer to Hopkins as "the ex-President of the New York American Music Association."[22]

THE TEN CONCERTS

The list of works for each concert is not necessarily in the order in which they were performed—in most cases unknowable. Only works known to have been actually performed are listed. A piano piece, for example, by Gustave Satter was scheduled to be heard on the concert of 30 April 1858; his appearance was announced in two advertisements. (Odell in his history of the New York stage recorded that Satter took part.) He did not, and no Satter work was performed. The forms of personal names, the credits, and the titles of compositions are given as they appeared in the period sources searched.

FIRST SEASON

First Concert
—16 February 1856—

Advertisement: None
Notice: A
Reviews: B, C, D
Place: Rooms of the Mendelssohn Union, Clinton Hall (Astor Place)
Program: "Nine pieces" (B), among them:
    Symphony ("Life"): ....C. Jerome Hopkins
      andante
    Sonata for Violin and Piano: ....Charles Hommann
      adagio
      scherzo

Second Concert
—3 April 1856—

Advertisement: None
Notice: E
Reviews: F, G
Place: Stuyvesant Hall
Program:
    Quintet for Strings ....Charles Hommann
    Two songs: ....Richard Storrs Willis
        "Sleep the kind angel"
        "Spring song"
            Annie Kemp, singer
            William Dressler, piano
    Piano solo: *Galop di Bravura*..........................Louis Moreau Gottschalk
        Candido Berti, piano
    Symphony ("Life"): ....C. Jerome Hopkins
        Third movement
    Song: (title?) ....T. Franklin Bassford
        Mrs. Clara M. Brinkerhoff, singer
    Piano solo: *Ballade*..T. Franklin Bassford
        (Bassford, piano?)
    Song: "Alone" ....Louis Moreau Gottschalk
        Mrs. Clara M. Brinkerhoff, singer
        Louis Moreau Gottschalk, piano
    Vocal quartet: *Gondolier's Serenade* ....William Mason
    (Encore: *The Last Hope*, composed and performed by Louis Moreau
      Gottschalk)

Third Concert
—30 May 1856—

Advertisement: H
Notice: I
Reviews: J, K
Place: Dodworth's Academy (806 Broadway)
Program:
    Quintet for Strings ....Charles Hommann
    Aria: "Alone" from *Rip Van Winkle* ....George F. Bristow
        Mr. C. W. Wooster, baritone
    Song: (composer and title?)
        Mrs. Jameson, singer
    Song: "Switzerland! My Switzerland" ....James Monroe Deems

    Miss K. V. Comstock, singer
Cornet solo: (title?) ....Allen Dodworth (?)
    Allen Dodworth, cornet
Song: (title?) ....C. Jerome Hopkins
    Annie Kemp, contralto
Vocal quartet: *Marco Bozarris* ....William Henry Fry
Piano solo: *Silver Spring* ....William Mason
    (William Mason, piano?)
Soprano solo, chorus, vocal fugue: (title?) ....C. Jerome Hopkins
Sonata in D-flat for Violin and Piano: ....Charles Hommann
    andante
    Julius Meyer, violin
    C. Jerome Hopkins, piano
("Mr. Morgan conducted at the piano ") (K)

SECOND SEASON

First Concert
—30 December 1856—

Advertisements: L, M
Notice: None
Reviews: N, O
Place: Dodworth's Academy
Program:
    Song: (title?) ....George F. Bristow
        Dr. Charles Guilmette, bass
    Anthem: (title?) ....William H. Walter
        Chorus
    Song: "A Death-Bed Rhapsody" ....C. Jerome Hopkins
        Dr. Charles Guilmette, bass
    Choral work: *Christmas Carol* ("The Shepherds of Bethlehem") ....
                                                         John Henry Hopkins, Jr.
    Chorus

Second Concert
—27 February 1857—

Advertisement: P
Notice: Q
Reviews: R, S, T, U
Place: Dodworth's Academy

Program:
   Consecration Anthem ....Edward Hodges
     Solo quartet:
        Mrs. Emma G. Bostwick, soprano
        Miss Robjohn, alto
        James A. Johnson, tenor
        Dr. Charles Guilmette, bass
     Chorus
     Edward Hodges, piano
   Two piano solos: ....William Mason
    Amitié pour amitié
    Etude de Concert
     William Mason, piano
   Song: "Has Summer Pass'd Away?" ....C. Jerome Hopkins
     Mrs. Bostwick, soprano
     Henry C. Timm, piano
   Aria from *Rip Van Winkle*: (title?) ....George F. Bristow
     Dr. Charles Guilmette, bass
   Duetto Dramatico, for clarinet and piano ....J. N. Pychowski
     Kiefer or Stark, clarinet
     Candido Berti, piano
   Song: "Still, Still the Same" ....T. J. Cook
     Miss C. M. Sheppard, soprano
   Poesie Symphonique, *Les Preludes* ....Franz Liszt
     William Mason, piano
     Candido Berti, piano
   Soprano solo with chorus: *Hymn to the Virgin* .....James Monroe Deems
     Miss C. M. Sheppard, soprano
     Chorus
   Stabat Mater: "Fac ut ardeat" ....William Henry Fry
     Dr. Charles Guilmette, bass
     Chorus
   Serenade ....(Anonymous)
        Words by Mrs. Childs (Lydia Maria Child?)

Third Concert
—17 April 1857—

Advertisements: V, W
Notice: X (Notes: Y, Z)
Reviews: AA, BB
Place: Dodworth's Academy
Program:

Quartet in d minor ....Charles Hommann
    Mr. Reiff
    Mr. Grosse
    Mr. Wedermeyer
    "Assisted by an amateur" (AA)
Piano solo: *Allegro de Concert* ....J. N. Pychowski
    Candido Berti, piano
Anthem: (title?) ....William H. Walter
Piano solo: *Fantasie* ....Richard Hoffman
    Richard Hoffman, piano
Song: (title?) ....William Mason
    Miss C. M. Sheppard, soprano
Vocal quartet: (title?) ....William Mason
    Mrs. Thomas, soprano
    Miss Robjohn, alto
    Mr. Loomis, tenor
    Mr. Tucker, bass
Piano solo[s?]:
    Valse di Bravura ....Louis Moreau Gottschalk
    [*Serenade* ....Gottschalk or Hoffman?]
    (?, piano)

Fourth Concert
—21 May 1857—

Advertisement: None
Notice: *Musical World* 17:321 (Saturday, 23 May 1857), 323
Reviews: DD, EE, FF
Place: Dodworth's Saloon
Program: "Ten musical productions" (see *Musical World* above)

Part 1

Mass in D Major: *Kyrie Eleison* ....R. F. Halsted
    Miss [or Mrs.] Crump
    James A. Johnson
    Chorus
Piano solo: *Souvenirs d'Andalousie* ....Louis Moreau Gottschalk
    Candido Berti, piano
Song: "Ave Maria" ....William A. King
    Miss Henrietta Simon
Grand Scena and Aria ....Anthony Reiff, Jr.
    Dr. Charles Guilmette, bass
Song: "Come Love With Me" ....James A. Johnson

James A. Johnson, singer
Hymn 186 (Book of Common Prayer), soprano solo and chorus ....
                  C. Jerome Hopkins
  [apparently credited on the printed program as by "Jerome"]
  Miss Henrietta Simon, soprano
  Chorus

Part 2

Hymn to the Virgin ....James Monroe Deems
  Miss [or Mrs.] Crump
  James A. Johnson
  Chorus
Fantasie sur "Lucrezia" and "Lucia" ....Seide [or Siede]
  Mr. F. J. Eben, flutist
Song: ("Song" may have been the title) ....William H. Walter
  James A. Johnson
Duet from the opera *Esther* ....James Monroe Deems
  Miss Henrietta Simon
  Dr. Charles Guilmette
("Conductor at the piano, Mr. William A. King") (FF)
("Conductor of chorus, Dr. Charles Guilmette") (FF)

THIRD SEASON

First Concert
—12 November 1857—

Advertisements: GG, HH
Notice: II
Reviews: JJ, KK
Place: Dodworth's Saloon
Program: "Nine pieces" (JJ)
 Nebuchadnezzar (oratorio): 3 selections ....James Monroe Deems
  1. Duet for bass and contralto
  2. Chorus
  3. Soprano solo with chorus
    The Misses Gellie
    Mr. Stephen W. Leach
    Chorus
 Sonata for Violin and Piano ....J. N. Pychowski
  J.N. Pychowski, piano
  Theodore Thomas, violin

Vocal duet: "We Are Wandering O'er the Mountains" ....
William Vincent Wallace
    The Misses Gellie
Glee: (title?) ....(Anonymous)
(Vocal duet?): *Nocturne* ....Mr. Willet (?)
Song: (title?) ....Mr. D. D. Griswold (?)
Song: (title?) ....Mr. [or Mrs.] E. A. Payne (?)
Vocal quartet: (title?) ....George Henry Curtis

Second Concert
—11 February 1858—

Advertisement: LL
Notice: MM
Reviews: NN, OO, PP, QQ, RR
Place: Hope Chapel (720 Broadway)
Program:
    Anthem: *Hide Not Thy Face* ....Samuel Parkman Tuckerman
    1. Quartet
    2. Chorus (fugue)
        Miss Fanny Stockton
        Mrs. Westervelt
        Mr. Peck
        Dr. Charles Guilmette
        Chorus
    Song: "The Winds That Waft My Sighs to Thee" ....
William Vincent Wallace
        Mrs. Clara M. Brinkerhoff
    Violin solo: *Fantasie on "La Fille du Regiment"* ....Henry C. Cooper
        Henry C. Cooper, violin
    Two piano solos: ....Richard Hoffman
      Reverie (Twilight)
      Marche Funebre
        Richard Hoffman, piano
    Song: "Ave Maria" ....Carlo [or Charles] Bassini
        Miss Fanny Stockton, singer
    Violin solo: *Recollections of Scotland* ....Henry C. Cooper
        Henry C. Cooper, violin
    Grand Scena ed Aria: "Jerusalem, or St. Peter the Hermit" ....LaBarre
        Dr. Charles Guilmette, bass
    Drinking Chorus, with two soprani obligati ....Thomas Ward
        Mrs. Clara M. Brinkerhoff
        Miss Fanny Stockton

Chorus
("Mr. [William A.] King presided at the piano") (OO)

Third Concert
—30 April 1858—

Advertisements: SS, TT
Notice: None
Reviews: UU, VV, WW
Place: Dodworth's Saloon
Program:
    First Trio for Piano, Violin, and Violoncello ....George F. Benkert
        Candido Berti, piano
        Mr. Simon, violin
        Mr. Bergner, cello
    Maria di Rohan: Cavatina ....Donizetti
        Miss Hattie Andem
    Song: "The Three Ages of Love" ....Loder
        Mr. George Simpson
    Vocal quartet: *This is the Hour* ....S. O. Dyer
        Mr. Johnson's Quartet Party
    Song: "Sing to Me, Love, I'm Sad Tonight" ....William Mason
        Miss Hattie Andem
    Sonata for Violin and Piano: ....Charles Hommann
      scherzo
      finale
        Candido Berti, piano
        Mr. Simon, violin
    Song: "Oh! Who Can Guess My Emotion" ....Mendelssohn
        James A. Johnson
    The Peri: recitative and aria from the American opera .....James G. Maeder
        Mr. George Simpson
    Vocal quartet: *Slumber, Dearest* ....Mendelssohn
        Mr. Johnson's Quartet Party
    Harp solo: (title?) ....(Composer?)
        Aptommas, harp
("Mr. W. A. King at the piano, furnished by Messers. Steinway & Sons")
(VV)

THE SIXTY-NINE PARTICIPANTS

These are not complete biographies but largely the barest of sketches to show the subject's relation to the NYA-MA. Where I know of their existence, I have suggested sources of fuller information. Most abbreviations should be self-evident, such as an author's last name with a page reference (all such authors and specific books are in the Bibliography).

For citations to *The American Musical Directory, 1861* and the *National Cyclopedia of American Biography*, I have included page numbers because the order of categories and names in these two sources is not alphabetical.

The numbers in George C. D. Odell's *Annals of the New York Stage* refer to volumes 6-8 and frequency of listing in the indexes of those volumes. This should give the reader an indication of the approximate duration of a professional career in New York City. The information in Odell, however, should not be taken as definitive. It was apparently derived mainly from advertisements, which in the case of the NYA-MA, were haphazard and confusing, when not missing altogether. (There are three listings for the NYA-MA in volume 6, and one in volume 7.) One should be careful, too, to overlook Odell's highly personal point-of-view, out of place in a reference work. (Here he comments on the second concert of NYA-MA's first season: "I missed the first of these 'soirees,' if, indeed it was recoverable. It is annoying to burden a page with record of mediocrity" (Odell, 6:504).)

The following entries contain every critical mention of a person that could be found in the sources searched, though no excerpt was duplicated here if used in the body of the article.

The order of information in the sketches: name of the participant, frequently amplified, as it appeared in the sources searched; birth and death dates when known; capacity in which the subject participated in NYA-MA concerts; date(s) of NYA-MA concerts in which the subject participated; optional biographical and career notes; excerpts from critical comments; and references.

Adem, Miss Hattie. Singer, 30 April 1858. From a notice of a concert to take place that night: "Miss Adem is a young lady of our city and this, her first appeal to the musical public, deserves attention" (*New York Daily Tribune*, 16 February 1858, 6). She sang "Parto, parto, ma tu, ben mio" from Mozart's *La Clemenza di Tito* and an aria from William Vincent Wallace's *Maritana* at the opening concert (20 November 1858) of the New York Philharmonic's 1858-59 season (Krehbiel, 116).

> . . . a mezzo-soprano with a good voice but indifferent method (UU).

Odell, 6:2; 7:9; and 8:0

Appy, Henri. Violinist-composer. Was scheduled to appear 21 May 1857, but did not.

> Mr. Appy was so un-appy [*sic*] as to be detained in Philadelphia (FF).

Aptommas. (1829-1919). Harpist, 30 April 1858.

> Aptommas always repays one the trouble of going to see him (*New York Musical Record*, 10 January 1858).

> . . . a solo for the harp was nicely handled by Mr. Aptommas (WW).

Blom; Odell 6:12; 7:11; and 8:0.

Bassford, T. Franklin. Composer, 3 April 1856. Bassford is the American composer performed by the NYA-MA perhaps most cloaked in obscurity. As far as we know, he left only two published songs and two published piano pieces. Richard Storrs Willis did not publish his thumbnail sketches of current NYA-MA participants until 1857, the season after Bassford appeared. Biographical information on him is in no reference book, library file, or municipal source I have searched. However, if we assume he was a relative of the well-known Gottschalk pupil William K. Bassford (1838-1902)—pianist, organist, and composer—T. Franklin Bassford was probably related to Abraham Bassford, father of William K. and an early New York manufacturer of pianos and of the perhaps surprisingly related billiard tables, active until 1860 (Groce, 191). New York city directories are not much help in that they list T. Franklin Bassford only once: the issue for 1856/57. (This does not necessarily mean, of course, that he was a resident for only this period, for listing in the directories could be casual and dependent on several factors.) That listing indicates his profession simply as "music," and the address given is identical with Abraham's.

William K. Bassford's obituary in the *American Art Journal* (see Bibliography under Thoms) mentions that William K. was "surrounded by music from his youth" (Thoms, 226). One can well imagine that, for not only was his father a piano manufacturer, but there was composer-pianist T.

Franklin, and Abraham, Jr. and Julian, both active in their father's business. Another relative, Samuel W. Bassford, composer of a few published pieces, taught music and was an organist. The obituary also mentions that William K. inherited "considerable property" (Thoms, 226), that he "went through one or two fortunes," that he indolently visited "the trout streams, [sailed] his yacht, and [enjoyed] the finest brand of Havanas obtainable" (Thoms, 227).

> Messrs. Berti (encored), Bassford, and Hopkins were . . . received with favor, and the soiree altogether was a success—with the drawback of an extraordinary length of time between pieces (F). . . .

> Mr. Bassford's pretty song [title?] was neatly sung by Mrs. Brinkerhoff who . . . secured an encore. [His] "Ballade" was fairly composed and executed (G).

For T. Franklin Bassford, see Odell 6:7 and 7, 8:0. For William K. Bassford, see Odell 6, 7:0; 8:2.

Bassini, C. (1815-1870). Composer, 11 February 1858. Carlo (or Charles) Bassini, singing teacher in New York and, by 1861, Brooklyn, wrote the book *Bassini's Art of Singing* (Boston: Oliver Ditson, 1857), edited by Richard Storrs Willis. His song "Ave Maria," sung at the 11 February 1858 concert, was published in New York in 1858 by William Dressler, another performer in the NYA-MA concerts.

> [Bassini's "Ave Maria"] was well-written and original (OO).

> The song by Signor Bassini is cleverly composed and very appealing. The public know chiefly of the author as a popular and uncommonly successful teacher thus far. They would like him quite well in his capacity as composer, judging from what we know of his quality as a musician. We trust he may find time to let us hear oftener from him as a writer (RR).

The American Musical Directory, 1861, 176; Moore, 15.

Benkert, G. F. (1831-?). Composer, 30 April 1858. There are several references to George Frederick Benkert in the District of Columbia Historical Records Survey's *Bio-bibliographical Index*, the most informative from Upton's *Art-Song in America*:

> [He] spent five years in Germany, and a Mass of his is said to have been performed with great success under Helmsberger in Vienna, with orchestra and a chorus of a hundred voices. His chief importance in our eyes, perhaps, lies in the fact that he was the teacher of John Philip Sousa, who, according to Rupert Hughes, considers him the most complete musician our country has ever known. His first song (at the age of eighteen), "Look Not," is of no interest, while "Pretty Jenrry Wren" of the next year, 1850, although simple, shows more individuality. "Grüss Gott'" (1857) is a good, musicianly song containing some excellent part writing (Upton, 54).

His piano trio that was performed by the NYA-MA got unfavorable notices or was ignored altogether. At least he could take pride in the *Daily Times* advertisement that called its upcoming rendering "the first public performance in this city of an American Piano Trio" (SS).

One piano piece and seven songs by Benkert are in The New York Public Library for the Performing Arts. Several of these pieces have Philadelphia imprints.

> The programme chiefly consisted of a very poor trio for Piano, Violin, and Violoncello, by G. F. Benkert, which but for the masterly handling ... would hardly have been endurable (WW).

Bergner, Mr. (1827?-1900). Cellist, 30 April 1858. Frederick Bergner, who came to New York in 1849 from Baden, Germany, was a famous cellist who played in Theodore Eisfeld's Quartet series in the 1850s and, beginning in 1861 (Krehbiel, 74), was cellist in the William Mason-Theodore Thomas group that performed European chamber music. Bergner appeared with the orchestra of the New York Philharmonic Society about a dozen times as soloist, and was a member of its Board from 1864 until the end of his life. Mrs. Richard Hoffman remembered that he sometimes played trios with her husband (Hoffman, 23-24). Odell, 6:2; 7:22; 8:13.

Berti, Candido. Pianist, 3 April 1856; 27 February 1857; 17 April 1857; 21 May 1857; 30 April 1858 (Berti was also scheduled for the concert of 30 May 1856, but did not appear). Reviewing the concert of 21 May 1857, Richard Storrs Willis did future researchers a great favor by providing thumbnail biographical sketches that had been prepared by Jerome Hopkins of some of the group's composers and performers. I have included all of them in this biographical section where appropriate. Berti is identified by Willis as one of the promising <u>might-bes</u> of art, who is giving the enthusiasm to law-study which he formerly applied to music. Meantime, however, he avails himself, as any young enterprising man would, of the pecuniary advantage which his musical accomplishment affords him to help him on in the expense of student life; . . . we cordially recommend him to such private families and schools as would like to secure a high-bred, gentlemanly-mannered and very capable teacher (FF, 354-55).

Later in the same review, in a section written by Edward Hodges, the author stated that Berti "put forth such skill and taste upon the piano [in his performance of Gottschalk's *Souvenirs d'Andalousie*] in such a manner as to call down an encore" (FF, 355).

In the February 1885 *Musical Courier*, Jerome Hopkins listed Berti as having died a suicide (quoted in Slonimsky, 255).

We cannot close this brief notice without making "honorable mention" of Mr. Candido Berti's share in the concert. As a pianist he bids fair to take his stand in the very first rank, and his rising merit is none the less commendable for its combination with genuine modesty of deportment (O).

Odell, 6:3; 7:1; 8:1.

Bostwick, Mrs. Emma G[illingham]. Singer, 27 February 1857. Daughter of the English emigrant George Gillingham (1770-1822?), she was a soprano who "had captivated audiences in the 1820s" (Lawrence, 599). She was a volunteer in the Trinity Church choir in the 1850s before it became an all-male group in 1859 (Messiter, 359). Lawrence, 599-600; Odell, 6:22; 7:1; 8:4.

Brainerd, Miss. Singer, 16 February 1856 (?). We know that the popular Maria S. Brainerd was scheduled to sing but we do not know if or what she sang on the first concert. Said the *Times* editorial on 16 February 1856: "There will be a quartette party, several pianists, Miss Brainerd, and a host of other artists. Commences at 8 o'clock. Clinton Hall. Fifty cents" (A). Odell, 6:16; 7:25; 8:16.

Brinkerhoff, Mrs. Clara M. (1830?- ?). Singer, 3 April 1856; 11 February 1858. She was a professional concert and oratorio singer (never opera) in New York after her debut there when she was about sixteen. Before she married C. E. L. Brinkerhoff on 25 December 1848, her maiden name was Rolph, being the London-born daughter of Mr. and Mrs. John A.

Rolph. After her career as a soprano, she taught voice. Several entries for her can be found in the *Bio-bibliographical Index*, the preceding information from one of them (Jones, 23).

> The singing of Mrs. Brinkerhoff, especially in Mr. Gottschalk's charming song "Alone" . . . was vehemently encored (F).

> The hall appertaining to the *lower* regions, it was exceedingly difficult for Mrs. Brinkerhoff to accomplish her task. But an experienced and well cultivated voice is not easily foiled in what it undertakes (G).

Odell, 6:4; 7:2; 8:4.

Bristow, George Frederick (1825-1898). Composer, 30 May 1856; 30 December 1856; 27 February 1857.

> [He sang] a rather difficult baritone ["ballad" from Bristow's opera *Rip Van Winkle*], a descending cadence in it reminding one of Rip's yawns when he came out of his long sleep. The main theme, however, is tender, and was sung by Dr. Guilmette with much feeling (U).

Blom; DAB; Hitchcock; NCAB 23:194; Sadie.

Comstock, Miss K. V. Singer, 30 May 1856. Probably the Kate Comstock referred to by Odell.

> "Switzerland! My Switzerland" by James Monroe Deems was sung by Miss Comstock with much expression. This young lady's somewhat enfeebled health must account for her difficult respiration, which does not detract from her excellent method as pupil of Bassini. Calisthentics and exercise appertains more strickly [*sic*] in the present state of Miss Comstock's voice than vocal exercises (K).

Odell, 6:1; 7 (Kate Comstock):5; 8:1.

Cook, T. J. Composer, 30 May 1856; 27 February 1857. Though identified by *Dwight's Journal of Music* in December 1856 as a "Broadway music publisher" (VIII), Cook is not listed in Dichter-Shapiro, Redway, or Wolfe. Nor is he listed as a music publisher in AMD, rather as a compiler of music for church (99). He and his brother J. C. Cook did, however, have a publisher's imprint apparently briefly in the 1850s: the piano piece that seems to have been his big hit as a composer, *Three Bells Polka*, was issued with the double imprint Berry and Gordon (297 Broadway, New York City) and Cook & Brother (843 Broadway, New York City), [1856?]. He was probably like a number of musicians of his generation in that he dabbled in several amusical venues in order to make a decent living.

Two of his song collections were *The Original Glee and Anthem Book*, with Theodore E. Perkins, assisted by Thomas Hastings (New York: Huntington, 1861) and *The Union: Music for the Church and the Fireside* (New York: F. J. Huntington, 1863).

> [T. J. Cook's song "Still, Still the Same"] is neat and pleasing (K).

> ["Still, Still the Same" is] a fair song, but marred occasionally by stiffness in the main theme. Some snuff-box variations in the accompaniment give variety to the piece, particularly when [it] is played so as to attract more than half the attention of the audience (U).

Cooper, Henry C. (1784-1872). Violinist-composer, 11 February 1858. This English violinist, "one of the greatest of living artists" (OO), to quote William Henry Fry from 1858, is unfortunately not included in any edition of *Grove's Dictionary* or other standard reference works I have examined. When Cooper—"just arrived from England" (MM)—performed with the NYA-MA, he had apparently appeared briefly before a New York audience only once ("we listened to him last summer at the Academy of Music" (OO), wrote Fry).

Perhaps eager to establish an American reputation, he appeared *gratis* at the 11 February 1858 concert performing his own fantasy on Donizetti's opera *Daughter of the Regiment* and his own *Recollections of Scotland*, both for violin and piano. He would appear that April as soloist with the New York Philharmonic in Spohr's Violin Concerto in A, op. 47 (Krehbiel, 116).

Later in the month of February 1858, Cooper was an assisting artist at a concert by the bass Charles Guilmette. The *Tribune* wrote of this concert that

> Mr. H. C. Cooper, the violinist . . . being added to three of Mr. Eisfeld's quartet party (Messrs. Noll, Reyer and Bergner), there was but one opinion among the critics, which was that never before was such quartet playing heard on this side of the Atlantic (*New York Daily Tribune*, Saturday, 27 February 1858, 7).

> [Mr. Cooper's] excellent playing is much more interesting when illustrating the beauties of the tone muse of Molique, de Beriot and Mendelssohn, than in his own compositions (QQ).
>
> [Mr. Cooper's] playing, for depth of manly feeling and genuine art and purity has never been surpassed (NN).

Odell, 6, 7, 8:0.

Crump, Miss (or Mrs.). Singer, 21 May 1857.

> Mrs. Crump afforded much pleasure by the sweetness of her voice and the delicacy of her execution. She evinced no small degree of power also, in the opening piece, a "Kyrie" by Dr. R. F. Halsted (FF).

Odell, 6, 7, 8:0.

Curtis, George Henry (1821-1895). Composer, 12 November 1857. This song-book compiler and composer of the cantata *Elutheria* (vocal score published in 1851), *The Forest Melody* (performed in 1858), and other works, was a public-school teacher and close friend of George Frederick Bristow. A detailed review of the NYA-MA's concert of 27 February 1858 signed "G. H. C." was published in the *New York Musical World* of 7 March 1858 (U).

> In the vocal quartet by Mr. Curtis, the singers did not do the composer justice. It was the worst performed piece of the evening. The tenor several times lost his pitch and place, and the whole was generally confused. No opinion can be formed of a composition under such circumstances (KK, 723).

Jackson, 298-99.

Deems, J[ames] M[onroe] (1818-1901). Composer, 30 May 1858; 27 February 1857; 21 May 1857; 2 November 1857. "J. M. Deems is a Virginian; studied, we believe abroad, is a teacher, lives in Charlottesville, is a cornet-player, has composed and scored an opera and oratorio, and is a member of the N. Y. Musical Fund society," wrote Willis in the 6 June 1857 issue of the *New York Musical World* (FF). Well, yes and no. This was the slightly garbled prose introduction to New York City concert audiences of a man who lived in Baltimore for most of his life, thus not making a great name in the New York musical world, but who nevertheless had a "remarkable career" (Mathews, 300).

He was born and he died in Baltimore, did study abroad (Dresden), taught at the University of Virginia in Charlottesville (1849-58), and did play the cornet as well as the clarinet and French horn. He was called "General" because he fought in the Civil War and emerged a Brigadier General.

Deems's compositions were performed on NYA-MA concerts on four occasions covering the three seasons, rivalling only William Mason, Jerome Hopkins, and Charles Hommann in exposure. Those compositions included excerpts from his oratorio *Nebuchadnezzar*, a duet from his opera *Esther*, and *Hymn to the Virgin*, which was performed on two concerts.

There are several references to Deems in the *Bio-bibliographical Index*, among the fullest being that in Mathews (pp. 298-300), which also includes a photo of Deems.

> The oratorio is written in the Anglo-Germanic style, and is a work of decided merit. The three numbers were well performed (KK). . . .

> "Hymn to the Virgin" and [the] Duet from "Esther," show decided ability. We should say [Deems's] talent were as well worth cultivating as that of any composer on the programme (FF, 355).

Jackson, 300-01.

Dodworth, Allen (1817-1896). Composer?-cornetist, 30 May 1856.

> Mr. Dodworth, on the cornet, excited much approval (J).

> Mr. Dodworth's tone is mellow and agreeable and his execution finished, with the exception of some occasional notes which are slightly blurred (K).

Hitchcock; Lawrence, 105-06.

Dressler, William (1826?-1914). Accompanist, 3 April 1856. If Dressler's obituary in the *New York Times* of 3 July 1914 is accurate, he was born in Nottingham, England, and came to the United States in the early 1850s as accompanist to the Norwegian violinist Ole Bull. Dressler settled in New York City, pursuing a variety of musical jobs, like so many fellow musicians of the time. Other than a prolific composer of songs and piano pieces, he compiled song-books, such as *Temperance Echoes* (New York: J. L. Peters, 1874), published and sold music (*American Musical*

Directory listed him as a music dealer, 94) and, perhaps most consistently of all, played the organ in many churches. Occasionally, Dressler's pursuits can be found in combination, as in his *Thanksgiving Anthem*, op. 80, for chorus and solo quartet, "dedicated to Rev. Joel Parker, Pastor of the Fourth Avenue Presbyterian Church, New York, by the organist William Dressler" (New York: William Dressler's Music Store, 933 Broadway, 1859). Dressler's *New York Times* obituary says he was organist at St. Peter's Church in Jersey City, N. J. for eighteen years.

Like composer-teacher Ellsworth C. Phelps (1827-1913) and composer-organist George W. Warren (1828-1902), Dressler had a musician son, the composer Louis Rafael Dressler (1861-1932).

Dyer, S. O. Composer, 30 April 1858. This is probably the Samuel O. Dyer listed in the *American Musical Directory* as a teacher of piano, organ, and singing (108), as organist at Brooklyn's "Congregational Church on Church and Clinton Avenue" (159), and as a piano tuner (172). If so, his middle name was Owen; he was son of the distinguished compiler of tunebooks and a church-anthem book Samuel Dyer (1744-1833). Samuel Owen Dyer was born in Norfolk, Va. in 1819, and died in Brooklyn, N.Y. in 1894.

S. O. Dyer was composer of the vocal quartet *This Is the Hour* heard at NYA-MA's last concert. Metcalf, 209-10; Odell 6, 7, 8:0.

Eben, F[elix] J. Flautist, 21 May 1857. There is a portrait and a one-sentence identification of Eben in Fairly: "Thought to be of German descent, he emigrated to America in about 1849, where he became a leading flautist and conductor, attaining much fame in New York towards the end of the century" (Fairly, 36). According to Krehbiel, Eben played the flute obligato for Mrs. Bostwick in William Vincent Wallace's song "The Happy Birdling" in the 7 April 1852 concert of the New York Philharmonic (Krehbiel, 107).

> Mr. Eben plays a most resonant and pure-toned Boehm flute, which he well understands witching the music out of. Mr. Eben is of German birth and education (F, 355).

American Musical Directory, 116; Odell, 6:4; 7:10; 8:6.

Fry, William Henry (1813-1864). Composer, 30 May 1856; 27 February 1857.

The composer's aim in [*Marco Bozarris*] was apparently to subjugate the musical to the rhetorical sensibility. Rhetorically speaking,

Marco Bozarris was well recited; of course a certain sacrifice of the music was necessary (K).

[In] "Fac ut Ardeat" . . . secular effects only are obtained, the chorus sustaining but a meagre part, and the solo so entirely absorbing the attention as to "crush out" the chorus, leaving them among the audience at the close. The solo is well defined in character, that is for the stage, and was feelingly rendered by Dr. Guilmette (U, 148).

Blom; Hitchcock; NCAB 8:143; Sadie.

Gellie, Misses. Singers, 12 November 1857. A Miss Gellie and a Miss M. Gellie sang in the Trinity Church choir from 1853 until it changed to an all-male group in 1859 (Messiter, 310). They are, no doubt, the "Misses Gellie" of the advertisements for, and *Musical World* review of, the 12 November 1857 concert.

The two Misses Gellie sang very charmingly the Wallace duet (K, 723). . . .

Odell, 6:0; 7:6 (Mary Gellie), 8 (Miss Gellie); 8:0.

Gottschalk, Louis Moreau (1829-1869). Composer-pianist, 3 April 1856; composer, 17 April 1857; 21 May 1857. As pianist and secondarily as composer, Gottschalk was, of course, the first big international "star" of American music. He and his music still hold much for many over a century after his death: his life story has been told in the *American Masters'* series on the PBS television network; his autobiography, *Notes of a Pianist*, edited and titled by his sister Clara and published posthumously in 1881 (later re-edited by Jeanne Behrend in 1964 and published by Knopf); his complete piano music was published in 1969; many smaller collections of his music have been published; and numerous recordings of his music have been made. His great abilities, widely recognized during his lifetime, are now legendary.

When Gottschalk appeared on the NYA-MA concert of 3 April 1856, he was also busy completing a series of sixteen other concerts that began on 20 December 1855 and was to end 7 June 1856. On 7 February 1857 he left New York City on a Caribbean tour with the fourteen-year-old soprano Adelina Patti. Although Patti returned to the United States in 1858, Gottschalk, apparently weary of his life as a piano-virtuoso, decided to stay out of the country for five years. In 1861, having been influenced by matters related to the Civil War, he was prompted to return to the United States. He made his second New York City "debut" on 11 February 1862.

Blom; Hitchcock; Sadie.

Griswold, Mr. D[avid] D. Composer?-singer, 12 November 1857. David Griswold was a New York singer (Lawrence, 600) and a composer of songs (AMD, 98). From the ads and Willis's review—the only one to mention Griswold—it is not really clear if Griswold sang a song he had composed.

> A song by Mr. Griswold was pleasing and easy. We think, however, the composer carries the voice too uniformly high (KK, 723).

Odell, 6:1; 7:6; 8:2.

Grosse, Mr. Violinist, 17 April, 1857. Otto Grosse is listed as a New York violinist in AMD, 142.

> The [Hommann] quartet for stringed instruments was performed excellently by Messers. Reiff, Grosse, and Wedermeyer, assisted by an amateur (AA).

Odell, 6, 7, 8:0.

Guilmette, Charles [A.]. Singer, 30 December 1856; 27 February 1857; 21 May 1857; 11 February 1858. Writing under the date 15 December 1856, the New York correspondent of *Dwight's Journal of Music* mentioned in his column that

> the Pyne and Harrison Opera Troupe made their debut [of the season] at Nibo's . . . in a dismal comic opera called "The Valley of Andorre." Louisa Pyne is a favorite, and was well received, as was Mr. Guilmette (debut). (*Dwight's Journal of Music*, 10/12 (Saturday, 20 December 1856, 93))

Within about two weeks, Guilmette had left Pyne-Harrison, sung at the first concert of the second season of the young NYA-MA, and had settled (or would shortly settle) in New York City. Nothing else is known about the life of this probable Englishman, although he did become busy immediately on the New York musical scene by giving concerts and by appearing as an assisting artist. The *American Musical Directory* listed him as a teacher at New York's Cooper Institute (161) and as a private teacher of "vocal physiology" (177).

> This gentleman's voice and manner steadily win upon the public favor (U, 148).

> Of Dr. Guilmette we need scarcely speak. His "basso profundo" always *tells* with good effect, and an audience does not tire of witnessing his occasional descent into the "lower deep" of the gamut (Hodges in "FF," 355).

> A grand scene and aria by Labarre, a French composer, [was] passionately delivered by Dr. Guilmette, amid loud applause (OO).

Odell, 6:3; 7:15; 8:0.

Halstead, Dr. R. F. Composer, 21 May 1857. "Dr R. F. Halstead is a New York physician," Richard Storrs Willis wrote in his review of the 21 May 1857 concert, giving program notes supplied him by Jerome Hopkins. "[He also] plays the organ in Church of the Holy Apostles. Native American. Never abroad" (FF, 354).

> His "Kyrie" indicates fine musical feeling and a refined and cultivated taste. It is somewhat over-spiced with dissonance, however, the flat-sixth, particularly, in its various harmonic combinations, being over-used and over-dominant,

he sniffed, giving Dr. Halstead a showy professional tongue-lashing.

> Dr. Halstead will soon, doubtless, fall into a more diatonic style of writing (FF, 354).

In his review, Willis included another review written by "our more capable confrere, Dr. H [odges, organist-music director at Trinity Church]," who wrote of Halstead's Kyrie that it "would have been more satisfactory had it been connected with less sacred words" (FF, 355).

Hodges, Edward (1796-1867). Composer-accompanist, 27 February 1857.

> [Hodges' *Consecration Anthem*] is a solid composition in strict ecclesiastical style, and was extremely well performed (S).

> The opernning quartet movement of Hodges' *Consecration Anthem* is clearly conceived and is, by far, the most elaborately worked out of all the four movements. . . . The second and third movements

afforded an opportunity to hear the chorus contrasted and combined with the quartet . . . but in both of these movements, as well as the concluding fugue, the want of the organ . . . was keenly felt. . . . We were glad to see the venerable doctor at the piano (U, 148). . . .

Baker (1984); Blom; Hitchcock; Sadie.

Hoffman, Richard (1831-1909). Composer, 17 April 1857; composer-pianist, 11 February 1858.

. . . a pianist who is good enough to be the best in any capital of the world if his modesty would permit him to claim his proper position (NN).

. . . a young master whose modesty was only equal to his merit. We were not prepared. . . to find Mr. Hoffman excelling as he showed he can, in the character of a piano-forte composer. His two pieces; one "Reverie," Twilight [New York: Wm Hall & Son, n. d.] very beautiful, and another, "Marche Funebre" [Mayence: Chez les fils B. Schott, n.d.] . . . so good, that produced in Europe before writers for the piano have increased as at present, would have established the reputation of the composer. . . . As it came from young Hoffman's elegant fingers, it was worthy of any composer in Europe (OO).

The composer-pianist played his two pieces with the taste and elegance which always distinguish him. Both compositions are significant of their subject and suggestive to the fancy. The second might bear a little curtailing, perhaps, without detriment (RR).

DAB; Hitchcock; *New York Times* (obituary, 19 August 1909, 7).

Hommann, Charles. Composer, 16 February 1856; 3 April 1856; 30 May 1856; 17 April 1857; 30 April 1858. This Philadelphia resident (in the early 1850s) is a now-obscure but important figure in nineteenth-century American music. As composer in the 1830s or 1840s of possibly the first American symphony, Hommann deserves careful investigation and his life thorough documentation. (Bristow's *Sinfonia*, op. 10, dates from 1848; his Second—or *Julien*—Symphony, op. 24, from 1854.)

Hopkins was obviously a fierce believer in Hommann's music. One would be interested to know how he came to know the music. Did Hommann, for example, simply submit scores for consideration by the NYA-MA? The Hommann-Hopkins letter mentioned earlier casts little light on the subject, though one passage does suggest some familiarity: "Mr. Hupfeld desires me to convey his compliments to you," writes Hommann. This is a reference to Charles Frederick Hupfeld (Hupfield) (1787-1864), the Philadelphia composer-conductor, who published some of Hommann's shorter works and a *Te Deum*, and who was his brother-in-law. Had Hopkins met him in Philadelphia?

Strengthening the idea of a New York City acquaintanceship between Hommann and Hopkins, however, is the fact that Hommann was located in Brooklyn by June 1855 (Hitchcock, 2:416). In the letter, Hommann apologizes for not attending the NYA-MA's first concert due to illness; he apparently felt this was in order because he lived relatively close. He obviously did not attend the second concert either ("which I hope was successful"), but no apology since he could hardly have been expected to journey from Philadelphia at that time for one concert. After all, the letter was written from that city on 8 April 1856, not long after the concert, return address suggesting impermanence, however: "for the present at 49 Filbert [?] St."

> The other work of any importance [besides the Hopkins symphony "Life"] was a Sonata for violin and piano by C. Hommann. Two movements were played [at the concert] . . . both of which display good perception of the classic form, but little freshness. . . . We are anxious to hear more from Mr. Hommann (B).

> A quintett by Mr. Hommann of Philadelphia was the principal feature (F).

Hitchcock; Sadie.

Hopkins, Charles Jerome (1836-1898). Composer, 16 February 1856; 3 April 1856; 30 May 1856; 30 December 1856; 21 May 1857; composer-accompanist, 27 February 1857; pianist, 30 May 1856. While his biography is given briefly in the sources noted below, the NYA-MA's founder and president awaits full attention. From a few known incidents in his life and from his writings, mainly found in his periodical *The Orpheonist and Philharmonic Journal*, we know that he was probably one of the most explosive, flamboyant, and out-spoken characters in American—no, world—music history. Read, for example, Slonimsky's *A Thing or Two About Music*, 250-56, for a report of some of Hopkins' escapades. While completely unscholarly and played for laughs in the usual Slonimsky manner, his report gives some idea of what Hopkins must have been like. The following passage from Hopkins' delightful, outrageous pamphlet *Music and Snobs; or A Few Funny Facts Regarding the Disabilities of*

Music in America, published thirty years after the death of the NYA-MA, provides an example of his prose style:

> Misrepresented, maligned and robbed by careless, ignorant or mercenary Editors, snubbed by Managers, underpaid by Church Committees, and cheated by Publishers, while totally incapable of "backing," rehearsing, engineering, publishing, and popularizing their works *themselves*; everybody calling them "presumptuous egoists" or "musical quacks," and no one able or willing to examine and test the results of their painful brains' sweat, I hold that serious American composers are indeed fifty per cent worse off than any European musicians of like ambition ever were or ever could be, and that any such Americans should "succeed" before their ninetieth birthday under existing circumstances is indeed a sixty-fold miracle, *unless* they sell their self-respect and independence as many have to do, thus becoming a sort of intellectual prostitutes, to make a living (Hopkins, *Music*, 19).

Yet, Hopkins could be thoughtful and vivid, as these passages he wrote after Gottschalk's death demonstrate:

> The newspapers announce the death of Gottschalk, the greatest American pianist who has yet appeared.... He was one of the few original and remarkable artists of this century.... We have seen his audiences rise and wave handkerchiefs, while shouting "*bravo*," "*encore*," and kindred words. Again we have witnessed the bursting forth of applause in the middle of the music two or three times in one piece, while he was playing.... In losing Gottschalk, the sweet singer as well as the thunderer of the piano, we, as a nation, have sustained a heavy, perhaps irreprable [*sic*] loss, for we think the incentive to extra great virtuosity are decreasing in this country every day. [*The Orpheonist and Philharmonic Journal* 6/39 (2 February 1870): 3]

> After the Mass, the body of the pianist and composer was borne from the church and interred by the side of his brother Edward in Greenwood Cemetery. And as we wandered our way homeward through the rain, pondering upon the possibilities of the late pianist's talents, had they been directed in a different channel towards a worthier goal, the lines echoed in our ears—"For of all sad words of tongue or pen, The saddest are these: It might have been!" [*The Orpheonist and Philharmonic Journal* 7/42 (5 November 1870): 3]

We were, unfortunately, too late to hear the opening movement of Mr. Hopkins symphony called "Life." For some remarkable reason, the concert commenced before the usual hour (B).

The Symphony of "Life" by Mr. Hopkins expressed well that struggle through which we all are put to gain an eminence in this world. He is struggling through art; his aim is high and pure, and in the language of the German miners in ascending from below to pure air, we will say to him, *"Glück auf"* (G).

The accompaniment [in the song by Hopkins] of stringed instruments with the piano we think was a mistake. . . . But young composers have to try their hand at a great many things before they settle down into their best style (K).

[The soprano solo, chorus, and vocal fugue by Mr. Hopkins were] creditably written. The fugue, however, was an imitation properly—not a fugue (K).

Dr. Guilmette made a portion of ["A Death-Bed Rhapsody," by Hopkins] very effective; but we must confess that we could not discover what we may call the *rationale* of the composition. The rhapsody of a death-bed, we should presume, would be a monologue (O).

The 186th Hymn . . . we think . . . the best thing we have heard from Jerome [Hopkins], although composed, we understand, before he was instructed in harmony (FF, 355).

Baker (1984); Hitchcock; NCAB 4:134; Sadie.

Hopkins, John Henry, Jr. (1820-1891). Composer, 30 December 1856. Jerome Hopkins' older brother, John Henry Hopkins, Jr. was well established in New York City when Jerome got there at age twenty (or perhaps younger).

The concert we perceived closed with the performance of a *Christmas Carol* ("The Shepherds of Bethlehem"), which we unfortunately could not stay to hear. We have [a published copy], however, before us. . . . We do not err in attributing it to the versatile brain and ready pen of our highly esteemed and reverend friend the Editor of the *Church Journal.* . . . The composition, albeit the author subscribes himself "Junior" [in the NYA-MA printed program] smacks very strongly of the harmonies of the "olden time" (O).

Baker (1984); Jackson, 309-10.

Jameson, Mrs. R. S. Singer, 30 May 1856. (Also scheduled to sing 17 April 1857, but did not appear.) In 1861, Mrs. Jameson sang professionally at New York's Church of the Puritans (Congregational) (AMD, 219). She is probably the same person that Vera Lawrence refers to as "Mrs. Jamieson," 533, 536.

> Mr. Berti not appearing, Mrs. Jameson took his place in the programme. She appeared somewhat embarrassed at the change, which feeling, however, did not extend itself to her singing (K).

> Mrs. Jameson (for whom a needless apology was previously offered by the Secretary) sang with exquisite pathos (O).

Odell, 6:5; 7:4; 8:0.

Johnson, James A. Singer, 27 February, 1857; 30 April, 1858; singer-composer, 21 May 1857.

> [In Hodges' *Consecration Anthem*] Mrs. Bostwick, Miss Robjohn, James, the son of John (apostoloically named), and Dr. Guilmette formed a telling quartet (U, 148).

> Mr. Johnson is music director at Dr. Muhlenberg's church, an American, a teacher in the common schools, and an efficient and zealous musician (DD).

> We have heard better things of his than the song he sang ["Come Love With Me"] (FF).

> Mr. Johnson's voice seems to improve rather than deteriorate. He is, whenever and wherever he appears, a welcome vocalist (Hodges in FF, 355).

Odell, 6:2; 7, 8:0.

Kemp, Annie. Singer, 3 April 1856; 30 May 1856.

> Miss Annie Kemp was vehemently encored (FF).

Miss Annie Kemp is a charming daughter of the Muses with a beautiful voice to perform their behests. Mrs. Seguin, her teacher, has succeeded well with her rich contralto and bringing it under control—a difficult matter generally with this style of voice. As she stood in Stuyvesant Hall, which is a remarkably unattractive place, she looked like a pretty bird in a shabby cage. She sang [the two songs by Willis] with such feeling as to secure for herself enthusiastic applause and an encore. We predict for this fine young singer a decided success as concert-singer and trust we may very soon hear her again (G).

We have noticed before this charming young contralto, whose music flows out with all the ease of an Alboni as even when welling up from the chest as deep as G sharp and G (K).

Odell, 6:3; 7, 8:0.

Kiefer, Mr. (K. or X.). Clarinetist, 27 February 1857. There is something of a confusion here. Although a notice in the *Daily Tribune* of the 27 February 1857 performance (Q), a review of that performance in *Dwight's Journal of Music* (S), and a review in the *Gazette* (T) mention Kiefer's participation, Willis's review in the *World* (U) mentions in a lengthy passage devoted to his dislike of the clarinet, that the performers of the Pychowski duo were Berti, piano, and Stark, clarinet.

That Frederick Stark was a clarinetist around this time in New York City is confirmed by the *American Musical Directory*, where he is listed as both a teacher of violin and clarinet (127) and simply as a clarinet player (152). There is no Kiefer listed in that source. There is also a "Fred'k Starck (viollin, clarinet)" in the 1856/57 city directory; there is no Kiefer listed.

However, a Mr. X. Kiefer played the solo in a *Concertino for Clarinet and Orchestra* by Theodore Eisfeld at a New York Philharmonic concert on 8 March 1858, the composer conducting. There is a notice of this concert in the Saturday, 6 March 1858 (p. 6), *Daily Tribune*, and a review (presumably by Fry) of that concert in the edition of Monday, 8 March 1858 (p. 5). Kiefer: Odell, 6:1 (clarionet); 7:1 (clarionet); 8:1 (opera [?]). Stark: Odell, 6:1; 7, 8:0.

King, William A. (1817?-1867). Composer-pianist, 21 May 1857; accompanist-conductor, 12 November 1857; 11 February 1858; 30 April 1858. On 12 May 1867 the *New York Times* carried the following story under the headline "Death of an Organist":

The twenty-ninth Precinct police found William A. King, the well-known organist, lying dead on the sidewalk near the corner of Thirty-first Street and Fourth Avenue at an early hour yesterday. Deceased was 50 years of age and is supposed to have died of exhaustion and exposure [*New York Times*, 12 May 1867, 8]. . . .

In the February 1858 issue of the *Musical Courier*, Jerome Hopkins wrote that King had gone to a "drunkard's grave" (quoted in Slonimsky, 255).

So ended the life of a man who was probably one of the most talented performers in New York at that time. Many also thought King a good composer. Richard Storrs Willis wrote in June 1857:

> We happened in at Grace Church [where King was organist] one sleepy summer afternoon some years hence, and heard him play an introductory voluntary to about a dozen people, which put fairly into notes would suffice to make the reputation of any man (FF, 355).

King was born in London, England, the son of M. P. King (Moore, 75). He came to the United States in 1834 (Not in 1835, as given in Moore), a man in his late twenties, and quickly became a fixture on the New York music scene, giving concerts as virtuoso pianist and organist, assisting at the concerts of other artists, and serving as "longtime organist at Grace Church" (Lawrence, 73), when it was located at Broadway and Rector Street (a site it occupied until 1846).

His flashy piano piece *Variations on the Star-Spangled Banner*, with a "finale a la valse," the sheet music announced, was published in 1835 in New York City by Firth & Hall. It was one of about twenty publications of King's that appeared before his death, many of them editions of his collection *New York Grace Church Collection of Sacred Music*.

In 1845 King was organist at St. Peter's Roman Catholic Church (Lawrence, 302), but he was presumably back at Grace Church by the time the first edition of the published collection mentioned was published (Boston: Ditson, 1852; the phrase "organist at Grace Church, New York," follows his name on the title page). When King appeared in NYA-MA concerts in 1857 and 1858, he was not working as organist. Wrote Willis in June 1857: "His talent for organ playing . . . is now unapplied . . . wishing a seventh of the time, at least, to himself" (FF, 355). He would relinquish that seventh again, however; the *American Musical Directory* lists King as organist at St. George's Episcopal Church (162). Odell, 6:7; 7:5; 8:2.

Labarre. Composer (French), 11 February 1858. This is probably Théodore Labarre (1805-1870).

Leach, Mrs. G[eorgiana] S[tuart]. Mrs. Leach was a singer scheduled for the concert of 17 April 1857 but cancelled, though one would never know this from the *Gazette* of 2 May 1857, whose critic wrote (out of inattentiveness or actual failure to attend the concert): "Miss Leach acquitted herself admirably in the song" (AA).

Leach, Mr. Stephen W. Singer, 12 November 1857. Odell, 6:18, 7:2; 8:0.

Loder. Composer, 30 April 1858. Edward James Loder (1813-1865) was a prolific English composer who never came to the United States. New York City resident George Loder (1816-1868), undoubtedly a relative, was also English, born in Bath, just as Edward James Loder was. The latter was a standard English-language composer of the day, his songs and operas being performed in the United States as well as England. Blom; Sadie.

Loomis, Mr. Singer, 17 April 1857. Probably the tenor of this name in the Trinity Church choir in the 1840s and 1850s (Messiter, 47). Odell, 6, 7, 8:0.

Maeder, J[ames] G[aspard] (1809-1876). Composer, 30 April 1858. (The *Bio-bibliographical Index* has this British-American theater conductor-composer's name incorrectly spelled "Meader.") In 1834 in New York City, he married the famous London-born actress Clara Fisher, who outlived her husband by twenty-two years, dying in Metuchen, New Jersey in 1898 (see entry for Clara Fisher in NCAB 10:471). Hitchcock; Lawrence, 103.

Mason, William. Composer, 3 April 1856; 17 April 1857; 30 April 1858; composer-pianist, 30 May 1856; 27 February 1857; pianist, 27 February 1857.

> The *Gondolier's Serenade* by William Mason is an effective quartette, exhibiting the well-known resources of this author, and swaying easily among rich musical combinations. It is somewhat in the instrumental style; but this is quite as pleasing when well done by singers, as the vocal style proper. The quartette was encored (G).
>
> An inevitable encore followed this popular piece [Mason's *Silver Spring*], which was responded to, however, with a piece for which

the audience less cared and were less pleased with—a very common error of those who play in public (K).

"Amitié pour Amitié" [Boston: Nathan Richardson at the Exchange, 1854] is a charming piece, and though published as an impromptu, shows marks of a more careful composition than later works by this author. The "Etude de concert" [New York: William Hall & Son, 1856; dedicated to Gottschalk] was more pretentious, but far less unique. Both were effectively played (U).

Baker (1984); Blom; Hitchcock; NCAB 7:423; Sadie.

Meyer, Julius E[ward] (1822-1899). Violinist, 30 May 1856. He played the *andante* movement from Hommann's Violin Sonata with Jerome Hopkins as pianist. Meyer apparently came to the United States from Germany in 1852, and became known as a vocal teacher in Brooklyn, living there for forty years (Pratt, 26).

Beginning in 1867, and lasting for a period of about five years, Meyer was the first voice teacher of Emma Thursby (1845-1931). A biography of Thursby includes the following information on Meyer's early training at the Leipzig Conservatory under Mendelssohn:

> The instrument of his attention was the violin. Yet it was his fine baritone voice and his unusual ear for music . . . that had persuaded Mendelssohn to regard him as a born singing teacher. . . . [Thursby] always remained thankful to him, particularly for the knowledge he gave her of the music of Germany, and for the great aid his violin accompaniment gave to her purity of tone (Gipson, 70).

Odell, 6:1 (vocalist); 7:0; 8:1.

Morgan, Mr. George Washborne (1822-1892). Accompanist-conductor, 30 May 1856. From Willis's review of the concert, we know that Morgan conducted (K). He could likely have done so on other occasions without having been mentioned by critics. Apparently a most talented musican, Morgan came to this country from his native England in 1853, pausing in his musical pursuits to fight with the Union Army in the Civil War (Morgan's obituary in the *American Art Journal*).

Morgan was involved with much organ-playing activity in Boston and New York City, including thirteen years at Grace Church on and off before 1868 (Stewart, 263). According to Jones (103), Morgan's harpist daughter Maud made her debut in 1876; Stewart (263) says she was engaged as harpist by Grace Church in 1896, four years after her father's death. Odell, 6:2 (W. Morgan: 1); 7:16; 8:26.

Payne, [Mr. or Mrs.] E. A. Composer?-singer, 12 November 1857. A mid-nineteenth century American composer named Edward A. Payne is represented by three published songs in the Music Division, The New York Public Library for the Performing Arts.

> A pleasant and simple song was also that of Mr. E. A. Payne (KK, 723).

Odell, 6:0; 7:1 (Mrs. E. A. Payne); 8:5 (Anna Payne, contralto).

Peck, Mr. Singer, 11 February 1858. Peck was in the solo quartet that sang *Hide Not Thy Face*, an anthem by Samuel P. Tuckerman. He was probably the "Mr. Peck" or "Mr. E. M. Pecke," both of whom sang in the Trinity Church choir in 1858 (Messiter, 315). Odell, 6, 7, 8:0.

Pychowski, J[an] (or John) N[epomucene] (1818-1900). Composer, 27 February, 1857; 17 April 1857; composer-pianist, 12 November 1857. Several references for this Bohemian-American composer-teacher-pianist are in *Bio-bibliographical Index*. *Baker's Biographical Dictionary* (1919 edition, 731) cites Pychowski as having arrived in New York City in 1850, and having lived in Hoboken, New Jersey from 1855 until his death. He was apparently mainly a piano teacher. Amy Fay claimed that Pychowski revolutionized her technique after studying with him for only the summer of 1861 in Genesco, New York (Mathews, 138).

> [Pychowski's *Duetto Dramatico* for clarinet and piano] is a very odd piece. It might have been called a caprice for these two instruments, more properly. It treated two main themes in a style surprising, but not eminently pleasing. It contains much straining after unusual effect by means of sudden transitions of key, a device we do not much admire, though quite in vogue among the disciples of the transcendental school (U, 148).

> Among the compositions which we heard on the present occasion, the *Sonata* for piano and violin, by [Jan N. Pychowski] ranks highest. It is not what we should call a real *Sonata*, but each part, separately considered, offers many interesting traits. The lack of unity in the style, the mixture of French, Italian, and German music, of old and modern style, produces uneasiness in the mind of the listener; nevertheless, the whole shows good musical ability,

spirit, and intelligence on the part of the author. The *Romance* is the most satisfactory piece [in it], inasmuch as it presents the most unity. It had to be repeated. The work was most satisfactorily performed by the author and Mr. Theodore Thomas (JJ).

A grand sonata for piano and violin by Pychowski was also performed. We have often had occasion to speak of Pychowski. He is one of our cleverist musical writers. Like most of his countrymen, he is fond of the minor and his style is passional [passionate?]. He is full of science and ingenious invention—rather too full. If he could be persuaded to let himself alone—so to speak—he would prove more obviously melodious and popular. An artist sometimes forgets, in the advance he has made in science, how far he has left the world behind him. The sonata in question is running over with conceits of all kinds, challenging admiration rather than exciting general musical sympathy. The *Romance* was the best movement and was deservedly re-demanded (KK, 723).

Reiff, Anthony (Anton), Jr. (? -1916). Violinist, 17 April 1857. Composer, 11 May 1857. Both Messrs. Reiff, Sr. and Jr. were rather typical journeymen musicians of nineteenth-century New York City. Both were secondary, if important, players on the scene. Neither is widely remembered. Anthony Reiff, Sr. (d. 1880), mainly a bassoonist, immigrated from Germany to New York City (see various references in Lawrence for his performing career). He became vice-president of the fourth Philharmonic Society of New York, an organization he helped form in 1842 (Shanet, 82), and vice-president of New York City's Musical Fund Society when it was founded in 1849 (AMD, 250). Reiff, Sr. also taught music and was cited as a "professor of music to the New York Institution for the Blind" in his *Institution March* for piano (New York: F. Riley, 1846; classmark *MYD-box, Music Division, New York Public Library).

Anthony Reiff, Jr., like his father, had an interest in music. He was an opera conductor as young as eighteen and conducted occasionally for the Pyne-Harrison troupe (see his *New York Times* obituary, listed in the Bibliography). The *Times* obituary claims he "introduced opera to Australia," a reference to the fact that he was orchestra conductor in the company formed by Edward Lyster that began the first opera seasons in Melbourne in 1861, the first in the country of Australia (see Love, especially 98-99). Reiff's successor in 1863 as Lyster's opera conductor was George Loder, mentioned earlier.

Reiff, Jr. played the violin and must have been a rather accomplished pianist as well. For example, at his farewell concert in Australia on 24 August 1863, he performed Gottschalk's *The Banjo* (Love, 99).

In 1914, Reiff, Jr. was described as "a well-known New York musician" and, charmingly, as "a familiar figure on Riverside Drive" (his last address was on 103rd Street) (Wielich, 26). His *Times* obituary called him the "oldest living member of the New York Philharmonic Society."

> The quartet in D minor for stringed instruments [by Hommann] was performed excellently by Messers. Reiff, Grosse, and Wedermeyer, assisted by an amateur (AA).

> [The Anthony Reiff, Jr.] "Grand Scena and Aria" we could not get into the significance of, despite Dr. Guilmette's painstaking rendering (FF, 355).

Robjohn, Miss. Singer, 27 February 1857; 17 April 1857. In the first concert mentioned here, Miss Robjohn sang in the Hodges anthem; in the second, she sang in the unnamed Mason vocal quartet.

A Miss E. Robjohn was an alto in the Trinity Church choir beginning in 1853 (Messiter, 59, 310), and was undoubtedly a relative of William James Robjohn (1843-1920), the composer, who came with his parents about 1858 to the United States where his aunt and organ-building uncle already lived. William James Robjohn was among the first and best boy sopranos in the Trinity choir, joining it in 1858 (Messiter, 75).

> [The vocal quartet that performed Hodges' anthem was a telling one] except that the alto was perhaps a trifle too small in volume by the side of singers of greater age and experience (U, 148).

Odell, 6, 7, 8:0. Entries for Ada and Fanny Robjohn, and for W[illiam] J[ames] Robjohn are in Odell 7 and 8, respectfully.

Satter, Gustave (1832-1879?). Composer-pianist, 30 April 1958 (scheduled to appear but did not).

Sheppard, Miss Caroline M. Singer, 27 February 1857; 17 April 1857.

> Miss C. M. Sheppard made her debut [at NYA-MA concerts?] as a soprano with tolerable success (S, 189).

> Not that Miss Sheppard did not do justice to [T. J. Cook's song "Still, Still the Same"], but it is the fate of all songs so constructed that either the vocal or the instrumental part must be measureably sacrificed (U, 148).

> Miss Sheppard gave her part [in Deems's *Hymn to the Virgin*] with care, and the accompanying chorus was well sung (U, 148).

> Miss Sheppard sang acceptably, at short notice, both of Mrs. Leach's song (BB).

Odell, 6:2; 7, 8:0 [Odell, 8:8 (Mrs. George Sheppard)].

Siede, [Julius?]. Composer, 21 May 1857. Felix J. Eben played Siede's flute fantasy on themes from the Donizetti operas *Lucrezia Borgia* and *Lucia di Lammermoor* in the same concert as Anthony Reiff, Jr.'s *Grand Scene and Aria*. It is likely that he is the Julius Siede (in DD, but "Seide" in FF) that became flutist in the orchestra that Reiff put together and conducted for William Lyster's famous season of opera in Melbourne, Australia, in 1861 (see Love, 31, e.g.).

Simon, Mr. Violinist, 30 April 1858.

> [The Benkert piano trio] which, but for the masterly playing by Messers. Berti, Simon, and Bergner, would hardly have been endurable (WW).

Odell, 6, 7, 8:0.

Simon, Miss Henrietta. Singer, 21 May 1857. Although she had much to do in the last concert of the second season—she sang King's "Ave Maria," Hopkins' *Hymn 186*, and with Dr. Guilmette, the duet from Deems's opera *Esther*—Miss Simon received no critical mention. Odell, 6:2; 7, 8:0.

Simpson, George. Singer, 30 April 1858. This durable tenor is listed in the *American Musical Directory* as a professional singer (175) and tenor in the professional quartet at Grace Church (221). He was still singing in that quartet in 1891 (*Year Book of Grace Church*, 1890/91, 54).

Two months before his appearance with the NYA-MA, he received the following notice: "As Mr. Simpson is hardly twenty, with much voice . . . and what the Italians would call abandonment, he ought to have a brilliant career before him" (*New York Daily Tribune*, 18 February 1858, 6).

> [One volunteer for the occasion was] George Simpson (a gentleman who possesses a thoroughly English tenor voice, and who can sing ballads exquisitely) (UU).

> Two pretty songs [by Loder and Maeder were sung] by our rising tenor Mr. George Simpson (WW).

Odell, 6:3; 7:35; 8:34.

Stark (or Starck). Clarinetist. See **Kiefer**.

Stockton, Miss Fanny. Singer, 11 February 1858.

> ["Ave Maria" by Bassini was] nicely sung by Miss Stockton—excepting a nasal tendency in the upper notes she should correct (OO).

> Miss Stockton has a nice voice, well-trained (RR).

Odell, 6:0; 7:14; 8:12 (some opera roles).

Thomas, Mrs. Singer, 17 April 1857. She participated in the unnamed vocal quartet composed by William Mason. Odell, 6:0; 7:6 and 8:1 (Mrs. J. E. Thomas).

Thomas, Theodore (1835-1905). Violinist, 12 November 1857.

> [Pychowski's Sonata for Violin and Piano] was most satisfactorily performed by the author and Theodore Thomas (J).

Baker (1984); Blom; Hitchcock; Sadie.

Timm, H[enry] C[hristian] (1811-1892). Accompanist, 27 February 1857. In light of his presidency of the Philharmonic Society of New York (1848-63) and his German citizenship for the first twenty-four years of his life, Timm's participation in a NYA-MA concert is a little surprising, especially considering his contretemps with Bristow over American music earlier in the 1850s. Of course, he did appear in the relatively minor role of accompanist to one song; maybe it was the singer of that song, Mrs. Emma Bostwick, many times a soloist with the Philharmonic, who persuaded him. The song was by Jerome Hopkins who thanked Timm publicly in 1858. Hopkins' first song compilation is dedicated to Timm, "to whose kind encouragement at the commencement of his artistic career, the author is indebted" (*A Collection of Sacred Song*. New York: sold by Daniel Dana, Jr., 1859. See verso of title page).

["Has Summer Pass'd Away?" by Jerome Hopkins, was] a delicate little song, and most beautifully rendered by Mrs. Bostwick. Indeed, young Mr. President, there is everything in having a lively interpreter of a new song . . . and a conscientious accompanist. Vive le Timm! (UU)

Baker (1984); Hitchcock; Howard, 153-54; Lawrence, 85-86.

Tucker, Mr. Singer, 17 April 1857. A Mr. H. Tucker was in the Trinity Church choir as of 1853 (Messiter, 315). "Henry Tucker," the composer (?) of "Weeping Sad and Lonely, or When this Cruel War Is Over" (1863) and "Sweet Geniveve" (1869), is listed in the *American Musical Directory* as a song composer (98) and as a private music teacher (122).

[William] Mason's quartet was sung by Mrs. Thomas, [Miss] Robjohn, and Messers. Loomis and Tucker with spirit and power (AA).

Odell, 6:0; 7:2 (H. Tucker); 8:3 (Henry Tucker).

Tuckerman, S[amuel] P[arkman] (1819-1890). Composer, 11 February 1858. This wealthy pupil of English-born Edward Hodges, organist and music director at New York's Trinity Church from 1839 to 1858, succeeded him at Hodges' suggestion.

[Tuckerman] played one Sunday . . . and one only, resigning immediately afterwards. . . . [He] was of a restless disposition, and always found it difficult to settle down to church work. Fortunately, or unfortunately, as it may be, he had private means which allowed him to do as he pleased (Messiter, 64).

The anthem—original—"Hide Not Thy Face" by S. P. Tuckerman, Mus. Doc. is extremely well written. It is rigidly within the sanctions of English ecclesiastical music: it has good, sober, orthodox harmonies. It contains two parts—a quartet . . . and a chorus—the quartet being much better appointed than the chorus, which wanted clear outline and division of statement (OO).

[Tuckerman's anthem] was the best ensemble composition of the evening. It is in chastened church style, well wrought and imbued with deep religious feeling. We hope . . . the public may hear it again (RR).

Baker (1984); Blom; NCAB 12:260; Sadie.

Wallace, William Vincent (1812-1865). Composer, 12 November 1857; 11 February 1858.

> The two Miss Gellies sang very charmingly Wallace's duet "We Are Wandering O'er the Mountains," which was repeated (KK, 723).

> We remarked upon last week—the same song having been gracefully sung by Mrs. Brinkerhoff at Mr. Eisfeld's concert, [RR; Willis is referring here to the Wallace song "The Winds That Waft My Sighs to Thee," words by H. W. Challis (New York: William Hall & Son, 1856)]

Baker (1984); Blom; Sadie.

Walter, William H[enry] (1825-1893). Composer, 30 December 1856; 17 April 1857; 21 May 1857. Walter was Secretary of the NYA-MA, and compositions by him were performed on three concerts of the second season. A biography of Walter has not been written and apparently the only allusions to him are found in various writings about New York's Trinity Church and Walter's own publications. The first reference to Walter appeared in 1847, when he published his "Songs of the Flowers" (New York: Van Gelder & Riley), a setting of a Fitz-Greene Halleck poem, followed the next year by "When Through Life Unblest We Rove" (New York: Riley & Co.), a setting of a Thomas Moore poem.

Walter studied organ with Edward Hodges (Messiter, 64. See entry on Hodges above), and was an organist at Trinity Church.

> During the summer of 1850 two young musicians became organists in [Trinity] Parish who afterward attained eminence in their chosen professions; Mr. William H. Walter was appointed to St. Paul's Chapel and Mr. George F. Bristow to St. John's (Dix, 346).

By 17 April 1855, upon the recommendation of Hodges, Walter was appointed permanent organist at the Consecration of Trinity Chapel (25th Street, between Broadway and Sixth Avenue). On that day Hodges's *Consecration Anthem* was performed. On 6 June 1855 Walter was serving as organist at Columbia College.

> Mr. W. H. Walter, we hear with much pleasure, has recently been appointed organist of Columbia College, 49th Street. The duties of his new office will not clash with those devolved upon him at

Trinity Chapel, as the College Chapel is not open for service on Sundays [Walter also cited in FF, 355 as an "Organist at Columbia College"].

Walter and Hodges were known to have exchanged church positions. In a letter from Hodges to W. H. Harrison (probably a Trinity Church vestryman) dated 21 June 1855 (original in the archives of Trinity Church; uncataloged photocopy in the Music Division, New York Public Library for the Performing Arts), Hodges discusses the exchange which lasted "for about two months" (see Messiter, 63) and various dissatisfactions he experienced, including his requests for a raise for himself (Hodges was earning $2000 per annum) and Walter as well: "Mr. Walter cannot possibly afford to work for the church as cheaply as I have done. Do consider this for his family's sake."

On 1 September 1858, Walter took part in a festive occasion at Trinity Chapel:

> ... a grand celebration, civic and national, on the completion of the Atlantic cable ... began with a solemn service at Trinity Church. ... Dr. Walter played the opening voluntary, introducing the national airs "Hail, Columbia" and "God Save the Queen" ... (Messiter, 66-67).

Walter continued as an organist at Trinity Church until at least 1861 while persuing his interests as a "composer and arranger of music for church" (*American Musical Directory*, 99). In 1886, he was cited in his work *Mass in C or Communion Service* as "Mus. Doc" and "Organist of Columbia Chapel."

Walter's publications include, in addition to the works cited above, an Easter anthem titled *Christ Our Passion* (New York: William Hall & Son, 1853); *Selections of Psalms, Together with the Canticles, Occasional Anthems, and Proper Psalms for Certain Days* (New York: Daniel Dana, Jr., 1857); *Manual of Church Music* (New York: D. Appleton, 1860; third edition, New York: S. T. Gordon, 1868); *Carols and Hymns* (New York: Protestant Episcopal Sunday School and Church Book Society, 1862); *Canticle and Chants* (New York: S. T. Gordon, 1863); *O How Amiable* (New York: Beer and Schirmer, 1865); *Introits and Anthems by Modern Composers, Prepared for the Services of the Evangelical Lutheran Church*, edited by Walter (Philadelphia, 1875); *Mass in C or Communion Service* (New York: C. F. Walter, 1886).

> Among the pieces performed was an anthem [*Christ Our Passion?*] by Mr. Wm. H. Walter, the organist of Trinity Chapel. It was a respectable but not very striking composition (O).

> The next concert takes place on the [17th], when several new compositions, among them an elaborate anthem by W. H. Walter, organist of Trinity Chapel, will be produced (Z).

> The chief pieces performed [17 April 1857] were an anthem by W. H. Walter, organist of Trinity Chapel. . . . (BB)

> W. H. Walter is a New Yorker, a pupil of Dr. Hodges, is organist at Trinity Chapel and teaches the organ and harmony. Judging by this "Song" [title?], his ability lies far more in the sacred than the secular style (FF).

Ward, Dr. Thomas (1807-1873). Composer, 11 February 1858. Born into a wealthy family in Newark, New Jersey, and graduating from medical school in New York City in 1829, Ward practiced his profession only two or three years, "devoting the rest of his life to literary pursuits." He had a private theater constructed in his house where he gave theatricals for a paying public, the receipts going to charity. (Information on Ward and the quotation are from his entry in NCAB 10:247.)

> [Dr. Ward's drinking chorus was] badly executed, and . . . we could not form an opinion (OO).

> Not a little interest was felt in the chorus by Dr. Ward. . . . It was so inadequately rendered, from a lack of drill, that one really could form but little idea of its real merits (RR).

Wedermeyer, Mr. Violist?, 17 April 1857.

> The quartet for stringed instruments [by Hommann] was performed excellently by Messers. Reiff, Grosse, Wedermeyer, assisted by an amateur (AA).

Odell, 6, 7, 8:0

Westerfelt, Mrs. [H. L.]. Singer, 11 February 1858. She sang the alto part in the solo quartet section of the Tuckerman anthem "Hide Not Thy Face." AMD, 175. Odell, 6:0; 7:8, 8:0.

Willet, Mr. Singer?, 12 November 1857. The only mention of this name is in an enigmatic sentence in Willis's review of the 12 November 1857 concert: "Mr. Willet brought forward a nocturne in the shape of a pleasing vocal duet" (KK, 723). This could be the music and instrument dealer William E. Millet listed in the *American Musical Directory* (94, 96), or possibly the Emile Millet listed in that source as a professional singer and teacher of singing (176). Odell, 6, 7:0; 8:1 (Kate M. Willet).

Willis, Richard Storrs (1819-1900). Composer, 3 April 1856. Willis was not only a member of NYA-MA's "consulting committee," but also a composer of songs. Two songs were performed on 3 April 1856: "Sleep the Kind Angel" (Boston: Oliver Ditson, 1849) and "Spring Song." The concert was reviewed by Willis, who gracefully praised the singer Annie Kemp and mentioned the accompanist William Dressler. No mention was made of the songs.

Much of the information available on the NYA-MA's concerts is due to Willis's reviews. Baker (1984); Hitchcock.

Wooster, Mr. C. W. Singer, 30 May 1856. This is probably the "George W. Wooster" listed by Odell.

> *Alone* [from Bristow's opera *Rip Van Winkle* was] creditable . . . the performance [by Mr. Wooster] of amateur excellence (K).

Odell, 6:1 and 7:7 (George W. Wooster); 8:0.

---

[1] In the various period reviews and articles concerning the Association, the use of a hyphen between the words "American" and "Music" was haphazard. I have decided to use it consistently in this article. Furthermore, I abbreviate the whole as NYA-MA. A hyphen was consistently used between the words "New" and "York" in the majority of years preceding the twentieth century. I use the modern standard version.

[2] See the anonymous *Musical Courier* article about this group listed in the Bibliography.

[3] American solo piano music fared better. Pianists, not having boards of directors to contend with, played what they wished. A Gottschalk might be "roasted" by the critics for playing mostly his own compositions instead of the "classics" by Bach and Beethoven, for instance, or, say, the then-contemporary music of Chopin, but play them he did—just as Thalberg played largely his own pieces when he came to New York in 1857.

[4] See, for example, the long professorial article "Fry Versus Dwight: American Music's Debate Over Nationality," *American Music* 3/1 (Spring 1985), 63-84, which reads like a pious, idealistic lecture based on secondary opinions.

[5] Letter codes following this and other quotes or bits of information correspond to those used in the section titled "Sources."

[6] According to Delmer Rogers, Bristow helped "organize a new group, the New York American Music Association." "Nineteenth Century Music in New York City as Reflected in the Career of George Frederick Bristow" (Ph.D. diss., University of Michigan, 1967), 87. Of the several writers who have mentioned the Association, Rogers was perhaps the first. His coverage of the group, however, is brief. Further, it should be noted that Rogers' statement that the Association ended in February 1858 (quoting *Dwight's Journal of Music* of 27 February 1858 in a passage that was probably from a press release) is not correct. Actually, after the Association announced its demise in February, they gave a final concert on 30 April 1858.

[7] In his book on William Mason, Kenneth Graber refers to this document as a "manifesto." *William Mason (1829-1908): An Annotated Bibliography and Catalog of Works* (Warren, Mich.: Harmonie Park Press, 1989), 332.

[8] John Henry Hopkins, Jr., *The Life, of the Late Right Reverend John Henry Hopkins, First Bishop of Vermont, and Seventh Presiding Bishop* (New York: Scribner, 1910), 306.

[9] Not that the *Tribune* carried *no* reviews of the NYA-MA's concerts, but they were short and reportorial, like the two-sentence review on 1 January 1857 (N) of the 30 December 1856 concert or the three-sentence review on 3 March 1857 (R) of the 27 February 1857 concert, one that Fry could have reviewed as he surely attended to hear a solo with a chorus from his then-unperformed *Stabat Mater*. The day after this concert the *Tribune* (p. 6) ran a review of a lecture for the Board of Education given the preceding evening by Richard Storrs Willis, Fry's enemy from the *Santa Claus Symphony* affair. Fry would hardly have been interested.

[10] It should be noted, however, that the composer performed most at the NYA-MA concerts was William Mason with seven titles. Hopkins was probably glad to have this well-known young man (with the famous family name) appear and perform some of his popular piano pieces.

[11] *The Edwin A. Fleisher Collection of Orchestral Music in the Free Library of Philadelphia; a Cumulative Catalogue, 1929-1977* (Boston: G. K. Hall, 1979), 413.

[12] *New York Daily Tribune*, 16 February 1856, [1].

[13] John G. Doyle, *Louis Moreau Gottschalk, 1829-1869: A Bibliographical Study and Catalog of Works* (Detroit: Information Coordinators, 1982), 327.

[14] *New York Daily Times*, 3 April 1856; *New York Daily Tribune*, 3 April 1856.

[15] Only two published titles by him are listed in the *National Union Catalog, Pre-1956 Imprints*, one for a song, one for a piano piece.

[16] Billed as "Alone," this was probably Rip's aria at the beginning of Act III, "Alone, all alone in my wide world of sorrow," an excerpt later published separately (New York: Wm. Hall & Son, 1870).

[17] This vocal quartet, *Marco Bozarris*, based on the popular poem of the same title (published 1825) by Fitz-Greene Halleck (1790-1867), is not among Fry's works listed in William Treat Upton's faulty, old-fashioned biography *William Henry Fry: American Journalist and Composer-Critic* (New York: Thomas Y. Crowell, 1954; reprint, New York: Da Capo, 1974), nor is it referred to in the body of the book.

[18] In a "Musical Correspondence" section dated "New York, March 17, 1857," *Dwight's Journal of Music* reported that the NYA-MA "has recently appointed as Conductor Dr. Charles Guilmette, late of the Pyne and Harrison opera troupe, and now a resident of this city" (Y).

[19] There is a bit of confusion regarding another Deems work, *Hymn to the Virgin*, performed on this concert. When it was performed on the earlier concert of 27 February 1857, it was billed as a soprano solo with chorus; at its repeat here on 21 May 1857, it was sung by a female *and* a male soloist with chorus.

[20] A printed program for this second concert exists in the New-York Historical Society. A photocopy is in the Music Division, The New York Public Library for the Performing Arts (class-mark: *MNY-Amer.).

[21] This work, about Ponce de Leon and the search for the Fountain of Youth, ran for two weeks, 13-25 December 1853, at the Broadway Theatre, New York City, Maeder conducting. George C. D. Odell, *Annals of the New York Stage* (New York: Columbia University Press, 1931), 6:200. At least four musical excerpts from it were published in 1852.

[22] *New York Musical World and Times*, 6 November 1858, 706.

SOURCES

In the sources below for background information, only the *New York Musical World and Times*, with one important exception, was drawn upon. The order is chronological. In those for each of the three concert seasons, the two newspapers are always cited before the periodicals. Within each kind of source—advertisement, notice, review—the order is alphabetical and then chronological.

My list may not be exhaustive; there may be other references to the NYA-MA in the newspapers and periodicals I searched, as well as those I did not search.

Background Information

I *New York Musical World and Times* 8/9 (Saturday, 4 March 1854), 100.
II _____ 8/10 (Saturday, 11 March 1854), 110.
III _____ 8/11 (Saturday, 18 March 1854), 121-22.
IV _____ 8/12 (Saturday, 25 March 1854), [133].
V _____ 8/13 (Saturday, 1 April 1854), [145], 148, 153.
VI _____ 8/15 (Saturday, 15 April 1854), 172.
VII _____ 8/16 (Saturday, 22 April 1854), 183-84.
VIII *Dwight's Journal of Music* 10/12 (Saturday, 20 December 1856), 93.

Concert Information

First Season

A *New York Daily Times*, Saturday, 16 February 1856, 4. (Notice/editorial)
B _____, Monday, 18 February 1856, 4. (Review)
C *New York Daily Tribune*, Monday, 18 February 1856, 7. (Review)
D *New York Musical World* 14/256 (Sunday, 23 February 1856), [85]. (Review)
E *New York Daily Tribune*, Wednesday, 2 April 1856, 4. (Notice)
F *New York Daily Times*, Friday, 4 April 1856, 4. (Review)
G *New York Musical World* 14/263 (Saturday, 12 April 1856), [171]. (Review)
H *New York Daily Tribune*, Friday, 30 May 1856, [1]. (Advertisement)
I *New York Daily Times*, Friday, 30 May 1856, 4. (Notice)
J *New York Daily Tribune*, 2 June 1856, 7. (Review)

K   *New York Musical World* 15/271 (Saturday, 7 June 1856), [273]. (Review)

Second Season

L   *New York Daily Times*, Tuesday, 30 December 1856, 6. (Advertisement)
M   *New York Daily Tribune*, Tuesday, 30 December 1856, 2. (Advertisement)
N   _____, Tuesday, 1 January 1857, 6. (Review)
O   *New York Musical World* 17/302 (Saturday, 10 January 1857), 19. (Review)
P   *New York Daily Tribune*, Friday, 27 February 1857, [1]. (Advertisement)
Q   _____, Friday, 27 February 1857, 7. (Notice)
R   _____, Monday, 3 March 1857, 7. (Review)
S   *Dwight's Journal of Music* 10/24 (Saturday, 14 March 1857), 188-89. (Review)
T   *New York Musical Review and Gazette* 8/5 (Saturday, 7 March 1857), 68. (Review)
U   *New York Musical World* 17/310 (Saturday, 7 March 1857), 147-48. (Review)
V   *New York Daily Times*, Friday, 17 April 1857, 3. (Advertisement)
W   *New York Daily Tribune*, Friday, 17 April 1857, [1]. (Advertisement)
X   _____, Friday, 17 April 1857, 8. (Notice)
Y   *Dwight's Journal of Music* 10/25 (Saturday, 21 March 1857), 196. (Notice)
Z   _____, 11/2 (Saturday, 11 April 1857), 12. (Notice)
AA *New York Musical Review and Gazette* 8/9 (Saturday, 2 May 1857), 132. (Review)
BB *New York Musical World* 17/317 (Saturday, 25 April 1857), 259. (Review)
CC _____, 17/321 (Saturday, 23 May 1857), 323. (Notice)
DD *Dwight's Journal of Music* 11/11 (Saturday, 13 June 1857), 84. (Review)
EE *New York Musical Review and Gazette* 8/12 (Saturday, 13 June 1857), 178. (Review)
FF *New York Musical World* 17/323 (Saturday, 6 June 1857), 354-55. (Review)

Third Season

GG   *New York Daily Times*, Thursday, 12 November 1857, 6. (Advertisement)
HH   *New York Daily Tribune*, Thursday, 12 November 1857, 2. (Advertisement)
I I   _____, Thursday, 12 November 1857, 6. (Notice)
JJ   *New York Musical Review and Gazette* 8/24 (Saturday, 28 November 1857), 372.
KK   *New York Musical World* 18/347 (Saturday, 21 November 1857), 722-23. (Review)
LL   *New York Daily Times*, Thursday, 11 February 1858, 6. (Advertisement)
MM   *New York Daily Tribune*, Thursday, 11 February 1858, 7. (Notice)
NN   *New York Daily Times*, 16 February 1858, 5. (Review)
OO   *New York Daily Tribune*, Saturday, 13 February 1858, 5. (Review)
PP   *Dwight's Journal of Music* 12/22 (Saturday, 27 February 1858), 382. (Review)
QQ   *New York Musical Review and Gazette* 9/4 (Saturday, 20 February 1858), 51. (Review)
RR   *New York Musical World* 19/6 (Saturday, 20 February 1858), 116. (Review)
SS   *New York Daily Times*, Friday, 30 April 1858, 3. (Advertisement)
TT   *New York Daily Tribune*, Friday, 30 April 1858, 2. (Advertisement)
UU   *New York Daily Times*, Monday, 3 May 1858, 4. (Review)
VV   *New York Musical Review and Gazette* 9/10 (Saturday, 15 May 1858), 146.
WW   *New York Musical World* 19/19 (Saturday, 8 May 1858), 291. (Review)
XX   Odell, George C. D. *Annals of the New York Stage* 7:100. (Notice)

BIBLIOGRAPHY

"The American Music Society: Its People, Plans and Purposes." *Musical Courier* 57/6 (5 August 1908): 22-23.

The American Musical Directory, 1861. New York: Thomas Hutchinson, 1861. Reprint, New York: Da Capo Press, 1980.

"Anthony Reiff Dies." *New York Times* (7 October 1916): 11.

Baker, Theodore. *Baker's Biographical Dictionary of Musicians.* 7th edition. Revised by Nicolas Slonimsky. New York: Schirmer Books, 1984.

_____. *Biographical Dictionary of Musicians.* 3rd edition. Revised by Alfred Remy. New York: G. Schirmer, 1919.

Bialosky, Marshall. "A Brief History of Composers' Groups in the United States." *College Music Symposium* 20/2 (Fall 1980): [29]-40.

Blom, Eric, ed. *Grove's Dictionary of Music and Musicians.* 5th edition. New York: St. Martin's Press, 1954.

"Death of Richard Hoffman." *Musical Courier* 59/8 (25 August 1909): 15.

Dichter, Harry, and Elliott Shapiro. *Early American Sheet Music: Its Lure and Its Lore, 1768-1889.* New York: R. R. Bowker, 1941.

Dictionary of American Biography. New York: Charles Scribner's Sons, 1928-37.

District of Columbia Historical Records Survey. *Bio-bibliographical Index of Musicians in the United States of America since Colonial Times.* Washington, D.C.: Music Section, Pan American Union, 1941. Reprint, New York: AMS Press, 1972.

Dix, Morgan. *A History of the Parish of Trinity Church in the City of New York.* Vol. 4. New York: G. P. Putnam's Sons, 1906.

Doyle, John G. *Louis Moreau Gottschalk, 1829-1869: A Bibliographical Study and Catalog of Works.* Detroit: Information Coordinators for the College Music Society, 1982.

The Edwin A. Fleisher Collection of Orchestral Music in the Free Library of Philadelphia: A Cumulative Catalog, 1929-1977. Boston: G. K. Hall, 1979.

Elson, Louis C. *The History of American Music*. New York: Macmillan, 1904.

Engel, Carl. "Views and Reviews." *Musical Quarterly* 18/1 (January 1932): 178-83.

Fairley, Andrew. *Flutes, Flautists and Makers (Active or Born Before 1900)*. London: Educational Music, 1982.

"George Washbourne Morgan." *American Art Journal* 59/14 (16 July 1892): 347-48.

Gipson, Richard McCandless. *The Life of Emma Thursby, 1845-1931*. New York: The New-York Historical Society, 1940. Reprint, New York: Da Capo Press, 1980.

Gottschalk, Louis Moreau. *Notes of a Pianist*. Ed. Jeanne Behrend. New York: Knopf, 1964. Reprint, New York: Da Capo, 1979.

Graber, Kenneth. *William Mason (1829-1908): An Annotated Bibliography and Catalog of Works*. Warren, Mich.: Harmonie Park Press for the College Music Society, 1989.

Groce, Nancy. "Musical Instrument Making in New York City During the Eighteenth and Nineteenth Centuries." Ph.D. diss., University of Michigan, 1982. Reprint, under the title *Musical Instrument Makers of New York: A Directory of Eighteenth and Nineteenth Century Urban Craftsmen*, Stuyvesant, N.Y.: Pendragon Press, 1991.

Hipsher, Edward Ellsworth. *American Opera and Its Composers*. Philadelphia: Theodore Presser, 1927. Reprint, New York: Da Capo Press, 1978.

Hitchcock, H. Wiley, and Stanley Sadie, eds. *The New Grove Dictionary of American Music*. 4 vols. New York: Grove's Dictionaries, 1986.

Hodges, Faustina Hasse. *Edward Hodges*. New York: G. P. Putnams Sons, 1896. Reprint, New York: AMS Press, 1970.

Hoffman, Richard. *Some Musical Recollections of Fifty Years; with a Biographical Sketch by His Wife*. New York: Scribner, 1910. Reprint, Detroit: Information Coordinators, 1976.

Hopkins, Jerome. *Music and Snobs; or a Few Funny Facts Regarding the Disabilities of Music in America.* New York: R. A. Saalfield, 1888.

Hopkins, John Henry, Jr. *The Life, of the Late Right Reverend John Henry Hopkins, First Bishop of Vermont, and Seventh Presiding Bishop.* New York: F. J. Huntington, 1873.

Howard, John Tasker. *Our American Music: A Comprehensive History from 1620 to the Present.* New York: Crowell, 1931; 4th ed., 1965.

Hughes, Rupert. *Contemporary American Composers.* Boston: L. C. Page, 1900.

Jackson, Richard. *Democratic Souvenirs: An Anthology of 19th-century American Music.* New York: C. F. Peters for The New York Public Library, 1988.

"Jerome Hopkins." *New York Daily Times* (6 November 1898): 7.

Johnson, H. Earle. "Gustave Satter, Eccentric." *Journal of the American Musicological Society* 16/1 (Spring 1963): 61-73.

Jones, F. O. *Handbook of American Music and Musicians, Containing Biographies of American Musicians and Histories of the Principal Musical Institutions, Firms, and Societies.* Canaseraga, N.Y.: F. O. Jones, 1886. Reprint, New York: Da Capo Press, 1971.

Krehbiel, Henry Edward. *The Philharmonic Society of New York: A Memorial.* New York: Ewer, 1892.

Lawrence, Vera B. *Strong on Music: The New York Music Scene in the Days of George Templeton Strong.* Vol. 1: *Resonances, 1836-1850.* New York: Oxford University Press, 1988.

Love, Harold. *The Golden Age of Australian Opera: W. W. Lyster and His Companies, 1861-1880.* Sydney: Currency Press, 1981.

Lowens, Irving. "The Library of Congress and Gustave Satter: A Cautionary Tale." *Journal of the American Musicological Society* 18/1 (Spring 1965): 73-77.

McCarthy, S. Margaret. "Amy Fay: The American Years." *American Music* 3/1 (Spring 1985): 52-62.

Mathews, William S. B., ed. *One Hundred Years of Music in America: An Account of Musical Effort in America During the Past Century.* Chicago: Howe, 1889.

Messiter, A. H. *A History of the Choir and Music of Trinity Church, New York, from Its Organization to the Year 1897.* New York: Edwin S. Gorham, 1906. Reprint, New York: AMS Press, 1970.

Metcalf, Frank J. *American Writers and Compilers of Sacred Music.* New York: The Abingdon Press, 1925. Reprint, New York: Russell & Russell, 1967.

Moore, John W. *A Dictionary of Musical Information.* Boston: Oliver Ditson & Co., 1876.

Morehouse, Clifford P. *Trinity: Mother of Churches.* New York: Seabury Press, 1973.

The National Cyclopedia of American Biography. New York: J. T. White, 1893-1948. Reprint, Ann Arbor, Mich.: University Microfilms, 1967-71.

The National Union Catalogue, Pre-1956 Imprints. London: Mansell Information Publishing, 1968-81.

Odell, George C. D. *Annals of the New York Stage.* Vol. 6 (1850-57); vol. 7 (1857-65); vol. 8 (1865-70). New York: Columbia University Press, 1927-49. Reprint, New York: AMS Press, 1970.

Pratt, Waldo Seldon, ed. *Grove's Dictionary of Music and Musicians. American Supplement.* New York: The Macmillan Co., 1935.

Redway, Virginia Larkin. *Music Directory of Early New York City.* New York: The New York Public Library, 1941.

Rogers, Delmer Dalzell. "Nineteenth Century Music in New York City as Reflected in the Career of George Frederick Bristow." Ph.D. diss., University of Michigan, 1967.

Sadie, Stanley, ed. *The New Grove Dictionary of Music and Musicians.* 20 vols. London: Macmillan, 1980.

Shanet, Howard. *Philharmonic: A History of New York's Orchestra.* New York: Doubleday, 1975.

Slonimsky, Nicolas. *A Thing or Two About Music.* New York: Allen, Towne & Heath, 1948. Reprint, Westport, Conn.: Greenwood Press, 1972.

Spillane, Daniel. *History of the American Pianoforte.* New York: the author, 1890. Reprint, New York: Da Capo Press, 1969.

Stewart, William Rhinelander. *Grace Church and Old New York.* New York: E. P. Dutton, 1924.

Thoms, William M. "Passing of W. K. Bassford, American Composer." *American Art Journal* 81/15 (Saturday, 10 January 1903): 226-27.

Upton, William Treat. *Art-Song in America: A Study in the Development of American Music.* Boston: Oliver Ditson, 1930. Reprint, New York: Johnson Reprint Co., 1969.

Wielich, Ludwig. "Philharmonic's Early Days." *Opera Magazine* 1/2 (February 1914): 26-28.

Wolfe, Richard J. *Secular Music in America, 1801-1825: A Bibliography.* 3 vols. New York: The New York Public Library, 1964.

THE BEGINNINGS OF BACH IN AMERICA
J. Bunker Clark

This country began its life as a colony of England.[1] After the Declaration of Independence in 1776, it continued as a cultural colony of England for many years. Even though there were important settlements of Germans in some areas, the artistic leadership in the United States remained the larger east coast cities—notably Boston, New York, Baltimore, Philadelphia, and Charleston—where could be purchased the latest fashions in clothing, books, art, and sheet music, imported from London. And it was to these cities that professional musicians came—also mainly from London—to further their careers. Therefore, until well into the nineteenth century, our musical taste largely paralleled that of our mother country.

So it is that American music publishers of secular music, beginning in the late 1780s, followed English taste. And most of their publications consisted of reprints or new editions of keyboard music and songs issued by London publishers of the time. Even when our own immigrant professional composers performed and published songs and piano music, it was based on the same English taste. Such names as James Hewitt, Benjamin Carr, Rayner Taylor, and Alexander Reinagle had first received their training and had their first professional successes in London.

Johann Sebastian Bach was almost unknown to the English musical public, as was the case in the United States. Such was not true, however, of Handel. It is well known that Handel captured the musical public of England during his lifetime, and some say that England has never recovered from Handel's impact ever since, to the present day. Handel was equally well known to American colonial audiences, and his music appeared frequently in early American publications. The bibliography of published secular music in the United States to 1800 by Oscar Sonneck lists five works of Handel, including two from *Water Music* and one air from *Acis and Galatea*.[2] Haydn, who made two extended trips to England in the 1790s, is even better represented with seventeen items, including a piano arrangement of the "celebrated Andante" from the Surprise Symphony.[3] The bibliography by Richard Wolfe of secular music published in the first quarter of the nineteenth century has no fewer than fifty-six Handel items, and Haydn is up to eighty.[4]

In comparison, there are three works by Bach published through 1800—but this is the "London" Bach, Johann (John) Christian. He rises to nine for the period 1801-25. The number of American publications for his father, in the whole period through 1825, remains exactly zero. John Rowe Parker's *A Musical Biography: or Sketches of the Lives and Writings of Eminent Musical Characters* (1825)[5] brought together significant aspects of popularly known composers, including Handel, Haydn, Mozart, Purcell, Arne, Beethoven, Clementi, and Rossini. But there was no mention of Bach—either of Leipzig or of London.

An account of musical tastes in one of the major east coast cities, Philadelphia, will illustrate the absence of Bach from the musical scene. Louis Madeira gives some information in his 1896 book on music in Philadelphia and the Musical Fund Society to 1858.[6] Philadelphia, of course, was well-populated with Germans. One of the post-war events occurred on 4 May 1786: a grand concert at the Reformed German Church. Yet it included no German music—instead, Handel's "Hallelujah Chorus" and an anthem by American-born William Billings. Another concert on 29 May 1787 had a piano sonata (unspecified) by Haydn, and this was even before Haydn had gone to London. After the turn of the century, in 1801, there was a choral concert, with orchestra, at the University of Pennsylvania that included excerpts from both *Messiah* and Haydn's *Creation*. Among the professional immigrants, with the English Carr, Taylor, and Reinagle, was the German Charles Hupfeld (Hupfield, Huffeldt, Huffield), who arrived at the age of fourteen in Philadelphia that same year. He was to be a major force in the promotion of orchestra and chamber music from about 1815, but obviously he had no knowledge of Johann Sebastian Bach to spread. Perhaps the only professional American musician to have heard of and probably knew at least some details about J. S. Bach was Alexander Reinagle. He had met and subsequently corresponded with Carl Philipp Emanuel Bach in 1785, just before he emigrated to the United States in 1786.[7]

A number of musical societies was founded in Philadelphia in its post-war years. The Urania Society was devoted to the promotion of church music beginning in 1787 until after 1800; there was a Harmonic Society beginning in 1802; a Haydn Society founded the year of the composer's death, 1809; a Handelian Society by 1815; and a St. Cecilia Society in 1824. But no Bach Society. The Musical Fund Society, modeled after a London organization of the same name, was founded in 1820 by eighty-five distinguished citizens and musicians, with a twofold purpose: "reform the state of neglect into which the beautiful art of music had fallen" and for the "provision of a fund for relieving decayed musicians." At its first concert on 24 April 1821 there were works by Romberg, Sale, Gilles, Danby, Rode, Bishop, Clarke, Mehul, and even the *Tancredi* overture by Rossini and Beethoven's Symphony in C. But no Bach. The third concert on 10 June 1822 had Haydn's *Creation*; one in April included Mozart's overture to *Figaro*. For the opening of its own hall on 29 December 1824 was performed Handel's *Dettingen Te Deum*. A document of that year mentions Bach, but that he is in the same phrase as Abel indicates that this is again the London, not the Leipzig, Bach. In short, even as late as 1858 (Madeira's cutoff date) J. S. Bach was apparently unknown in Philadelphia.

Boston is a little better, but not by much. There was an important German name, Johann Christian Gottlieb Graupner, born in Hanover. But before he came to the United States, specifically Charleston, Norfolk, Salem, and New York, before settling in Boston in 1798, he played in the London orchestra (as did James Hewitt) under the direction of Haydn for the introduction of the "London" symphonies in 1791. Graupner, in Boston, was also a publisher, and in 1806 he issued a pianoforte tutor, *Rudiments of the Art of Playing on the Piano Forte*. The book has not only instructions on how to play the piano, but also short examples of pieces for the student. Some of the composers are the usual, reflecting taste at the time: Handel (air from *Atalanta*), Pleyel, Hook, Scarlatti, Haydn, and even a gavotte by Corelli. The miracle is the last piece: "Polonoise," by "Sebastian Bach." It is from the first French Suite in E major. Graupner was no creative tastemaker, however: this is one of the pieces he lifted from Clementi's *Introduction to the Art of Playing on the Piano Forte*, first published in London in 1801. Indeed, most of Graupner's instructions, along with some of the pieces, are pirated from Clementi's book. Nonetheless, Graupner has the honor of publishing the first work of J. S. Bach in the United States.

Like Philadelphia, Boston had its share of musical societies. Its most important one is not named the Bach and Haydn Society, but instead the Handel and Haydn Society. Founded in 1815, it gave its first concert Christmas night that year. Among the founding members was the same Graupner. In 1817 it gave performances of Handel's *Messiah* and Haydn's *Creation*. A minuet by Beethoven was performed in Boston as early as September 1818, by the Philharmonic Society, which had been founded in 1810 (Graupner, a double bass player, also was involved), and Sophia Hewitt, daughter of James Hewitt, is credited with the first public performance in the United States of a Beethoven piano sonata (op. 26) on 27 February 1819. Mendelssohn's oratorios were included in the 1840s—*St. Paul* in 1843 and *Elijah* in 1848.

Not until 1871, however, was any of Bach's oratorio music heard in Boston. On 13 May 1871 the Handel and Haydn Society presented selections from the *St. Matthew Passion*.[8] The entire work was heard on 11 April 1879. On 11 November 1883 the Society did the cantata *Ein feste Burg*, here entitled "A Stronghold Sure," and on 27 February 1887 half of the Mass in B minor.[9]

This information on nineteenth-century music in Boston is largely derived from several books by H. Earle Johnson.[10] His last book, *First Performances in America*,[11] is the most useful concerning Bach's major choral and orchestra works. It seems that the major figure behind the introduction of orchestral works of Bach to the United States was the conductor Theodore Thomas.[12] Born in Germany, he came to the United States as a ten-year-old in 1845. Thomas began his conducting career in 1859 and emphasized the music of those we now consider German classics, especially Beethoven, Schumann, Liszt, and Wagner. He even organized his own orchestra, the Theodore Thomas Orchestra, in 1869, which toured extensively over the "Thomas Highway" in the United States and Canada. Thomas also directed the first Cincinnati May Festival in 1873 and continued this function until his death. He was named conductor of the New York Philharmonic Orchestra in 1877-91, then created the Chicago Symphony Orchestra, and Orchestra Hall was opened for it in December 1904, a few weeks before Thomas's death in 1905.

Along with the German classics already named, Thomas was a champion of then little-known J. S. Bach. Of 36 works for orchestra introduced to American audiences, Thomas premièred no fewer than twelve—more than any other conductor. (See appendix, below.) Thomas was only the most prolific; others conducting American premières of Bach included such German-American conductors or soloists as Walter and Leopold Damrosch (2 each), Hans von Bülow, Carl Zerrahn (3), Benjamin J. Lang (3), and Anton Seidl (1).

The introduction of Bach chorale settings to the United States was subtle, but the individual deserving credit is A. N. Johnson (1817-1892), whose musical career began as a protégé of Lowell Mason in the fields of public school and church music in 1838-39. Johnson may have first encountered Bach's music when studying in Frankfurt am Main with the Swiss composer Xaver Schnyder von Wartensee in 1842-43; he had sung Bach in the Cäcilien-Verein there. In 1849, Johnson became alienated from Mason (until then Mason's lecturer in thorough-bass and harmony for the annual music convention sponsored by the Boston Academy of Music, 1844-48) in part because he knew of Mason's plagiarism, in his 1834 *Manual of the Boston Academy of Music for Instruction in the Elements of Vocal Music on the System of Pestalozzi*, of G. F. Kübler's 1826 book on Pestalozzi. In 1853 Johnson also earned the enmity of John Sullivan Dwight, editor of *Dwight's Journal of Music*, for countering Dwight's attacks on "native Americanism."[13]

Nonetheless, Johnson was the first to introduce Bach chorales to America, in his *Instructions in Thorough Base: Being a New and Easy Method for Learning to Play Church Music upon the Piano Forte or Organ* (Boston, 1844; later eds. to 1894)[14] — sixteen "German chorals," as he simply designated them — even though he included neither titles nor that they were settings by Bach.[15] With his brother James Jr., A. N. Johnson founded a journal *The Musical Gazette* (sometimes titled *Boston Musical Gazette*) in 1846, which in its first volume includes articles about Bach, mostly excerpted from the 1802 biography by Johann Nikolaus Forkel, as translated to English in 1820.[16] The complete Forkel biography, from the same 1820 translation, was later printed serially in *Dwight's Journal of Music*.[17] But probably because of the split with Dwight, Johnson's early advocacy of Bach was not acknowledged in the article "Bach's Chorals" in *Dwight's Journal*, 13 September 1856.[18]

The American musician important for the spread of Bach's organ music was John Knowles Paine (1839-1906). In 1858 Paine sailed for Berlin (in the company of Alexander Wheelock Thayer, who was returning to continue work on his pioneer Beethoven biography). Paine's principal teacher in organ, composition, and counterpoint was Karl August Haupt, who, not only the outstanding organ virtuoso of his time, was also, according to Paine's biographer John Schmidt, "an enthusiastic disciple of Bach — in whose style he improvised variations on the organ — and he instilled this enthusiasm in his students."[19] Paine's Prelude and Fugue in G minor, composed the following year in Berlin, was closely modeled after Bach.[20] After three years, Paine returned to the United States. According to an article in the *Boston Musical Times*,

> Mr. Paine plays with remarkable clearness and vigor, and his pedal playing is most admirable. Bach's fugues were given with a rare power we have not heard excelled, and a trio sonata of the same composer, in which two manuals and the pedals are simultaneously employed, was played with a clearness and individuality of parts, and at the same time so elegantly interwoven and shaped into a perfect whole, as to at once indicate the talent of the performer, as well as the lofty genius of the composer. . . . [Paine] is a devoted worshiper of . . . Johann Sebastian Bach. He revels in the wealth of the life-long labor of the illustrious master. He would have the world love Bach as he loves him, and he sincerely believes that the world has only to know him as he knows him to love him equally as well. He is a missionary of Bach, and Bach has no more enthusiastic a worshiper, nor so admirable an interpreter in the United or Disunited States of America.[21]

Paine left Portland, Maine, his home, shortly thereafter, and took a position as organist at West Church in Boston in November 1861.[22] In 1862, at the age of 23, he accepted an offer to be teacher of sacred music, director of music, and organist at Harvard—albeit not with academic status. The impact of Bach on Harvard began with the first private hearing of the new pipe organ, made by the German firm of E. F. Walcker, at Harvard's Music Hall on 31 October 1863. Paine was one of the organists for the occasion, and he played Bach's Toccata in D minor. For the public inauguration two days later, Paine played Bach's Grand Toccata in F[23] and the E-flat Trio Sonata, followed by Eugene Thayer (of Worcester) performing Bach's Grand Fugue in G minor. (The second half of the program, reflecting traditional English and American taste, began with two choruses from Handel's *Israel in Egypt* and ended with the "Hallelujah Chorus.")

The pattern of spreading the gospel of Bach was thus established at Harvard. In succeeding concerts on this organ in 1864, Paine played fourteen works of Bach (see appendix for a list[24]), closely followed in number by ten of his own. That was the year he was given a regular faculty appointment. Two years later, in 1866, his student George L. Osgood prepared one of the commencement speeches, with the title "Thesis: Condition of the Appreciation of the Music of Sebastian Bach."[25] Highlights of Paine's subsequent career at Harvard were his appointment as assistant professor in 1873, and his promotion two years later as the first full professor of music at Harvard.[26]

Paine's reputation as advocate of Bach is reflected in this piece in *Dwight's Journal* of 7 June 1865:[27]

> THE QUESTION SETTLED! A certain "Aylmer" writes a musical letter to the *Springfield Republican*, about the late "Choral Festival" in New York, in which he tilts against the windmill of Bach's Fugues, with such annihilating vehemence, that the opinion of Mozart and Mendelssohn, and all the really great composers, not excepting jovial Rossini, must henceforth pass for nothing. Read! Master Paine, and tremble, and be silent evermore:
>
> Mr. C. J. Hopkins gave the Toccata in F, which has claimed an ex-officio place upon many of the programmes of the Boston Music Hall, and—shades of Bach, forgive—it was, as usual with fugues, a chaos of sound and fury, signifying nothing. It is all very well to talk of the fugue as classical. Is it any more classical than the chromatic scale? And is there any music in the chromatic scale itself? If any disciple of Bach can tell what the fugue means, he will seem to many to hold a more reasonable position after he has interpreted it, than while he rails at the multitude for their lack of

appreciation.

Read, Master Dresel, and forsaking the wrong way, humbly crave permission to sit at the feet of Master Gamaliel Gottschalk! As for you, Master Robert Franz, what can you do but leave editing of Bach, and devote the rest of your life to pious meditation on the operas of Verdi, or the pretty Offertoires of Batiste; or come over here and fatten on the broad fields and pastures green of Yankee psalmody? Peradventure, in due time, you may become sleek and prosperous enough to exchange the German Doctorate for a fresh "Mus. Doc." from some New York University.

Indeed, Otto Dresel, who emigrated from Germany to settle in Boston in 1852, seems to have been important in making Bach's harpsichord (piano) works better known in the United States—at least in Boston.[28] Dresel was involved with several performances of Bach's Concerto for "3 pianos," as reported in *Dwight's Journal* for 5 March 1853 (played by Dresel, Alfred Jaëll, and William Scharfenburg, in Boston), 28 January 1854 (Dresel, J. Trenkle, and Carl Bergmann, with the Germania Orchestra, Boston).[29] The issues of 14 and 21 March 1857 announce the publication in Wolfenbüttel of Chrysander's edition of Bach's piano works, presumably available in American music shops. *Dwight's Journal*, 22 July 1865,[30] describes Dresel's thirteen piano concerts of the previous season, in which the following works by "T. S. BACH" [*sic*] are listed:

Concerto for three pianos in C major, accompaniments
  arranged by Mr. Dresel for a fourth, (Messrs. Dresel, Leonhard,
  Lang and Parker), twice given.
Concerto for three pianos, in D minor (as above).
Gavotte, from Orchestral *Suite* (arranged by Mr. D. for two pianos).
Pastoral Symphony, arranged (as above) from the Christmas
  Oratorio. Twice.
Sarabande and Rondo, from *Partita* in C minor.
Fugue, in C minor, ("Well-tempered Clavichord," Part I. No. 2).
Prelude and Fugue, C-sharp minor, (Do. I. 4.)
Prelude and Fugue, F minor, (Do. II. 12).
Organ Prelude and Fugue in A minor.
Fugue, in C-sharp major, (Well-temp. Cl. I. 3).
Prelude, in E-flat minor, and Fugue in G-sharp minor.

The important American pianist and composer William Mason (1829-1908) played Bach even earlier; at the age of seventeen or eighteen,

his father [Lowell Mason] suggested that he learn Bach's Fugue in

F-sharp major and offered him a grand piano if he did so. This task William soon accomplished. It is said that the only other musician in America who could play this piece without his notes, was Stephen Henry Cutler [Henry Stephen Cutler], then organist of Trinity Church.[31]

Mason also did his share of playing Bach later in his career: for example, the Triple Concerto in D minor on 25 April 1873, with Anton Rubinstein and Sebastian Bach Mills; on 19 May 1877, with Anna Essipoff and F. Boscovitz; and 5 January 1878, with the Theodore Thomas Orchestra and pianists Richard Hoffman and Ferdinand Dulcken—all at Steinway Hall, New York City. Mason also prepared several editions of Bach's works, including an 1894 edition of the Inventions, published by G. Schirmer.[32]

The publication of Bach's music became more important after mid-century. The *Complete Catalogue of Sheet Music and Musical Works, 1870*,[33] a collected listing of available scores by the principal publishers, includes the following (of which the first two are in the category of songs; the others listed under "Rondos, Fantasies, Variations, &c."):

Herald comes, behold (song; Boston: Oliver Ditson)
Mein gläubiges Herz/My heart ever faithful (Boston: Oliver Ditson)
Allegro from Italian Concerto (Chicago: Root & Cady)
Gavotte, D minor (Boston: Oliver Ditson; Boston: G. D. Russell)
Gavotte, G minor (Boston: G. D. Russell)
Gavotte from second violin sonata, B minor (Boston: G. D. Russell)
Saraband and Burlesca (Boston: G. D. Russell)
Saraband and rondo (Chicago: Root & Cady)
Saraband and scherzo (Boston: G. D. Russell)
Saraband passepied and air (Boston: G. D. Russell)
Piano pieces (Chicago: Root & Cady):
    No. 1. Prelude, G minor
    No. 2. Sarabande and rondo, E-flat [same as above]
    No. 3. Symphony, G minor
    No. 4. Allegro from Italian Concerto, F [same as above]

In the section "Piano Studies and Exercises," the *Wohltempierte Clavier* appears as for sale by Oliver Ditson of Boston, available in separate volumes or complete, as well as the Fifteen Inventions. G. D. Russell, also of Boston, separately published fifteen of the preludes from the "Well-Tempered Clavichord."[34]

Ditson's edition of *Das wohltemperirte Clavier* first appeared in 1850, and six years later its edition of Bach's chorale settings.[35] It also issued the

Passion Music, According to the Gospel of St. Matthew, with text in German and English, in 1869, the year the Handel and Haydn Society took it up in earnest.[36] The international firm of C. F. Peters published *Johann Sebastian Bach's Kompositionen für die Orgel*, edited by Friedrich Conrad Griepenkerl and Ferdinand Roitzsch, in New York in 1852. (A complete listing of nineteenth-century American publications of Bach remains to be compiled.)

The most important impetus to the performance of Bach's choral works in the United States was provided by an American Moravian, J. Fred Wolle.[37] His great-great grandfather Matthias Weiss came to Bethlehem, Pennsylvania, in 1743—in the second group of Moravians to settle that important Moravian community. Weiss's son John George Weiss was likewise a musician: church organist, violinist of the Collegium Musicum, and teacher of music in the boys' school. His daughter married Francis Wolle, a Moravian clergyman, a botanist and inventor of the first machine to manufacture paper bags. Our subject, John Frederick Wolle, born in Bethlehem in 1863, was fortunate in being able to travel to Munich in 1884 to study at the Royal Conservatory and with its director Josef Rheinberger. Wolle's interest in Bach, however, had begun as an organ student of David Wood, blind organist of Philadelphia, in 1883-84, and only intensified with his studies under Rheinberger. Especially impressive to the young student was a performance of the *St. John Passion* in Munich in spring 1885. When Wolle returned to Pennsylvania, he became organist at the Moravian Church in Bethlehem, and in 1887-1905 of Lehigh University.

Wolle's career as conductor had begun as early as 1882 (before his trip abroad), when he organized a chorus of girls, and the following year when he organized the Bethlehem Choral Union. When Wolle came back, with the Munich performance of the *St. John Passion* in mind, he guided his Choral Union in the first complete performance of the same work in the U.S., on 5 June 1888. The next was of the *St. Matthew Passion*, 8 April 1892.[38] Thereafter, Wolle proposed to the Bethlehem Choral Union that they perform the B-minor Mass. The difficulties of the work, however, were overwhelming to the singers. Yet Wolle insisted the whole work be done— or nothing. He failed, and the Bethlehem Choral Union went out of existence in 1892. Nevertheless, Wolle was able to organize a performance of parts of Bach's *Christmas Oratorio*, with his Moravian Church Choir, on 18 December 1894.

Yet the seeds were sown. With the organizational enthusiasm of Wolle and others, a call for a new organization, the Bethlehem Bach Choir, was given in September 1899. Rehearsals began that winter, and the first Bach Festival planned for spring. So on 27 March 1900, at the Moravian Church, the complete B-minor Mass was given for the first time in the United States: at 4 p.m. the Kyrie and Gloria, and beginning at 8 that evening the rest. The chorus of eighty was accompanied by an orchestra of thirty, and Wolle conducted from the organ. Other Bach works followed; for example, the complete *Christmas Oratorio* was heard in the festival of 1901, for the first time in this country.

A. N. Johnson for publishing chorale settings and articles, Oliver Ditson as music publisher, John S. Dwight for further attention in his journal, Theodore Thomas for orchestra music, John Knowles Paine for organ music, J. Fred Wolle for choral music. Thus began a tradition of Bach publication and performance, which continues to this day.

Indeed, Bach now seems to have risen above Handel in importance, reversing the situation in the early years of this country. At my own university, for Bach's 300th birthday, 21 March 1985, I participated in a faculty concert with varying chamber groups and choir on campus, at the same hour that there was a faculty organ recital of Bach downtown. Two days later, the local organists organized a Bach marathon. In contrast, on Handel's birthday on 23 February, the only local event I'm aware of was at a party, of non-musicians, I attended. I interrupted the festivities when I proposed a toast to George Frideric's 300th birthday. With this commemoration, lasting some ten seconds, the party continued with unrelated conversation. So much for Handel. At least he's always been with us. Bach has finally come into his own.

APPENDIX

Bach Premières by Theodore Thomas

1865	Organ Toccata in F, arr., New York Symphony
	Organ Passacaglia in C minor, arr., Thomas Symphony Soirée, New York
1867	Suite in D, Thomas Symphony Soirée, New York
1869	Motet *Ich lasse dich nicht*, by Johann Christian Bach (then thought to be by J. S. Bach), New York
1874	Brandenburg Concerto 3, Thomas Orchestra, New York
	Suite 2 in B minor, Thomas Orchestra, Boston
1875	Concerto for 2 violins in D minor, Thomas Orchestra, Philadelphia
	Magnificat in D, Cincinnati May Festival
1876	Suite 1 in C, Thomas Orchestra, New York
1880	Prelude, Adagio, Gavotte, Rondo, arr., Brooklyn Philharmonic
1882	Cantata 11, *Lobet Gott in seinen Reichen*, May Festival, Chicago

1886   Mass in B minor (11 selections), Cincinnati May Festival
1887   Organ Fugue in A minor, arr., Thomas Orchestra, New York

Organ Works Performed by John Knowles Paine, 1864

Prelude in E-flat, BWV 551
Prelude and Fugue in G (probably BWV 541)
Prelude in C
Toccata and Fugue in D minor, BWV 565
Toccata in F, BWV 540
Passacaglia in C minor, BWV 582
Pastorale, BWV 590
Trio Sonata in C minor, BWV 526
Canzona in D minor, BWV 588
Schmücke dich, BWV 654
Aus tiefer Not, BWV 686
O Mensch bewein' dein' Sünde gross, BWV 622
An Wasserflussen Babylon, BWV 653
Christ, unser Herr, zum Jordan kam, BWV 684

---

[1] This article originated as a paper given on 10 May 1986 to the Midwest Chapter of the American Musicological Society, University of South Dakota, Vermillion.

[2] Oscar George Sonneck, *A Bibliography of Early Secular American Music (18th Century)*, rev. and enlarged by William Treat Upton (Washington, D.C.: Library of Congress Music Division, 1945; reprint, New York: Da Capo, 1964), 509.

[3] Ibid.

[4] Richard J. Wolfe, *Secular Music in America, 1801-1825: A Bibliography*, 3 vols. (New York: New York Public Library, 1964), nos. 3331-3386, 3478-3557.

[5] (Boston: Stone & Fovell, 1825; reprint, Detroit: Information Coordinators, 1975). J. S. Bach's name, however, was mentioned in another publication that same year. *A Universal Dictionary* (New York, 1825) describes him as "an eminent German musician. . . ." For this information I am indebted to Karl Kroeger, "Johann Sebastian Bach in Nineteenth-Century America," *Bach* 22/1 (Spring-Summer 1991): 34 n. 3. This article, originating as a lecture given 11 March 1988, is recommended

for those wishing more information on Bach in America.

[6]Louis Madeira, *Annals of Music in Philadelphia and History of the Musical Fund Society from Its Organization in 1820 to the Year 1858* (Philadelphia: J. B. Lippincott, 1896; reprint, New York: Da Capo, 1973).

[7]Oscar G. Sonneck, "Zwei Briefe C. Ph. Em. Bachs an Alexander Reinagle," *Sammelbände der international Musikgesellschaft* 8 (1906-07): 112-14.

[8]Its first American publication had been only two years earlier, in Boston, by Oliver Ditson, with English translation by John Sullivan Dwight. A facsimile of this piano-vocal score's title page is in Roger L. Hall, "Early Performances of Bach and Handel in America," *Journal of Church Music* 27/5 (May 1985): 7. The performance was previewed, then reviewed, in *Dwight's Journal of Music* 31, no. 3 (6 May 1871) through no. 9 (29 July).

[9]All of these dates, except the last, are represented in the pages of *Dwight's Journal of Music*, 41 vols., 1852-81 (reprint, New York: Arno Press, 1967), edited and published in Boston by John Sullivan Dwight. See the comprehensive index by Richard Kitson, *Dwight's Journal of Music, 1852-1881*, 6 vols., Répertoire International de la Presse Musicale (Ann Arbor: UMI, 1991), specifically vol. 4, pp. 952-55. Most of the Bach items are reprints of articles originating abroad, or concern concerts there. Bach reached his summit in *Dwight's* in 1879. First, for the issue of 1 March, an article "Bach-Biting" appeared, written by "W.F.A.," concerning the inability of uneducated listeners to appreciate Bach's music; and on 29 March an account was given concerning a concert marking Bach's birthday the previous 21 March.

[10]H. Earle Johnson, *Musical Interludes in Boston, 1795-1830* (New York: Columbia University Press, 1943; reprint, New York: AMS Press, 1967); *Hallelujah, Amen!: The Story of the Handel and Haydn Society of Boston* (Boston: Bruce Humphries, 1965; reprint, New York: Da Capo, 1981).

[11]H. Earle Johnson, *First Performances in America: Works with Orchestra*, Bibliographies in American Music, 4 (Detroit: Information Coordinators, 1979).

[12]The latest biography on Thomas is Ezra Schabas, *Theodore Thomas: America's Conductor and Builder of Orchestras, 1835-1905* (Urbana: University of Illinois Press, 1989).

[13]For further information, see Jacklin Bolton Stopp, "A. N. Johnson, Out of Oblivion," *American Music* 3/2 (Summer 1983): 152-70, and "Johnson versus Mason: Musical Politics, 1843 Style," *Quarterly Journal of Music Teaching and Learning* 3/3 (Fall 1992): 54-60.

[14]My thanks to Jacklin Bolton Stopp for loaning me her copy of the 1871

edition, and for ensuring the accuracy of this account. Bach's chorale settings are on pp. 43-45 and 68-71 of the 1844 publication. Dr. Stopp is writing a book on her favorite subject, with the working title *More Than a Footnote: The Musical Career of A. N. Johnson*. She concludes that Johnson, in *Instructions in Thorough Base*, identified the sixteen settings only as "German chorals" not only because Bach was little-known to Americans, but also because he wanted his publication to succeed without trading on any foreign name. The only earlier American book on thorough bass was Johnson's former student Isaac Baker Woodbury, *The Elements of Musical Composition and Thorough Base* (1843), which includes, and acknowledges, translated writings by the German theorist Friedrich Schneider.

[15] The chorale at the top of p. 58, for example, is Bach's setting of "Du Lebensfürst, Herr Jesu Christ," BWV 248/12, which sometimes has the text "Ermuntre dich, mein schwachen Geist"; this chorale is illustrated in the section "Johnson's Advocacy of Bach" in the introduction by Jacklin Bolton Stopp to H. S. Cutler and A. N. Johnson, *American Church Organ Voluntaries* (New York, 1852; reprint, Richmond, Va.: Organ Historical Society, 1987), x-xi.

[16] (London: T. Boosey & Co., 1820). The translation, perhaps by A. C. F. Kollmann, is available in Hans T. David and Arthur Mendel, eds., *The Bach Reader*, rev. ed. (New York: Norton, 1966), 293-356. Specifically, the articles are: "John Sebastian Bach" (family background and marriages, from chapter 1, credited to "*Forkel's life of John Sebastian Bach*"), no. 2 (16 February): 10-11; "Anecdote of Sebastian Bach" (a shorter account of the Potsdam visit, from Forkel's chapter 2 of "*—Life of Bach*"), and "Bach's Organ Playing" (from chapter 4), no. 3 (2 March): 21; "J. S. Bach, as a Teacher" (from chapter 7), no. 4 (16 March): 28-29; "Bach as a Citizen" (from chapter 8), no. 5 (30 March): 37; "Bach's Works" (adapted from Forkel's chapter 9), no. 7 (27 April): 53-54; "Handel and Bach" (not from Forkel), no. 14 (3 August): 109-10; "John Sebastian Bach" (an account of his visit to Potsdam, from Forkel's chapter 1, acknowledged as taken from the [London] *Musical World*), no. 20 (26 October): 153-54; "John Sebastian Bach" (a more detailed account of his travel to Lübeck to study with "Dieteisch" Buxtehude than in Forkel), no. 24 (21 December): 185-87. My thanks to James R. Heintze for obtaining copies of these articles at the Library of Congress, after I had tried unsuccessfully for several years to find this journal by correspondence and interlibrary loan. The index to the journal also includes the article "Bach's System of Fingering," but it does not appear in the Library of Congress copy on the specified p. 2.

[17] Vol. 8, no. 4 (27 October 1855) through no. 16 (19 January 1856).

[18]An earlier, unrelated, *Boston Musical Gazette* 1/16 (28 November 1838): 128, included this short paragraph:

> *Modesty of John Sebastian Bach.*—John Sebastian united with his distinguished talents and science as singular and praiseworthy a modesty. Being one day asked how he had contrived to make himself so great an organist, he answered, "I was industrious; whoever is equally sedulous, will be equally successful." One of his pupils complaining that the exercise he had set for him was too difficult, he smiled and said, "Only practice diligently, and you will play it extremely well; you have full as good fingers on each hand as I have; and nature has given me no endowments that she has not freely bestowed upon you. Judging by myself application is every thing."

This same anecdote was also printed earlier the same year in New York's *Musical Review* 1/8 (27 June 1838): 93. (Both were kindly supplied by James R. Heintze.) For an earlier American notice of Bach, dated 1825, see note 5, above.

[19]John C. Schmidt, *The Life and Works of John Knowles Paine*, Studies in Musicology, 34 (Ann Arbor: UMI Research Press, 1980), 36.

[20]There is also a clear influence of Bach on Paine's Mass in D, published in 1866, especially the Gloria (the whole recorded on New World NW 262-263 and compact disc 80262-2).

[21]Quoted in Schmidt, 42.

[22]Schmidt, 43-44. *Dwight's Journal of Music*, 1 February 1862, 350-51, has a review of an organ recital Paine gave the previous Monday at an unspecified location, which included Bach's Prelude and Fugue in A minor, "Chorale variations, for two manuals and double pedals [*sic*; for two feet]," Trio Sonata in E-flat, and Toccata in F.

[23]This work, as orchestrated by Heinrich Esser, was played by the Harvard Musical Association on 19 April 1866, according to *Dwight's* the following 28 April. The reviewer had "often heard it on the great organ of the Music Hall by Mr. Paine and others" (p. 229).

[24]Schmidt, 56.

[25]Schmidt, 67. *Dwight's*, 15 March 1879, 45-46, describes a performance of the motet "Sing unto the Lord a New-Made Song," for double chorus, by the Boylston Club the previous 25 February, conducted by Osgood.

[26]The conventional wisdom is that Paine was the first professor at an American university, but actually there were earlier ones, according to

information from Mary Jane Corry (SUNY-New Paltz) printed in the *Newsletter* of the Institute for Studies in American Music 14/2 (May 1985): 4. Edward Wiebe became professor of music at Vassar College in 1865, Frédéric Louis Ritter professor of vocal and instrumental music in 1867 and simply professor of music in 1873—again at Vassar—and Hugh Archibald Clarke was appointed professor of the science of music at the University of Pennsylvania in 1875.

[27]Vol. 24, no. 21: 376.

[28]On Dresel (1826-1890), see *The New Grove Dictionary of American Music* (1986), s.v. "Dresel, Otto," by John Gillespie; or John and Anna Gillespie, *A Bibliography of Nineteenth-Century American Piano Music* (Westport, Conn.: Greenwood Press, 1984), 239.

[29]According to *Dwight's* 8/23 (8 March 1856): 180, it was also performed in New York by William Mason and Bergmann—and no third name; and again in Boston by B. J. Lang with Messrs. Leonhard and Parker, accompanied by a string quartet—vol. 32/1 (6 April 1872): 214.

[30]Vol. 25, no. 9: 69.

[31]Quoted from an obituary in Kenneth Graber, *William Mason (1829-1908): An Annotated Bibliography and Catalog of Works*, Bibliographies in American Music, 13 (Warren, Mich.: Harmonie Park Press, 1989), 41.

[32]Graber, nos. 681, 689-90; the editions: nos. 791-95.

[33](Board of Music Trade, 1871; reprint, New York: Da Capo, 1973).

[34]The above works are found on the following pages: 49, 203, 304, 334, 341, 386, 388, 409.

[35]The chorale publication is cited in *Dwight's* 10/11 (13 December 1856): 86.

[36]*Dwight's* 29/15 (9 October 1869): 118. An admonishment for choristers to attend rehearsals faithfully, by "C.," appeared the previous issue, 25 September, p. 111. The first public performance of excerpts, as noted above, took place on 13 May 1871.

[37]Information on Wolle comes from Raymond Walters, *The Bethlehem Bach Choir: An Historical and Interpretative Sketch* (Boston: Houghton Mifflin, 1918; reprint, New York: AMS Press, 1971).

[38]Not of its U.S. premiere in complete form, however. The Handel and Haydn Society began performing excerpts 13 May 1872, then complete in 1879; Theodore Thomas conducted it at the Cincinnati May Festival, 17 May 1882; and Philadelphia's Cecilian Society on 12 March 1885. See above, and Johnson, *First Performances*, 16-17.

INDEX

Abel, Karl Friedrich, 19-20, 339
Acis and Galatea, 337
Adams, John, 3, 10, 76
Adams, John Quincy, 106
Adem, Hattie, 294-95
Adgate, Andrew, 14
Aitken, John, 22, 207
Alexander, Robert, 85
Allegro de Concert, 283
Allen, William Henry, 91-92
Alley, Joseph, 135
"Alone," 281
Amilie; or the Love Test, 175-76, 185, 187
Amitié pour Amitié, 315
Anderson, John, 111
André, Major John, 27
Anthems, Hymns, etc., 207
Anthems, list, of, 161-68
Antiphonaire de Saint Gregaire, 225
Appy, Henri, 295
Aptommas, Thomas, 106, 295
Armonica, 12
Arne, Thomas, 20, 175-76, 338
Arnold, Samuel, 151
Artaxerxes, 20
Auber, Daniel-François-Esprit, 176, 186-87
Austin, Elizabeth, 175, 193, 195
"Austrian Retreat," 103
"Ave Maria" (Bassini), 296, 320

"Ave Maria" (King), 319
Bach, Carl Philipp Emanuel, 338
Bach, Johann Christian, 19, 338, 346
Bach, Johanna Sebastian, 337-51; list of works, 343-44, 346-47
Baini, Giuseppi, 224
Balatka, Hans, 237-38, 241, 246
Balfe, Michael William, 175, 186-87
balls, *see* dancing
Baltimore Olio and American Musical Gazette, 214, 226
Baltimore Olio Waltz, 226
Bangs, F., 107
Banjo, 317
Barber of Seville, 253
"Barcarole," 187
Barron, James, 83, 90-91, 109-10
Barron, Samuel, 77
Bassford, Abraham, 295
Bassford, Samuel W., 296
Bassford, T. Franklin, 282, 295-96
Bassford, William K., 295
Bassini, Carlo, 296, 320
Bassini's Art of Singing, 296
"Battle," 84
"Battle of Waterloo," 102
"Battle Song," 238
Beals, John, 12
Beaumont, J., 62
Bedinger, Daniel, 90

Beethoven, Ludwig van, 223, 241, 252, 338-40
Bella Arsène, 20
Bellini, Vincenzo, 176, 187, 236
Benedict XIII, Pope, 206
Benedict, XIV, Pope, 207
Benkert, G. F., 296-97, 319
Bergmann, Carl, 343
Bergner, Frederick, 297, 319
Berti, Candido, 272-73, 282, 296-98, 312
Bethlehem Bach Choir, 345-46
Bethlehem Choral Union, 345
"Bid Me Discourse," 185-86
Biddle, John, 5
Billings, William, 152, 276, 338
Birch, Thomas, 63-64
"Birks of Aberfeldie," 185-86
Bishop, Henry Rowley, 175-76, 185
Blundell, Mary, 173-74, 179-80, 183, 189-91, 195
Board of Music Trade, 209
Boccherini, Luigi, 78
Bohemian Girl, 236, 253
"Bonaparte Entering Paris," 101
"Bonnie Briar Bush," 185-86
Boon Children, 107
Borghi, Luigi, 19
Boston Academy of Music, 340
Boston Handel and Haydn Society Collection of Church Music, 64, 67
Boston Melodeon, 138
Boston Musical Gazette, 341
Bostwick, Emma G., 273-74, 298, 303, 311, 321
Boye, W. de, 106
Brainerd, Maria S., 298
Bremner, James, 12
Bremner, John, 12
Breval, Jean-Baptiste, 19

"Bridge of Sighs," 137
Bridgewater Collection of Sacred Music, 67
Brinkerhoff, Clara M., 281, 296, 298-99
Bristow, George Frederick, 266-67, 270, 273, 278, 283, 299, 301, 307, 322, 325
Brown, Elizabeth, 133
Brown, Thomas, 133
Brown, William, 12-18, 20-23
Bruner, John, 22
Bülow, Hans von, 340
Bull, Ole, 106, 239-40, 246, 248, 302
Bunch of Grapes, 5
Burrows, William Ward, 76-77, 79, 82
Buskirk, Lawrence Van, 52

Campbell, James, 235-36
Cannon, John Brazier, 86
Cantata Erl King, 253
Canticle and Chants, 323
Capron, Henri, 12-22
Carols and Hymns, 323
Carr, Benjamin, 96, 103, 158, 207-08, 223, 337
Carr, Joseph, 94
Carroll, John, 203
Carusi, Gaetano, 75-131, 226
Carusi, Joseph, 80-81
Carusi, Lewis, 75, 81, 103-04, 108, 116
Carusi, Nathaniel, 75, 81, 86, 102, 108, 115
Carusi, Philippa, 75, 116
Carusi, Samuel, 75, 81, 86, 101-02, 105-06, 108, 226
Carusi's Saloon, *see* Washington Assembly Hall
Catholic Advocate, 204, 206, 209

Index

Catholic Harp, 223-24
Catholic Music With Latin Words, 215-22
Cenerentola, 176
Cenis, Mr., 25, 30
Centuri, Signor, 106
"Charity," 84
Charleston Theatre, 181, 189
Chauncey, Isaac, 96-98, 100
Chesapeake (frigate), 89-92, 109
Chestnut Street Theatre, 177, 181-82
Cheverus, John, 207
Chicago Brass Band, 234-35
Chicago Philharmonic Society, 234, 237, 245, 247
Choice Selection of Evangelical Hymns, 53-54
Chopin, Frederic, 252
Choral-Buch, 49, 54-55, 63-64
Christ Our Passion, 323-24
Christhilf, George, 22-24
Christmas Carol, 310
Christmas Oratorio, 345-46
Christy Minstrels, 137
Church Melodist, 136
Church of the Holy Apostles, 306
Cincinnati Polka, 226
Cinderella, 176, 187
circus (Baltimore), 94-95
"Circus Tunes," 94
City Tavern, 3-47
Clari, or the Maid of Milan, 176
Clark's Inn, 5
Clementi, Muzio, 60, 78, 338
Clemenza di Tito, 294
Clinton, Henry, 28
Coach and Horse, 5
Cobbler and the Fairy, 253
Cole, John, 153
Collection of Church Tunes, 49, 60, 63-70

Collection of Evangelical Hymns Made from Different Authors, 51-52
Collection of Favorite Songs, 22
Collection of Hymns, and a Liturgy, 54, 63
Collection of Sacred Music, 223, 320
Collegium Musicum (Bethlehem), 345
Colliere, L. Coradie, 226
Columbia College, 322
Columbia Musical Association, 107
"Come Love With Me," 311
"Come Take the Harp," 101
Compilation of the Litanies and Vespers, 207
Complete Catalogue of Sheet Music and Musical Works, 344
Comstock, Kate V., 283, 299
Concertino for Clarinet and Orchestra, 312
Congressional Cemetery, 116
Consecration Anthem, 306, 311, 322
Consecration Service, 274
Cook, T. J., 270, 273, 299-300, 318
Cooper, Daniel A., 135
Cooper, Henry C., 279, 284, 300-01
Corelli, Arcangelo, 20, 78, 339
Cramer, Johann Baptist, 19
Creation, 96, 246, 252, 338-39
Creighton, John Orde, 97, 99-101
Crispino e la Comare, 248
Cross, Benjamin Carr, 223
Crown Diamonds, 253
Crowninshield, Benjamin, 97
Crump, Miss, 301

Curtis, George Henry, 270-71, 277, 301
Custis, Nelly, 14
Cutler, Henry Stephen, 344
Cutler, Rev. Manasseh, 6-7
Czar and Zimmerman, 253

Dalley, Gifford, 8, 11-12, 16
Damrosch, Leopold, 340
Damrosch, Walter, 340
dancing, in Philadelphia, 24-32
Daughter of the Regiment, 300
Davaux, Jean-Baptiste, 19
Davisson, Ananias, 153-54, 158
Davy, John, 176
Death-Bed Rhapsody, 310
Deems, James Monroe, 283-84, 299, 301-02, 319
Dempster, William, 234
Déserteur, 20
Dettingen Te Deum, 339
Diabelli, Anton, 225
Diadeste, 187
Dibdin, Charles, 175
Dickens, Charles, 174
Diehlman, Henry, 107
Dodge, Ossian E., 107
Dodworth, Allen, 283, 302
Don Giovanni, 252
Donizetti, Gaetano, 187, 225, 300, 319
D'Ormy, Martini, 106
Downey, Thomas, 100
Dramatic Association, 107
Dresel, Otto, 343
Dressler, William, 296, 302-03
Duenna, 20
Duetto Dramatico, 283, 316
Duff, Mr., 102
Dulcken, Ferdinand, 344
Durang, John, 22
Dwight, John Sullivan, 266, 340
Dwight, Timothy, 158

Dwight's Journal of Music, 247, 269, 275-76, 280, 305, 312, 340-43
Dyer, Samuel O., 303
Dyhrenfurth, Julius, 236-37

"Easter Anthem," 60
"Easter Hymn," 60
Eaton, William, 86
Eben, Felix J., 303, 319
Eckhard, Jacob, 49, 54-55, 63-64
Edition of the Songs of Scotland, 186
Eichner, Ernst, 19
Eisfeld, Theodore, 266, 297, 300, 312
Elementarbuch der Harmonie und Tonsetzkunst, 138
Elijah, 241-42, 339
Ellery, William, 11
Elutheria, 301
Epple, Henry, 9, 12, 14, 26
Erben, Henry, 57
Erben, Peter, 49-73
Ernani, 248, 253
Ernst, John Frederick, 51
Erskine, Thomas, 19-20
Esch, Louis von, 60
Esther, 284, 302, 319
Estvan, Countess, 106
Ethiopian Serenaders, 107
Etude de Concert, 315
Evans, George, 8

Fabj, Signor, 107
Fading, Still Fading, 226
Farmer's Wife, 186
Faust, 236, 248, 253
Fay, Amy, 268
Federal Ballet, 26
Federal Minuet, 26
Fenwick, Benedict J., 204
Feste Burg, 340

Index 357

Fiala, Josef, 19-20
Fidelio, 253
Field, Joel, 209
Figaro, 339
Fiorillo, Federigo, 19
First Religious Society, 133-34
Fisher, Clara, 314
Flora, or The Gypsy's Frolic, 284
"Flowers of the Forest," 185-86
folk hymns, 149
Forest Melody, 301
Forkel, Johann Nikolaus, 341
Formes, Karl, 239
Forrage, Stephen, 12, 23, 265
Forrest, Alexander, 86
Foster, Stephen, 138, 209
Four Hungarian Singers, 107-08
Fox, Mary, 11
Fox, Thomas, 136
Fra Diavolo, 176, 185-87, 248, 253
Francis, William, 25
Franklin, Benjamin, 12
Franks, Rebecca, 27
Frederick the Great, 19
"Freien Geister," 238
French, Jacob, 152
Freyschutz, 252
Frothingham, Andrew, 133
Fry, William Henry, 266-68, 275, 278-79, 283, 300, 303-04
Funeral March, 252

Gallesio, Charles, 93
"Galley Slave," 84
Galop di Bravura, 282
Gansbacher, Johann, 225
Gaviniès, Pierre, 13
Gazza Ladra, 187
Gehot, Jean, 17
Geib, John, 57
Geissenhainer, Anastasius T., 63

Geissenheimer, F. W., 54
Gellie, Miss, 304
Genevieve, 253
Gérard, Alexander, 12
Germania Männerchor, 238, 245
Germania Musical Society, 107
Germania Orchestra, 343
Giardini, Felice de, 157-58
Gilldorff, F., 98, 101
Gillingham, George, 298
Giornovichi, Giovanni, 19
Gockel, August, 106
"God Save the Queen," 323
Gondolier's Serenade, 282, 314
Good Will Club, 107
"Goodnight, Love," 187
Gossec, François-Joseph, 19, 86
Gottschalk, Louis Moreau, 106, 239, 268, 272-73, 281-82, 295, 298-99, 304-05, 309, 315, 317
Gould, Hannah Flagg, 137
Gould, John Edgar, 136
Gould, Nathaniel Duren, 135, 139
Grace Church, 313, 315-16
Graham, John, 96
Grand Fugue in G minor (Bach), 342
"Grand March & Rondo," 60
Grand Toccata in F (Bach), 342
Grande Duchesse, 253
Graupner, Johann Christian Gottlieb, 339
Grayson, William John, 112-13
Great Fire (Chicago), 231, 243, 249
Green, J., 151
Grétry, Andre Ernest, 19
Griepenkerl, Friedrich Conrad, 345
Griswold, David D., 305
Grosse, Otto, 305, 318, 324
"Grüss Gott," 297

Gualdo, Giovanni, 12
Guarnaccia, D. Domenico, 85, 88, 108
Guignon, P., 135
Guilmette, Charles A., 274, 283-84, 299-300, 304-06, 310-11, 318-19
Guitar Without a Master, 138
Guy Mannering, 176

Hadfield, George, 105
"Hail Columbia," 84, 102, 323
Half Moon, 5
Hall, John, 77-81, 83, 88, 90
Halsted, R. F., 301, 306
Hamilton, Alexander, 14
Hamilton, Andrew, 26
Hamilton, Thomas, 174
Handel, George Frederick, 59, 62, 96, 157-58, 223, 337-39, 342, 346-47
Handel and Haydn Society, 64, 339-40
Handelian Society, 338
Hankins, John, 231
"Happy Birdling," 303
Harmoneons, 107
Harmonic Society, 233, 338
"Harmony Piece," 101
Harrison, Mr., 104
Harrison, W. H., 323
Hartung, William, 22
Harvard Music Hall, 342
"Has Summer Pass'd Away?," 321
Hastings, Thomas, 300
Haupt, Karl August, 341
Hauser, William, 156
Haydn, Franz Joseph, 19, 21, 96, 101-02, 223, 225, 246, 252, 337-39
Haydn Society, 338
"Hearts of Oak," 84
Heine, William, 107

Heinrichs, Johann, 27
Heller, Robert, 106
Henderson, Archibald, 111
Henni, Martin, 224
Henry, John, 16
Herwig, Leopold, 107
Hesperian Harp, 156
Hewitt, James, 64, 337, 339
Hewitt, John Hill, 208
Hewitt, Sophia, 339
Hide Not Thy Face, 316, 321, 324
Higgins, Hiram Murray, 245
Himmel, F. H., 225
Hobart, John Henry, 58
Hodges, Edward, 56-57, 270, 274, 283, 298, 306-07, 311, 318, 321-23
Hoffman, Josiah Ogden, 112
Hoffman, Richard, 279, 297, 307, 344
Holliday Street Theatre, 181
Hollins, George Nicholas, 99-100
Holten, Samuel, 11-12
Homans, Benjamin, 96
"Home That I Love," 137
Hommann, Charles, 103, 280-81, 305, 307-08, 315, 324
Hood, Thomas, 137
Hook, James, 60
"Hope Told a Flattering Tale," 101-02
Hopkins, Jerome, 266, 268-69, 270, 272, 280, 283, 285, 296-98, 306-10, 313, 315, 319, 321, 342
Hopkins, John Henry, Jr., 274, 310-11
Hopkins, John Henry, Sr., 268, 274
Hopkinson, Francis, 12, 14
Hopper, Edward, 137
Howard, John Tasker, 268
"Howe's Strolling Players," 27

Index

Hummel, J. N., 223
"Hunter's Song," 238
Hupfeld, Charles, 103, 308, 338
Hutchinson Family Singers, 107, 137-38
Hymn and Prayer-Book, 51
"Hymn for Whitsunday," 60
Hymn 186, 319
Hymn to the Virgin, 302, 319
hymns, see *A Collection of Church Tunes*

I Was Glad, 274
"I'm Ouer Young to Marry Yet," 185-86
"In Sweetest Harmony," 64
Independence (frigate), 97
Indian Queen, 5-6, 9
Inglis, John, 29
Institution March, 317
Instructions in Thorough Base, 341
Introduction to the Art of Playing on the Piano Forte, 339
Introits and Anthems by Modern Composers, 323
Inventions (Bach), 344
Israel in Egypt, 342

Jackson, George Pullen, 149
"Jackson's March," 102
"Jackson's Victory," 101
Jacobi, John Christian, 50
Jaëll, Alfred, 343
Jameson, Mrs. R. S., 311
Jefferson, Thomas, 77-78
"Jefferson's March," 78, 83
"Jesus, Saviour, pilot me," 137
Joan of Arc, 187
Johann Sebastian Bach's Kompositionen für die Orgel, 345
"John Anderson, My Joe," 185-86

Johnson, A. N., 137, 340-41, 346
Johnson, James A., 311
Jones, William, 108
Juhan, Alexander, 12-14, 16-18, 21-22
Julien, Paul, 106

Kammel, Antonín, 19
Kelly, Patrick, 104
Kemp, Annie, 311-12
Kent, Mr., 62
Kentucky Harmony, 153
Keyser, John, 22
Kiefer, Mr., 312
King, E. J., 154, 158
King, William A., 312-13, 319
Kitchen, James, 8
Klemm, Johann G., 51
Knap, Nathaniel, 133
Kozeluch, Leopold, 186
Kübler, G. F., 340
Kuchen, Friedrich, 226
Kunze, John Christopher, 51-53
Kutzstock, David, 22

Labarre, Théodore, 314
Lachnith, Ludwig Wenzel, 19
Lacy, Michael Rophino, 176
Lambillotte, Louis, 224-25
"Land Far Away," 185-86
Lang, Benjamin J., 340
Last Hope, 281-82
"Last Rose Summer," 185-86
Latham, W. H., 182
Law, Andrew, 152
Lazare, Martin, 106
Leach, Mrs. Georgiana Stuart, 314, 318
Leach, Js., 62
Leach, Stephen W., 314
Leavitt, Josiah, 134
Lee, George Alexander, 186
Lennox, Peter, 5

Leopard (frigate), 91
"Let Thine Eyes on Mine Mildly Beaming," 187
Linley, Thomas, 20
Liszt, Franz, 246, 252, 271, 340
Livingston, Henry, 27-28
Loder, Edward James, 226, 314
"Look Not," 297
Loomis, Mr., 314, 321
Loreley and Lurline, 252
Loria, D. Pasquale, 79-80, 85, 108
Loria, Frencesco, 79
Loria, Salvador, 109
Love in a Village, 176
"Love Like a Shadow Flies," 185-86
"Lovely Lady Mine," 187
Lover, Samuel, 186, 188
Lucia di Lammermoor, 319
Lucrezia Borgia, 248, 319
Lutheran Book of Worship, 49
Lutheran hymnals, 50-56
Lyster, William, 319

McCurry, John G., 156
McKean, Thomas, 11
McLean, John, 23
McVickers Theater, 236, 240
Madan, Martin, 151-52, 157
Madison, Dolley, 87
Madison, James, 87, 97-99
"Madison's March," 102
Maeder, James G., 186, 285, 314
Maid of Artois, 186
Malloney, Philip, 23
Manual of Church Music, 323
Manual of the Boston Academy of Music, 340
"March and Rondo," 95
March & Waltz at the Battle of Waterloo, 103
Marche Funebre, 307
Marco Bozarris, 303

Marine Band, *see* U. S. Marine Band
Marino Faliero, 187
Maritana, 294
Marriage of Figaro, 176
Marryat, Frederick, 174
Martha, 236, 253
Martineau, Harriet, 174
Martinez, Signior, 233-34
Martini, Giovanni, 20
Mason, John, 98
Mason, Lowell, 137, 340, 343
Mason, William, 266, 272-73, 275, 282, 314-15, 318, 320-21, 343-44
Masonic Assembly Rooms, 9, 16
Mass in B minor (Bach), 340, 345
Mass in C (Walter), 323
Mass in C Major (Tauman), 225
Mass in Three Parts, 223
Mass of the Holy Ghost, 223-24
Masses, Vespers, Litanies, 223
Mathews, W. S. B., 246-48
Mauro, Ignazio di, 109
Mauro, Philip, 104
Max Robespierre, 252
Mayer, Ph. F., 54
Mazeppa (Gottschalk), 282
Mazzei, Filippo, 78
Meade, John, 91
"Meet Me in the Willow Glen," 185-86
"Meeting of the Waters," 185-86
Meineke, Charles, 153, 226
Melodeon Without a Master, 139
Melodien der deutschen evangelischen Kirchenlieder, 67
Mendelssohn, Felix, 225, 241, 246, 252, 315, 339, 342
Mendelssohn Quintette Club, 246
Mendelssohn Society, 280
Mercadante, G., 225

Index

"Meschianza," 28-29
Messiah, 59, 96, 338-39, 342
Meyer, Julius E., 282, 315
Midnight March, 226
Midsummer-Night's Dream, 252
Miller, W. E., 151
Mills, Sebastian Bach, 344
Miranda, Francisco de, 15
Modern Harp, 136
Moller, John Christoph, 17, 20
Moller, Lucy, 17
Monsigny, Pierre-Alexandre, 20
Moore, Benjamin, 61
Moore, Mr., 134
Moore, Thomas, 137, 186, 322
Morgan, George Washborne, 315
Morgan, Justin, 152
Morgan, Maud, 315-16
Morris, Robert, 14
Mount Vernon, 86
Moyston, Edward, 8, 16, 31
Mozart, Wolfgang Amadeus, 21, 86, 246, 294, 338-39, 342
Muhlenberg, Henry Melchior, 50-51
Murray, Charles, 174
Music and Snobs, 308-09
Musical Biography, 338
Musical Fund Society (Philadelphia), 103, 338-39
Musical Fund Society (New York), 317
"Musical Gift," 138
Musical Independent, 245-47
Musikverein, 238
Muzzy, Helen, 107
"My Boy Tammie," 185-86
"My Companions are Warn'd," 185

National Church Harmony, 135
National Greys, 107
National Theatre, 175-78, 181

Nebuchadnezzar, 284, 302
Neukomm, Sigismund, 225
New Constitution March, 26
New Edition with an Appendix of Masses, 208
Newland's Collection of Sacred Music, 223
New York American-Music Association, 265-336
New York Grace Church Collection of Sacred Music, 313
New York Philharmonic, 266-67, 294, 297, 300, 303, 318, 320, 340
Niblo's Garden, 283
Niblo's Grand Saloon, 185
Niblo's Theatre, 178, 181
Night in Grenada, 252
Nightingale Ethiopians, 107
Nilsson, Christina, 239
Noeren, J. M., 226
Norma, 236, 238, 253
Novello, Vincent, 223
Novello's Cantica Vespers, 223
"Now a Poor and Simple Maid Appears," 185

O How Amiable, 323
Oberon, 252
Oeller's Hotel, 17, 32
"O'er Shepherd Pipe & Rustic Dell," 187
"Oh Dear! What Can the Matter Be?," 84
"Oh Hasten, Dearest Lady," 187
"Oh! Susanna," 138
"Oh! Think Not Less I Love Thee," 226
"Oh Whistle and I'll Come to You My Lad," 185-86
"Old Uncle Ned," 138
Olympic Theatre, 94

Onís, Don Luis de, 96
Orchestral Union, 238
Organ Without a Master, 138-39
Original Glee and Anthem Book, 300
Orpheonist and Philharmonic Journal, 308
Orpheus aux Enfers, 253
Osgood, George L., 342
Ossian's Bards, 107
"Our Souls by Love," 151
"Overture to Adrina," 101
Overture to Henry the Fourth, 20

Paine, John Knowles, 341-42, 346
panharmonicon, 95
Papa, Joseph, 80, 108
Pardi, John, 95
Park Theatre, 175, 192, 195
Parker, Joel, 303
Parker, John Rowe, 338
Parodi, Teresa, 106
Parry, John, 186
Passion Music, 345
"Pastoral Aria," 187
Paterno, Antonio, 80, 108
Patti, Adelina, 239, 304
Patti, Carlotta, 239
Payne, E. A., 316
Peale, Charles Willson, 29
Peck, Mr., 316
Peene, J., 62
Penn, John, 12, 14
Perez, Señor, 107
Pergolesi, Giovanni Battista, 78
Peri, or The Enchanted Fountain, 285
Perkins, Theodore E., 300
Peters' Catholic Harmonist, 225
Peters' Catholic Harp, 214
Phelps, Ellsworth C., 303
Philadelphia Dancing Assembly, 26, 28

Phile, Philip, 14, 18, 22-24
Philharmonic Society, 339
Philipps, Thomas, 186
Pike, Mr., 24
"Pilot," 136
Pinkney, William, 97
Plumstead, William, 9
Polonoise, 339
Ponceau, Stephen du, 14
Poor Soldier, 20
Porter, Alexander, 114
Porter, David, 97
Postillion of Longjumeau, 187
Pré Aux Clercs, 187
Prelude and Fugue in G minor (Paine), 341
Preludes (Liszt), 271-72
President (ship), 79, 81-83
President of the United States March, 26
"Pretty Jennry Wren," 297
Proch, H., 226
Proctor, Thomas, 11-12, 22
"Proudly and Wide My Standard Flies," 185
Prunner, George, 23
Psalmodia Germanica, 50-51
Pulizzi, Antonia, 109
Pulizzi, Felice, 79-80, 85, 87, 89, 109
Pulizzi, Francesco, 79, 108
Pulizzi, Venerando, 79, 109
Purcell, Henry, 223, 338
Pychowski, J. Nepomucene, 283, 316, 320
Pyne, Louisa, 305

Quakers, 26
Quartet in D minor (Hommann), 318
"Quartetto, with Yankee Doodle," 102
Quidant, Alfred, 282

Index

Quitman, F. H., 54

Radieuse, 282
Rakemann, L., 107
Randolph, Peyton, 14
Rapp, George, 208
"Rapture Dwelling," 185-86
"Rapture Fills My Joyful Heart," 187
Recollections of Scotland, 300
Reiff, Anthony, Jr., 317-18, 324
Reiff, Anthony, Sr., 317
Reinagle, Alexander, 12-14, 16-22, 32, 337-38
Rendon, Don Francisco, 25
Reverie, 307
Rheinberger, Josef, 345
Richardet, Samuel, 8
Rip Van Winkle, 283, 299, 325
Ritter, Frederick, 224
Rives, William Cabell, 114
Rob Roy, 176
Robjohn, Miss, 311, 318, 321
Rodgers, John, 84, 88, 97
Roitzsch, Ferdinand, 345
Rolph, John A., 298-99
"Romance," 187, 317
Romeo and Juliet (Gounod), 248
Rooke, William Michael, 175
"Rory O'Moore," 185-86, 188
Rose et Colas, 20
Rosetti, Antonio, 19
Rosina, 20
Rossini, Gioachino, 176, 187, 225, 252, 338-39
Roth, Philip, 22-24
Rotti, Philip, *see* Roth, Philip
Rubinstein, Anton, 344
Rudiments of the Art of Playing on the Piano Forte, 339
Russell, G. D., 344

Sable Harmonists, 107

Sacred Harp, 154, 156, 158
Sacred Music Being a Collection of Anthems in Score, 62
Sacred Music for the Use of Singing Societies, 62
Sacred Music in Two, Three, and Four Parts, 61, 63, 66
Santa Claus Symphony, 267
Sardo, Gaetano, 79, 108
Sardo, Giuseppe, 89, 100, 109
Sardo, James, 79, 108
Sardo, Michele (Michael), 79, 85, 87
Sarti, Giuseppe, 19
Satter, Gustave, 285, 318
"Savourneen Deelish," 185-86
Schetky, J. George, 20, 22, 103
Schmidt, John, 341
Schmittbauer, Joseph, 19
Schneider, Friedrich, 138
Schnyder, Xaver von Wartensee, 340
Schonenberg, Professor, 107
Schroeter, Johann Samuel, 19
Schubert, Franz, 225, 246, 252
Schultz, Nicholas (?), 12, 23-24
Schumann, Robert, 252, 340
Scott, Winfield, 98
Seidl, Anton, 340
Select Sacred Music Suitable for the Catholic Church Service, 209-15
Selection of Psalm and Hymn Tunes, 60
Selections of Psalms, Together with the Canticles, 323
Seminary Class Book, 138
Sequin, Anne, 182-83
Sequin, Edward, 174-75, 182, 187
Shaw, George Bernard, 242
Shepherds of Bethlehem, 274
Sheppard, Caroline M., 318
Shield, William, 20, 175

Sicard, Stephen, 25-26
Sicilian Vespers, 253
Siede, Julius, 319
Siege of Rochelle, 187
Sign of the Conestoga Wagon, 6
Sign of the Rainbow Tavern, 9, 12, 26
Signorelli, Corrado, 80, 108
Signorelli, S. Antonio, 80, 108
Silver Spring, 283, 314
Simon, Mr., 319
Simon, Henrietta, 319
Simpson, George, 285, 319-20
Sinfonia, 307
Six Irish Melodies by Thomas Moore, 186
Six Sonatas for the Piano-forte or Harpsichord, 21
"Sleep the Kind Angel," 325
"Smile On," 137
Smith, Daniel, 3, 8, 28
Smith, Margaret Bayard, 78
Smith, Robert, 86-88, 90
Smith's Masonic Lodge, 10
Social Harp, 156
Society for Cultivating Church Music, 58
Sofge, Henry D., 226
Sonata for Violin and Piano (Hommann), 308
Sonata for Violin and Piano (Pychowski), 316, 320
Song Messenger of the North-West, 243-45
"Songs of the Flowers," 322
Sonnambula, 176, 187, 236-37, 253
"Sons of Alknomack," 84
Sousa, John Philip, 297
Southwark Theater, 9, 27
Souvenirs d'Andalousie, 298
Spangenberg, Conrad, 12, 22, 24
Spohr, Louis, 300

Spontini, Gasparo, 224-25
Spoth, Edward, 226
"Spring Song" (Willis), 325
St. Cecilia Society, 338
St. John Passion, 345
St. Matthew Passion, 340, 345
St. Paul, 339
Stadler, Abbe G. J., 225
Stamitz, Carl, 19-20
"Star Spangled Banner" (Hewitt), 64
Stark, Frederick, 312
State House Inn, 5
Steffey, J. W., 156
Steinway Hall, 344
Stickney, E. L., 134
"Still, Still the Same," 300, 318
Stockton, Fanny, 320
Stoddard, J. T., 226
Stoddert, William Benjamin, 76
Stradella, Alessandro, 225
Strakosch, Maurice, 106
Strebeck, George, 51-53
Sumner, Jezaniah, 152
"Sweet Little Cherub," 84
"Switzerland! My Switzerland," 283, 299
Symphony in C (Beethoven), 339
Szemeleng, Chevalier de, 106

"Tak Yer Auld Cloak About Ye," 185-86
Tancredi, 339
Tasso, 252
Taylor, Rayner, 13, 96, 103, 223, 337
Te Deum (Hommann), 280, 308
Temperance Echoes, 302
Temple, S., 152
Templi Carmina, 64
Terziani, Pietro, 224
Thanksgiving Anthem, 303
Thayer, Alexander Wheelock, 341

Index

"Then Since Time Flies So Fast Away," 185
"There's a Good Time Coming," 137
"This Blooming Rose at Early Dawn," 64
This Is the Hour, 303
Thomas, Mrs., 320-21
Thomas, Theodore, 240, 283, 317, 320, 340, 344, 346-47
"Though I Leave Now in Sorrow," 185
Three Bells Polka, 300
Three Rondos for the Piano Forte or Harpsichord, 14, 23
Tillier, Joseph, 19
Timm, Henry C., 267-68, 320-21
Toccata in D minor (Bach), 342
Toeschi, Carlo Giuseppe, 19
Topp, Alida, 246
Tournament Galop, 282
Traviata, 253
Treatise on Dancing, 30-31
Tremner, Fruntz (Fritz), 22-24
Treniner, Mr., *see* Tremner, Fruntz
"Trifler, Forbear," 185
Trinity Church (N.Y.), 273-74, 283, 298, 304, 314, 316, 321-23
Tripolian War, 81, 83, 110
Trippe, E., 101
Triumphal Symphony, 252
Trollope, Frances, 174
Trovatore, 236, 240, 248, 253
Tucker, Mr., 321
Tuckerman, Samuel Parkman, 274, 316, 321-22
tunebooks, list of, 159-60
Twelfth Night, 186

Union: Music for the Church and the Fireside, 300

Upton, George P., 232, 236-42, 247
Urania Society, 338
Urso, Camilla d', 239, 248
U.S. Congress, 109-15
U.S. Marine Band, 75-78, 109

Vai, Signor, 107
Valley Harmonist, 156
Valley of Andorre, 305
Valse di Bravura, 282
Vanhal, Jan, 19
Varano, Gaetano, 77
Variations on the Star-Spangled Banner, 313
Vie Parisienne, 253
Vieuxtemps, Henri, 106
Violin Sonata (Hommann), 315
Virginia Sacred Minstrel, 158
Vogler, Abbe, 225
Vries, Rosa de, 106

Wagner, Richard, 246, 340
Wallace, William Vincent, 265, 294, 303, 322
Wallack, James, 176-78
Walter, William Henry, 271, 274, 322
Ward, Thomas, 284, 324
Warren, George W., 303
Wartmann, H. T., 156
Washington Assembly Hall, 105-08
Washington Associates, 107
Washington Dancing Assemblies, 76
Washington (frigate), 96-99
Washington German Yeagers, 107
Washington Harmony, 136
Washington Light Infantry, 107
Washington Philharmonic Society, 107-08

Washington Theatre, 104
"Washington's March," 102
Water Music, 337
Watts, Isaac, 53, 154
"We Are Wandering O'er the Mountains," 322
"We Never Aught Demand from the Fair," 185
We Three Kings of Orient, 268, 274
Webb, B. J., 204-05, 209
Webbe, Samuel, 223
Webster, F. J., 209
Wedermeyer, Mr., 318, 324
Weiss, John George, 345
Weiss, Matthias, 345
"Well if I Must Speak My Mind," 187
Wendling, Johann, 19
West and Peal's Old Original Campbell Minstrels, 107
West, George R., 107
Westerfelt, Mrs., 324
Wharton, Franklin, 77, 82, 85-89
"When Edward Left His Native Plain," 60
"When Through Life Unblest We Rove," 322
White, Anna Samson, 135
White, B. F., 154-57
White, Edward Little, 133-47
White, Gilman, 133, 135
White, Mary Ann, 133-34
White, Thomas B., 134-35
White House, 78, 108
White Spirituals in the Southern Uplands, 149
"Who Hath Not Mark'd?," 185
Wickliffe, C. A., 108
Wiesenthal, Thomas Van Dyke, 226
Wilkinson, James, 92-93
Will, John, 62

Willet, Mr., 325
William Tell, 252
Willig, George, 208
Willis, Richard Storrs, 266, 269-71, 275, 277-78, 286, 295-97, 301, 306, 312, 315, 325
Williston, Ralph, 53-54
"Winds That Waft My Sighs to Thee," 322
Winter, Peter, 225
Wohltempierte Clavier, 344
Wolle, Francis, 345
Wolle, John Frederick, 345-46
Wood, David, 345
Wood, Joseph, 175, 193, 195
Wood, Mary Anne Paton, 175, 193, 195
Wooster, C. W., 283, 325
Work, Henry C., 244
"Wrecker's Daughter," 137

"Yankee Doodle," 84, 102, 138

Zampa, 252
Zerrahn, Carl, 340
Zingarelli, Nicolo, 225

CONTRIBUTORS

J. Bunker Clark is professor emeritus of music history at the University of Kansas. He is the editor of *Anthology of Early American Keyboard Music, 1787-1830* (Recent Researches in American Music, vols. 1-2, 1977), *Nathaniel Giles: Anthems* (Early English Church Music, vol. 23, 1979), and *American Music through 1865* (Three Centuries of American Music, vol. 3, 1990). His books include *Transposition in Seventeenth Century English Organ Accompaniments and the Transposing Organ* (1974) and *The Dawning of American Keyboard Music* (1988). He serves as editor of the series Detroit Studies in Music Bibliography and Detroit Monographs in Musicology/Studies in Music, published by Harmonie Park Press.

James Deaville received his Ph.D. from Northwestern University with a dissertation about the music criticisms of Peter Cornelius. Currently Chair of the Department of Music at McMaster University, he has written articles and read papers about Schumann, Liszt, Wagner, American music, music criticism, and women and music. He edited a four-volume descriptive catalogue of the *Allgemeine Wiener Musik-Zeitung*, is co-editor of the new journal *Criticus Musicus* and is a contributor to *Die Musik in Geschichte und Gegenwart* and *The New Grove Dictionary of Opera* (1992).

James R. Heintze is music librarian at The American University in Washington, D.C. and editor of the series Bibliographies and Monographs in American Music published by the College Music Society. He has written numerous articles and reviews and was a contributor to *The New Grove Dictionary of Music and Musicians* (1980) and *The New Grove Dictionary of American Music* (1986). His recent books include *Esther Williamson Ballou: A Bio-Bibliography* (1987), *Igor Stravinsky: An International Bibliography of Theses and Dissertations, 1925-87* (1988), *American Music before 1865 in Print and on Records: A Biblio-Discography* (1990), and *Early American Music: A Research and Information Guide* (1990).

Richard Jackson, born in New Orleans, was head of the Americana Collection in the Music Division of The New York Public Library at Lincoln Center. He is a specialist in the life and music of that other New Orleanean, Louis Moreau Gottschalk. Other than articles and bibliographies, Jackson has published several collections of American music, perhaps most notably a group of previously unknown Gottschalk piano works (1976), his collected songs (1992), and the well-received *Democratic Souvenirs* (1988).

Sterling E. Murray is professor and chair of the Department of Music History in the School of Music, West Chester University, West Chester, Pa. He earned his Ph.D. in musicology from the University of Michigan. His research interest is eighteenth-century music—on both sides of the Atlantic. He has prepared editions and written several articles about the music of the Bohemian composer known as Antonio Rosetti (1750-1792) and the musical activities of the Oettingen-Wallerstein court. In addition, Dr. Murray has written on various aspects of the music of Franz Joseph Haydn and Wolfgang A. Mozart. He has also published his studies on aspects of early American psalmody and musical activities in eighteenth-century Philadelphia. Dr. Murray's research has been published in *Music and Letters*, *Musical Quarterly*, *Musik in Bayern*, *The New Grove Dictionary of Music and Musicians* (1980), *Journal of the American Musicological Society*, *Notes* (Music Library Association), and *Journal of Musicology* among others. Most recently, Harmonie Park Press has published the second edition of his *Anthologies of Music: An Annotated Index*.

David W. Music is assistant dean of the Performance Division and associate professor of church music at Southwestern Baptist Theological Seminary, Fort Worth, Texas. His publications include articles in the fields of hymnology, church music, and musicology in a variety of journals and books. He has been Editor of *The Hymn*, the journal of the Hymn Society in the United States and Canada, since 1990, and has served on the editorial boards of Studies in Puritan American Spitituality and *Southwestern Journal of Theology*. He has recently been appointed to the editorial board of Bibliographies and Monographs in American Music. A composer, arranger, and editor of church music, his published compositions include pieces for choir, handbells, recorder, and a hymn tune.

Barbara Owen holds degrees from Westminster Choir College and Boston University, and has also studied in Germany and Italy. She has given lectures, recitals, and seminars throughout the United States as well as in England and Japan, and has published articles in *American Music*, *The*

American Organist, The Hymn, and other periodicals. Author of *The Organ in New England* (1979), *E. Power Biggs, Concert Organist* (1987) and *The Mormon Tabernacle Organ* (1990), she has also contributed articles to *The New Grove Dictionary of Music and Musicians* (1980), *The New Grove Dictionary of Musical Instruments* (1984), and *The New Harvard Dictionary of Music* (1986). She is active as a teacher, lecturer, recitalist and organ consultant, and has since 1963 served as Director of Church Music for the First Religious Society of Newburyport.

Katherine K. Preston is a member of the faculty at the College of William and Mary, Williamsburg, Virginia. She has received numerous awards and fellowships including those from the Smithsonian Institution, American Antiquarian Society, Newberry Library, Philadelphia Center for Early American Studies, and the Sonneck Society for American Music. She has served on the editorial boards of *American Music* and *College Music Symposium*, and as a member of the Board of Directors of the Sonneck Society, and has recently been appointed to the editorial board of Bibliographies and Monographs in American Music. She has published articles, reviews, and has contributed to *The New Grove Dictionary of American Music* (1986) and *The New Grove Dictionary of Opera* (1992). Her book *Music for Hire: A Study of Professional Musicians in Washington, D.C., 1877-1900* was published by Pendragon Press in 1992. In 1993 her work *Opera on the Road: Traveling Opera Troupes in the United States, 1825-1860* was published by the University of Illinois Press.

Richard D. Wetzel is on the faculty of the School of Music of Ohio University and is active as a composer. His works include a suite for alto saxophone and piano, a fantasy for bassoon and organ, a woodwind quintet, a song cycle for soprano, flute and piano. His liturgical music is found in *The Worshipbook* (Presbyterian, 1972), *The Hymnal* (United Church of Christ, 1974), and *The Hymnal* (Episcopal, 1982). His research emphasis is in American music, specifically German-American music and musicians and music publishing during the nineteenth century. His *Frontier Musicians on the Connoquenessing, Wabash, and Ohio: A History of the Music and Musicians of George Rapp's Harmony Society (1805-1906)* (1976) is a definitive work on German-American communal music, and among his articles are those published in *The New Grove Dictionary of Music and Musicians* (1980), *The New Grove Dictionary of American Music* (1986), *The Hymn, American Music,* and *Monatsheft.* He is currently preparing a monograph on the publisher-composer William Cumming Peters (1805-1866). Dr. Wetzel holds a Ph.D. in musicology from the University of Pittsburgh.

Edward C. Wolf is professor of music history and chair of the Department of Music at West Liberty State College, West Liberty, West Virginia. His primary research interests have been in American Lutheran church music and musical practices, as well as in the activities of German singing societies and their influence upon American musical life before World War I. He has published articles in several national periodicals, including *The Musical Quarterly*, *American Music*, and *Journal of Research in Music Education*. He was also a contributor to *The New Grove Dictionary of American Music* (1986). He is active as a music educator, and for the past eighteen years has been editor of the West Virginia Music Educators Association state magazine, *Notes a tempo*. Dr. Wolf holds a Ph.D. in musicology from the University of Illinois.